7th Joint SIGHUM Workshop on Computational Linguistics for Cultural Heritage, Social Sciences, Humanities and Literature (LaTeCH-CLfL 2023)

Dubrovnik, Croatia
5 May 2023

ISBN: 978-1-7138-7384-6

Printed from e-media with permission by:

Curran Associates, Inc.
57 Morehouse Lane
Red Hook, NY 12571

Some format issues inherent in the e-media version may also appear in this print version.

Association for Computational Linguistics
209 N. Eighth Street
Stroudsburg, Pennsylvania 18360

Phone: 1-570-476-8006
Fax: 1-570-476-0860

acl@aclweb.org

Additional copies of this publication are available from:

Curran Associates, Inc.
57 Morehouse Lane
Red Hook, NY 12571 USA
Phone: 845-758-0400
Fax: 845-758-2633
Email: curran@proceedings.com
Web: www.proceedings.com

EACL 2023

The 7th Joint SIGHUM Workshop on Computational Linguistics for Cultural Heritage, Social Sciences, Humanities and Literature

Proceedings of LaTeCH-CLfL 2023

May 5, 2023

Introduction

Welcome to our workshop! If you have been here earlier: good to have you back. If this is your first visit: make yourself at home. This event, which has been around in a few forms for nearly two decades, always covers a tantalizingly wide palette of topics. It is not different this year.

First off, there is the usual helping of articles on the broad subject of literature. There are papers on literary devices: antonomasia (you want to find out more), rhymes and adverbial markers. Also, quote detection and quote attribution; authorship verification; a look at models of humour; an analysis of emotional narratives; scent mining (a study of olfactory information in texts).

Next, we have three papers on ancient languages, Latin twice and Greek once; and two papers on the diachronic study of language – English science writing over 300 years, and the gender of book authors over 200 years.

Then there is a paper on biases in Named Entity Recognition, two papers on text and current politics (the European refugee crisis and the Russian invasion of Ukraine), and work on exploring Social Science archives via question-answering.

Last but not least, it turns out not only that action on climate change costs a colossal amount of money but that such money can be the subject of incorrect reporting. We have a paper just about that.

As you can see, there is something for everyone (all things considered) but do keep an open mind and read all nineteen papers. You will be glad you did.

Do not forget to visit our Web site HERE – and check out past workshops too.

Stefania, Anna, Nils, Stan

The program

9:00-10:30: Talks I

Named Entity Annotation Projection Applied to Classical Languages
Tariq Yousef, Chiara Palladino, Gerhard Heyer and Stefan Jänicke

Linking the Neulateinische Wortliste *to the anonymous Knowledge Base of Interoperable Resources for Latin*
Federica Iurescia, Eleonora Litta, Marco Passarotti, Matteo Pellegrini, Giovanni Moretti and Paolo Ruffolo

Fractality of informativity in 300 years of English scientific writing
Yuri Bizzoni and Stefania Degaetano-Ortlieb

10:30-11:15: Coffee break / SIGHUM Business Meeting

11:15-12:45: Talks II

GPoeT: a Language Model Trained for Rhyme Generation on Synthetic Data
Andrei Popescu-Belis, Àlex R. Atrio, Bastien Bernath, Etienne Boisson, Teo Ferrari, Xavier Theimer-Lienhard and Giorgos Vernikos

Scent Mining: Extracting Olfactory Events, Smell Sources and Qualities
Stefano Menini, Teresa Paccosi, Serra Sinem Tekiroğlu and Sara Tonelli

"Who is the Madonna of Italian-American Literature?": Extracting and Analyzing Target Entities of Vossian Antonomasia
Michel Schwab, Robert Jäschke and Frank Fischer

12:45-14:15: Lunch break

14:15-15:45: Posters

Standard and Non-standard Adverbial Markers: a Diachronic Analysis in Modern Chinese Literature
John Lee, Fangqiong Zhan, Wenxiu Xie, Xiao Han, Chi-Yin Chow and Kam-Yiu Lam

Quote Detection: A New Task and Dataset for NLP
Selma Tekir, Aybüke Güzel, Samet Tenekeci and Bekir Haman

Improving Long-Text Authorship Verification via Model Selection and Data Tuning
Trang Nguyen, Charlie Dagli, Kenneth Alperin, Courtland Vandam and Elliot Singer

Direct Speech Quote Attribution for Dutch Literature
Andreas van Cranenburgh and Frank van den Berg

Large Bibliographies as a Source of Data for the Humanities ? NLP in the Analysis of Gender of Book Authors in German Countries and in Poland (1801-2021)
Adam Pawłowski and Tomasz Walkowiak

Using Text Classification with a Bayesian Correction for Estimating Overreporting in the Creditor Reporting System on Climate Adaptation Finance
Janos Borst, Thomas Wencker and Andreas Niekler

Detecting intersectionality in NER models: A data-driven approach
Ida Marie Lassen, Mina Almasi, Kenneth Enevoldsen and Ross Deans Kristensen-McLachlan

OdyCy – A general-purpose NLP pipeline for Ancient Greek
Jan Kostkan, Márton Kardos, Jacob Palle Bliddal Mortensen and Kristoffer Laigaard Nielbo

Exploring Social Sciences Archives with Explainable Document Linkage through Question Generation
Elie Antoine, Hyun Jung Kang, Ismaël Rousseau, Ghislaine Azémard, Frederic Bechet and Geraldine Damnati

Towards a More In-Depth Detection of Political Framing
Qi Yu

Our kind of people? Detecting populist references in political debates (paper from Findings)
Christopher Klamm, Ines Rehbein and Simone Paolo Ponzetto

Bridging Argument Quality and Deliberative Quality Annotations with Adapters (paper from Findings)
Neele Falk and Gabriella Lapesa

15:45-16:30: **Coffee break**

16:30-18:00: Talks III

Emotion Recognition based on Psychological Components in Guided Narratives for Emotion Regulation
Gustave Cortal, Alain Finkel, Patrick Paroubek and Lina Ye

Wartime Media Monitor (WarMM-2022): A Study of Information Manipulation on Russian Social Media during the Russia-Ukraine War
Maxim Alyukov, Maria Kunilovskaya and Andrei Semenov

What do Humor Classifiers Learn? An Attempt to Explain Humor Recognition Models
Marcio Lima Inácio, Gabriela Wick-Pedro and Hugo Goncalo Oliveira

Organizing Committee

Organizers

Stefania Degaetano-Ortlieb, Saarland University
Anna Kazantseva, National Research Council Canada
Nils Reiter, University of Cologne
Stan Szpakowicz, EECS, University of Ottawa

Program Committee

Program Committee

Beatrice Alex, University of Edinburgh, Edinburgh Futures Institute, School of Literatures, Languages and Cultures, School of Informatics
Melanie Andresen, Universität Stuttgart
Jinyeong Bak, Sungkyunkwan University
Yuri Bizzoni, Aarhus University
Paul Buitelaar, University of Galway
Miriam Butt, University of Konstanz
Thierry Declerck, DFKI GmbH
Stefanie Dipper, Ruhr-Universität Bochum
Jacob Eisenstein, Google
Anna Feldman, Montclair State University
Mark Finlayson, FIU
Heather Froehlich, The Pennsylvania State University
Francesca Frontini, Istituto di Linguistica Computazionale A. Zampolli"- ILC Consiglio Nazionale delle Ricerche - CNR
Udo Hahn, Friedrich-Schiller-Universitaet Jena
Serge Heiden, ENS de Lyon
Labiba Jahan, Augustana College
Fotis Jannidis, Universität Würzburg
Dimitrios Kokkinakis, University of Gothenburg
Stasinos Konstantopoulos, NCSR Demokritos
Markus Krug, University of Wuerzburg
John Lee, City University of Hong Kong
Chaya Liebeskind, Jerusalem College of Technology , Lev Academic Center
Thomas Lippincott, Johns Hopkins University
Barbara Mcgillivray, King's College London
David Mimno, Cornell University
Syrielle Montariol, EPFL
Vivi Nastase, University of Geneva
Borja Navarro-colorado, University of Alicante
Claes Neuefeind, University of Cologne
Kristoffer Nielbo, Center for Humanities Computing, Aarhus University
Pierre Nugues, Lund University
Petya Osenova, Sofia University St. Kl. Ohridskiand IICT-BAS
Janis Pagel, Department of Digital Humanities, University of Cologne
Andrew Piper, McGill University
Petr Plechac, Institute of Czech Literature CAS
Thierry Poibeau, LATTICE (CNRS and ENS/PSL)
Jelena Prokic, Leiden University
Georg Rehm, DFKI
Martin Reynaert, ILLC - Universiteit van Amsterdam / DCA - Tilburg University
Pablo Ruiz Fabo, LiLPa, Universite de Strasbourg
Marijn Schraagen, Utrecht University
Pia Sommerauer, Vrije Universiteit Amsterdam
Elke Teich, Universität des Saarlandes
Ulrich Tiedau, University College London

Menno Van Zaanen, South African Centre for Digital Language Resources
Rob Voigt, Northwestern University
Albin Zehe, University of Wuerzburg
Heike Zinsmeister, Universität Hamburg

Additional Reviewers

Kaveh Aryan Poo, King's College London
Kenneth Enevoldsen, Aarhus University
Andrea Farina, King's College London
Olumide Ojo, Instituto Politécnico Nacional

Table of Contents

Standard and Non-standard Adverbial Markers: A Diachronic Analysis in Modern Chinese Literature

John S. Y. Lee[1], Fangqiong Zhan[2], Wenxiu Xie[3], Xiao Han[4], Chi-Yin Chow[3], Kam-Yiu Lam[3]

[1]Department of Linguistics and Translation, City University of Hong Kong, Hong Kong SAR
[2]National Institute of Education, Nanyang Technological University, Singapore
[3]Department of Computer Science, City University of Hong Kong, Hong Kong SAR
[4]Faculty of Social Sciences and Humanities, Universiti Kebangsaan Malaysia, Malaysia
{jsylee,cskylam}@cityu.edu.hk, fangqiong.zhan@nie.edu.sg, vasiliky@outlook.com, p122876@siswa.ukm.edu.my, tedchow@gmail.com

Abstract

This paper investigates the use of standard and non-standard adverbial markers in modern Chinese literature. In Chinese, adverbials can be derived from many adjectives, adverbs and verbs with the suffix "de". The suffix has a standard and a non-standard written form, both of which are frequently used. Contrastive research on these two competing forms has mostly been qualitative or limited to small text samples. In this first large-scale quantitative study, we present statistics on 346 adverbial types from an 8-million-character text corpus drawn from Chinese literature in the 20th century. We present a semantic analysis of the verbs modified by adverbs with standard and non-standard markers, and a chronological analysis of marker choice among six prominent modern Chinese authors. We show that the non-standard form is more frequently used when the adverbial modifies an emotion verb. Further, we demonstrate that marker choice is correlated to text genre and register, as well as the writing style of the author.

1 Introduction

In many languages, adverbs can be derived from words of other parts-of-speech and are morphologically marked in the derivation process. In English, the '-ly' suffix is used to derive the adverb 'happily', for example, from the adjective 'happy'. Analogously, in Chinese, the '-de' suffix[1] can form adverbials from many adjectives, adverbs, and verbs. For example, the adverbial phrase *gaoxing-de* 'happily' is derived from the adjective *gaoxing* 'happy'. This paper analyzes the use of this adverbial marker, which has a standard written form (地 *de*) and a non-standard written form (的 *de*), with no difference in pronunciation. We will henceforth refer to the standard form as DI[2], and the non-standard form as DE.

The DE vs. DI choice is a language phenomenon that remains poorly understood. Unlike the case for Germanic vs. Latinate affixes in English text (Bauer, 2001), the choice is not directly tied to vocabulary, since every suffixed adverbial in Chinese can be rendered in one of the two competing forms, which we will refer to as the "DE-adverbial" (e.g., *gaoxing-DE* 高兴的 'happily') and the "DI-adverbial" (e.g., *gaoxing-DI* 高兴地 'happily'). It is not related to phonological factors, which can explain suffix choice in nonce-word nominalization (Cutler, 1980), such as the choice between the suffix '-ness' or '-ity' following an adjective. Nor is there a clear semantic distinction, as is the case for prefix choice in negation (Kjellmer, 2005), such as the choice between the prefix 'non-' or 'un-' for an adjective. It is also not a language change "from below" (Claes, 2015), since the standard form DI was proposed by the elites, at the beginning of the 20th century. Unlike language regularization phenomena, the non-standard form persisted and is frequently used even to this day.

It has been suggested that the choice is motivated by stylistic and expressional effects (Zhang, 2012). More often associated with actions, DI emphasizes the manner of the action, whereas DE emphasizes other elements of the situation, such as the agent, patient, instrument, time, and place, etc. For example, in the sentence *ta manman-DI zou* 他慢慢地走 'he slowly walked', the DI-adverbial highlights the slowness. In contrast, in the sentence *ta gaoxing-DE paole* 他高兴的跑了 'he happily ran away', the DE-adverbial not only characterizes the action but also brings out the attitudinal status of

[1]More exactly, '-de' is an enclitic since it is used here to form a phrase rather than a word. However, we will use the more common term "suffix" in this paper.

[2]The shorthand DI is based on the character's pronunciation *di* in other contexts.

Proceedings of the 7th Joint SIGHUM Workshop on Computational Linguistics for Cultural Heritage, Social Sciences, Humanities and Literature (LaTeCH-CLfL2023), pages 1–9

the subject 'he'.

Previous studies have postulated that marker choice may be due at least in part to habit or social factors, or even some randomness (Zhang, 2012). In contrast, we set out to focus on the DE vs. DI marker choice that is intentionally made. To do so, we examine adverbials in the writings of six prominent authors in Chinese literature in the 20th century. Unlike most previous research, which offered only anecdotal examples and limited quantitative analysis to small samples (Ho, 2015), we present statistics on 346 adverbial types from an 8-million-character corpus of literary texts. Specifically, we address the following research questions:

Semantic analysis : Whether adverbial marker choice is influenced by the semantic category of the head word, i.e. the verb modified by the adverbial (Section 5);

Diachronic analysis : Whether adverbial marker choice can reflect the writing style of an author (Section 6).

2 Metrics for adverbial marker choice

Similar to other languages, Chinese adverbials can be non-derived, or derived from base words of various parts-of-speech, typically through reduplication and suffixation (Biq and Huang, 2016). During suffixation, the base word is morphologically marked with the DI (地 *de*) suffix, analogous to the English '–ly' suffix. For example, the adjective *gaoxing* 高兴 'happy' serves as the base word of the adverbial *gaoxing-DI* 高兴地 'happily'. As an alternative to the standard form DI, the adverbial marker is also written as the non-standard DE (的 *de*).

Following previous analyses on Chinese adverbial markers, we adopt the **DE ratio** as the quantitative metric. This ratio is the percentage of suffixed adverbials, in a text or a collection of texts, that use DE rather than DI. More precisely, the ratio is the number of DE-adverbials in the text, divided by the total number of DE- and DI-adverbials.

The DE ratio can be computed for a specific *base word*, by restricting the counts to adverbials derived from that base word. A base word is called "DE-leaning" if its DE ratio exceeds 50%, and "DI-leaning" otherwise. The percentage of DE-leaning base words, out of all base words in the text, can also characterize marker choice. This metric gives equal weight to each base word, in contrast to the DE ratio which can be swayed by the more frequent base words. Together, the two metrics provide a more comprehensive view of adverbial marker usage.

3 Linguistic background

3.1 DE vs. DI as adverbial marker

The distinction between attributive and adverbial markers emerged during the Tang Dynasty (618-907 CE), with the suffix DI marking adverbials, and the suffix *de*, written as the character 底, marking attributives. These two markers began to be merged in the Yuan Dynasty (1271-1368 CE), and eventually gave way to DE. Adverbial constructions could be formed by affixing "any preformed idiomatic phrase or syntactic construction to DI or DE" in vernacular Chinese before the 20th century (Gunn, 1991, p.264). Vernacular novels such as *Water Margin*, *Dream of the Red Chamber* and *Unofficial History of the Scholars* used mostly DE and only sporadically DI (Sun, 1995).

The Vernacular Movement started in China in 1919. In translating foreign literature, Chinese intellectuals were exposed to languages in which adjectives and adverbs can be distinguished by their suffix. They proposed to use DE to mark attributives and DI to mark adverbials (Table 1). As adverbial suffixation became more widespread after 1919, most writers observed this division of labor to some extent. The DE/DI convention fluctuated in the 1930s during the Latinization movement, and also in the 1950s during the 'normalization' movement, an effort to regulate standard Mandarin. By the end of that decade, the convention had become well established (Cordes, 2014, p.116) and was eventually endorsed by almost all grammar books.

Both DE and DI remain in frequent use today. Seeing the division as artificial, some scholars nonetheless advocated unified use of DE and claimed that it would neither cause ambiguity nor reduce reading speed and comprehension. Others argued that unified use would cause ambiguity in sentence structure, since DE and DI are syntactically different markers.

3.2 Corpus-based studies on marker choice

Most corpus-based studies on adverbials in literary texts concentrated on the frequency of suffix use (Cordes, 2014) and its productivity in adverbial derivation (Kubler, 1985). In the only study on marker choice in literary text, Ho (2015) reported

Type	Marker	Status	Example
Adverbial	DI	standard	*gaoxing-DI shuo* 高兴地说 'happily say'
	DE	non-standard	*gaoxing-DE shuo* 高兴的说 'happily say'
Attributive	DE	standard	*gaoxing-DE rizi* 高兴的日子 'happy day'

Table 1: Standard and non-standard adverbial marker in Chinese; the latter shares the same character as the attributive marker

that Qiong Yao always used DE, Eileen Chang always used DI, while Lu Xun's DE ratio was 91.8%. The analysis was based however on only three texts per author.

The most in-depth study to-date focused on adverbials derived from adverbs (Zhang, 2012). Four factors for marker choice were identified: conventional usage, random usage, syntactic usage, and conscious usage. "Conventional usage" governs lexicalized adverbials, where the suffix can be viewed as part of a fixed expression. "Random usage" means the writer makes the choice unconsciously from habit, background and knowledge, which may in turn depend on social factors such as educational level, age, and gender. For example, a higher level of education is a strong predictor for DI. Thirdly, "syntactic usage" refers to cases where the syntactic environment determines the choice. For example, when the adverbial modifies a deverbal object, DE is favored to "harmonize" with a verb in nominalized form. Most relevant to this study is "conscious usage", where the writer deliberately makes the choice for stylistic purposes. Statistics from two corpora of contemporary Chinese suggested that the choice is correlated with adverb categories (Zhang, 2012).

The present study differs from previous research by focusing on marker choice in literature, in which marker choice was likely more carefully and intentionally made, and by presenting a diachronic analysis of well-known authors.

4 Data

There is no publicly available, large-scale corpus of Chinese text with annotations on adverbial markers. This section describes the automatic creation of such a corpus to support this study. After presenting the textual material of the corpus (Section 4.1), we describe the adverbial identification algoritm (Section 4.2) and its evaluation (Section 4.3).

Author	# texts	# characters
Guo Moruo	40	255,198
Lao She	405	1,752,079
Lu Xun (non-translation)	283	652,788
Lu Xun (translation)	107	2,205,225
Mao Dun	76	1,439,051
Shen Congwen	241	1,846,914
Yu Dafu	44	317,356
Total	1,196	8,468,611

Table 2: Statistics on the six authors represented in our corpus

4.1 Textual material

Literary texts are ideal for studying adverbials since the marker choices therein are more likely to be consciously rather than randomly made. We compiled a corpus of literary texts written during and after the Vernacular Movement, when the DE/DI choice was formalized. We downloaded from the *Baiwan Shuku* website[3] all texts written by six prominent Chinese authors: Guo Moruo, Lao She, Lu Xun, Mao Dun, Shen Congwen and Yu Dafu. As shown in Table 2, this corpus consists of over 8 million characters in 1,089 texts.

Just as there are lexical differences between translational and non-translational Chinese text (Xiao, 2010), there can potentially be differences in marker choice, since translators are exposed to the adverbial suffixes in the source text. More generally, adverbial constructions could be influenced by literal translations from Japanese and European languages (Gunn, 1991, p.264). To determine if the influence from translation might be a confounding variable in our study, we divided the writings of Lu Xun, who has the largest amount of translation works among the six authors in our corpus, into the "translation" and "non-translation" portions (Table 2).

[3] http://www.millionbook.com/mj/index.html

Semantic category	DE ratio	% DE-leaning
`Communication`	54.7%	78.6%
`Caused-motion`	58.1%	57.1%
`Perception`	58.7%	74.4%
`Cognition`	69.5%	75.0%
`Emotion`	**84.9%**	**84.8%**

Table 3: DE ratio of adverbials modifying verbs in different semantic categories, and the % of DE-leaning base words

Author	DE Ratio	% DE-leaning
Mao Dun	19.2%	12.7%
Guo Muoro	29.3%	25.4%
Lu Xun	57.2%	62.2%
Yu Dafu	81.4%	83.4%
Lao She	86.5%	90.8%
Shen Congwen	97.6%	99.3%
Overall	60.7%	61.2%

Table 4: DE ratio and percentage of DE-leaning base words by author

4.2 Automatic adverbial identification

Existing adverbial identification algorithms (Xing et al., 2020) assume the standard marker DI. In a word-segmented Chinese text, DI-adverbials can be reliably identified by searching for DI and its preceding word. For DE-adverbials, however, a similar search for DE would yield low precision, since it also matches DE that marks attributives.

We adopted the adverbial identification algorithm proposed by Xie et al. (2021), based on word segmentation, POS tagging and dependency parsing by the HanLP Chinese parser.[4] This algorithm first identifies candidate base words, i.e. defined as all words followed by DE or DI. It then retrieves its head word, i.e. the parent of the candidate base word in the dependency tree. If the part-of-speech (POS) of the head word is a noun, DE marks an attributive and the instance should be excluded; if the head word is an adjective or verb, DE marks an adverbial and the instance should be included.

4.3 Evaluation

To ensure an adequate level of annotation accuracy, we evaluated the performance of the adverbial identification algorithm. A native speaker of Chinese with formal training in linguistics examined 1196 occurrences of three candidate base words[5] in the writings of Guo Moruo, Mao Dun, Lao She, and Lu Xun. Each occurrence was labeled as one of the following: base word in a DE-adverbial; base word in a DI-adverbial; adverb with no suffix; or, not used as an adverb.

As expected, the extracted adverbials were almost always true positives, with precision at 100% for DI-adverbials and 97.25% for DE-adverbials. Recall for DI-adverbials reached 93.56%, with the false negatives mostly caused by word segmentation errors on the base word. Recall was lower for DE-adverbials (79.20%) because of POS ambiguity for the head word.

5 Semantic categories of head word

The verb modified by the adverbial, which we refer to as the "head word", may influence the choice of adverbial marker. Specifically, we examine if there is any correlation between the semantic category of the head word and marker choice. We adopted the frame categories in Mandarin VerbNet (MVN)[6] as the semantic taxonomy for testing this hypothesis. A widely used verbal semantic database, MVN uses a schema-based meaning representation and constructional patterns for its frames (Liu and Chiang, 2008).

MVN provides a list of verbs for each frame. Our analysis centers on the five top-level frames (Table 3) with the largest number of verbs attested in our corpus. In the `Communication` frame (64 verbs), a speaker conveys a message or interlocutors make a conversation. The `Caused-motion` frame (39 verbs) is concerned with an agent causing a figure to move. `Perception` (47 verbs) involves a perceiver perceiving a phenomenon through his or her body part. A cognizer in the `Cognition` frame (21 verbs) either conducts a mental/intellectual activity, or undergoes a mental/intellectual state. Finally, the `Emotion` frame (62 verbs) describes the emotional state of an experiencer or affectee, which may be provoked by a stimulus or caused volitionally by an affector.

As shown in Table 3, the `Emotion` verbs have notably higher DE ratio (84.9%) and DE-leaning base words (84.8%) than other categories. The large number of stative verbs, which highlight the description of the situation (Zhang, 2012), may account for the preference for the non-standard

[4] https://github.com/hankcs/pyhanlp

[5] 慢慢 *manman* 'slow', 客气 *keqi* 'courteous' and 高兴 *gaoxing* 'happy'

[6] http://verbnet.lt.cityu.edu.hk

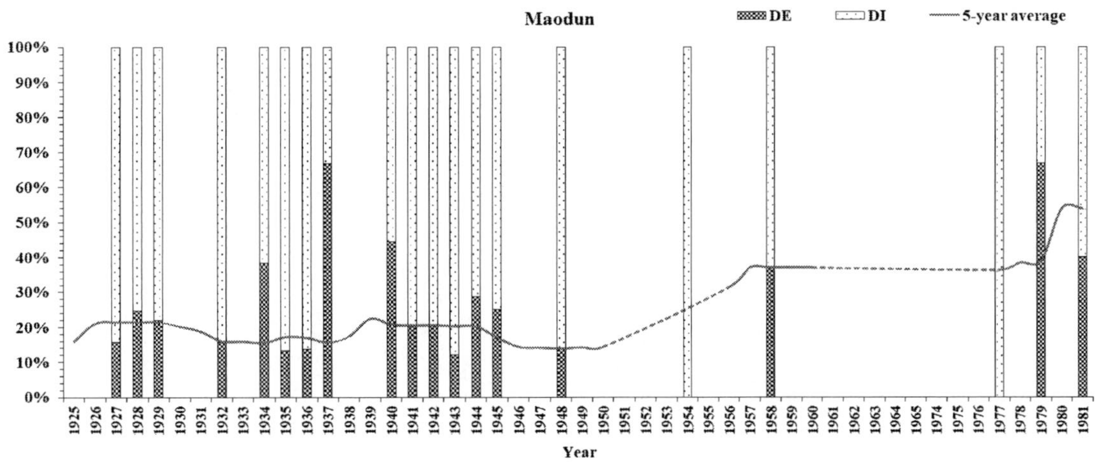

Figure 1: DE ratio of Mao Dun

marker. This explanation would also be consistent with the fact that the `Cognition` category, which also contains many stative verbs, attained the second-highest ratio (69.5%). In comparison, categories with more dynamic verb phrases, such as `Caused-motion`, are more likely to use DI.

6 Analysis

Our analysis focuses on the four authors with the most text in our corpus (Table 2), namely, Lu Xun, widely regarded as the founder of modern Chinese literature; followed by Shen Congwen, Lao She and Mao Dun, who inherited his innovations but also developed their own distinctive styles. Literary critics have distilled their writing styles as follows: "historical" and "political" for Mao Dun; "melodramatic" and "farcical" for Lao She; and "lyrical" and "nativist" for Shen Congwen (Wang, 1992, p.292).

We automatically annotated all adverbials in our corpus with the adverbial identification algorithm. The overall marker choice by the authors are shown in Table 4, ranging from Shen Congwen who was highly partial to DE, to Mao Dun who heavily leaned DI. A diachronic analysis reveals significant evolution in marker choice for some of the authors. Figures 1 to 5 plot the DE ratio for each year during which the author's works contained at least 5 instances of DE-/DI-adverbials. The overall trend, which can be obscured by yearly fluctuations, is often better visualized with a moving average. Hence, the figures also provide curves that plot the average DE ratio within the 5-year window centered on each year.

6.1 Preference for standard marker

Mao Dun consistently preferred the standard marker DI throughout his career. Both his DE ratio (19.2%) and percentage of DE-leaning base words (12.7%) are by far the lowest among the six authors. As a moving average, his DE ratio rarely exceeded 20% before 1950 and increased only slightly thereafter (Figure 1).[7]

Mao Dun played a major role in introducing Western literary ideas and masterpieces to China. His conscientious adoption of the standard adverbial marker is consistent not only with his compliance with the new punctuation standards (Tan, 2006), but also his advocacy for "European-style" grammar. Further, Mao Dun is celebrated for his "historical" novels, which interweave real and fictional episodes. Relative to other genres, these novels are favorable to DI usage with their description of historical events.

6.2 Preference for non-standard marker

At the other end of the spectrum lies Shen Congwen, who hardly adopted the DI and scored 97.6% in DE ratio. His strong preference for the non-standard marker endured throughout his career (Figure 2).[8] Indeed, all but two base words are DE-leaning in his writing (99.3%).

Shen Congwen is known for his "lyrical style", a style that exhibits "features of poetic expression",

[7]The occasional spikes were caused by relatively small samples sizes, between 8 to 11 instances for the years 1934, 1937, 1940, 1944 and 1945.

[8]The only exception was in 1949, when there were 2 DE instances and 3 DI instances.

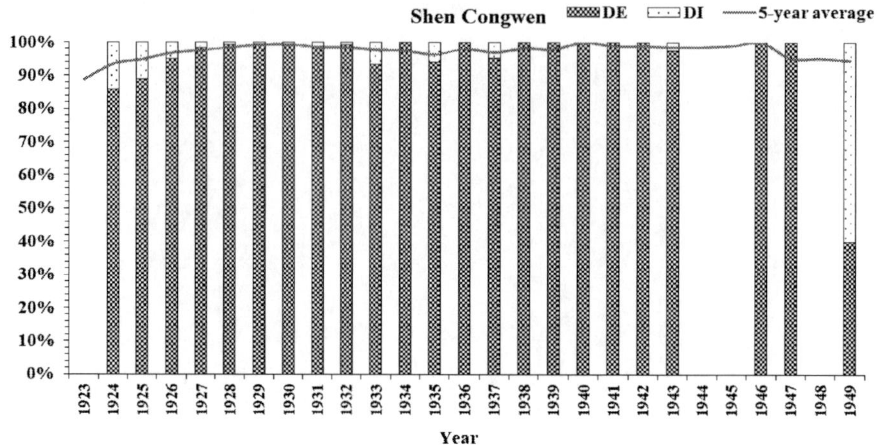

Figure 2: DE ratio of Shen Congwen

with "emphasis on an intensified expression of emotion" (Wang, 1992, p.224). The strong association of emotion verbs to the non-standard marker (Section 5) is consistent with his high DE ratio. Furthermore, in Modern Chinese literature, Shen is considered the most important of the "native soil" writers, who emphasized regional identity in their writing. Shen captured the landscape and lives of his provincial home in West Hunan. Since his works focused on local communities and regional culture, his literary language was likely less influenced by foreign languages. On the contrary, it may have been influenced more by classics such as the *Dream of the Red Chamber*, along with their DE usage, since Shen combined classical Chinese writing techniques with the vernacular style. Both factors would contribute to the absence of the standard marker in his writing.

6.3 From non-standard to standard marker

Second only to Shen Congwen, Lao She has a DE ratio of 86.5%. Lao She mostly used the non-standard marker: 90.8% of his base words are DE-leaning. Although Lao She at first glance resembles Shen in marker usage, diachronic analysis reveals a dramatic change over his career.

Until 1946, Lao She's pattern is comparable to Shen Congwen, with DE ratio consistently over 90% as a moving average (Figure 3). Among the first to adopt the vernacular in fiction, Lao She is known for his incorporation of colloquialisms, especially Beijing idiomatic speech, in his writing. Many adverbial phrases and onomatopoeia employ the non-standard marker, as is the case for a majority of the examples given by (Cui, 2008, p.87-90) to illustrate his oral style of writing. Furthermore, Lao She exhibited "emotional spectacle", "gestural hyperbole", and "verbal extravagance", in contrast to the "emotional restraint", "symbolic subtlety", and "linguistic economy" of Lu Xun (Wang, 1992, p.18). The prevalence of DE can thus be partially explained by the association of emotion verbs to the non-standard marker (Section 5).

The early 1950s saw the beginning of the 'normalization' movement, which appeared to have a significant effect on Lao She's marker choice. Lao She began to decrease the amount of regional speech and local dialect in his writing in favor of the style of the "common language" or Putonghua (Gunn, 1991, p.115). Reflecting this change, his DE ratio drastically decreased from over 70% to only 20% in 1952. Thereafter the standard marker remained his preferred choice, in line with the fact that his last novel, published in 1961, contained much fewer non-standard sentences than earlier ones (Cui, 2008, p.236).

6.4 From non-standard to standard and back

Figures 4 and 5 show the marker usage in the non-translation and translation works of Lu Xun, who has an overall DE ratio of 57.2%, with 62.2% of his base words DE-leaning (Table 4). The similarity between these two figures visualizes the fact that translation did not have a statistically significant impact on marker choice (cf. Section 3.2).

Three phases in Lu Xun's marker usage may be discerned from these figures. An initial period, dominated by the non-standard marker, lasted from

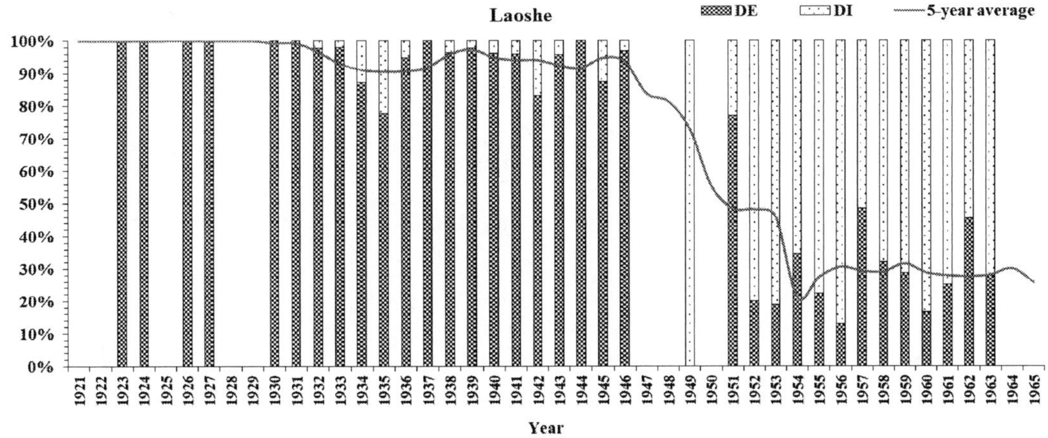

Figure 3: DE ratio of Lao She

1917 to 1924. Lu Xun's preference for DE in this period explains the 91.78% DE ratio reported by Ho (2015), which is much higher than the 57.2% in our corpus (Table 4). The ratio in Ho's study considered only three texts, all of which were written during this period; in contrast, our corpus also includes works from the two subsequent periods.

As Lu Xun absorbed mixed language features during the Vernacular Movement, he entered a second period around 1924-25. The DE ratio dropped[9] from 86.4% in 1924 to 23.9% in 1925, a dramatic change reflecting the "innovative work in style" in 1925 noted by Gunn (1991, p.95). The standard marker became prevalent, for example, in the novels *The Divorce*, *Articles under the Lamplight* and *What Happened to Nora After She Left*. His DE ratio would remain low into the early 1930s with his literary language under the influence of Europeanization.

In the 1930s, Lu Xun returned to the non-standard marker as he became an activist advocating for reform and simplification of the Chinese language. The call for a "mass language" gathered steam towards the end of the Vernacular Movement, with the goals of eradicating illiteracy and giving ordinary people access to writing. Subsequently the Latinized New Writing movement blurred the distinction between the two markers, leading to the re-emergence of the unified use of DE. An advocate of Latinization, Lu Xun reverted to non-standard market, returning to the high DE ratio in the initial period.

[9]Lu Xun also used more DI than DE in 1923, but there were only 5 samples in that year.

7 Conclusion

We have presented the first large-scale, quantitative study on adverbial markers in modern Chinese literature. Drawing on over 8 million characters of literary texts, we investigated the usage of standard and non-standard adverbial markers among six major authors in the 20th century. A semantic analysis reveals that the non-standard marker DE is more frequent when when the adverbial modifies a head word that expresses emotion, compared to other semantic categories. Further, a diachronic analysis shows that marker choice is correlated to text genre and register, for example Mao Dun's preference for the standard marker and Shen Congwen's preference for the non-standard. Marker choice also reflects the evolution of writing style amidst historical linguistic developments, as shown in the case of Lu Xun and Lao She.

This research can be extended in several dimensions. The influence of the base word can be further examined. More fine-grained semantic taxonomies on head words can potentially yield new insights. Finally, as language change continues to affect marker choice, it would be interesting to study whether and how contemporary writers differ from their counterparts in the 20th century.

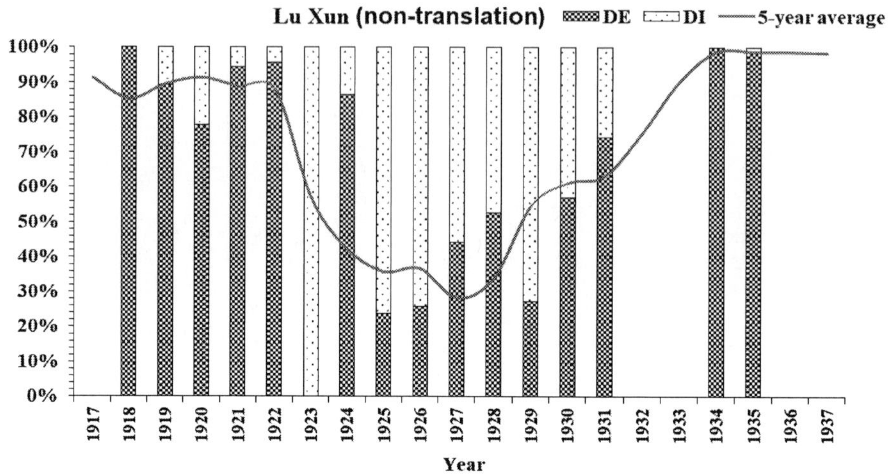

Figure 4: DE ratio of Lu Xun (non-translation)

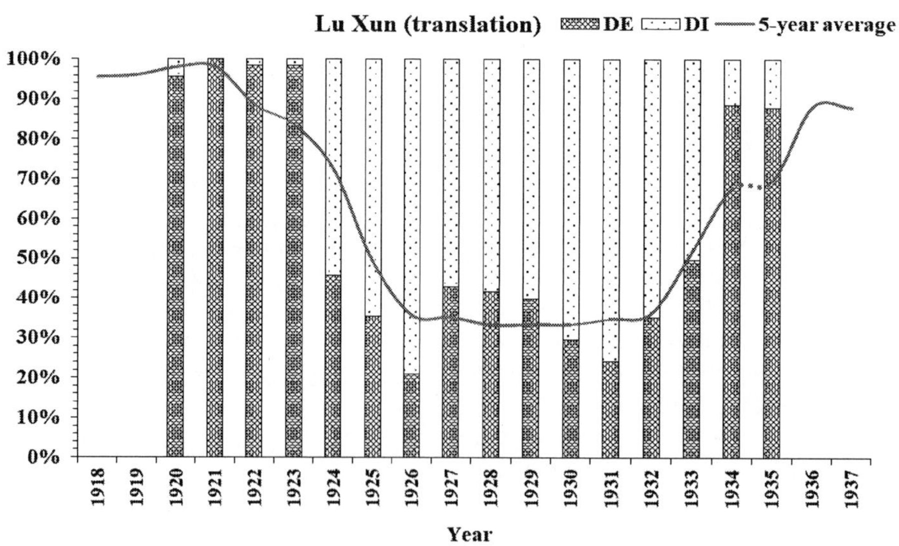

Figure 5: DE ratio of Lu Xun (translation)

References

L. Bauer. 2001. *Morphological productivity*. Cambridge University Press, Cambridge, UK.

Y-O Biq and C-R Huang. 2016. *Adverbs: A reference grammar of Chinese*. Cambridge University Press, Cambridge, UK.

J. Claes. 2015. Competing constructions: The pluralization of presentation haber in Dominican Spanish. *Cognitive Linguistics*.

R. Cordes. 2014. *Language change in 20th century written Chinese – the claim for Europeanization*. PhD Dissertation, Universität Hamburg.

Y. Cui. 2008. *The Style of Lao She and Modern Chinese: A Study of Lao She's Literary Language in his Fictional Works*. PhD Dissertation, University of London.

A. Cutler. 1980. Productivity in work formation. In *Proceedings of Sixteenth Regional Meeting of the Chicago Linguistic Society*.

E. M. Gunn. 1991. *Rewriting Chinese: style and innovation in twentieth-century Chinese prose*. Stanford University Press, Stanford, CA.

J. Ho. 2015. From the use of three functional words examining author's unique writing style – and on dream of red chamber author issues. *BIBLID*, 120(1):119–150.

G. Kjellmer. 2005. Negated Adjectives in Modern English. *Studia Neophilologica*, 77(2):156–170.

C. Kubler. 1985. *A study of Europeanized grammar in modern written Chinese*. Student Book Company, Barline.

Meichun Liu and T. Y. Chiang. 2008. The construction of mandarin verbnet: A frame-based study of statement verbs. *Language and Linguistics*, 9(2):239–270.

R. Sun. 1995. The variation of the structural particle DE and DI [in Chinese]. *Journal of Yangzhou Normal University (Humanities and Social Science)*, 4:80–82.

K. C. Tan. 2006. *A study of the language of Mao Dun (1896-1981) [in Chinese]*. Institute Thesis (Ph.D.) National Institute of Education, Nanyang Technological University, Singapore.

D. D.-W. Wang. 1992. *Fictional realism in twentieth-century China: Mao Dun, Lao She, Shen Congwen*. Columbia University Press.

R. Xiao. 2010. How different is translated Chinese from native Chinese? A corpus-based study of translation universals. *International Journal of Corpus Linguistics*, 15(1):5–35.

Wenxiu Xie, John S. Y. Lee, Fangqiong Zhan, Xiao Han, and Chi-Yin Chow. 2021. Unsupervised adverbial identification in modern chinese literature. In *Proc. 5th Joint SIGHUM Workshop on Computational Linguistics for Cultural Heritage, Social Sciences, Humanities and Literature*, page 91–95.

D. Xing, E. Xun, C. Wang, G. Rao, and L. Ma. 2020. Construction of adverbial-verb collocation database based on large-scale corpus. In *Proc. Chinese Lexical Semantics Workshop (CLSW) 2019, LNAI 11831*, page 585–595.

Yisheng Zhang. 2012. On the Selection of Adverbial Markers in Contemporary Chinese. *Hanyu Xuebao*, 40:32–43.

GPoeT: a Language Model Trained for Rhyme Generation on Synthetic Data

Andrei Popescu-Belis[1,2], **Àlex R. Atrio**[1,2], **Bastien Bernath**[2],
Étienne Boisson[2], **Teo Ferrari**[1], **Xavier Theimer-Lienhard**[2] and **Giorgos Vernikos**[1,2]

[1]HEIG-VD / HES-SO, Yverdon-les-Bains, Switzerland
[2]EPFL, Lausanne, Switzerland
{andrei.popescu-belis, alejandro.ramirezatrio, georgios.vernikos}@heig-vd.ch

Abstract

Poem generation with language models requires the modeling of rhyming patterns. We propose a novel solution for learning to rhyme, based on synthetic data generated with a rule-based rhyming algorithm. The algorithm and an evaluation metric use a phonetic dictionary and the definitions of perfect and assonant rhymes. We fine-tune a GPT-2 English model with 124M parameters on 142 MB of natural poems and find that this model generates consecutive rhymes infrequently (11%). We then fine-tune the model on 6 MB of synthetic quatrains with consecutive rhymes (AABB) and obtain nearly 60% of rhyming lines in samples generated by the model. Alternating rhymes (ABAB) are more difficult to model because of longer-range dependencies, but they are still learnable from synthetic data, reaching 45% of rhyming lines in generated samples.

1 Introduction

The quality of texts generated by language models (LM) has improved tremendously in recent years. While their factual accuracy is still open to debate, this is not an issue when using LMs with a creative purpose, in particular to generate works of art such as poems. In the recent past, LMs were put to use for poetry generation in several studies (Hopkins and Kiela, 2017; Lau et al., 2018; Van de Cruys, 2020; Wöckener et al., 2021; Uthus et al., 2022; Ormazabal et al., 2022), which found that fluency and intelligibility reached satisfactory levels. However, poems often exhibit structural, text-level properties that are still quite difficult to manage by LMs: rhyming patterns and division into verses and stanzas. While not all poems make use of these properties, a convincing LM for poetry generation should be able to deal with them.

In this paper, we focus on the first property and propose a method to adapt an LM so that it generates rhyming verses, with modest computing requirements. We start from an unconstrained autoregressive LM, in our case GPT-2, which we fine-tune first on a poetry corpus of about 120 MB to improve its style (Section 3). We design a rule-based system which modifies text generated by the LM so that it obeys a given rhyming pattern while retaining acceptable fluency, and we generate two datasets of 160k lines (6 MB) each with the AABB and ABAB patterns (Section 4). We further fine-tune the LM on these synthetic datasets in order to generate rhyming verses with the respective patterns, thus showing that they can be learned by a moderately-sized LM (Section 5).

We also introduce a rhyming metric (see Section 2) based on an English rhyming dictionary, and use it throughout the study to count the proportion of perfect and assonant rhymes generated by a model. We find that this is very low (11%) for the LM fine-tuned on natural poetry with variable rhyming patterns, but increases to around 60% when the LM learns only the AABB pattern from synthetic data. The ABAB pattern is more challenging, but can still be learned, reaching around 45% rhyming lines. In the conclusion (Section 7), we discuss some issues related to the integration of the rhyming LMs into an existing, operational system for interactive poetry generation.[1]

Our contributions are the following:

- a metric computing how many lines have perfect or assonant rhymes that conform to a given pattern in English;
- a rule-based algorithm to generate rhyming lines of a given pattern, based on a GPT-2 LM fine-tuned on poetry;
- a demonstration that even medium-scale LMs can be fine-tuned to learn a rhyming pattern from machine-generated poems;
- evidence that local rhyming patterns are more easily learned than those implying longer-range dependencies.

[1]Source code available at github.com/heig-iict-ida/crpo.

Proceedings of the 7th Joint SIGHUM Workshop on Computational Linguistics for Cultural Heritage, Social Sciences, Humanities and Literature (LaTeCH-CLfL2023), pages 10–20

2 Measuring the Number of Rhymes

A criterion for measuring the number of rhyming verses is key for the present study. We present a metric that distinguishes between perfect rhymes, assonant rhymes, and no rhymes, using a rhyming dictionary derived from an English pronunciation dictionary. We test it on a corpus of human poetry annotated for rhyme and show that its accuracy is sufficient for use in this study.

2.1 Definitions of Rhymes

Following a widespread definition,[2] also adopted by Van de Cruys (2020), a perfect rhyme is the identity of the final vowel and consonant sounds of a word, starting with the first vowel of the last stressed syllable. An assonant rhyme is the identity of the final vowels in the last stressed syllable, but not of the ending consonant.

Since the addition of stress information would reduce the amount of available candidates for a rhyme, we simplify the definition of a rhyme between words w_1 and w_2 as follows, using the phonetic representation of each word $phon(w)$.

1. We have a *perfect rhyme* if $phon(w_1)$ and $phon(w_2)$ end with the same vowel followed by the same consonant(s), if any.
2. We have an *assonant rhyme* if $phon(w_1)$ and $phon(w_2)$ end with the same vowel, followed by one or more non-identical consonants.
3. Otherwise, the lines *do not rhyme*.

2.2 Construction of the Rhyming Dictionary

To apply the preceding definitions, and to generate rhymes according to them, we build a rhyming dictionary starting from the Carnegie Mellon Pronouncing Dictionary of English.[3] The dictionary contains pronunciations of 123,631 English words. Each word is associated with a series of phonemes coded using ASCII letters only, for example 'K AE M P EY N' for the word 'campaign'.

We distinguish 15 phonemic vowels (e.g., 'AH', 'AW', 'EY', 'OY') and consider all other phonemes as consonants. To each word from the dictionary we associate two strings.

1. The last phonemic vowel and all the consonants following it (if any), to allow testing for perfect rhymes.
2. The last phonemic vowel only, whether it is followed or not by consonants, to allow testing for assonant rhymes.

Examples of entries in our rhyming dictionary are therefore ('campaign' → 'eyn', 'ey'), ('copycodes' → 'owdz', 'ow'), ('vanilla' → 'ah', 'ah'), ('do' → 'uw', 'uw'), and ('wouldn't' → 'ahnt', 'ah').

To help with rule-based generation of rhymes, we create two dictionaries that invert the first one, for efficiency reasons. One has the strings defining the perfect rhymes as keys and the corresponding words as values – for instance ('eyn' → ..., 'campaign', 'overtrain', 'plane', ...) – and the other one has the strings defining the assonant rhymes as keys and the corresponding words as values. The first additional dictionary has 1,356 keys (word endings for perfect rhymes) and an average number of 91 words per key, while the second one has only 15 keys (the number of phonemic vowels) and an average of 6,507 words per key, ranging from 576 to 34,037.

2.3 Definition of the Metric

The proposed metric for rhymes follows from the definitions above, and makes use of the first dictionary. Given two words – the ending words of two lines of poetry – we compare their entries in the dictionary. If the first strings are identical, then we count a *perfect rhyme*. If they are not, we examine the second strings, and if they are identical, then we count an *assonant rhyme*. If not, then we consider that the words do not rhyme. The order of testing is important, because for words ending with a vowel, such as ('vanilla' → 'ah', 'ah') and ('Godzilla' → 'ah', 'ah'), both entries match, but we want to consider this as a perfect rhyme.

To apply the metric, the lines of the poem are first tokenized using NLTK's `word_tokenize()` function.[4] If a line finishes with punctuation, we discard it and examine the last word of the line. If the line ends with a contraction (such as 'wouldn't') we join back the two resulting tokens generated by `word_tokenize()`. If a word does not appear in the pronunciation dictionary, then we search for the most similar one in terms of string edit distance using the `get_close_matches()` function from the 'difflib' Python package (a time-consuming operation). We experimented with restricting the similarity search to the initial parts of words, because changing the end changes the rhyme, but did not

[2] See e.g. rhymenow.com/types-of-rhymes.

[3] Freely available from svn.code.sf.net/p/cmusphinx/code/trunk/cmudict/sphinxdict/cmudict_SPHINX_40.

[4] From www.nltk.org.

		Our metric		
		Perfect rhyme	Assonant rhyme	No rhyme
Human annotation	Rhyming	27,174 (78.8%)	680 (2.0%)	6,628 (19.2%)
	Not rhyming	4,209 (1.3%)	25,163 (7.9%)	290,633 (90.8%)

Table 1: Confusion matrix for rhyming detection by our metric vs. human annotation.

observe significant differences when validating the metric.

2.4 Validating the Metric

We validated our metric on the Chicago Rhyming Poetry Corpus[5] which includes English poems annotated with their rhymes. For each poem, the annotation marks the last word of each line with an index number, and co-indexes rhyming words. For instance, a three-line stanza could be annotated as "house pain souse" followed by "1 2 1", indicating that its lines end respectively with the words 'house', 'pain' and 'souse' and that the first line rhymes with the third one.

From the corpus, we derive ground-truth pairs of rhyming and non-rhyming words. For each annotated stanza with k line-ending words, we consider all $k(k-1)/2$ pairs of words and separate them using the annotations in rhyming or non-rhyming pairs. During this process, we found a small number of annotation inconsistencies, and we checked how many words are actually present in our pronunciation dictionary. As for some poets the total number of unknown words is quite high, we exclude them from the dataset, on the grounds that their vocabulary or spelling is too different from modern use.[6]

In fact, the human assessment of rhymes may not be 100% reliable, due to the evolution of pronunciation and the imperfections of the annotation process. Additionally, some pairs annotated as non-rhyming may in fact rhyme, but have not been annotated as such since they do not fit the rhyming schema of the poem. The creation of a validation corpus can thus be improved, but the goal is to obtain the most reliable rather than the largest possible dataset, in order to validate the metric. Overall, we obtained 34,482 rhyming word pairs and 320,005 non-rhyming ones.

We assessed if our metric, given each word pair, can correctly label it as rhyming or non-rhyming. As the metric distinguishes perfect from assonant rhymes, we may or not merge these two categories. Results are shown in Table 1. If we merge perfect and assonant rhymes, our metric finds 80.8% of the rhymes (most of them perfect) but also labels 9.2% of non-rhyming words as rhyming ($F_1 = 0.61$). To maximize the F_1-score, it would seem preferable not to count assonant rhymes (then $F_1 = 0.83$) but in what follows we will count both types of rhymes.

Upon inspection, recall errors are often due to words that are absent from the pronunciation dictionary, and when replaced with similarly-spelled ones, their pronunciations differ. For instance, 'marinere' → 'mariner' no longer rhymes with 'hear', or 'thro" → 'throw' no longer rhymes with 'flew'. In other cases, the pronunciation in our dictionary does not match the one considered by the poet: 'stood' rhymes with 'blood' and 'thus' rhymes with 'albatross' according to the corpus, but not in our dictionary. As for precision errors, a large part of them are assonant rhymes which are not annotated in the corpus. For instance, 'there'-'around'-'howl'd'-'swound' is annotated as ABCB but we detect an assonance because the last three words have the same final vowel. Finally, annotation mistakes in the corpus can lead to both types of errors, e.g. 'close'-'beat'-'sky'-'eye'-'feet' is annotated as ABCCC in the corpus but correctly labeled by us as ABCCB.

3 An Auto-regressive Language Model Fine-Tuned on Poetry

Our starting point is GPT-2 (Radford et al., 2019), a general-purpose decoder LM for English. We use the Python implementation provided by the Huggingface library (Wolf et al., 2019).[7] We enable the model to generate poetry by fine-tuning it first on a corpus of English poetry (3.1), and then by designing constraints so that its output has the form of a poem, with lines and stanzas (3.2). We evaluate the frequency of rhymes in the output of this model using our metric (3.3), before moving

[5] github.com/sravanareddy/rhymedata

[6] These are, by decreasing numbers of unknown words: Spenser, Lovelace, Drayton, Jonson, Kipling, and Byron.

[7] huggingface.co/gpt2

on to its specific training for rhyming in the next sections.

3.1 Fine-tuning GPT-2 on Poetry

We use the *Gutenberg Poetry Corpus*[8] composed of approximately 3 million lines of poetry extracted from hundreds of poetry books from Project Gutenberg. Unlike the Chicago Rhyming Poetry Corpus used for validation in Section 2.4, we do not filter out any author. We convert the corpus from the JSON format it into raw text, with poetry lines separated by newline characters ('\n') and no blank lines. Therefore, all information about stanzas, poems and books is removed, and we also delete quotation marks and dashes. However, to emphasize the importance of lines, we prefix each line with a '<start>' tag, which will help generation. The result is a text file with 3,085,063 lines (142 MB). On this data, we fine-tune the smallest GPT-2 model (124M parameters) for three epochs, which takes ca. 3 hours on a single Nvidia GeForce RTX 3080 GPU.

3.2 Setting the Poem's Form

Generating text in a form that is typical of poetry is essential for considering rhyming patterns because without a division into lines (verses) there are no line endings that can rhyme. A general discussion of form constraints is out of the scope of this paper (see Section 4.1 of Popescu-Belis et al., 2022), and we summarize the approach as follows.

We give the desired structure of the poem – number of stanzas, number of lines in each stanza, and number of syllables in each line – to the following algorithm. The first two parameters are easy to constrain, by inserting one or two newline characters. However, it is harder to constrain GPT-2 to generate a pre-specified number of syllables in a line. We generate the poem line by line, with decoding by sampling according to the word probability generated by GPT-2, modulated by a temperature factor. To generate line k, we provide GPT-2 with lines $1, 2, \ldots, k-1$ as context. To obtain the expected number of syllables S_E in line k, we loop through the following steps:

1. Require GPT-2 to generate a line L with a fixed number of tokens, computed from S_E using a ratio of 1.5 syllables per token.[9]
2. Count the actual number of syllables S_L of the line L, using an algorithm for English by Emre Aydin (found at eayd.in/?p=232).
3. Exit the loop with L if $S_L = S_E$, or after 10 iterations.

3.3 Number of Rhymes of the Baseline

Using the GPT-2 model fine-tuned on poetry, we evaluate the number of rhyming verses as a term of comparison with further models. As we cannot make any prior assumption on the rhyming pattern, we simply group the generated verses into pairs (or couplets) by inserting a newline every other verse. When applying our metric to a set of 4,000 couplets generated in this way, we find that only 4.3% have perfect rhymes, while 6.6% have assonant rhymes, and the remaining 89.1% do not rhyme at all.

4 Synthetic Data with Rhymes: Rule-based Generation

We use a rule-based approach to modify the poems generated by the previous model so that they follow a given rhyme scheme, which is specified in conventional form (e.g. AABB, ABAB or ABBA). This is part of our earlier interactive system for poetry generation (Popescu-Belis et al., 2022) which combines LMs with rules governing form, rhymes, topics and emotions.

The rule-based rhyming algorithm parses the scheme, and for every second line of a rhyme (e.g., given AABB, for the second and fourth lines), it modifies the last word so that it rhymes with the last word of the previous line. The inverted rhyming dictionaries presented in Section 2.2 and the fine-tuned GPT-2 model are used as follows.

The algorithm obtains from the first dictionary the perfect rhyme ending the word to replace, and it searches the second dictionary for all the words that share this perfect rhyme. If none is found, the words sharing the respective assonant rhyme are used instead. Each word is inserted in the entire line and the result is submitted to GPT-2, which generates a likelihood score for each of these sequences. The replacement word leading to the highest score is selected. Therefore, to generate rhyming poems, we first generate a non-rhyming one and then we re-generate the last words so that they rhyme according to the given patters.

Using this strategy, we generate large numbers of poems, first with the AABB rhyming pattern, and later with the more challenging ABAB pattern. For

[8] github.com/aparrish/gutenberg-poetry-corpus

[9] Technically, the decoder is given a *maximum* length, but in practice, we never observed end-of-sequence symbols, so this length is always reached.

each pattern we generate 20,000 quatrains (four-line stanzas) resulting in about 6 MB of text. Some cleaning of the data is necessary because some lines are made mostly of punctuation or include special characters. About 0.04% of the lines are removed. To simplify training, we insert a blank line after lines AA and then BB of the quatrain, so that the training data is made of rhyming couplets only. Alternatively, to learn ABAB, we insert a blank line after each quatrain. Our metric found that the first dataset has a rhyming accuracy of 97.8%, which is expected because the rhyming algorithm and the metric make use of the same dictionary.

Moreover, as the LM must capture dependencies between words at the end of lines regardless of the punctuation, we hypothesize that if we remove punctuation at the end of the verses in the training dataset, the LM would better learn rhyming patterns. The results below confirm this hypothesis.

5 Learning Rhyming Patterns from Synthetic Data

5.1 Learning the AABB Pattern

Our first experiment with fine-tuning GPT-2 on synthetic data studies the simplest rhyming pattern, where two consecutive lines rhyme. As stated above, the synthetic data is made of couplets, and this is what we expect the fine-tuned model, called GPoeT, to generate as well.

To measure the proportion of rhyming verses, we consider only the couplets and exclude isolated lines, or stanzas with an odd number of lines. This ensures that we always test the rhyming of paired lines in the sample data. During fine-tuning, we generate ca. 50 kB of text every 10 epochs and measure the proportion of rhyming lines on this sample.[10] Cleaning the isolated lines removes ca. 20% of the text, a number which stays quite constant during fine-tuning (red curve in Figures 1 and 4). In other words, the model produces couplets in 80% of the cases.

The evolution of the rhyming capabilities of GPoeT during fine-tuning is shown in Figure 1. The improvement with respect to the baseline (fine-tuned on the Gutenberg Poetry Corpus only) is very substantial, from a proportion of perfectly rhyming couplets of 4.3% to 56.2% (a factor of 13). When counting both types of rhymes, GPoeT generates 59% of rhyming couplets vs. 7.6% for the baseline

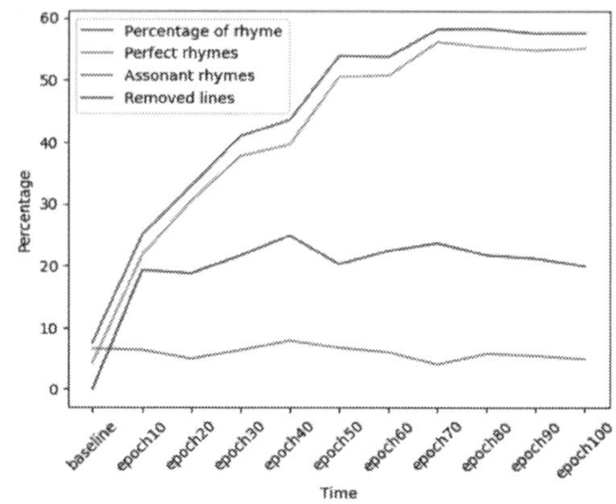

Figure 1: Proportion of perfect and assonant rhymes generated during the fine-tuning of GPoeT on AABB synthetic data, for 100 epochs.

(a factor of 7.7). The proportion of perfect rhymes rises quickly and then converges to around 56% after 70 epochs, while the proportion of assonant rhymes remains quite constant, likely because the data used for fine-tuning has only perfect rhymes. From the evolution of the curves, the system has likely reached its maximal performance.

The learning rate decreases linearly with the number of steps, from 5×10^{-5} to 9×10^{-7} along 10 epochs. After 10 epochs we reset the learning rate to the initial value. In this way, we force larger updates of the parameters at regular time intervals, which makes the model more robust, following our insights from low-resource machine translation (Atrio and Popescu-Belis, 2022). This may improve training, as opposed to a learning rate that decreases too quickly. We can see in Figure 2 that the validation loss globally decreases over time, with small increases every 10 epochs when the learning rate is reset.

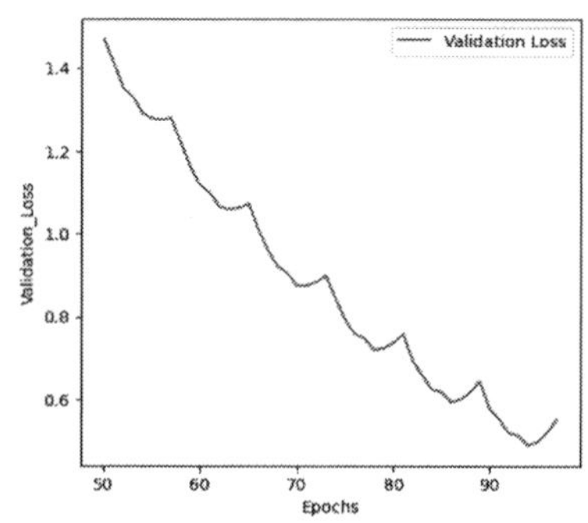

Figure 2: Evolution of the validation loss while learning the AABB pattern.

[10]On one GPU, 10 epochs take about 25 minutes.

We validate the use of quatrains stripped of the final punctuation for training, hypothesizing that such tokens may hinder the learning of rhymes. We compare the proportion of rhymes generated by GPoeT after fine-tuning for 10 epochs on the synthetic quatrains when the final punctuation is kept *versus* deleted. The results shown in Table 2 confirm that deleting the punctuation from the training data is beneficial, and GPoeT was trained beyond 10 epochs on this data only.

	Final punctuation	
Metric	**kept**	**deleted**
Perfect rhymes	13.8%	18.4%
Assonant rhymes	8.1%	7.2%
No rhyme	78.1%	74.4%

Table 2: Scores after 10 epochs on fine-tuning on data with or without punctuation at the end of the lines.

We also experiment with a promising approach for accelerating fine-tuning. We alternate between (1) training on the full synthetic dataset for 20 epochs, and (2) training on a dataset containing only the last word of each line (i.e. pairs of rhyming words) for 10 epochs. The second stage is much quicker, and as the obtained scores are similar, we believe that training only on the rhyming words of lines should be studied in more detail in the future.

5.2 Sample Outputs of GPoeT

We provide below two unedited excerpts selected from the sample generated by the last GPoeT checkpoint.

The prince of men in arms he heard
So bold, so bold the warrior plundered

That she herself in sorrow cried
My God! who made the earth so bide

She sees no other sun above
Nor in that cloudless sky doth dove

My God! who made the earth so fair
And on this cloudless night hath mair

To the sound of your sweet voice
As of a little bird at choice

As in a trance the dreamer hears
At length a voice, so deep, so here's

That in itself it seems a sound
It is as if a great brown ground

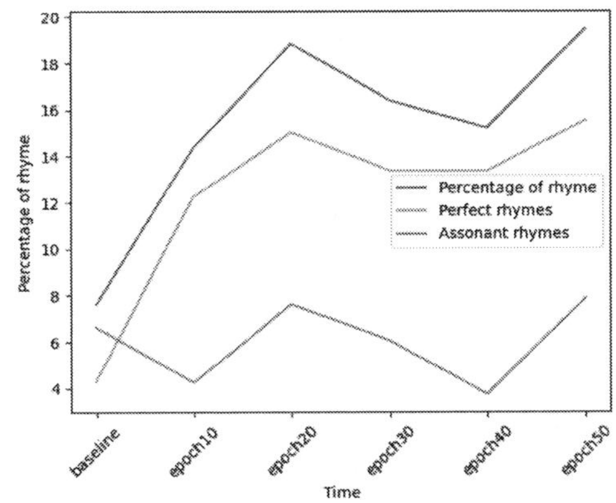

Figure 3: Proportion of perfect and assonant rhymes when training on natural AABB data for 50 epochs.

5.3 Learning from Natural Data

In this experiment, we attempt to teach GPoeT the AABB rhyming pattern using natural rather than synthetic data. We extract from the above-mentioned Chicago Rhyming Poetry Corpus all couplets with consecutive rhyming lines, resulting in a dataset of 2.25 MB of text, mainly with perfect rhymes (75% according to our metric). All other parameters are identical to those of the previous section.

The evolution of the proportions of perfect rhymes and assonant rhymes generated every 10 epochs during training is shown in Figure 3. The proportions are significantly smaller than in the previous experiment, and as the total proportion of rhymes never surpassed 20%, we only represent 50 epochs in the figure. While the model still outperforms the baseline (which has only 7.6% of rhyming verses), it is noticeably less successful than the previous one. It is likely that the smaller amount of data (by a factor of 3) and the larger variety of the vocabulary used by human poets vs. GPT-2 are the main causes of the lower performance.

5.4 Learning the ABAB Pattern

The ABAB rhyming pattern seems more challenging to learn, as line-endings which should rhyme are further apart, separated by one verse. In this experiment, we use our second synthetic dataset, with ABAB quatrains, without separating them into couplets. Quatrains are separated by a blank line. All other parameters are identical to those of the first experiment.

We train the model until the scores stabilize,

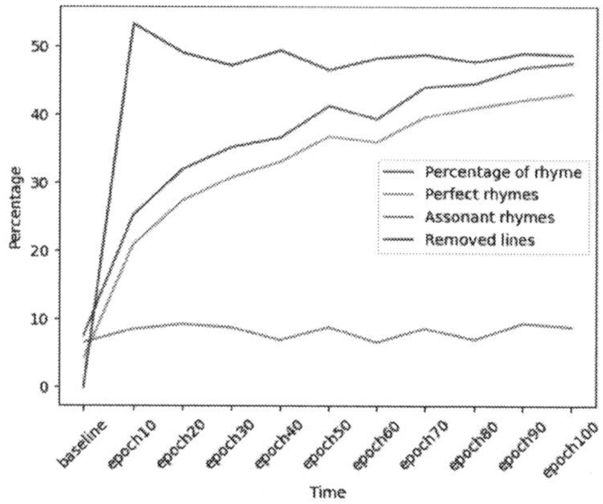

Figure 4: Proportion of perfect and assonant rhymes generated every 10 epochs when training on ABAB synthetic data.

which is around 80 epochs, as shown in Figure 4. The proportion of perfect rhymes rises quickly and converges at around 40%, with a total number of rhyming verses (perfect and assonant) around 45%. Among these, 82.6% are perfect rhymes. As before, to evaluate rhyming, we delete solitary lines, i.e., lines that are not in a quatrain. The proportion of lines retained is 51%, which is much less than above (80%), likely because it is harder to learn to generate a quatrain than a couplet. However, when it generates a full quatrain, the model has clearly learned the ABAB rhyming scheme, although to a lesser extent than the AABB scheme (45% compared to 59%).

6 Related Work

Before the advent of deep neural LMs, various combinations of rule-based approaches and n-gram LMs have been tried. For instance, McGregor et al. (2016) defined a poem generation system which included a phonological model "to impose a sense of prosody" but not dealing with rhymes. In fact, rhyming was not considered the most urgent problem to solve as LMs were struggling with fluency and, especially, meaning.

Large neural LMs have brought high expectations regarding their capacities to generate structured texts such as poems, and clearly improved fluency for high-resource languages. Poem generation with GPT-2 (Radford et al., 2019) was discussed, for instance, by Branwen and Presser (2019) in a blog entry shortly after the model was made available. More recently, ChatGPT (OpenAI, 2022) has tremendously improved the quality and relevance of generated text. However, anecdotal evidence shows that it cannot reliably generate a given rhyming pattern.[11] GPT-4 (OpenAI, 2023), an even larger LM, is likely to improve this capability, as initial analyses seem to show (Bubeck et al., 2023, Sections 1.1 and 6.2).

LMs based on recurrent neural networks (RNNs) were trained by Hopkins and Kiela (2017) on 1.5 MB of English sonnets, first with a single phonetic model and HMM-based phonetic-to-orthographic transliteration, and then with decoupled models for content vs. form. Rhymes from the first model were exemplified, but not evaluated, while the second approach targeted only rhythm, but not rhyme.

'Deep-speare' (Lau et al., 2018) is a LSTM-based system trained on sonnets (2,685 poems), which includes a dedicated orthographic rhyming model, distinct from the LM and from the rhythmic model. The model learns to distinguish rhyming from non-rhyming words in non-annotated quatrains, and during generation it is applied like our rule-based algorithm to select line endings that rhyme. Evaluation is done over word pairs from the CMU pronunciation dictionary, using rules similar to ours to determine ground truth; on this task, their system reaches 0.91 F_1-score.

Wöckener et al. (2021) trained an end-to-end unidirectional word-level RNN on quatrains from the Chicago Rhyming Poetry Corpus. The RNN obeys user-specified constraints such as rhyme, alliteration, sentiment, text length, and time period. These are represented as a feature vector c and concatenated to every input representation to compute $P(w_t|w_0^{t-1}, c)$. Evaluation of rhymes is done with a supervised model (Haider and Kuhn, 2018). They also attempt to fine-tune GPT-2 on pseudo-quatrains from Project Gutenberg, but find that the model does not learn the relevant patterns. They observe an accuracy of 7.5% for rhyming, when compared with a random baseline of 4.2%.

For Chinese, one of the earliest systems using

[11] When asked 'What are the possible rhyming patterns?", ChatGPT enumerates several patterns with definitions and examples, but with factual mistakes such as "ABAB: In this pattern, each line rhymes with the line that comes after it." Moreover, the example generated by ChatGPT for the ABAB pattern is an ABCB stanza. When prompted to "write one quatrain about the ocean, make the first verse rhyme with the third one, and the second with the fourth", ChatGPT generates three fluent quatrains, but with incorrect rhyming patterns (AAAB, CCDE, and FFAA). Moreover, ChatGPT seems unable to reliably generate verses (or even plain sentences) with a fixed number of syllables or words larger than about 7.

RNNs was proposed by Zhang and Lapata (2014), starting from user-provided keywords and generating a quatrain line-by-line, with pre-defined line lengths and tonal patterns. Rhyming is only enforced between the second and fourth lines, simply by disallowing the decoder to select ending characters that do not rhyme. The constraints are similar to the method of Yan et al. (2013) who used a generative summarization approach. Li et al. (2018) built a Chinese poem generator using a variational encoder and adversarial training, starting from a title. Poems were evaluated for topic consistency, fluency, and meaning, but not explicitly for rhyming. Yang et al. (2019) studied the problem of generating a poem from prose and compared LSTM to Transformer models, but did not model explicitly rhymes, nor evaluated them.

PoeTryMe is a rule-based interactive poem generation system initially designed for Portuguese and later extended to Spanish and English (Gonçalo Oliveira, 2017). In the interactive version,[12] assistance is provided to users for selecting end-of-line words that rhyme, through a dictionary. In the standalone Twitter bot (`@poetartificial`), candidates which happen to contain rhyming lines more than others are rewarded. Poem Machine (Hämäläinen, 2018) is an assistant for Finnish, which provides help for rhyming via a phonetic dictionary, but does not select rhyming words automatically. Our own CR-PO system for French (Popescu-Belis et al., 2022), combined a general LM with topic and emotion-specific LMs, and with rules for constraining form and rhymes (the latter are used in this paper).

Hafez was one of the first systems to combine interaction and deep neural LMs (Ghazvininejad et al., 2016, 2017). The system gets the desired features from the user, including keywords and sentiment, transforms them into transducers, and uses a RNN filtered by these transducers to generate a quatrain. Rhyming words are generated early in the process, using word2vec similarity and a phonetic representation, typically in an ABAB pattern, and afterwards they constrain the generation of the poem. Henceforth, rhyming is always ensured.

Van de Cruys (2019, 2020) proposed a RNN encoder-decoder architecture with attention, with GRUs, for English and French poems. The model is trained to generate a line of poetry given the preceding one, with a decoder part that models the new line in reverse order. The advantage of starting from the last word, as for Hafez, is that it can be sampled with a probability distribution that incorporates rhyming constraints, using a rhyming dictionary similar to ours, with an additional bias to avoid repeating the consonant group preceding the final vowel [+ consonant]. In the experiments, the ABAB CDCD pattern is always used. Human judges ranked a set of 40 generated poems almost as high as human ones on several parameters. No scores are provided for rhyming alone, likely because it is nearly perfect given the architecture, but the rhyming component improved scores of 'poeticness' and human-likeliness.

PoeLM (Ormazabal et al., 2022) uses a decoder (GPT-style with 350M parameters) to learn rhythm and syllables from a large corpus of prose in Spanish and Basque. Input text is segmented into phrases, and for each set of phrases of a sentence a set of tags is prepended to the sentence, e.g. `<LEN:11><END:ura>` for an 11-syllable phrase finishing with '-ura'. PoeLM learns these control tags and can leverage them to generate lines of poetry of desired length and endings. However, as the model does not learn rhyming rules (i.e. identity of syllables) but only identifies actual syllables, poem generation must start by specifying exactly the ending syllables of each line. Evaluation is done by completing the initial line of human poems with PoeLM, and then asking human judges which version they prefer.

ByGPT5 (Belouadi and Eger, 2022) is a character-level Transformer-based decoder, with generation conditioned on rhyme, meter, and alliteration. The model is initialized on the decoder of ByT5 (Xue et al., 2022), trained on large amounts of data, and then fine-tuned on a machine-labeled corpus of pseudo-quatrains in English and German, separately. Meter and rhyme are evaluated with classifiers trained on labeled data. Overall, according to automatic and human measures, ByGPT5 produces better results than ByT5 and subword-level models such as GPT-2 and mT5.

7 Discussion and Conclusion

The rhyme-generating LM presented here, GPoeT, is intended for integration in our interactive poem generation system (Popescu-Belis et al., 2022). While the experiments above show that rhyming patterns can be learned from synthetic data, several issues remain to be solved in future studies.

[12] See poetryme.dei.uc.pt.

Our rule-based rhyming algorithm operates on a poem already generated by a LM with several other parameters as input, e.g. a title or first verse, a desired theme or emotion, and a poetical form (such as a sonnet). We must now integrate GPoeT in this pipeline, and ensure that the generated rhymes are not altered by the other constrains of the system. Moreover, we must ensure that the lexical diversity of GPoeT is not reduced by its training on synthetic data.

We intend to address the problem of generating a desired form using the rule-based algorithm presented in Section 3.2, which takes advantage of a maximum length for the LM decoder. It may seem straightforward to replace GPT-2 with GPoeT in this algorithm, in order to obtain rhyming lines of a desired length, but our initial experiments have shown that rhymes are less satisfactory when the desired length is very different from the synthetic data GPoeT was trained on.

Moreover, while our rule-based rhyme generator can be easily adapted to any rhyming pattern, this is not yet the case for GPoeT, which is trained on one pattern at a time in our proof-of-concept. The solution lies probably in using a labeling system to indicate which lines must rhyme, and then training a GPoeT model to learn the effects of labels rather than a single rhyming pattern, in the style of the CTRL model (Keskar et al., 2019).

In this paper, we demonstrated that rhyming is learnable with LMs that can be efficiently fine-tuned and queried with very moderate computing requirements. The key to effective fine-tuning is the use of synthetic data, which we showed how to generate in much larger amounts than what human poets have ever written. However, not all rhyming patterns are learned equally well: a pattern that exhibits longer-term dependencies such as ABAB is harder to learn than a more local one such as AABB. Overall, LMs that are able to deal with rhyme, and later with form, are part of our ongoing effort to design an interactive poetry generator, with the aim of enhancing (but not replacing) human creativity.

Limitations

The technical limitations of this study were discussed to some extent at the beginning of the conclusion (Section 7) and will result in future investigations regarding the generation of specific poetic forms (and line lengths) and on-the-fly selection of rhyming patterns. Our study relies on a phonetic dictionary of English, along with rhyming definitions related to the English-speaking culture: these must be redesigned when porting the system to a new language. The results may have been limited by the use of a rather small LM and reduced computing time, but this also has the advantage of reduced power consumption, and makes it possible to demonstrate the system on a standalone portable workstation.

Ethics Statement

The ethical issues broadly related to the of LMs for text generation also apply to poetry: the generation of offensive content, the reproduction of unethical stereotypes learned from the data, and the substitution of human creativity by machines. While we do not have quick answers to these large societal questions, we observed that due to its training on classic poetry, GPoeT is not likely to generate offensive content (for instance, filtering out bad words has proven unnecessary). Our goal is not the fully-autonomous generation of poems, but co-creation of poetry with human users, who have to steer the system towards a desired form and topic. Our approach is intended to stimulate human creativity, not to replace it.

Acknowledgments

We would like to thank the Swiss National Science Foundation (SNSF) for its support through the Digital Lyric (n. 184330) and the DOMAT projects (n. 175693). We are grateful for the support received from the HES-SO through the PhD fund (AGP n. 107554 and 119509) and from the Institute for ICT at HEIG-VD. We thank EPFL Professors Martin Jaggi and Nicolas Flammarion for the opportunity to conduct a project in their CS-433 machine learning course, and the three anonymous LaTeCH-CLfL reviewers for their helpful suggestions.

References

Àlex R. Atrio and Andrei Popescu-Belis. 2022. On the interaction of regularization factors in low-resource neural machine translation. In *Proceedings of the 23rd Annual Conference of the European Association for Machine Translation (EAMT)*, pages 111–120, Ghent, Belgium. European Association for Machine Translation.

Jonas Belouadi and Steffen Eger. 2022. ByGPT5: End-to-end style-conditioned poetry generation with token-free language models. *arXiv preprint arXiv:2212.10474*.

Gwern Branwen and Shawn Presser. 2019. GPT-2 neural network poetry. *Demo Tutorial*.

Sébastien Bubeck, Varun Chandrasekaran, Ronen Eldan, Johannes Gehrke, Eric Horvitz, Ece Kamar, Peter Lee, Yin Tat Lee, Yuanzhi Li, Scott Lundberg, et al. 2023. Sparks of artificial general intelligence: Early experiments with GPT-4. *arXiv preprint arXiv:2303.12712*.

Marjan Ghazvininejad, Xing Shi, Yejin Choi, and Kevin Knight. 2016. Generating topical poetry. In *Proceedings of the Conference on Empirical Methods in Natural Language Processing (EMNLP)*, pages 1183–1191, Austin, Texas. Association for Computational Linguistics.

Marjan Ghazvininejad, Xing Shi, Jay Priyadarshi, and Kevin Knight. 2017. Hafez: an interactive poetry generation system. In *Proceedings of ACL 2017, System Demonstrations*, pages 43–48, Vancouver, Canada. Association for Computational Linguistics.

Hugo Gonçalo Oliveira. 2017. O Poeta Artificial 2.0: Increasing meaningfulness in a poetry generation Twitter bot. In *Proceedings of the Workshop on Computational Creativity in Natural Language Generation (CC-NLG 2017)*, pages 11–20, Santiago de Compostela, Spain. Association for Computational Linguistics.

Thomas Haider and Jonas Kuhn. 2018. Supervised rhyme detection with Siamese recurrent networks. In *Proceedings of the Second Joint SIGHUM Workshop on Computational Linguistics for Cultural Heritage, Social Sciences, Humanities and Literature*, pages 81–86, Santa Fe, New Mexico. Association for Computational Linguistics.

Mika Hämäläinen. 2018. Poem Machine – a co-creative NLG web application for poem writing. In *Proceedings of the 11th International Conference on Natural Language Generation*, pages 195–196, Tilburg University, The Netherlands. Association for Computational Linguistics.

Jack Hopkins and Douwe Kiela. 2017. Automatically generating rhythmic verse with neural networks. In *Proceedings of the 55th Annual Meeting of the Association for Computational Linguistics*, pages 168–178, Vancouver, Canada. Association for Computational Linguistics.

Nitish Shirish Keskar, Bryan McCann, Lav R Varshney, Caiming Xiong, and Richard Socher. 2019. CTRL: A conditional transformer language model for controllable generation. *arXiv preprint arXiv:1909.05858*.

Jey Han Lau, Trevor Cohn, Timothy Baldwin, Julian Brooke, and Adam Hammond. 2018. Deep-speare: A joint neural model of poetic language, meter and rhyme. In *Proceedings of the 56th Annual Meeting of the Association for Computational Linguistics*, pages 1948–1958, Melbourne, Australia. Association for Computational Linguistics.

Juntao Li, Yan Song, Haisong Zhang, Dongmin Chen, Shuming Shi, Dongyan Zhao, and Rui Yan. 2018. Generating classical Chinese poems via conditional variational autoencoder and adversarial training. In *Proceedings of the 2018 Conference on Empirical Methods in Natural Language Processing (EMNLP)*, pages 3890–3900, Brussels, Belgium. Association for Computational Linguistics.

Stephen McGregor, Matthew Purver, and Geraint Wiggins. 2016. Process based evaluation of computer generated poetry. In *Proceedings of the INLG 2016 Workshop on Computational Creativity in Natural Language Generation*, pages 51–60, Edinburgh, UK. Association for Computational Linguistics.

OpenAI. 2022. ChatGPT: Optimizing language models for dialogue. *OpenAI Blog*.

OpenAI. 2023. GPT-4 technical report. *arXiv preprint arXiv:2303.08774*.

Aitor Ormazabal, Mikel Artetxe, Manex Agirrezabal, Aitor Soroa, and Eneko Agirre. 2022. PoeLM: A meter- and rhyme-controllable language model for unsupervised poetry generation. In *Findings of the Association for Computational Linguistics: EMNLP 2022*, pages 3655–3670, Abu Dhabi, United Arab Emirates. Association for Computational Linguistics.

Andrei Popescu-Belis, Àlex Atrio, Valentin Minder, Aris Xanthos, Gabriel Luthier, Simon Mattei, and Antonio Rodriguez. 2022. Constrained language models for interactive poem generation. In *Proceedings of the Thirteenth Language Resources and Evaluation Conference*, pages 3519–3529, Marseille, France. European Language Resources Association.

Alec Radford, Jeffrey Wu, Rewon Child, David Luan, Dario Amodei, and Ilya Sutskever. 2019. Language models are unsupervised multitask learners. *OpenAI Blog*.

David Uthus, Maria Voitovich, and R.J. Mical. 2022. Augmenting poetry composition with Verse by Verse. In *Proceedings of the 2022 Conference of the North American Chapter of the Association for Computational Linguistics: Human Language Technologies: Industry Track*, pages 18–26, Hybrid: Seattle, Washington + Online. Association for Computational Linguistics.

Tim Van de Cruys. 2019. La génération automatique de poésie en français. In *Actes de la Conférence sur le Traitement Automatique des Langues Naturelles (TALN) PFIA 2019. Volume I : Articles longs*, pages 113–126, Toulouse, France. ATALA.

Tim Van de Cruys. 2020. Automatic poetry generation from prosaic text. In *Proceedings of the 58th Annual Meeting of the Association for Computational Linguistics*, pages 2471–2480, Online. Association for Computational Linguistics.

Jörg Wöckener, Thomas Haider, Tristan Miller, The-Khang Nguyen, Thanh Tung Linh Nguyen, Minh Vu Pham, Jonas Belouadi, and Steffen Eger. 2021. End-to-end style-conditioned poetry generation: What does it take to learn from examples alone? In *Proceedings of the 5th Joint SIGHUM Workshop on Computational Linguistics for Cultural Heritage, Social Sciences, Humanities and Literature*, pages 57–66, Punta Cana, Dominican Republic (online). Association for Computational Linguistics.

Thomas Wolf, Lysandre Debut, Victor Sanh, Julien Chaumond, Clement Delangue, Anthony Moi, Pierric Cistac, Tim Rault, Rémi Louf, Morgan Funtowicz, and Jamie Brew. 2019. HuggingFace's Transformers: State-of-the-art natural language processing. *arXiv preprint arXiv:1910.03771*.

Linting Xue, Aditya Barua, Noah Constant, Rami Al-Rfou, Sharan Narang, Mihir Kale, Adam Roberts, and Colin Raffel. 2022. ByT5: Towards a token-free future with pre-trained byte-to-byte models. *Transactions of the Association for Computational Linguistics*, 10:291–306.

Rui Yan, Han Jiang, Mirella Lapata, Shou-De Lin, Xueqiang Lv, and Xiaoming Li. 2013. i, Poet: Automatic Chinese poetry composition through a generative summarization framework under constrained optimization. In *Proceedings of the 23rd International Joint Conference on Artificial Intelligence (IJCAI)*, pages 2197–2203. AAAI Press.

Zhichao Yang, Pengshan Cai, Yansong Feng, Fei Li, Weijiang Feng, Elena Suet-Ying Chiu, and Hong Yu. 2019. Generating classical Chinese poems from vernacular Chinese. In *Proceedings of the 2019 Conference on Empirical Methods in Natural Language Processing and the 9th International Joint Conference on Natural Language Processing (EMNLP-IJCNLP)*, pages 6155–6164, Hong Kong, China. Association for Computational Linguistics.

Xingxing Zhang and Mirella Lapata. 2014. Chinese poetry generation with recurrent neural networks. In *Proceedings of the 2014 Conference on Empirical Methods in Natural Language Processing (EMNLP)*, pages 670–680, Doha, Qatar. Association for Computational Linguistics.

Quote Detection: A New Task and Dataset for NLP

Selma Tekir and **Aybüke Güzel** and **Samet Tenekeci** and **Bekir Ufuk Haman**
Izmir Institute of Technology
Dept. of Computer Engineering
35430 Izmir, Turkey
{selmatekir, aybukeguzel, samettenekeci, bekirhaman}@iyte.edu.tr

Abstract

Quotes are universally appealing. Humans recognize good quotes and save them for later reference. However, it may pose a challenge for machines. In this work, we build a new corpus of quotes and propose a new task, quote detection, as a type of span detection. We retrieve the quote set from Goodreads and collect the spans through a custom search on the Gutenberg Book Corpus. We run two types of baselines for quote detection: Conditional random field (CRF) and summarization with pointer-generator networks and Bidirectional and Auto-Regressive Transformers (BART). The results show that the neural sequence-to-sequence models perform substantially better than CRF. From the viewpoint of neural extractive summarization, quote detection seems easier than news summarization. Moreover, model fine-tuning on our corpus and the Cornell Movie-Quotes Corpus introduces incremental performance boosts. Finally, we provide a qualitative analysis to gain insight into the performance.

1 Introduction

Human beings have aesthetic appeal. They create and enjoy different works of art. Among these, literary works contain the highest form of bookish experience. People enjoy reading novels and highlighting textual segments that are distinctive and memorable, which we can term quotes. Humans can readily recognize good quotes and save them for later reference. However, it may pose a challenge for machines since the quote detection task relies mostly on semantic features such as memorability and distinctiveness.

The Goodreads website[1] stores a collection of quotes that are extracted from different resources to meet users' expectations. This community-wide interest has led us to propose a work in this context.

This paper proposes a new NLP task, quote detection, as a variant of span detection, and releases a benchmark quotes dataset. In the literature, there is a movie quotes corpus for binary quote classification (Danescu-Niculescu-Mizil et al., 2012). There is also a similar task of quotation detection and classification (Pareti et al., 2013, Papay and Padó, 2020, Vaucher et al., 2021) where the aim is to extract/identify direct, indirect, or mixed speech parts from the text. Quote detection is different and unique in that spans represent the free-standing textual segments that are distinctive and favorable for later reference (Table 1). A similar trend has been in the Viral Texts Project, which interrogates the qualities that cause literary texts to go viral by their reprints in newspapers (Cordell and Smith, 2022). Furthermore, quotes are different from subtexts as subtexts underlie a new meaning connected with a speaker's motive in particular.

To challenge the problem, we first formulate it as a sequence tagging problem and work with a statistical baseline, conditional random field (CRF). Secondly, we regard it as a type of summarization. To have a baseline performance, we experiment with two neural sequence-to-sequence models; the pointer-generator network (Vinyals et al., 2015) and Bidirectional and Auto-Regressive Transformers (BART) (Lewis et al., 2020), respectively. The solutions' performances confirm that the task is relatively easier than the existing summarization problems but is a difficult sequence tagging problem.

The main contributions of this paper are: (a) a corpus of 5015 quotes with their 10 sentence-length left and 10 sentence-length right contexts; (b) a distinctiveness analysis based on language model log-likelihoods and comparison against movie quotes (the Cornell Movie-Quotes Corpus); (c) experimental results from summarization and sequence tagging methods; (d) a qualitative analysis to give insight on errors (whether they are mainly precision

[1] goodreads.com/quotes

Proceedings of the 7th Joint SIGHUM Workshop on Computational Linguistics for Cultural Heritage, Social Sciences, Humanities and Literature (LaTeCH-CLfL2023), pages 21–27
May 5, 2023 ©2023 Association for Computational Linguistics

or recall-based).

2 A Corpus of Quotes

To construct the quote dataset, we rely on two primary resources. The first one is the Goodreads platform which shares a voted collection of quotes. The collection consists of $348,085$ instances, each with Quote, Title, Author, Likes, and Tags columns. We download this collection from Kaggle[2]. As humans recognize good quotes and user rating is an indicator for recognition, we exclude the rows with ≤ 10 likes from the dataset. Another filtering criterion is the language of quotes. We detect the language with the help of Python's NLTK library and remove the non-English quotes. After these two filtering steps, the quote dataset includes $100,837$ rows.

The second resource is the free eBook library Project Gutenberg[3]. We download books in plain text format to check whether a quote appears in the referenced book. For this purpose, we search the title and author of the relevant books in the search section of the Project Gutenberg site and collect the book's plain text links. Then, we scrape plain texts using plain text links by the BeautifulSoup library of Python. We remove the quotes that do not comply with the UTF-8 standard and that give a page not found error (404 error). We also exclude song lyrics and philosopher speeches as we cannot extract the contexts they appear from Project Gutenberg. Finally, we discard quotes from some books of contemporary literature that are not accessible. After filtering, the total number of rows is reduced to 8670.

To search for a quote in the plain text of the target book, we first trim the standard book header and footer using regular expressions. Then, we have a custom search based on the F1 score. We compute the F1 score based on overlap-based precision and recall definitions to determine the best possible match. In our context, precision is the ratio of the number of shared words to the total number of words in the target span, and recall is defined as the ratio of the number of shared words to the total number of words in the ground truth (quote). We also consider the lengths of quotes in this procedure, having faced the fact that a quote can be a phrase within a sentence, a single sentence, or a text made up of a group of sentences. Therefore, we process a sliding window of quote length when searching for the closest sentence or sentences in the book text. For example, if the quote consists of three sentences, we calculate the F1 score by sliding over three sentences in the text and return the three-sentence span with the highest score as the most similar context for the quote.

The next step is the validation of the returned spans. We arrange quotes in different bins based on F1 score thresholds to decide whether each span corresponds to the wanted quote. The match becomes better as the threshold increases, but the dataset size shrinks. We observe that F1 scores increase as the quote lengths decrease. On the other hand, there is no noticeable difference in the quotes' lengths in each bin. We choose the optimum F1 score threshold as 50%, with an average 2.40 sentence count, 22.97 word count per sentence, and 5015 quotes in total.

In the construction of the final collection (T50[4]), each quote is enclosed by 10 left and 10 right sentences. The appendix A.1 includes an example instance.

2.1 Analysis on Distinctiveness of Quotes

Quotes are known to use distinctive vocabulary (Danescu-Niculescu-Mizil et al., 2012). To check the distinctiveness of our quotes dataset, we compare quotes and non-quotes contexts in terms of language use. In particular, we calculate negative log-likelihoods based on a state-of-the-art language model (GPT-2) (Radford et al., 2019) to measure their unique vocabulary use. We rely on the Mann-Whitney U non-parametric test of the null hypothesis that there is no difference between the negative log-likelihoods of quotes and non-quotes in our dataset to test the statistical difference. The test returns a p-value of $P < .001$, which confirms that we can reject the null hypothesis in favor of the alternative. Moreover, the negative log-likelihoods for quotes are higher than their non-quote counterparts, which means that the vocabulary choice in quotes is more discrete.

To further test the language characteristics of our quotes dataset, we run the analysis of variance (Table 2) where the groups are the Cornell Movie-Quotes Corpus quotes (Mov^{+}), their negative samples (Mov^{-}), our dataset's quotes (T50^{+}), and our dataset's non-quote contexts (T50^{-}). We first test the group null hypothesis and get a p-value

[2]kaggle.com/datasets/faellielupe/goodreads-quotes

[3]gutenberg.org

[4]https://cloud.iyte.edu.tr/index.php/s/YO407M8uAglLIY3

Task	Main Source / Structure of Input	Indicators	Examples
Quote Detection	Free-form literary texts (books, poems, lyrics)	Semantic features and distinctive vocabulary	- There is always something left to love. - No medicine cures what happiness cannot.
Quotation Detection	Excerpts from direct or indirect speech (news, political speech, dialog)	Quotation marks and speech verbs	- "I'm in love with you," he said quietly. - Authorities say that the risk still remains.

Table 1: Quote vs Quotation Detection

of $P < .001$ to reject it safely. When we consider pairwise differences, the results confirm a statistical difference between $T50^-$ and $T50^+$ and Mov^- and Mov^+. On the other hand, the test reveals no difference between $T50^+$ and Mov^+, which is another piece of evidence for quote recognition. The negative mean differences in the μ_d column in each row indicate that Group 1 has a lower negative log-likelihood than Group 2, which again shows that Group 1 has a higher probability of occurrence based on the language model.

Group 1	Group 2	μ_d	p-value	Reject
T50$^-$	**T50$^+$**	-43.98	0.001	**True**
T50$^-$	Mov$^-$	-31.91	0.001	True
T50$^-$	Mov$^+$	-65.38	0.001	True
T50$^+$	Mov$^-$	$+12.06$	0.507	False
T50$^+$	**Mov$^+$**	-21.39	0.063	**False**
Mov$^-$	**Mov$^+$**	-33.46	0.022	**True**

Table 2: ANOVA on negative log likelihoods. μ_d: mean difference, $^+$: quote, $^-$: non-quote

3 Experiments

3.1 Datasets

We experiment with two datasets as part of the evaluation. The first is the proposed corpus (T50), and the second is an adapted version of the Cornell Movie-Quotes Corpus (Danescu-Niculescu-Mizil et al., 2012). Although both datasets are similar in nature, they are in different domains; the former is on books while the latter is on movies. We briefly describe the latter in the following subsection.

3.1.1 Cornell Movie-Quotes Corpus

Cornell Movie-Quotes (Danescu-Niculescu-Mizil et al., 2012), is a dataset[5] of movie scripts with memorability annotations. It contains a total of 2197 memorable and non-memorable short text pairs. The dataset also includes 6282 movie quotes (IMDB memorable quotes), each linked to a movie script line.

As the proposed task is quote detection rather than quote classification, we need extended spans of quotes. Since the dataset includes the full movie scripts where the quotes appear, we expand each quote with its left and right contexts, which are 4 script lines each, creating a total length of 9.

3.2 Baselines

3.2.1 Conditional Random Fields (CRF)

As the first baseline, we utilize conditional random fields (CRF) (Lafferty et al., 2001) to catch the span of quotes. Accordingly, each training sample includes 10-length left and right contexts of the quote and the quote itself. CRF computes a feature vector for each word in the training instance and maximizes the likelihood of the output label given the feature vector. The feature vector consists of whether the current word is in the upper or title case or a digit, its first bi-gram and tri-gram, the part-of-speech (POS) tag, the left and right neighbors' case, and digit information with their POS tags. The motivation is that the model captures distinctive vocabulary by its character n-grams. Alternatively, we ran CRF with a feature vector of the word, word level bi-gram, word level tri-gram, their POS tags, 3rd person pronoun (indicator for generality), and the indefinite article (indicator for generality) because Danescu-Niculescu-Mizil et al. (Danescu-Niculescu-Mizil et al., 2012) worked with these features to quantify the level of distinctiveness of a quote. However, our experiments prove that character-level features perform better than their word-level counterparts for CRF. Thus, distinctive vocabulary plays a vital role in the discrimination of quotes. We label each token as previous (`P`), quote (`Q`), or next (`N`). We execute CRF for 500 iterations on T50 and movie datasets and evaluate the model's performance using ROUGE scores.

3.2.2 Pointer Generator Networks

The second baseline is a pointer generator network (See et al., 2017) for text summarization. It com-

[5] cs.cornell.edu/~cristian/memorability.html

bines an LSTM-based sequence-to-sequence model with a pointer network (Vinyals et al., 2015) to summarize news articles and can specify the weight of abstractive/extractive summarization as a variable. As the quote detection task is extractive in nature, we fine-tune and evaluate the model in a fully extractive form. The base model is pre-trained on CNN (Hermann et al., 2015) data without coverage loss (the coverage loss is responsible for making the output more abstractive). We fine-tune this model with the train partition of the T50 data for 5000 steps in batches of 16.

3.2.3 Bidirectional and Auto-Regressive Transformers (BART)

The last baseline is BART (Lewis et al., 2020). BART is a neural sequence-to-sequence model that aims to improve the masked language model and next-sentence prediction objectives within the end-to-end transformer architecture by shuffling the order of sentences and allowing longer sequences to be masked. The model is capable of identifying different types of transformations to the input and making predictions about overall sentence length.

3.3 Evaluation Metrics

Using a train-validation-test split of 0.7-0.1-0.2, sequence-to-sequence models are evaluated using recall-oriented overlap-based ROUGE (Lin, 2004) metrics. For the formal definitions of the evaluation metrics, see Appendix A.2.

3.4 Results

In our experiments with 5-fold cross-validation, the CRF baseline achieves average R1 scores of $20.28 \pm 2.99\%$ and $26.42 \pm 0.13\%$ on T50 and movie datasets, respectively. We report the detailed results, including the R2 and RL scores, in our code repository[6].

Given a test instance in T50, the T50 fine-tuned pointer generator network predicts the ground-truth quote with an R1 score of 43.51% (Figure 1 the leftmost diagram). When we apply the same fine-tuning to the Cornell Movie-Quotes data, we obtain an R1 score of 53.19% on movie quotes. Compared to the CNN pre-trained model result (39.53%) in news summarization, we observe performance improvements using task-specific fine-tuning with T50 and Cornell Movie Quotes.

[6]https://github.com/Darg-Iztech/pointer_summarizer
https://github.com/Darg-Iztech/quote-detection-crf

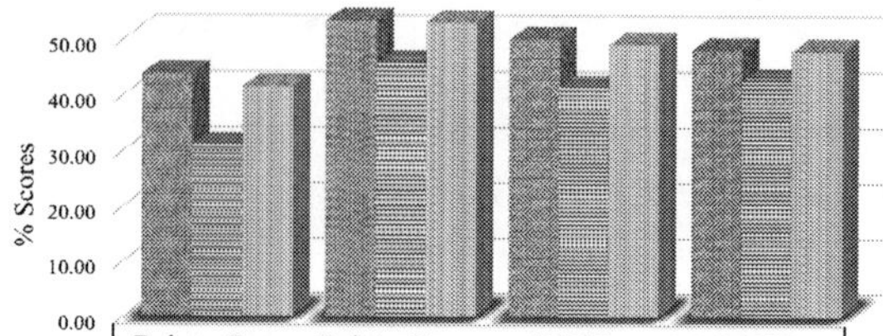

	PointerGen T50	PointerGen Movie Quotes	BART T50	BART Movie Quotes
R1	43.51	53.19	49.78	47.93
R2	30.72	45.52	41.06	42.36
RL	41.25	52.80	48.81	47.66

Figure 1: ROUGE Scores

We perform the same fine-tuning operations with BART on both datasets, resulting in R1 scores of 49.78% and 47.93% (Figure 1 rightmost). The result with the T50 dataset mirrors BART's improvement over the pointer generator network on the summarization benchmarks. However, BART falls behind the pointer generator network on Movie Quotes, which can be attributed to the domain and average length differences.

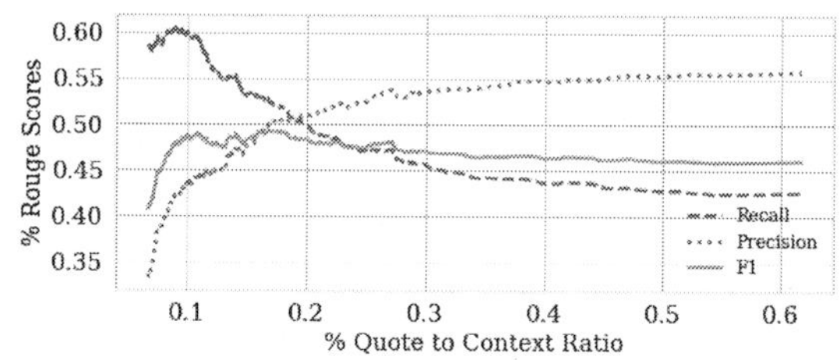

Figure 2: T50 Point-Gen Scores by the relative length

An essential factor for the model performance is the length of quotes. Figure 2 depicts the relationship of the obtained rouge scores with the quote-to-context length ratio. As can be seen from the plot, when the quote length gets higher relative to that of the context, precision increases as a word's probability of being inside the quote gets higher. On the other hand, it becomes difficult to pick all the words in the ground-truth quote correctly, which results in a fall in the recall. Moreover, the challenge remains in the recall, as can be observed by the parallel convergence of recall and F1 curves.

In general, longer quotes favor precision, while shorter ones favor recall. Given similar context lengths, a T50 quote (47 words on average) is almost twice as long as a movie quote (22 words on average). Length statistics for the T50 and Cornell Movie-Quotes datasets in all train, test and validation partitions are given in Table 3.

	T50				Mov			
	Context Lengths		Quote Lengths		Context Lengths		Quote Lengths	
	mean	std.	mean	std.	mean	std.	mean	std.
Train	590	266	47	49	107	62	21	24
Test	606	241	48	44	108	58	22	26
Val	593	263	46	46	109	70	21	24

Table 3: T50 and Movie Quotes Word Count Statistics

3.5 Qualitative Analysis

(a) Quote

let us fear ourselves. prejudices are the real robbers; vices are the real murderers. the great dangers lie within ourselves.

Prediction

let us never fear robbers or murderers. they are dangers from without, petty dangers. let us fear ourselves. prejudices are the real robbers; vices are the real murderers. the great dangers lie within ourselves.

(b) Quote

out of this pack-persecution he learned two important things: how to take care of himself in a mass-fight against him, and how, on a single dog, to inflict the greatest amount of damage in the briefest space of time.

Prediction

how to take care of himself in a mass-fight against him and how, on a single dog, to inflict the greatest amount of damage in the briefest space of time.

Figure 3: Quote prediction examples

Quantitative results prove that finding out quotes in endless contexts poses a difficulty in precision (e.g., 0.1 summary to context ratio in Figure 2), but while the quote to context ratio grows, recall becomes the determining factor.

We perform a qualitative analysis to observe what kind of errors is common in our experiments. We depict two cases (Figure 3) where the model is inclined to overshoot (a) and undershoot (b) the ground truth quotes. In the usual case, it extends the prediction from the beginning (a) or from the end where recall is perfect, but precision is low. Less often, the model undershoots the actual quote as in example (b) of the figure, yielding a perfect precision score and a low recall.

What we can reflect from these examples is that, generally, longer quotes favor precision, while shorter ones favor recall. When the context length is considered, recall increases as the quote-to-context length ratio decreases, and precision follows the opposite pattern. Thus, one can manipulate the context length to steer the recall-precision balance for the model training.

4 Conclusion & Future Work

What makes a sequence of words a quote? Although this question is hard to answer, we empirically show that it has a distinctive vocabulary using language model log-likelihoods on T50. This phenomenon was also confirmed by (Danescu-Niculescu-Mizil et al., 2012) on movie quotes. Moreover, the selected baselines show that it is possible to recognize a quote within its context.

Ultimately, this paper presents the quote detection task by releasing a new dataset with baseline performances. Our results state that quote detection is easier than news summarization using neural summarization. As for sequence tagging, detecting quotes by classifying the beginning and end tokens seems relatively more complicated. Thus, there is much room for improvement over mentioned baselines. We hope this task leads to the development of new methods and data sharing.

5 Limitations

The paper proposes a new task on quote detection and releases a dataset, and provides baselines to meet the purpose. The dataset includes the quotes that appear in books. Although we find similar patterns in movie quotes, the task's difficulty may differ for quotes in other contexts, e.g., lyrics and poems.

Moreover, the provided summarization and sequence tagging baselines give an idea about the difficulty level of the proposed task. They are in no way the best systems to solve the problem.

Finally, in constructing the dataset, each quote is enclosed by 10 left and 10 right sentences. This choice can be considered subjective, knowing that the quote lengths, context lengths, and their ratio have a role in the performance. Accordingly, we provide comments on this behavior in our quantitative and qualitative analyses.

Acknowledgements

The NVIDIA Corporation donated the Titan V used for this research.

References

Ryan Cordell and David Smith. 2022. Viral texts: Mapping networks of reprinting in 19th-century newspapers and magazines. http://viraltexts.org. Accessed: 2023-03-27.

Cristian Danescu-Niculescu-Mizil, Justin Cheng, Jon Kleinberg, and Lillian Lee. 2012. You had me at hello: How phrasing affects memorability. In *Proceedings of the 50th Annual Meeting of the Association for Computational Linguistics (Volume 1: Long Papers)*, pages 892–901, Jeju Island, Korea. Association for Computational Linguistics.

Karl Moritz Hermann, Tomáš Kočiský, Edward Grefenstette, Lasse Espeholt, Will Kay, Mustafa Suleyman, and Phil Blunsom. 2015. Teaching machines to read and comprehend. In *Proceedings of the 28th International Conference on Neural Information Processing Systems - Volume 1*, NIPS'15, page 1693–1701, Cambridge, MA, USA. MIT Press.

John D. Lafferty, Andrew McCallum, and Fernando C. N. Pereira. 2001. Conditional random fields: Probabilistic models for segmenting and labeling sequence data. In *Proceedings of the Eighteenth International Conference on Machine Learning*, ICML '01, page 282–289, San Francisco, CA, USA. Morgan Kaufmann Publishers Inc.

Mike Lewis, Yinhan Liu, Naman Goyal, Marjan Ghazvininejad, Abdelrahman Mohamed, Omer Levy, Veselin Stoyanov, and Luke Zettlemoyer. 2020. BART: Denoising sequence-to-sequence pre-training for natural language generation, translation, and comprehension. In *Proceedings of the 58th Annual Meeting of the Association for Computational Linguistics*, pages 7871–7880, Online. Association for Computational Linguistics.

Chin-Yew Lin. 2004. ROUGE: A package for automatic evaluation of summaries. In *Text Summarization Branches Out*, pages 74–81, Barcelona, Spain. Association for Computational Linguistics.

Sean Papay and Sebastian Padó. 2020. RiQuA: A corpus of rich quotation annotation for English literary text. In *Proceedings of the 12th Language Resources and Evaluation Conference*, pages 835–841, Marseille, France. European Language Resources Association.

Silvia Pareti, Tim O'Keefe, Ioannis Konstas, James R. Curran, and Irena Koprinska. 2013. Automatically detecting and attributing indirect quotations. In *Proceedings of the 2013 Conference on Empirical Methods in Natural Language Processing*, pages 989–999, Seattle, Washington, USA. Association for Computational Linguistics.

Alec Radford, Jeffrey Wu, Rewon Child, David Luan, Dario Amodei, Ilya Sutskever, et al. 2019. Language models are unsupervised multitask learners. *OpenAI blog*, 1(8):9.

Abigail See, Peter J. Liu, and Christopher D. Manning. 2017. Get to the point: Summarization with pointer-generator networks. In *Proceedings of the 55th Annual Meeting of the Association for Computational Linguistics, ACL 2017, Vancouver, Canada, July 30 - August 4, Volume 1: Long Papers*, pages 1073–1083. Association for Computational Linguistics.

Timoté Vaucher, Andreas Spitz, Michele Catasta, and Robert West. 2021. Quotebank: A corpus of quotations from a decade of news. In *Proceedings of the 14th ACM International Conference on Web Search and Data Mining*, WSDM '21, page 328–336, New York, NY, USA. Association for Computing Machinery.

Oriol Vinyals, Meire Fortunato, and Navdeep Jaitly. 2015. Pointer networks. In *Advances in Neural Information Processing Systems*, volume 28. Curran Associates, Inc.

A Appendix

A.1 Example: A Quote with its Span

Are you not happy in your? Naughty darling. At Dolphin's barn charades in Luke Doyle's house. Mat Dillon and his bevy of daughters: Tiny, Atty, Floey, Maimy, Louy, Hetty. Molly too. Eighty-seven that was. Year before we. And the old major, partial to his drop of spirits. Curious she an only child, I an only child. So it returns. ***Think you're escaping and run into yourself. Longest way round is the shortest way home.*** And just when he and she. Circus horse walking in a ring. Rip van Winkle we played. Rip: tear in Henny Doyle's overcoat. Van: breadvan delivering. Winkle: cockles and periwinkles. Then I did Rip van Winkle coming back. She leaned on the sideboard watching. Moorish eyes. Twenty years asleep in Sleepy Hollow.
@highlight
Think you're escaping and run into yourself. Longest way round is the shortest way home.

A.2 Evaluation Metrics

Given an n-gram length N, the ROUGE-N metric between a candidate document D_C and a reference document D_R is given by:

$$\text{ROUGE-N}(D_C, D_R) = \frac{\sum\limits_{r_i \in D_R} \sum\limits_{\omega \in r_i} T(\omega, D_C)}{\sum\limits_{r_i \in D_R} T(r_i)} \tag{1}$$

where r_i are the sentences in the reference document D_R, $T(\omega, D_C)$ is the number of times the specified n-gram ω occurs in the candidate document D_C, and $T(r_i)$ is the number of all n-grams in the specified reference sentence r_i.

To calculate ROUGE-L, we first calculate the recall (R_{lcs}) and precision (P_{lcs}) scores based on the longest common subsequences in the reference (D_R) and candidate (D_C) documents by:

$$R_{lcs}(D_C, D_R) = \frac{\sum_{r_i \in D_R} |\text{LCS}_{\cup}(D_C, r_i)|}{L(D_R)} \quad (2)$$

$$P_{lcs}(D_C, D_R) = \frac{\sum_{r_i \in D_R} |\text{LCS}_{\cup}(D_C, r_i)|}{L(D_C)} \quad (3)$$

where $L(D_R)$ is the number of words in D_R, $L(D_C)$ is the number of words in D_C, and $\text{LCS}_{\cup}(D_C, r_i)$ is the union of the longest common subsequences in D_R and D_C, which is given by:

$$\text{LCS}_{\cup}(D_C, D_R) = \cup_{r_i \in D_R} \{w | w \in \text{LCS}(D_C, r_i)\} \quad (4)$$

where $\text{LCS}(D_C, r_i)$ is the set of longest common subsequences in the candidate document D_C and sentence r_i from reference document D_R. Using R_{lcs} and P_{lcs}, ROUGE-L can be defined as:

$$\text{ROUGE-L}(C, R) = \frac{(1 + \beta^2) R_{lcs}(C, R) P_{lcs}(C, R)}{R_{lcs}(C, R) + \beta^2 P_{lcs}(C, R)} \quad (5)$$

where the parameter β controls the relative importance of the precision and recall. Because the ROUGE score favors recall, β is typically set to a high value.

Improving Long-Text Authorship Verification via Model Selection and Data Tuning

Trang Nguyen **Kenneth Alperin** **Cagri Dagli** **Courtland VanDam** and **Elliot Singer**
MIT Lincoln Laboratory
Lexington, MA US
{trang.nguyen, kenneth.alperin, dagli, courtland.vandam, es}@ll.mit.edu

Abstract

Authorship verification is used to link texts written by the same author without needing a model per author, making it useful for deanonymizing users spreading text with malicious intent. Recent advances in Transformer-based language models hold great promise for author verification, though short context lengths and non-diverse training regimes present challenges for their practical application. In this work, we investigate the effect of these challenges in the application of a Cross-Encoder Transformer-based author verification system under multiple conditions. We perform experiments with four Transformer backbones using differently tuned variants of fanfiction data and found that our BigBird pipeline outperformed Longformer, RoBERTa, and ELECTRA and performed competitively against the official top ranked system from the PAN evaluation. We also examined the effect of authors and fandoms not seen in training on model performance. Through this, we found fandom has the greatest influence on true trials, pairs of text written by the same author, and that a balanced training dataset in terms of class and fandom performed the most consistently.

1 Introduction

As more people turn to various online sources for their information, the ability to discriminate and discern authorship characteristics is critical to counter misinformation, plagiarism, and inappropriate aggregation. Understanding authorship is also essential to detecting individuals who make use of the anonymity afforded by the Internet to engage in harassment, impersonation, or criminal activities. Conversely, such technologies could also be applied in unethical ways such as the deanonymization of whistle-blowers, for example. Additionally, the identification of bots and information operation campaigns is essential in the areas of cyber and national security.

Authorship analysis includes multiple tasks that address different use cases. The goal of author identification/attribution is to identify if a document was written by one of a known set of authors and, if yes, specify the individual. Author verification compares two documents to determine if they were written by the same author, without directly identifying or providing author information.

Advancements in authorship analysis have been furthered by efforts in the community. PAN[1] is a yearly series of shared tasks on important text forensics topics, including authorship. The PAN author verification task from 2020 (Bevendorff et al., 2020) and 2021 (Bevendorff and et al., 2021) uses a fanfiction dataset. Fanfiction has many interesting traits with respect to its use for automated authorship verification: the documents are long-text, authors can write stories in different fandoms (e.g., Harry Potter or Star Trek), and authors may emulate a certain style when writing within a specific fandom.

Traditional approaches to authorship recognition often focus on modeling lexical choice (i.e. word usage) or stylometry separately. Modern, deep learning-based approaches are much more expressive. New developments in Transformers and other large language models have been incredibly impactful in natural language processing and have been used to great success in tasks such as machine translation, text generation, and question and answering. Open-source communities make using these models easy and accessible.

For author recognition, these more expressive models have the potential to learn both lexical and stylometric information at the same time. One challenge in realizing this potential, however, is context length. Authorship is a subtle task and the more information the model can integrate at one time, the more of this subtlety can be captured. Further, diversity in training data can also play a

[1] https://pan.webis.de/

Proceedings of the 7th Joint SIGHUM Workshop on Computational Linguistics for Cultural Heritage, Social Sciences, Humanities and Literature (LaTeCH-CLfL2023), pages 28–37
May 5, 2023

large role in the quality and robustness of trained models.

Accordingly, in this paper, we evaluate Transformer models for author verification on the long-text fanfiction data from PAN and attempt to understand the influence of topic and data tuning on performance. Our main contributions are the following:

- We evaluate four different Transformer models for author verification in terms of performance and their response to the fandom effect: standard models (RoBERTa, ELECTRA) and long-text models (Longformer, BigBird).
- We show that BigBird outperforms the other tested models and is competitive with systems submitted to PAN20/21.
- We demonstrate the impact of data tuning and preparation as an initial step into understanding how different aspects of a dataset influences model performance.

In the following sections, we first discuss work in the area of Transformers for authorship attribution and verification; outline the creation/tuning and statistical breakdown of our datasets; present our Cross-Encoder approach for verification; and then describe and discuss our experiments and results regarding the relative performance of multiple Transformer backbones, the fandom effect, and the performance of our BigBird Cross-Encoder on the official PAN20/21 test sets and how it is influenced by the dataset tuning.

2 Related Work

Previous approaches for author identification focused on traditional machine learning models with lexical information or stylometry, such as Burrow's Delta (Burrows, 2002). Deep learning approaches, like Transformers, have shown promising results for author identification. Fabien et al. (2020) developed a BERT approach and incorporated stylistic and hybrid features into their model to improve performance. Barlas and Stamatatos (2020) combined a multi-headed classifier (MHC) with pre-trained language models to evaluate their system's performance for cross-topic and cross-domain author verification (e.g., essays versus emails). They showed both the ELMo and BERT versions of their system outperformed a Recurrent Neural Network (RNN) baseline for cross-topic. Further in Barlas and Stamatatos (2021), they introduced transfer learning and evaluated an additional cross-fandom author identification scenario. This is different than our work, where we are using cross-fandom as our cross-topic scenario. In these experiments, their ELMo and ULMFiT systems outperformed their RNN baseline but was not SOTA for the target dataset.

Although pre-trained models overall appear promising for authorship analysis tasks, some work has been done that highlights possible limitations of these approaches. In Altakrori et al. (2021), the authors focused on the effect of topic and proposed a topic confusion task, where author and topic pairs are swapped between the train and test datasets.

Transformers' use in author verification has mixed results. Manolache et al. (2021) evaluated several BERT-like models for author verification using the PAN20/21 data with good success. However, their experiments also indicated these models relied on topical information rather than authorship characteristics. As in our work, the authors investigated how data partitioning affected model performance. However, this work was limited to dataset tuning based on disjoint authors or fandoms.

Ordoñez et al. (2020) used Longformer for the PAN20 challenge but had very different results on their test splits and the official PAN test set. Their model performed worse than the baselines provided by PAN. Conversely, in Peng et al. (2021), the authors used a BERT-based model for PAN21 (open-set scenario) and had promising results when compared to other models trained on the small dataset.

These works inspired us to explore how pre-trained Transformer models performed for author verification. PAN20/21 is a great source of long-text data, so we compared general Transformers with ones specialized for long-text. We also studied how fandoms and datasets affect performance.

3 Datasets

PAN offered data for closed and open-set author verification tasks. We used four training/validation sets and four test sets, with all training sets and two test sets derived from the PAN training data.

3.1 PAN20/21 Official Data Overview

The data used came from the PAN20 and PAN21 authorship verification tasks, which provided an official training dataset (with small/large versions) and two official test sets for the closed-set/open-set cases. These datasets consist of fanfiction text trial pairs. We used the large training set (PAN20 Shuffled), with 490k texts by 278k authors in 1.6k fandoms. The PAN test sets are smaller at 28.6k texts/12.6k authors and 49k texts/40k authors respectively. Both contain 400 fandoms. For each trial, PAN provides the fandoms and raw texts. Texts can appear in multiple trial pairs. In order to be as generalizable as possible, our models did not use the fandom information.

3.2 PAN20 Curated Datasets

To better study the effect of topic as a confounder, we resampled pairs from the official PAN20 training corpus to create new sets of splits for closed- and open-set verification conditions which we refer to as PAN20 Curated (Closed) and PAN20 Curated (Open), respectively. These datasets were created without prior knowledge about the structure of the official test datasets.

3.2.1 Curation and Post-Processing

We first separated the given trial pairs in the PAN20 large training set into texts by author and assigned unique story IDs to texts to create a pool of stories for resampling. We removed "inactive" authors with fewer than 20 associated texts in the corpus.

To investigate the role of topical variation, we designed splits to assess systems' abilities to model authorship within/across fandoms by bi-clustering stories based on authorship and fandom. We first formed the active-author-fandom matrix, and then performed spectral co-clustering to create four unique author-fandom co-clusters. Each quadrant (00, 01, 10, and 11) represents a unique grouping of stories with respect to author and fandom. The main clusters, 00 and 11, are completely disjoint in terms of authors and fandoms. Diagonal clusters, 01 and 10, contain the subset of texts that overlap in author/fandom of the main clusters.

For the closed-set verification scenario, PAN20 Curated (Closed), the training data consists of stories from the 00 and 11 author-fandom cluster conditions. Validation and test data are sampled from clusters 01 and 10. For the open-set scenario, PAN20 Curated (Open), the training data consists of story pairs sampled uniformly from the 00 author-fandom condition.

To reduce biases in the validation and test datasets, we did post-filtering to rebalance the number of authors and fandoms. We then sampled trial pairs from each cluster. Validation and test datasets are sampled from the filtered set of stories. We sampled uniformly across combinations of fandoms within trial pairs and set the open-set condition at 60% of all pairs.

3.3 PAN20 Equal Dataset

We created the PAN20 Equal training dataset to have an equal number of trials of each type: same author within the same fandom (TT WIN), same author between fandoms (TT BW), different authors within the same fandom (FT WIN), and different authors between fandoms (FT BW). Authors and their unique texts were randomly sampled and recombined to create trials for each type. The total number of trials per type was arbitrarily capped.

3.4 Statistical Breakdown of Datasets Used

To investigate how dataset tuning and features affect performance, we tabulated the trials, authors, and fandoms represented over each trial type. These can be seen in Table 1. We defined trials by two characteristics: whether the trial was a TT or FT pair, and whether the trial text was WIN or BW fandoms. The tables show the unique number of trials, authors, and fandoms for that trial type. The PAN20 Curated datasets (Closed and Open) have the most trials in both train and test, with PAN20 Curated Closed having the most with 780k/210k train/test. Most of the datasets have a smaller proportion of TT WIN trials, and the official PAN20/21 Test data sets and PAN20 Shuffled have none of this trial type. These three datasets also have a relatively small percentage of FT WIN.

Author distribution is fairly equal across the trial types for PAN20 Curated (Closed and Open) because this was a tuning focus. However, they contain few authors relative to the other datasets. PAN20 Shuffled contains the most unique authors at 227k total. The representation of authors in PAN20 Shuffled, PAN20 Equal, and the PAN20/21 Test data sets is skewed towards FT BW, as the data has a large number of single text authors and fandoms with few texts.

In terms of fandom distribution, all the training datasets contained a majority of the available 1600 fandoms, except for PAN20 Curated (Open) (with only 784) because of its post-processing. Similarly, the PAN20 Curated (Open) Test set also contained the fewest unique fandoms at 204, while PAN20 Curated (Closed) Test contained more than double the official test sets with 1151 fandoms. FT WIN trials had the least fandom representation, except

	PAN20 Curated (Closed)		PAN20 Curated (Open)		PAN20 Shuffled		PAN20 Equal	
Train Dataset Statistics	**TT**	**FT**	**TT**	**FT**	**TT**	**FT**	**TT**	**FT**
Trial Pairs WIN	18869	186885	10679	106640	0	18388	39538	39538
Trial Pairs BW	90179	481572	51204	241032	118392	83672	39538	39538
Total Trial Pairs	777505		409555		220452		158152	
Authors WIN	2584	2590	1446	1452	0	36776	14402	31531
Authors BW	2590	2592	1452	1452	36591	165045	18955	56560
Total Authors	2592		1452		227274		60366	
Fandoms WIN	1251	759	703	408	0	252	1525	1522
Fandoms BW	1383	1393	773	784	1600	1600	1593	1589
Total Fandoms	1393		784		1600		1597	
Test Dataset Statistics	**TT**	**FT**	**TT**	**FT**	**TT**	**FT**	**TT**	**FT**
Trial Pairs WIN	8184	49580	3760	6099	0	209	0	992
Trial Pairs BW	31404	120994	5572	10942	7786	6316	10000	9007
Total Trial Pairs	210162		26373		14311		19999	
Authors WIN	1594	1587	280	269	0	418	0	1984
Authors BW	1456	1615	249	280	2907	11139	7615	18014
Total Authors	1615		280		12636		27613	
Fandoms WIN	1044	531	200	115	0	5	0	20
Fandoms BW	1140	1151	196	198	399	400	400	388
Total Fandoms	1151		204		400		400	

Table 1: Unique trial, author, and fandom counts for train and test datasets

in PAN20 Equal where each trial type had roughly the same number of unique fandoms.

Our datasets had differences in the extent and focus of their tuning as shown by the trial type, author, and fandom distributions. This variation in datasets allowed us to more thoroughly evaluate our system approach and Transformer backbones.

4 System Approach

We proposed a Transformer-based Cross-Encoder model setup for authorship verification that allowed us to evaluate several Transformer backbones and compared them to the baseline from PAN. This baseline (called "naïve" in the PAN official results and "cosine" in ours) is based on Term Frequency-Inverse Document Frequency (TF-IDF) cosine similarity computed over word tokens.

4.1 Cross-Encoder Model

Our Cross-Encoder system was designed to use existing pre-trained models from HuggingFace (Wolf et al., 2020). With a cross-encoder, each trial pair is passed to the classifier without creating individual text embeddings.

Training and validation trial pairs are subsampled in a balanced fashion with respect to TT/FT. The exact number of pairs used for train/validation is specified during experiment setup. We evaluated the impact of sample size on performance but only show results for one subsample in this paper. Text pairs are tokenized using the associated Huggingface Transformer tokenizer then passed to the Transformer backbone for classification.

We also included an option for "windowing" trials prior to tokenization. When windowing, a window equal to half the maximum length (dependent on the specified token limit) is randomly chosen for each text in the pair. We predicted windowing would improve performance, particularly when using smaller token limits, since the window of text can be pulled from any part of the story and different windows of the same story are used over multiple epochs thereby increasing coverage. At inference time, scores from multiple windowings of a test pair are pooled and returned as the final test pair score.

4.2 Transformer Backbone

We performed experiments with four Transformer backbones. DistilRoBERTa and ELECTRA have a token limit of 512 but use different pre-training approaches. DistilRoBERTa is the distilled version

Model	Windowing	Learning Rate	Gradient Clip	Precision	Batch Size
BigBird	Y	3.00E-03	0	16	2
Longformer	N	5.00E-04	0	16	4
DistilRoBERTa	Y	3.00E-04	1	32	16
ELECTRA	Y	3.00E-04	0	16	4

Table 2: Optimal hyper-parameters for each transformer backbone

	Model	PAN20 Curated (Open) Test		PAN20 Test		PAN21 Test	
		EER	AUC	EER	AUC	EER	AUC
PAN20 Curated (Open) Train	**BigBird**	**0.067**	**0.982**	**0.08**	**0.976**	**0.081**	**0.975**
	Longformer	0.221	0.869	0.224	0.855	0.251	0.831
	DistilRoBERTa	0.192	0.893	0.226	0.856	0.192	0.889
	ELECTRA	0.261	0.815	0.326	0.739	0.311	0.754
	Cosine Baseline	0.235	0.841	0.293	0.778	0.274	0.797
PAN20Shuffled Train	**BigBird**	**0.082**	**0.976**	**0.072**	**0.979**	**0.048**	**0.990**
	Longformer	0.143	0.936	0.144	0.928	0.109	0.959
	DistilRoBERTa	0.258	0.818	0.230	0.853	0.172	0.907
	ELECTRA	0.270	0.813	0.221	0.862	0.178	0.904
	Cosine Baseline	0.237	0.838	0.297	0.780	0.281	0.798

Table 3: Results for Transformer-backbone Cross-Encoder Models for two training sets and three test sets

of RoBERTa (a model that builds and improves on the original BERT model) and uses Masked language modeling (MLM) and next sentence prediction (Sanh et al., 2019). ELECTRA uses the same underlying BERT model but is pre-trained on a task called replaced token detection (RTD), which was shown to be more efficient for some problem sets (Clark et al., 2020). We show the results from ELECTRA Large.

Longformer and BigBird are Transformers designed for longer text and have a token limit of 4096. Both are based on RoBERTa. Longformer's approach to self-attention is to use global attention and a sliding window for local context (Beltagy et al., 2020). Although Longformer can notionally have dilated windows, the HuggingFace implementation does not support this option. BigBird has a slightly different approach to self-attention, and uses a combination of global attention, windows for local context, and random attention (Zaheer et al., 2020).

5 Experimental Results and Discussion

Our approach was to evaluate our Cross-Encoder model using multiple Transformer backbones on datasets with different types of tuning, and then compare its performance to the PAN baseline systems. We first optimized the hyper-parameters for each backbone, then examined the model's performance and effect of fandom.

After identifying BigBird as the backbone with the best performance, we evaluated the Cross-Encoder model using the metrics from the PAN challenge across all combinations of the multiple dataset variants.

5.1 Setup and Hyper-Parameter Selection

We conducted all Cross-Encoder experiments by subsampling to 50k pairs for training and 2k pairs for validation. Using larger subsamples did not dramatically increase performance. Each Transformer used its maximum token limit. We used twenty epochs for training, with early stopping after three epochs of no improvement. We scored each test trial using five different window-pairs and average-pooling to report the final score for each test trial.

We ran experiments with the Cross-Encoder models and a range of hyper-parameters to identify the optimal hyper-parameters for each Transformer backbone. Hyper-parameters that differed among Cross-Encoder models are shown in Table 2.

The learning-rate, gradient clipping, batch size, and windowing all had significant impact on the system performance. The precision did not affect performance, but it along with the batch size were limited by the hardware available.

We found only the Longformer Cross-Encoder

did not improve with windowing, while only the DistilRoBERTa Cross-Encoder benefited from gradient clipping. The BigBird Cross-Encoder did best with a larger learning rate but required a smaller batch size.

5.2 Comparison of Transformer-Based Cross-Encoders

The area under the curve (AUC) and equal error rate (EER) of the Cross-Encoder models and cosine baseline for two training sets and three test sets are shown in Table 3. Note we do not show all the dataset combinations here for simplicity.

The BigBird Cross-Encoder model outperforms regardless of train and test dataset, while the ELECTRA backbone tends to have poor performance. All Transformer Cross-Encoders performed best in the PAN20 Shuffled train/PAN21-Test experiment, with EER ranging from 4.8% for BigBird to 17.8% for ELECTRA.

As shown in the detection error tradeoff (DET) plots in Figure 1, the training data used impacts relative performance of the DistilRoBERTa and Longformer Cross-Encoders. For PAN20 Curated (Open) train/PAN21-Test, DistilRoBERTa outperforms Longformer, which is unexpected given that Longformer is meant for long text. However, when trained with PAN20 Shuffled, results are as expected: the long-text-specific Longformer does better than the more general DistilRoBERTa.

The Longformer backbone's relative performance inconsistency appears due to sensitivity to the training dataset. The Longformer Cross-Encoder EER increased from 10.9% to 25.1% when training with PAN20 Shuffled versus PAN20 Curated Open for the PAN21-Test experiment. The ELECTRA Cross-Encoder model has a similar sensitivity, and its EER increased from 17.8% to 31.1%. Comparatively, the DistilRoBERTa system was more stable (17.2% –> 19.2%).

5.3 Fandom Effect

To further explore the effect of topic, we considered fandom match/mis-match at the pair level (i.e., between TTs and FTs). These results are shown in Table 4, again for PAN20 Shuffled Open train/test. Note that ELECTRA and Longformer Cross-Encoder results are not shown but are consistent with DistilRoBERTa. Systems show a similar pattern, with fandom appearing to have a particularly strong influence on performance of TT pairs. For the BigBird Cross-Encoder, the highest performing breakout experiment (TTs from within the same fandom, FTs from between fandoms) has an EER of 0.98%, which is much lower than the average EER of approximately 6.7%. This may be because for this condition, the system can lean on its ability to match similar topical content (within fandom TTs) and discriminate between different topical content (between fandom FTs). The breakout condition where this ability is not as useful is the lowest performing breakout condition (TTs from between fandoms, FTs from within the same fandom), where the performance is an order of magnitude worse (nearly 10% EER). In this case, matching/discriminating topical content is actually a hindrance to performance. A primary difference between these results and those of the other Transformer systems is that the BigBird Cross-Encoder has effectively eliminated the effect of within/between fandom for FTs. We focus on the BigBird Cross-Encoder system going forward due to its strong performance.

5.4 Datasets Comparison using BigBird Cross-Encoder

Table 5 shows the performance of our BigBird Cross-Encoder model and the cosine baseline for multiple combinations of the four training and four test datasets. This table includes two performance metrics for each experiment: AUC and the official PAN challenge score (the average of the AUC, F1, F0.5u, c@1, and Brier score). These scores were calculated using the offical PAN scoring code.[2]

Because PAN introduced the notion of "unanswered" trials in the challenge and scoring, we included two versions of our BigBird model: the original version and a modified version that manually sets scores that round to 0.5 to "unanswered" (denoted by *). This was done to evaluate the uncertainty of our system. Our original Cross-Encoder system does not leave trials unanswered, so we created the BigBird Cross-Encoder* to naively allow it to mark difficult trials.

The BigBird Cross-Encoder model did well for all dataset combinations and significantly outperformed the cosine baseline. Naively leaving trials unanswered with BigBird Cross-Encoder* generally increased the overall PAN score. BigBird Cross-Encoder* assigned less than 2% of total trials

[2] https://github.com/pan-webis-de/pan-code/tree/master/clef22/authorship-verification

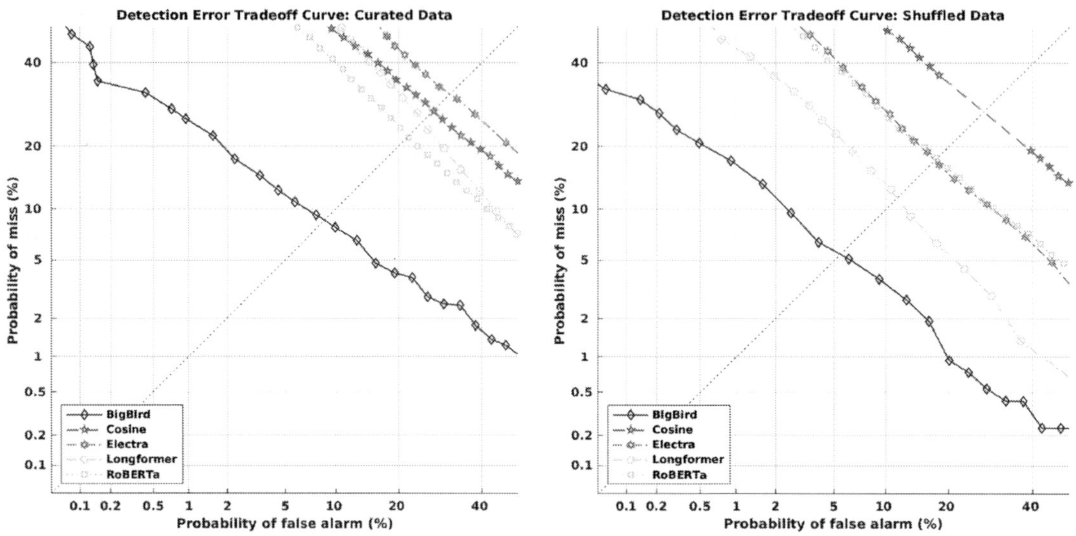

Figure 1: DET plots of Transformer-Based Cross-Encoder performance comparison for PAN21-Test trained using PAN20 Curated (Open) on the left and PAN20 Shuffled on the right. (Lines closer to the lower left are better)

			False Trials (FT)			
			Within Fandom		Between Fandom	
			AUC	EER	AUC	EER
DistilRoBERTa	True Trial (TT)	Within Fandom	0.981 ± 0.002	0.068 ± 0.006	0.994 ± 0.001	0.035 ± 0.005
		Between Fandom	0.783 ± 0.009	0.288 ± 0.009	0.864 ± 0.008	0.220 ± 0.010
BigBird	True Trial (TT)	Within Fandom	0.999 ± 0.001	0.009 ± 0.007	0.999 ± 0.001	0.0098 ± 0.006
		Between Fandom	0.967 ± 0.008	0.091 ± 0.016	0.966 ± 0.008	0.088 ± 0.015

Table 4: Performance breakdown to show fandom effect by trial type using PAN20 Curated (Open)

	Model	PAN20 Curated (Closed) Test		PAN20 Curated (Open) Test		PAN20 Test		PAN21 Test	
		AUC	PAN	AUC	PAN	AUC	PAN	AUC	PAN
PAN20 Curated (Closed) Train	BigBird	0.987	0.9215	-	-	0.980	0.9469	0.977	0.9381
	BigBird*	0.987	0.9268	-	-	0.980	0.9498	0.977	0.9421
	Cosine Baseline	0.805	0.7098	-	-	0.779	0.5635	0.798	0.6110
PAN20 Curated (Open) Train	BigBird	-	-	0.982	0.9416	0.976	0.9262	0.975	0.9352
	BigBird*	-	-	0.982	0.9452	0.976	0.9292	0.975	0.9384
	Cosine Baseline	-	-	0.841	0.7840	0.778	0.4474	0.797	0.6416
PAN20 Shuffled Train	BigBird	0.975	0.8976	0.976	0.9224	0.979	0.9416	0.990	0.9582
	BigBird*	0.975	0.9044	0.976	0.9264	0.979	0.9440	0.990	0.9596
	Cosine Baseline	0.806	0.5893	0.838	0.7212	0.780	0.7554	0.798	0.7610
PAN20 Equal Train	BigBird	0.983	0.9280	0.981	0.9426	0.982	0.9370	0.984	0.9416
	BigBird*	0.983	0.9325	0.981	0.9454	0.982	0.9390	0.984	0.9436
	Cosine Baseline	0.805	0.7020	0.837	0.7874	0.780	0.5234	0.797	0.7048

Table 5: BigBird Cross-Encoder performance for various dataset combinations. Scores in grey are best across systems

unanswered for all experiments, which was fewer than the cosine baseline (4.37% to 20.15% unanswered). This indicates the BigBird Cross-Encoder model has more separation in its TT and FT predictions than the baseline model.

No training set performed best across all test datasets. However, we did notice some patterns in the results. First, training datasets generally performed best with test sets that matched in terms of distribution of trials, authors, and fandoms, e.g., PAN20 Curated performed the best with the PAN20 Curated test sets, and PAN20 Shuffled performed best with PAN21-Test. While this does not hold for the case of PAN20-Test, this is a more complicated comparison because the results are a mixture of open- and closed-set verification.

The second observation is PAN20 Equal performed consistently for all test sets, even though it contains the fewest total trials and has fewer authors than PAN20 Shuffled. This could be a first step towards identifying a tuning approach for generalizable datasets. Although systems trained with this dataset do not always achieve top performance, they do outperform compared to other training sets in at least some of the individual performance metrics for all test sets except PAN21-Test. It is unlikely that the distribution of trials, authors, and/or fandoms in a test set of interest will always be known, so understanding what makes a training dataset more general is critical.

For the official PAN20-Test and PAN21-Test datasets, the best training datasets were PAN20 Curated (Closed) and PAN20 Shuffled respectively. Table 6 shows the BigBird Cross-Encoder performance using these training datasets compared to the official results of the PAN20/21 challenge top participant systems (Bevendorff and et al., 2021). These include hybrid neural-probabilistic, neural network-based, logistic regression, and graph-based Siamese network systems (Boenninghoff et al., 2020, 2021; Weerasinghe and Greenstadt, 2020; Embarcadero-Ruiz et al., 2021). Note here the systems submitted by the same team are not necessarily the same across PAN20 and PAN21 because some systems used for the PAN20 closed-set challenge relied on fandom information. The BigBird Cross-Encoder* model performed competitively with the top performers from the challenge, and can be used without modification for both tasks since it does not use fandom data. While this table shows our best results, the PAN score was > 0.9 for every training dataset we evaluated. Overall, for the PAN20/21 challenge the BigBird Cross-Encoder model performed very well, despite having a straightforward architecture and using a naive approach to leaving trials unanswered. There was limited benefit in using the tuned training datasets for PAN, potentially because the provided official training data matched distributions of the official test data so well. Future work will entail leveraging explainable AI techniques to understand black-box aspects of these models, including why BigBird is less affected by variations in training regminens.

6 Conclusion

We compared several Transformer backbones with our Cross-Encoder systems and found the choice in backbone dramatically impacted the feasibility of our Cross-Encoder model for long-text authorship verification. BigBird outperformed another long-text Transformer (Longformer) and two general Transformers that use different pre-training approaches (DistilRoBERTa and ELECTRA). Our experiments show that Longformer and ELECTRA are both sensitive to the tuning and preparation of training data. Our Longformer results were consistent with Ordoñez, et. al (2020); this sensitivity to datasets makes Longformer and ELECTRA non-ideal candidates for this task.

We found that fandom (which we considered equivalent to topic) is particularly important for TTs. TTs that are between fandom were significantly more difficult for our system to correctly predict than those that were within fandom. This fandom effect was seen to a lesser extent for FTs but was eliminated in BigBird Cross-Encoder. This visible fandom effect indicates that there is still room for future work to improve the model's ability to learn features of the author and reduce reliance on fandom.

Our BigBird Cross-Encoder performed very competitively with the official PAN20/21 scores and outperformed the top system for both the closed- and open-set verification tasks with only a naïve approach to leaving hard trials unanswered. These results show that BigBird may have great potential for author recognition work.

The BigBird Cross-Encoder performed well on PAN20/21 test sets without extra tuning, but different data tuning approaches affect system performance on test sets. For example, the minimally processed PAN20 Shuffled did not work the best for

	Team	Training	AUC	F1-Score	F0.5u	c@1	Brier	Overall
PAN20	boenninghoff20	large	0.969	0.936	0.907	0.928	-	0.935
	weerasinghe20	large	0.953	0.891	0.882	0.88	-	0.902
	boenninghoff20	small	0.94	0.906	0.853	0.889	-	0.897
	weerasinghe20	small	0.939	0.86	0.817	0.833	-	0.862
	BigBird Cross-Encoder*	PAN20 Curated (Closed)	0.980	0.938	0.947	0.934	0.946	0.950
PAN21	boenninghoff21	large	0.9869	0.9524	0.9378	0.9502	0.9452	0.9545
	embarcaderoruiz21	large	0.9697	0.9342	0.9147	0.9306	0.9305	0.9359
	weerasinghe21	large	0.9719	0.9159	0.9245	0.9172	0.9340	0.9327
	weerasinghe21	small	0.9666	0.9071	0.9270	0.9103	0.9290	0.9280
	BigBird Cross-Encoder*	PAN20 Shuffled	0.9900	0.9440	0.9620	0.9460	0.9560	0.9596

Table 6: Comparison of BigBird Cross-Encoder and PAN top performing systems

the PAN20 Curated test sets. Matching the distribution of trials, authors, and fandoms between train and test data led to the best performance, but this approach is not necessarily feasible for real-world applications. We found that the PAN20 Equal training data, which was tuned for equal trial types, performed consistently across all the test sets. More research is needed to determine what aspects of this tuning actually affects performance, and if PAN20 Equal is also generalizable to other test sets or the approach to other types of data.

Limitations

For our Cross-Encoder systems, the Transformer backbones we evaluated vary in their memory and GPU requirements, but the best performing backbone (BigBird) has greater hardware needs than may be available to some researchers. Similarly, BigBird requires more time for training and testing and could take multiple days to train. We also found that 50k trials were sufficient for training, but this amount of training data may not be available for all use cases.

Our experiments and findings focused on fandoms (or topics) and data tuning could be difficult to evaluate on other datasets because of the additional requirement for topic labels, which may not be found in all author attribution datasets. Depending on the data source, some documents may also have multiple topic labels, which is not considered in our work.

Ethics Statement

While there are many legitimate use cases for authorship analysis, it is also possible to use these approaches in a way that negatively impacts people's freedom, livelihood, or safety. For example, these models could be used to de-anonymize texts written by whistle-blowers, protesters, or other dissidents. People may also face personal embarrassment, social stigma, or loss of employment if they are linked with texts shared under the assumption of anonymity.

Acknowledgements

DISTRIBUTION STATEMENT A. Approved for public release. Distribution is unlimited. This material is based upon work supported under Air Force Contract No. FA8702-15-D-0001. Any opinions, findings, conclusions or recommendations expressed in this material are those of the author(s) and do not necessarily reflect the views of the U.S. Air Force. Delivered to the U.S. Government with Unlimited Rights, as defined in DFARS Part 252.227-7013 or 7014 (Feb 2014). Notwithstanding any copyright notice, U.S. Government rights in this work are defined by DFARS 252.227-7013 or DFARS 252.227-7014 as detailed above. Use of this work other than as specifically authorized by the U.S. Government may violate any copyrights that exist in this work.

References

Malik Altakrori, Jackie Chi Kit Cheung, and Benjamin CM Fung. 2021. The topic confusion task: A novel evaluation scenario for authorship attribution. In *Findings of the Association for Computational Linguistics: EMNLP 202*, pages 4242–4256.

Georgios Barlas and Efstathios Stamatatos. 2020. Cross-domain authorship attribution using pre-trained language models. In *IFIP International Conference on Artificial Intelligence Applications and Innovations*, pages 255–266.

Georgios Barlas and Efstathios Stamatatos. 2021. A transfer learning approach to cross-domain authorship attribution. *Evolving Systems*, 12(3):625–643.

Iz Beltagy, Matthew E. Peters, and Arman Cohan. 2020.

Longformer: The long-document transformer. *Computing Research Repository*, arXiv:2004.05150.

Janek Bevendorff and et al. 2021. Overview of pan 2021: Authorship verification, profiling hate speech spreaders on twitter, and style change detection. In *Advances in Information Retrieval*, pages 567–573.

Janek Bevendorff, Bilal Ghanem, Anastasia Giachanou, Mike Kestemont, Enrique Manjavacas, Ilia Markov, Maximilian Mayerl, Martin Potthast, Francisco Rangel, Paolo Rosso, et al. 2020. Overview of pan 2020: Authorship verification, celebrity profiling, profiling fake news spreaders on twitter, and style change detection. In *Experimental IR Meets Multilinguality, Multimodality, and Interaction: 11th International Conference of the CLEF Association, CLEF 2020, Thessaloniki, Greece, September 22–25, 2020, Proceedings 11*, pages 372–383. Springer.

Benedikt Boenninghoff, Robert M. Nickel, and Dorothea Kolossa. 2021. O2d2: Out-of-distribution detector to capture undecidable trials in authorship verification. *PAN@CLEF 2021*, arXiv:2106.15825.

Benedikt Boenninghoff, Julian Rupp, Robert M. Nickel, and Dorothea Kolossa. 2020. Deep bayes factor scoring for authorship verification. *CLEF 2020 Labs and Workshops*, arXiv:2008.10105.

John Burrows. 2002. 'delta': a measure of stylistic difference and a guide to likely authorship. *Literary and linguistic computing*, 17(3):267–287.

Kevin Clark, Minh-Thang Luong, Quoc V. Le, and Christopher D. Manning. 2020. Electra: Pre-training text encoders as discriminators rather than generators. *Computing Research Repository*, arXiv:2003.10555.

Daniel Embarcadero-Ruiz, Helena Gomez-Adorno, Ivan Reyes-Hernandez, Alexis Garcia, and Alberto Embarcadero-Ruiz. 2021. Graph-based siamese network for authorship verification. In *Notebook for PAN at CLEF 2021*.

Maël Fabien, Esaú Villatoro-Tello, Petr Motlicek, and Shantipriya Parida. 2020. Bertaa: Bert fine-tuning for authorship attribution. In *Proceedings of the 17th International Conference on Natural Language Processing (ICON)*, pages 127–137.

Andrei Manolache, Florin Brad, Elena Burceanu, Antonio Barbalau, Radu Ionescu, and Marius Popescu. 2021. Transferring bert-like transformers' knowledge for authorship verifications. *Computing Research Repository*, arXiv:2112.05125.

Juanita Ordoñez, Rafael A. Rivera Soto, and Barry Y. Chen. 2020. Will longformers pan out for authorship verification? In *Notebook for PAN at CLEF 2020*.

Zeyang Peng, Leilei Kong, Zhijie Zhang1, Zhongyuan Han, and Xu Sun. 2021. Encoding text information by pre-trained model for authorship verification. In *Notebook for PAN at CLEF 2021*, pages 1–5.

Victor Sanh, Lysandre Debut, Julien Chaumond, and Thomas Wolf. 2019. Distilbert, a distilled version of bert: smaller, faster, cheaper and lighter. *Computing Research Repository*, arXiv:1910.01108.

Janith Weerasinghe and Rachel Greenstadt. 2020. Feature vector difference based neural network and logistic regression models for authorship verification. In *Notebook for PAN at CLEF 2020*.

Thomas Wolf, Lysandre Debut, Victor Sanh, Julien Chaumond, Clement Delangue, Anthony Moi, Pierric Cistac, Tim Rault, Remi Louf, Morgan Funtowicz, Joe Davison, Sam Shleifer, Patrick von Platen, Clara Ma, Yacine Jernite, Julien Plu, Canwen Xu, Teven Le Scao, Sylvain Gugger, Mariama Drame, Quentin Lhoest, and Alexander Rush. 2020. Transformers: State-of-the-art natural language processing. In *Proceedings of the 2020 Conference on Empirical Methods in Natural Language Processing: System Demonstrations*, pages 38–45.

Manzil Zaheer, Guru Guruganesh, Avinava Dubey, Joshua Ainslie, Chris Alberti, Santiago Ontanon, Philip Pham, Anirudh Ravula, Qifan Wang, Li Yang, and Amr Ahmed. 2020. Big bird: Transformers for longer sequences. *Computing Research Repository*, arXiv:2007.14062.

Fractality of informativity in 300 years of English scientific writing

Yuri Bizzoni
Center for Humanities Computing
Aarhus University
yuri.bizzoni@cc.au.dk

Stefania Degaetano-Ortlieb
Language Science and Technology
Saarland University
s.degaetano@mx.uni-saarland.de

Abstract

Scientific writing is assumed to have become more informationally dense over time (Halliday, 1988; Biber and Gray, 2016). Given that scientific writing is intended for communication between experts, we hypothesize a tendency towards optimizing language use by striving for a balance between highly informative content and a conventionalized style of writing. We study this by means of fractal analysis, asking whether the degree of informativity has become more persistent with predictable patterns of gradual changes between high vs. low informational content, indicating a trend towards an optimal code for scientific communication. Specifically, surprisal is used to measure informativity and the Hurst exponent is used as a long-term dependence measure for fractality analysis, quantifying the degree of persistence of informativity in scientific texts.

1 Introduction

Fractals are the product of dynamic systems and refer to structures that are self-similar, i.e. repeat themselves on every level of scale, indicating recurrent patterns. While fractality has its origin in mathematics by researcher Benoît Mandelbrot, it has been applied to a wide range of fields which consider complex dynamic systems, such as biology (Das et al., 2016) or music (Sanyal et al., 2016). Language is a complex dynamic system that shows inherent fractal patterns, especially in language evolution, language processing, change in language use, acquisition or development (e.g., Cordeiro et al. (2015); Gao et al. (2016); Mohseni et al. (2021)). This dynamic perspective on language allows us 'to tease out the processes through which a phenomenon unfolds' (Halliday, 2007, 362).

In this paper, we are interested in how English written scientific communication has evolved over a period of $\sim$ 330 years from its beginnings (1660s) up to modern science (1990s). One general hypothesis for the development of scientific writing is that it has become increasingly informationally dense over time (Halliday, 1988; Biber and Gray, 2016), moving from increased clausal to increased phrasal complexity (i.e. from a verbal towards a heavy nominal style). Given that scientific writing is intended for communication between experts, we hypothesize a tendency towards optimizing language use by striving for a balance between highly informative content and a conventionalized style of writing. We measure the informativity of scientific texts using the information-theoretic measure of surprisal, i.e. a word's predictability in context. The more predictable a word is in its context, the less its informativity (e.g. function words are low in informativity as they are quite predictable given particular contexts, consider e.g. the expression *on behalf of*, were *of* is quite predictable given *on behalf*), while lower predictability indicates high informativity (as e.g. for scientific terms). By means of fractal analysis, we compute the Hurst exponent (Riley et al., 2012) of informativity arcs, asking whether over time the degree of informativity has become more persistent with texts showing gradually increasing and decreasing patterns of informativity (higher Hurst exponents) which repeat themselves in a text (indicated as self-similarity) or whether informativity tends to fluctuate within a text (low Hurst exponents) without a recurrent pattern.

2 Data and Methods

2.1 The Royal Society Corpus

Our data set consists of the Proceedings and Transactions of the Royal Society of London from the RSC corpus (Kermes et al., 2016; Fischer et al., 2020; Menzel et al., 2021), which covers a vast amount of English scientific writing from its beginnings in 1665 up to 1996. Given the prominent role of the Royal Society of London in scientific publishing, its articles have not only been used for diachronic linguistic studies (Atkinson, 1999;

Proceedings of the 7th Joint SIGHUM Workshop on Computational Linguistics for Cultural Heritage, Social Sciences, Humanities and Literature (LaTeCH-CLfL2023), pages 38–44
May 5, 2023 ©2023 Association for Computational Linguistics

Moessner, 2009; Biber and Conrad, 2014; Feltgen et al., 2017; Degaetano-Ortlieb and Teich, 2019; Degaetano-Ortlieb, 2021), but also for historical and cultural analysis (Hunter et al., 1989; Purver, 2013; Moxham and Fyfe, 2018; Degaetano-Ortlieb and Piper, 2019). The corpus consists of 47,837 texts, Table 1 showing the no. of texts and tokens across 50-year time spans.[1]

Years	Texts	Tokens
1665–1699	1.325	2.582.856
1700–1749	1.686	3.414.795
1750–1799	1.819	6.342.489
1800–1849	2.774	9.112.274
1850–1899	6.754	36.993.412
1900–1949	10.011	65.431.384
1950–1996	23.468	172.018.539

Table 1: Corpus size by texts and tokens according to approx. 50 years periods for the RSC corpus

In terms or processing, the RSC has been built in accordance with the FAIR principles (Wilkinson et al., 2016). While there is an extensive description of the corpus building procedure in Kermes et al. (2016) and Fischer et al. (2020) as well as a description of meta-data annotation in Menzel et al. (2021), we describe here some processing steps and information on meta-data relevant to this paper. Inspired by the principles of Agile Software Development (Cockburn, 2001; Voormann and Gut, 2008), corpus pre-processing, corpus annotation and linguistic analysis are intertwined and repeated cyclically. Thus, whenever problems with the corpus quality are detected by way of analysis, procedures are established to overcome these as good as possible. While we strive to maintain high quality data for the RSC, we recognize that there is always room for improvement, and we continually work towards enhancing the corpus dataset to the best of our ability. To tackle the problem of OCR-based text material, especially in the earlier periods, in version 6.0 of the RSC, we integrate the Noisy-Channel Spell Checker by Klaus et al. (2019) for a better recall and F-score at the cost of some loss in precision compared to a previously adopted method of pattern-based OCR post-correction. Considering meta-data, besides author and year of publication, which we use in this paper, there are various attributes on publication related information (e.g., journal, issn, text type), time slices (e.g., decades, 50-year periods) and textual information (e.g., pages, sentences) (cf. Fischer et al. (2020); Menzel et al. (2021)).

2.2 Informativity

Informativity is an information-theoretic notion measurable by surprisal (Shannon, 1948), which provides a useful tool for quantifying and analyzing informativity across linguistic contexts. Surprisal is defined as the negative log probability of an event measuring the amount of information conveyed by an event in bits:

$$S(w_t) = -\log P(w_t|w_{t-1}, w_{t-2}, w_{t-3}) \tag{1}$$

where $S(w_t)$ represents the surprisal of the current word w_t and $P(w_t|w_{t-1}, w_{t-2}, w_{t-3})$ represents the probability of the current word w_t given the previous three words $w_{t-1}, w_{t-2}, w_{t-3}$. The logarithm is typically taken in base 2, so that the unit of measure is bits of information. The intuition is that words with low probability convey more information than words with high probability. In the context of linguistic communication, an utterance with low surprisal conveys relatively little information, while an utterance with high surprisal conveys more information. We use surprisal to measure the degree of informativity of tokens in the RSC corpus. As the corpus presents noticeable variation in terms of corpus size and vocabulary size over time, we calculate the average surprisal value of each word in a given time period (here: decade), normalized by the vocabulary size:

$$\frac{\sum_{i=1}^{N} S(w_i)}{N} \tag{2}$$

where $S(w_i)$ is the surprisal value of word w_i, and N is the number of types in the corpus for the given time period. This controls for the effects of vocabulary size and corpus size on the average surprisal values, allowing us to make a fair comparison between time periods.

The probabilities needed for surprisal calculation are obtained by considering slices of decades, i.e. given a text, surprisal of each word in the text is calculated based on the probabilities of the words in context in the decade.[2]

2.3 Fractality

We measure the fractality of sequences with the Hurst exponent, computed on series of surprisal

[1] We excluded texts shorter than 200 sentences given that the Hurst exponent might not work well on very short sequences.

[2] Note that the RSC provides surprisal annotation at the token level based on decades, 50-year periods, and the whole corpus and given the pre-processed material.

values averaged on sentences for each RSC text. Recently, fractality has been applied to analyze dynamics in language use such as sentiment arcs in stories (Gao et al., 2016), on stylometric and sentiment features finding correlations to the perceived 'beauty' of a text (Cordeiro et al., 2015; Bizzoni et al., 2022), and for determining differences between fiction and non-fiction texts (Mohseni et al., 2021). A Hurst exponent >0.5 indicates relatively smooth transitions between highly informative and less informative sentences, i.e. rather gradual changes in informativity pointing to a relatively uniform information distribution (cf. uniform information density hypothesis (UID) (Jaeger and Levy, 2007; Jaeger, 2010)). These transitions will form patterns which are repeatedly encountered in a text (i.e. self-similarity of persistent trends). In our specific case of studying scientific writing, we would expect a rather high Hurst exponent, which would confirm our hypothesis towards striving for a balance between highly informative content and a conventionalized style of writing for expert-to-expert communication. On the other hand, a Hurst exponent <0.5 would suggest rather abrupt changes between more vs. less informative sentences (i.e. anti-persistent trends), which we would not assume to be the case.

We estimate the Hurst exponent by Adaptive Fractal Analysis (AFA) (Gao et al., 2011), by which time series (here: sentences in a text) are partitioned into overlapping segments of length $w = 2n + 1$, where neighboring segments overlap by $n + 1$ points. In each segment, the time series is fitted with the best polynomial of order M using standard least-squares regression. The fitted polynomials in the overlapping regions are then combined to yield a single global smooth trend (cf. Riley et al. (2012) for an introduction). The Hurst exponent is estimated based on the fluctuations around this trend and the scale at which these fluctuations occur. The original time series is denoted by $x_1, x_2, ..., x_T$ and the fitted polynomials for the ith and $(i+1)^{th}$ segments are denoted by $y_i(l_1)$ and $y_{i+1}(l_2)$, respectively, where $l_1, l_2 = 1, 2, ..., 2n + 1$. The fluctuations around the smooth trend's mean m can be measured by the residuals: $residual_i = x_i - m$. The scale-dependent fluctuations can be measured by the fluctuation function $F(n)$, which is given by:

$$F(n) = \sqrt{\frac{1}{n}\sum_{i=1}^{n} residual_i^2} \quad (3)$$

The Hurst exponent H is estimated as the slope of the regression line of $\log F(n)$ against $\log n$.

3 Analysis

Using the Hurst exponent, we ask whether the distribution of informativity within the RSC texts becomes more persistent over time, which would indicate a more uniform and smooth distribution of information within articles, i.e. a more persistent *informativity profile*.

Informativity is measured by surprisal (cf. Section 2.2). Example (1) shows a sentence with low informativity on average (4.6 of surprisal), where words are relatively predictable given their previous context (such as *Newton* given *Sir Isaac*). Example (2) shows a sentence which is higher in informativity on average (surprisal of 8.1), where *illustrated* is relatively unpredictable given its previous context (compare to the more explicit version *which occurred and which illustrated* which would lower the average informativity). Example (3) presents a highly informative sentence (surprisal of 10.9) due to the terms used in it.

(1) And$_{5.29}$ that$_{4.97}$ something$_{8.78}$ like$_{4.40}$ this$_{7.12}$ must$_{8.52}$ be$_{0.94}$ the$_{4.49}$ Case$_{6.92}$,$_{2.84}$ appears$_{12.91}$ from$_{2.61}$ what$_{0.92}$ Sir$_{5.25}$ Isaac$_{0.11}$ Newton$_{0.48}$ has$_{3.86}$ said$_{8.84}$ upon$_{1.98}$ this$_{2.42}$ Subject$_{3.67}$.$_{3.14}$ (J.T. Desaguliers 1724, average sentence surprisal 4.6)

(2) Another$_{10.09}$ effect$_{9.16}$ which$_{6.91}$ occurred$_{10.39}$ illustrated$_{15.13}$ the$_{4.10}$ same$_{5.28}$ point$_{7.44}$.$_{4.61}$ (M. Faraday 1846, average sentence surprisal 8.1)

(3) He$_{7.49}$ also$_{4.45}$ accepted$_{9.85}$ Van$_{12.92}$ Slyke$_{9.12}$ amino-N$_{23.48}$ determinations$_{16.54}$.$_{3.54}$ (R.L.M. Synge et al. 1990, average sentence surprisal 10.9)

We compute the Hurst exponent on the articles' sentence-based informativity arcs. Figure 1 and 2 show the lines of two arcs with extremely high ($H = 0.92$) vs. low ($H = 0.27$) exponents. Informativity is on the y-axis of Figure 1a and 2a with the time series of the texts (i.e. sentences) on the x-axis. Figure 2a shows high fluctuations around the mean with rather abrupt changes in surprisal values, while Figure 1a shows a much smoother trend, with smaller and gradual changes in informativity from low to high and vice versa. Figure 1b and 2b present a globally smooth trend signal, represented as a polynomial fit on the detrended informativity profile[3]. A detrended profile is a profile where the datapoints' values are subtracted to the mean;

[3]With linear trend (m1), quadratic trend (m2), and cubic trend (m3).

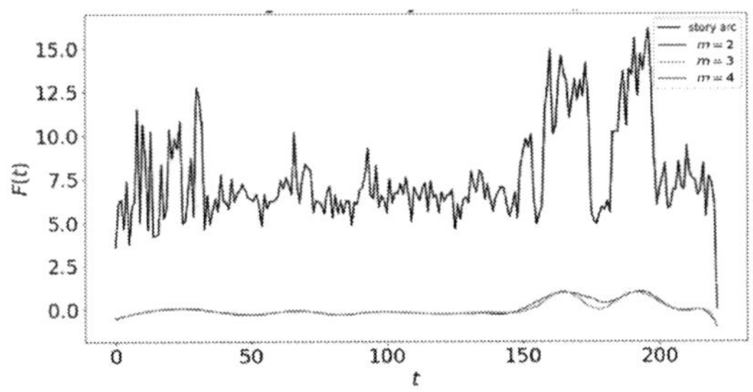

(a) Informativity profile of a text as its surprisal (y-axis) through the text (x-axis).

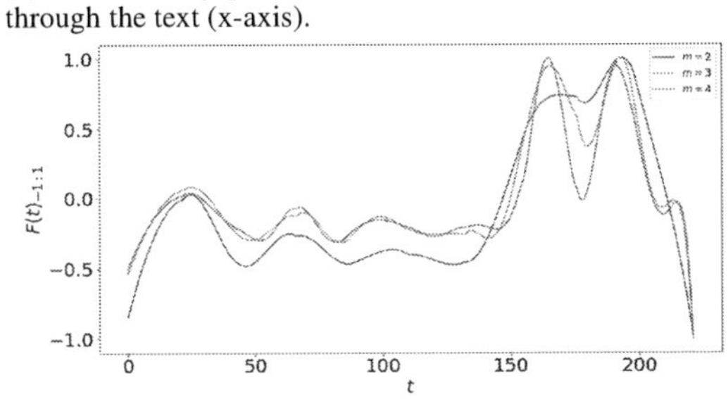

(b) Detrended profile: three alternative polynomial fits.

Figure 1: Informativity profiles (raw and detrended) of a text with high Hurst exponent ($H = 0.92$).

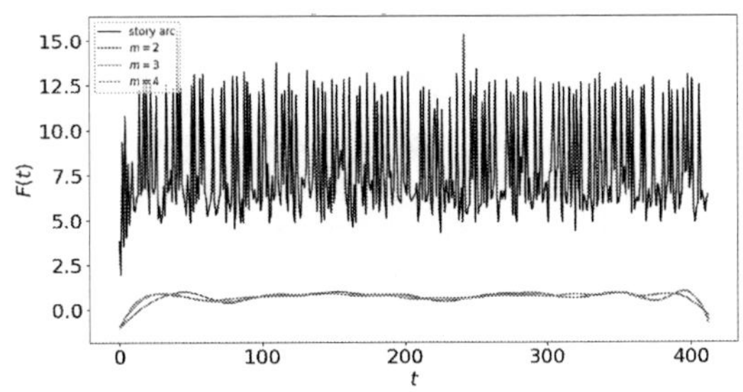

(a) Informativity profile of a text as its surprisal (y-axis) through the text (x-axis).

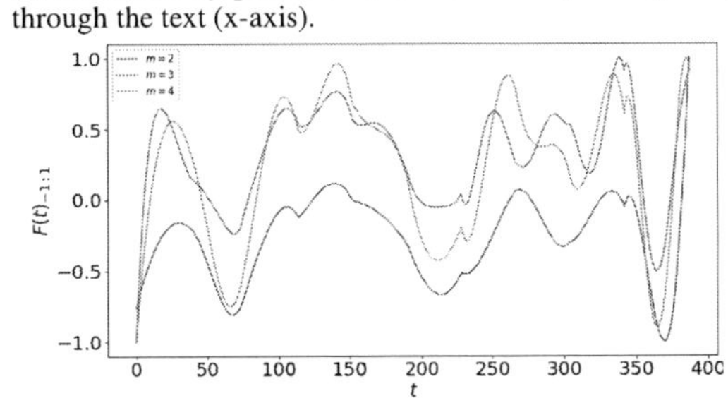

(b) Detrended profile: three alternative polynomial fits.

Figure 2: Informativity profiles (raw and detrended) of a text with low Hurst exponent ($H = 0.27$).[4]

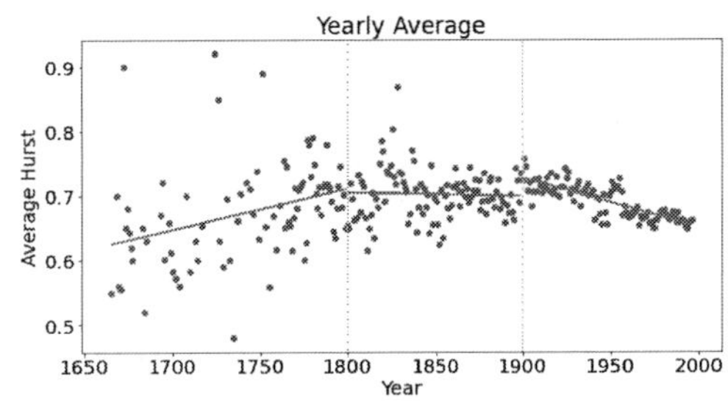

Figure 3: Hurst exponent of RSC texts over time averaged on each year.

polynomial fits on such a signal allow us to estimate the series' underlying systematic components and to forecast its long-term behaviour (see also Riley et al. (2012) on obtaining global lines, i.e. detrended lines).

In general, texts with a low Hurst exponent contain sentences with strongly varying averages in surprisal (low-high-low etc), while texts with a relatively high Hurst exponent are built up by sequences of sentences presenting a gradual increase or decrease in surprisal (low-lower-high-higher-highest-higher-high-lower-low etc). Thus, a Hurst exponent of >0.5 indicates long-term trends in the informativity profile of a text and more persistent patterns (e.g. a gradual increase in informativity followed by a gradual decrease or vice versa). A Hurst exponent of 0.5 indicates abrupt changes with unpredictable peaks and troughs in informativity, while a value of <0.5 suggests an anti-persistent trend, i.e. a trend reverting constantly to the mean through a "zig-zag"-like behaviour.

Figure 3 shows an overall trend of the Hurst exponent for the RSC texts averaged over each year, with the averaged exponent value on the y-axis and years on the x-axis. For almost all years the Hurst exponent is >0.5. From the 1650s to 1800 there is an increase, followed by a plateau until 1900 and a slight decrease until the 1990s. Spearman's correlation between average Hurst and the articles' publication date is positive and significant until roughly the late 18th century (0.43), negative and significant from the beginning of the 20th century (-0.79), and non-significant in-between. This indicates that the RSC texts show rather persistent informativity sequences, a tendency that becomes stronger through the 18th century, i.e. changes in informativity across the texts become more coherent showing recurrent patterns of change in a text. This is in line with psycholinguistic accounts on language processing. Given that smoother signals of informativity have shown to be related to less processing effort (Jaeger and Levy, 2007; Jaeger, 2010), the observed change might indeed indicate

[4] To best show mean-reverting patterns, (b) excludes the first and last ten sentences of the article.

change towards more coherent texts in English scientific writing to serve expert-to-expert communication, where a smoother signal indicates a more uniform distribution of information that goes beyond the sentence unit.

However, after a relatively stable period, informativity profiles become slightly less persistent in the 20th century. This could indicate a development of a scientific code at pressure given the highly demanding process of increased specialization, i.e. growing specialized domains, in which formulaic language and grammatical consolidation are combined with an increasingly diverse, domain-specific use of terminology. These high demands might introduce sharper changes in the informativity profiles of more contemporary articles, leading to the slight disrupt of the "smoothness" of the informativity trends, slightly lowering the overall Hurst score.

Finally, it is worth noting that while the texts' average Hurst exponent oscillates through macro-periods (here centuries), its variance and standard deviation decline steadily (Table 2 and Figure 4), i.e. the differences between the articles' informativity profiles becomes smaller – scientific authors converging on a particular range of informativity profiles.

Measure	Spearman corr.	Kendall corr.
Mean	0.160	0.076
Variance	-0.664* [-0.83, -0.4]	-0.517* [-0.74, -0.2]
Std	-0.619* [-0.8,-0.33]	-0.476* [-0.71,-0.13]

Table 2: Correlations between time and Hurst's decade-based average, variance, and standard deviation. All measures were taken starting from 1700, to avoid distortions induced by the data scarcity of the 17th century. *indicates p-values <0.05; confidence intervals for alpha=0.05 are in brakets.

4 Conclusion

We have modeled fractality for English scientific texts given their informativity over time on the RSC Corpus, showing a general trend towards the use of smoother informativity profiles. This is in line with previous accounts on information density, which hypothesize uniform distributions to ease processing cost (Jaeger and Levy, 2007; Jaeger, 2010). Here, we have shown that this also adheres at the textual level. Considering that scientific writing is meant for expert-to-expert communication, being subject to increased processes of specialization, more contemporary scientific writing shows

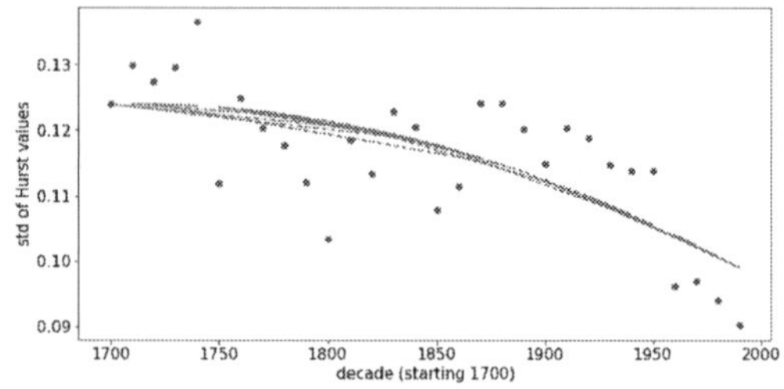

Figure 4: Standard deviation for each decade in our corpus starting 1700, with a polynomial fit. The standard deviation diminishes almost linearly, which seems to indicate a progressive stylistic convergence.

trends towards slightly less smoothed signals, with stronger alternations between more conventionalized, formulaic vs. highly specialized informational content. At the same time, we observed a strong converging trend indicated by a significant reduction in variance and standard deviation of the Hurst exponent. In future, we would like to see whether this notion of an optimized informativity signal is observable in the development of other registers. Also, there might be discipline-specific trends which would shed light on processes of specialization and diversification among scientific disciplines. Moreover, as we continuously work on enhancing corpus quality, we would like to have a through analysis of possible confounds that might have an impact on surprisal as well as fractality calculation. This will lead us to uncover more comprehensively source for changes in fractality. Also, as we here have applied one of the most simple ways of calculating fractality, we want to experiment with other measures in order to evaluate their performance for this task.

5 Acknowledgements

This research is funded by *Deutsche Forschungsgemeinschaft* (DFG, German Research Foundation) – Project-ID 232722074 – SFB 1102 and by *Velux Foundation* - Project *Fabula-Net* - Project-ID 35361. We would also like to express our sincere gratitude to the reviewers for their insightful comments and constructive feedback, which greatly contributed to the improvement of this paper.

References

Dwight Atkinson. 1999. *Scientific discourse in sociohistorical context: The Philosophical Transactions of the Royal Society of London, 1675-1975*. Erlbaum, New York.

Douglas Biber and Susan Conrad. 2014. *Variation in English: Multi-dimensional studies*. Routledge.

Douglas Biber and Bethany Gray. 2016. *Grammatical complexity in academic English: Linguistic change in writing*. Studies in English Language. Cambridge University Press, Cambridge, UK.

Yuri Bizzoni, Telma Peura, Mads Thomsen, and Kristoffer Nielbo. 2022. Fractal Sentiments and fairy tales - Fractal scaling of narrative arcs as predictor of the perceived quality of Andersen's fairy tales. *Journal of Data Mining & Digital Humanities*, NLP4DH.

Alistair Cockburn, editor. 2001. *Agile Software Development*. Addison-Wesley Professional, Boston, USA.

Joao Cordeiro, Pedro RM Inácio, and Diogo AB Fernandes. 2015. Fractal beauty in text. In *Progress in Artificial Intelligence: 17th Portuguese Conference on Artificial Intelligence, EPIA 2015, Coimbra, Portugal, September 8-11, 2015. Proceedings 17*, pages 796–802. Springer.

Nandan Kumar Das, Rajib Dey, Semanti Chakraborty, PK Panigrahi, and Nirmalya Ghosh. 2016. Probing multifractality in depth-resolved refractive index fluctuations in biological tissues using backscattering spectral interferometry. *Journal of Optics*, 18(12):125301.

Stefania Degaetano-Ortlieb. 2021. Measuring informativity: The rise of compounds as informationally dense structures in 20th century scientific english. In Elena Soave and Douglas Biber, editors, *Corpus Approaches to Register Variation*, chapter 11, pages 291–312. John Benjamins Publishing Company.

Stefania Degaetano-Ortlieb and Andrew Piper. 2019. The scientization of literary study. In *Proceedings of the 3rd Joint SIGHUM Workshop on Computational Linguistics for Cultural Heritage, Social Sciences, Humanities and Literature*, pages 18–28, Minneapolis, USA. Association for Computational Linguistics.

Stefania Degaetano-Ortlieb and Elke Teich. 2019. Toward an optimal code for communication: The case of scientific English. *Corpus Linguistics and Linguistic Theory*, 0(0):1–33. Online print.

Quentin Feltgen, Benjamin Fagard, and Jean-Pierre Nadal. 2017. Frequency patterns of semantic change: Corpus-based evidence of a near-critical dynamics in language change. *Royal Society Open Science*, 4(11):170830.

Stefan Fischer, Jörg Knappen, Katrin Menzel, and Elke Teich. 2020. The Royal Society Corpus 6.0. providing 300+ years of scientific writing for humanistic study. In *Proceedings of the International Conference on Language Resources and Evaluation (LREC) 2020, Marseille, France, May 2020*, pages 794–802.

Jianbo Gao, Jing Hu, and Wen-wen Tung. 2011. Facilitating joint chaos and fractal analysis of biosignals through nonlinear adaptive filtering. *PLOS ONE*, 6(9):1–8.

Jianbo Gao, Matthew L Jockers, John Laudun, and Timothy Tangherlini. 2016. A multiscale theory for the dynamical evolution of sentiment in novels. In *2016 International Conference on Behavioral, Economic and Socio-cultural Computing (BESC)*, pages 1–4. IEEE.

M.A.K. Halliday. 1988. On the language of physical science. In Mohsen Ghadessy, editor, *Registers of Written English: Situational Factors and Linguistic Features*, pages 162–177. Pinter, London.

M.A.K. Halliday. 2007. On the concept of 'Educational linguistics'. In Jonathan J. Webster, editor, *The collected works of M. A. K. Halliday, Volume 9: Language and education*, pages 354–367. Continuum, London. Originally published in: Giblett, R., & O'Carroll, J. (Eds.). (1990). Discipline, dialogue, difference: Proceedings of the Language in Education conference, Murdoch University, December 1989. Murdoch, Australia: Duration, pp. 23–42.

Michael Cyril William Hunter et al. 1989. *Establishing the new science: The experience of the early Royal Society*. Boydell & Brewer Ltd.

T. Florian Jaeger. 2010. Redundancy and reduction: Speakers manage syntactic information density. *Cognitive Psychology*, 61(1):23–62.

T. Florian Jaeger and Roger P. Levy. 2007. Speakers optimize information density through syntactic reduction. In Bernhard Schölkopf, John C. Platt, and T. Hoffman, editors, *Advances in Neural Information Processing Systems 19*, pages 849–856. MIT Press.

Hannah Kermes, Stefania Degaetano-Ortlieb, Ashraf Khamis, Jörg Knappen, and Elke Teich. 2016. The Royal Society Corpus: From uncharted data to corpus. In *Proceedings of the 10th LREC*, Portorož, Slovenia.

Carsten Klaus, Dietrich Klakow, and Peter Fankhauser. 2019. OCR post-correction of the Royal Society Corpus based on the noisy channel model. In *Proceedings of the 41. Jahrestagung der Deutschen Gesellschaft fuer Sprachwissenschaft (DGfS2019)*, University of Bremen, Germany.

Katrin Menzel, Jörg Knappen, and Elke Teich. 2021. Generating linguistically relevant metadata for the Royal Society Corpus. *Research in Corpus Linguistics*, 9(1):1–18.

Lilo Moessner. 2009. The influence of the Royal Society on 17th-century scientific writing. *ICAME journal*, 33:65–87.

Mahdi Mohseni, Volker Gast, and Christoph Redies. 2021. Fractality and variability in canonical and non-canonical English fiction and in non-fictional texts. *Frontiers in Psychology*, 12.

Noah Moxham and Aileen Fyfe. 2018. The Royal Society and the prehistory of peer review, 1665–1965. *The Historical Journal*, 61(4):863–889.

Margery Purver. 2013. *The Royal Society: Concept and Creation*. Routledge.

Michael A. Riley, Scott Bonnette, Nikita Kuznetsov, Sebastian Wallot, and Jianbo Gao. 2012. A tutorial introduction to adaptive fractal analysis. *Frontiers in Physiology*, 3:371.

Shankha Sanyal, Archi Banerjee, Anirban Patranabis, Kaushik Banerjee, Ranjan Sengupta, and Dipak Ghosh. 2016. A study on improvisation in a musical performance using multifractal detrended cross correlation analysis. *Physica A: Statistical Mechanics and its Applications*, 462:67–83.

Claude E. Shannon. 1948. A mathematical theory of communication. *Bell System Technical Journal*, 27:379–423, 623–656.

Holger Voormann and Ulrike Gut. 2008. Agile corpus creation. *Corpus Linguistics and Linguistic Theory*, 4:235–251.

Mark Wilkinson, Michel Dumontier, and IJsbrand Aalbersberg. 2016. The FAIR Guiding Principles for scientific data management and stewardship. *Nature – Scientific Data*, 3(160018).

Direct Speech Quote Attribution for Dutch Literature

Andreas van Cranenburgh
Center for Language and Cognition
University of Groningen
a.w.van.cranenburgh@rug.nl

Frank van den Berg
Klippa
Groningen, The Netherlands
frankvandenberg@klippa.com

Abstract

We present a dataset and system for quote attribution in Dutch literature. The system is implemented as a neural module in an existing NLP pipeline for Dutch literature (dutchcoref; van Cranenburgh, 2019). Our contributions are as follows. First, we provide guidelines for Dutch quote attribution and annotate 3,056 quotes in fragments of 42 Dutch literary novels, both contemporary and classic. Second, we present three neural quote attribution classifiers, optimizing for precision, recall, and F1. Third, we perform an evaluation and analysis of quote attribution performance, showing that in particular, quotes with an implicit speaker are challenging, and that such quotes are prevalent in contemporary fiction (57%, compared to 32% for classic novels). On the task of quote attribution, we achieve an improvement over the rule-based baseline of 8.0% F1 points on contemporary fiction and 1.9% F1 points on classic novels. Code, models, and annotations for the public domain novels are available under an open license at https://github.com/frenkvdberg/dutchqa.

1 Introduction

Quote attribution is the task of identifying the speaker of each quotation span in a given text. When applied to dialogue in literature, this enables us to study relations and interactions between characters, for example by extracting social networks (Elson et al., 2010; Labatut and Bost, 2019). Other applications to literature include examining gender differences (Underwood et al., 2018; Kraicer and Piper, 2019) or measuring information propagation (Sims and Bamman, 2020). Whereas the aforementioned studies all focus on English-language fiction, in this paper we focus on direct speech attribution in Dutch literature. An example can be seen in the following sentence:

(1) *"[Ik]$_1$ denk dat [je]$_2$ met [haar]$_3$ moet praten," zei [Tom]$_1$.* Speaker: [Tom]$_1$
"[I]$_1$ think [you]$_2$ should talk to [her]$_3$", [Tom]$_1$ said.

Example (1) has an **explicit** speaker mention (*Tom*). However, identifying the speaker is not always as easy (examples from Tolstoy's Anna Karenina):

(2) *"Maar, wat nu te doen?" vroeg [hij]$_1$ wanhopig.* Speaker: [Stepan]$_1$
"Well, what now?" [he]$_1$ asked disconsolately.

(3) *"[Mama]$_1$?, [ze]$_1$ is opgestaan," antwoordde [het meisje]$_2$.* Speaker: [Tanya]$_2$
"[Mamma]$_1$? [She]$_1$ is up," answered [the girl]$_2$.

(4) *"Het komt goed, [meneer]$_1$; [ze]$_2$ draait wel bij," zei [Matvey]$_3$.* Speaker: [Matvey]$_3$
"Bijdraaien?" Speaker: [Stepan]$_1$
"Ja, [meneer]$_1$." Speaker: [Matvey]$_3$
It's all right, [sir]$_1$; [she]$_2$ will come round," said [Matvey]$_3$.
"Come round?"
"Yes, [sir]$_1$."

The speakers of (2) and (3) are mentioned **by anaphor**. Sentences 2–3 of (4) are even more challenging, since they have an **implicit** speaker. Note that all of the above examples are direct speech, in which the exact words spoken by a person are reported. Although there exist systems for detecting and attributing indirect speech (Pareti et al., 2013; Salway et al., 2017) and free indirect discourse (Brooke et al., 2017), our focus in this work is strictly on direct speech.

For the task of Dutch quote attribution, van Cranenburgh (2019) presents a rule-based approach as part of the *dutchcoref* coreference resolution system. Quote attribution is relevant to coreference resolution, as the speaker and addressee of dialogue turns must be known to resolve first and second person pronouns in quoted speech correctly. Furthermore, after extending the dutchcoref system with three neural classifiers for the subtasks mention de-

Proceedings of the 7th Joint SIGHUM Workshop on Computational Linguistics for Cultural Heritage, Social Sciences, Humanities and Literature (LaTeCH-CLfL2023), pages 45–62
May 5, 2023

tection, mention attributes and pronoun resolution, van Cranenburgh et al. (2021) notes that in literature dialogue is particularly important; annotating and predicting speakers of direct speech was proposed as one of the directions for future work. Therefore, we implement a neural classifier for quote attribution, which we expect to outperform dutchcoref's rule-based approach.

Additionally, we perform an error analysis, where we look at whether certain speaker types are harder to classify: **explicit** (said Tom) vs. **anaphoric pronoun** (said he) vs. **anaphoric other** (said his friend) vs. **implicit**. Moreover, we will analyze whether the corpus of books that we use (RiddleCoref vs. OpenBoek) has an influence on the performance of the classifier.

2 Background

2.1 Quote attribution in the literary domain

Semino and Short (2004) present a taxonomy of speech and thought representation, and a corpus annotated with this taxonomy that includes fiction. Later work attempts to automate quote attribution. Glass and Bangay (2007) approach the task of quote attribution in the literary domain by combining a scoring technique and hand-coded rules to identify the speaker of quoted speech in fiction books. Their approach consists of three steps: identifying the speech verb for a quote, finding the actor for this speech verb and then selecting the correct speaker from a character list. While performing well, their system is limited to explicitly cued speakers and not able to identify implicit speakers. Elson and McKeown (2010) aim to automatically identify both quotes and the mentions of the speakers in a self compiled corpus of classic literature. However, their predictions rely on gold-label information at test time, which is not available in practice. O'Keefe et al. (2012) uses a sequence labeling approach, which proves successful for the news domain, but does not manage to beat their baseline accuracy on the literary domain. Subsequently, O'Keefe et al. (2013) reported on the impact of coreference resolution on the task of quote attribution, with Almeida et al. (2014) presenting a joint model of coreference resolution and quote attribution. Around the same time, the best system for literary quote attribution was the system by He et al. (2013), presenting a supervised machine learning approach. Instead of seeing the task as quote-mention labeling, they reformulated it to quote-speaker labeling. Their system was eventually outperformed by Muzny et al. (2017), who present a rule-based and statistical quote attribution system. Adding a supervised classifier to their deterministic sieve-based system proved successful on English literature, achieving an average F1-score of 87.5% across three novels. Yeung and Lee (2017) present a machine learning system that identifies not just the speaker of dialogue in literature, but also the addressee. Sims and Bamman (2020) reimplements the deterministic approach of Muzny et al. (2017), while also using coreference information and choosing to assign unattributed quotes to the majority speaker. Instead of evaluating system performance using accuracy and precision/recall, they measure the cluster overlap. Their system achieves an average F1-score of 71.3% across three different cluster metrics, when evaluated on their new dataset containing 1,765 quotes across 100 different literary texts. Byszuk et al. (2020) present an evaluation of direct speech attribution for 19th-century fiction in 9 languages by fine-tuning transformer-based sequence labeling models, which appear to be more robust to varying typographical conventions compared to rule-based approaches. Papay and Padó (2020) present a corpus of 19th century literature with rich dialogue annotations: direct and indirect speech are included, and not only speakers but also addressees and cue words are annotated. Yoder et al. (2021) present a neural pipeline tailored to English fan fiction, including character identification, coreference, and quote attribution. Most recently, Vishnubhotla et al. (2022) presented a dataset of all quotations in 22 English novels, with annotations for speaker, addressee, and other attributes. They also evaluate systems based on Muzny et al. (2017) and BookNLP,[1] and report lower scores (overall accuracy up to 63%) than with previous datasets, suggesting the task is more challenging than previously thought.

2.2 Quote attribution within dutchcoref

The dutchcoref system (van Cranenburgh, 2019; van Cranenburgh et al., 2021) performs quote attribution as part of its rule-based coreference resolution system, which follows the deterministic multi-sieve architecture of Lee et al. (2013). The system starts by identifying mention spans and attributes (animacy, gender, number). This is fol-

[1]BookNLP is a neural pipeline optimized for literature, cf. https://github.com/booknlp/booknlp

lowed by quote attribution and a sequence of rule-based sieves that make coreference decisions, ordered from most to least precise.

In the quote attribution component, direct speech is identified using punctuation: single and double quotation marks, and paragraphs that start with a dash. While this heuristic works for the majority of cases, there are rare cases where quotation marks are used for other things than direct speech. If no marker is found to indicate the end of direct speech, the system assumes the end of the paragraph is also the end of the quote. Furthermore, the system does not extract quotes within other quotes.

Speakers of direct speech are attributed where they are explicitly mentioned, such as when the subject of a reported speech verb is located next to a quote. Addressees are identified as well, as the addressee is set to the speaker of the previous or following quote. The system uses paragraph breaks in order to decide whether a speaker continues speaking or another participant takes the next turn. Even in a longer chain of implicit quotes, the system can still attribute the speakers and addressees, assuming that the same speaker pair keeps taking turns. Other heuristic rules for identifying speakers and addressees include recognizing certain vocative patterns and checking whether there is only a single human mention in the paragraph. These heuristic rules are similar to those reported in the paper by Muzny et al. (2017), although they do not discuss the identification of addressees.

The performance of dutchcoref's quote attribution component was reported using the first 1,000 quotes from the novel *De Buurman* by J.J. Voskuil. A low recall score of 43.3% was obtained, as almost half of the quotes were not assigned a speaker. However, the obtained precision score was high, scoring 81.7%. The low recall score can be explained by the decision to not assign unattributed quotes to the majority speaker, since the system was designed to favor precision. The error analysis revealed that most errors occurred where the speaker was implicit, with the quote attribution rules working well when speakers were mentioned explicitly.

As Muzny et al. (2017) obtained better results when combining the heuristic rules with a lightweight supervised classifier, a similar experiment was also tried for dutchcoref. van Cranenburgh (2019) trained a fastText classifier (Joulin et al., 2017) to classify the unattributed quotes, but the results were not encouraging, as there was not enough annotated data.

Seeing how a lack of training data caused the performance to be poor, we are curious how well a classifier can perform when we supply a sufficient amount of training data. Therefore, we annotated quotes appearing in fragments of 42 different Dutch-language novels and train our own classifier, which can then be implemented into the dutchcoref system as an independent module located before the second (string match) sieve. For the architecture of our classifier, we follow the approach of Muzny et al. (2017), although we replace the MaxEnt model with a feed-forward neural network. As adding neural classifiers to dutchcoref proved successful on the subtasks of mention detection, mention attributes and pronoun resolution (van Cranenburgh et al., 2021), we expect to see a similar improvement on the subtask of quote attribution.

3 Data and Material

For our experiments, we work with Dutch literary novels from both the RiddleCoref (van Cranenburgh, 2019) and the OpenBoek (van Cranenburgh and van Noord, 2022) corpora. For the task of quote attribution specifically, we needed to annotate the novels ourselves in order to obtain gold data. We will discuss both the corpora statistics and the annotation process below.

The RiddleCoref corpus was first presented in van Cranenburgh (2019) and consists of a selection Dutch (translated and original) contemporary literary novels from the *Riddle of Literary Quality* project (Koolen et al., 2020). This corpus contains a total of 33 documents, for which we use the train, development and test splits as defined in Poot and van Cranenburgh (2020). In total, there are 38,647 mentions in the corpus and on average 4,897.4 tokens per document. Unfortunately, the annotated texts from the RiddleCoref cannot be made publicly available due to copyright.

The OpenBoek corpus consists of public domain novels from Project Gutenberg enriched with several layers of annotation.[2] The corpus currently contains 9 fragments of Dutch-language novels and novellas. This corpus contains a total of 23,650 mentions, with an average of 11,502.4 tokens per document. The number of sentences per document (mean 643.3), as well as the number of tokens per document (> 10k), indicate that annotated OpenBoek fragments are longer than

[2] https://andreasvc.github.io/openboek/

the RiddleCoref fragments, or most other coreference datasets. These longer fragments lengths were chosen specifically with the challenge of long-document coreference resolution in mind.

4 Quote attribution annotation

Whereas gold standard coreference annotations (mentions and coreference clusters) were already available, this was not the case for the task of quote attribution. Therefore, we added quote attribution annotations as an extra annotation layer to the RiddleCoref and OpenBoek datasets. For the annotation we used the tool released by Muzny et al. (2017) along with our own annotation guidelines.[3] The guidelines can be summarized as follows:

1. We annotate all **direct** speech quotes, which often appear within quotation marks, or are preceded by a dash sign.
2. As for annotating mentions, the only mentions that should be annotated are the spans of text that refer to the speaker of a quote.
3. Each quote should be linked to the mention of that quote's speaker. A quote can only be linked to one mention, however one mention can be linked to multiple quotes.
4. In the case of multiple possible mention candidates for a quote's speaker, we will consistently choose the mention that is closest to the quote.
5. The mentions we annotate should always be outside the quotes they are connected to.

We only annotated the quotes and corresponding speaker mentions, but not the addressees for these quotes, as this is outside the scope of this paper.

Statistics In total, we annotated all 33 fragments from the RiddleCoref corpus and all 9 fragments from the OpenBoek corpus. Table 5 shows the number of quotes annotated per fragment. The RiddleCoref corpus contains a total of 1,864 quotes, whereas the OpenBoek corpus contains a total of 1,192 quotes. This results in an average of 56.5 quotes per fragment for the RiddleCoref corpus, versus an average of 132.4 quotes per OpenBoek fragment. The fact that the OpenBoek corpus seems to contain on average 2.3 times as much quotes per fragment is not surprising, as its fragments contain on average 2.1 times as many sentences per document. If we take this into account, the density of quotes per fragment is roughly the same for both corpora. We do however see that the number of quotes is more evenly distributed among the fragments of the OpenBoek corpora, whereas there seem to be more extreme outliers in the RiddleCoref corpus.

Inter-Annotator Agreement Ten fragments of 100 sentences from RiddleCoref had already been annotated at an earlier stage by the first author, allowing us to look at inter-annotator agreement with the annotations done for this project by the second author. Both annotators are native speakers of Dutch. For these 10 fragments of 100 words, we obtain an average F1-score of 83.7% (based on whether quotes are assigned to the correct speaker cluster, see Section 6). This is a lower bound, as the existing annotations were made before the annotation guidelines had been formalized. For more details and examples, see Section A.2.

5 Method

5.1 System architecture

We train a feed-forward classifier, using the aforementioned train and development split of the RiddleCoref corpus. This is a binary classifier that predicts for a given quote-mention candidate pair whether the mention is the speaker of the quote. Both the quotes and the candidate mentions are detected beforehand by the dutchcoref system, as we only focus on the attribution of each quote to the right speaker.

As candidate mentions, we only consider names, nouns and specific types of pronouns, that appear within a distance of at most one paragraph on either side of the quote. We restrict pronouns to personal and possessive pronouns, but unlike Muzny et al. (2017) we did not find restricting pronouns to only singular gendered pronouns to be helpful. Furthermore, mentions that appear within the quote are also excluded as its candidate mentions.

For each quote-mention pair, the classifier assigns a probability, which we use to select the most likely speaker for that quote. From all candidate mentions, we choose the mention with the highest probability. However, if this probability is lower than a pre-defined threshold (initially set at 0.2), no speaker is attributed to the quote.

Figure 1 provides an overview of our classifier. It consists of an input layer to which we apply a dropout of 0.2, followed by two dense hidden layers of 500 and 150 neurons, both with a dropout of 0.5. These layers both have ReLU activation

[3] https://github.com/frenkvdberg/dutchqa/blob/main/annotation_guidelines.pdf

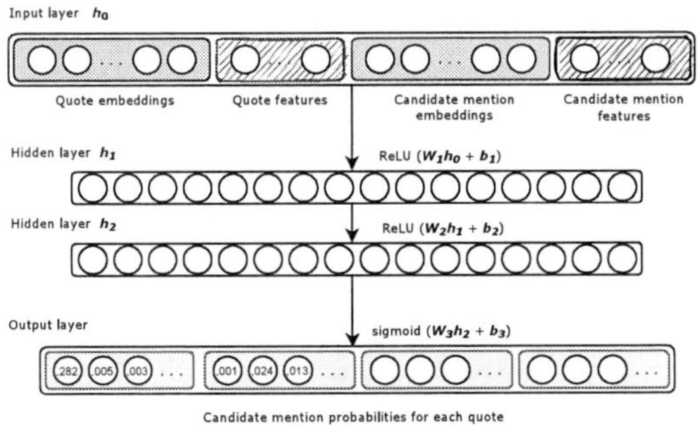

Figure 1: An overview of the classifier.

and batch normalization. For the output layer we use a sigmoid activation with L_2 regularization of 0.05. Furthermore, we use the Adam optimizer with a learning rate of 0.0001 and a batch size of 32. Lastly, we use early stopping to stop training when the model does not improve for 5 successive epochs.

Whereas van Cranenburgh (2019) favored precision over recall for their quote attribution component, we decide to experiment with tuning our classifier for different evaluation metrics. Using the same architecture with different features during training, we create a three variants of our classifier. Each focused on achieving the best performance on a specific metric, we present a *+precision*, *+recall* and *+F1* model. The features types are described in the next section; the classifier variants, along with their impact, are discussed in Section 6.1.

5.2 Features

Our classifier uses as input BERT embeddings and various handpicked features. For both the quotes and the mention candidates, we use BERT token embeddings produced by BERTje (de Vries et al., 2019), a pretrained, monolingual Dutch model. When a quote or a mention consists of multiple tokens, we take the mean of the embeddings of all tokens to use as input. As for the handpicked features, we will summarize each feature below.

Mention type of candidate mention; possible values: name, noun, pronoun.

Mention attributes For the mention attributes, we consider person, gender and animacy. The person attribute has three possible values: first, second, and third person. The gender attribute is either f (female), m (male), fm (mixed or unknown gender), or n (neuter). Lastly, animacy refers to whether the mention is human or non-human.

Quote length The number of tokens in the quote span.

Paragraph distance The number of paragraphs between the mention and the quote.

Token distance The number of tokens between the mention and the quote.

Quote distance The number of tokens between the end of the previous quote and the start of the current quote.

Mention occurrence in previous quote While we do not yet know the addressees for each quote, this feature might provide similar information. It looks at whether the candidate mention occurs within the previous quote, which means that it might be a speaker that is addressed before taking the next turn. Additionally, we store whether not the candidate mention itself, but a mention within the same cluster as the candidate mention has occurred within the previous quote.

Quotes in between The number of other quotes that appear between the current quote and the mention candidate.

Subject of speech verb Lastly, we check whether the candidate mention is the subject of a reported speech verb, for example 'says', 'asks' or 'replies'. Such verbs are also referred to as cue words (Pareti, 2012, 2016; Papay and Padó, 2020). Note that the reported speech verbs are not part of the annotations, but are detected using a predefined list mined from a large corpus of parsed novels using a syntactic query of the form "NP verb quoted-speech" in various orders (van Cranenburgh, 2019).

5.3 Baseline methods

In order to gain a better insight into the performance of our classifier, we compare it to three different baselines. We will describe the approach of these baselines below in order of complexity.

Closest mention baseline Always choose the mention that is closest to the quote in terms of token distance. This closest mention is still chosen from the pool of candidate mentions, meaning that it is required to either be a name, noun, personal pronoun or a possessive pronoun. Inspired by Bamman et al. (2014) and Muzny et al. (2017).

Embeddings-only baseline A classifier as in Section 5.1, using only the BERT token embeddings for the quotes and the mentions in order to predict the speaker for each quote.

Dutchcoref baseline Since our goal is to improve the quote attribution performance of the rule-based dutchcoref system with a neural classifier, we need to know how well the rule-based approach (cf. Section 2.2) performs.

6 Evaluation

As mentioned before, for the RiddleCoref corpus we use the same train, development and test splits as defined in Poot and van Cranenburgh (2020). For the OpenBoek corpus however, there is no predefined split. A first proposal for this corpus was to use the novel *Max Havelaar* as development and *Eline Vere* as test, leaving the other seven novels as the train split. However, we noticed some poor performance with regards to the quote extraction part, which means these novels might not be representative as evaluation data. Especially for the fragment *Eline Vere*, which is the only fragment in which quotes are always introduced by a dash sign instead of quotation marks, the quotes were often extracted incorrectly. In the fragment *Max Havelaar*, the quotes are introduced by both quotation marks and dash signs in a very inconsistent manner. Moreover, quotes do not always have ending quotation marks.

Since quote extraction works well for the seven other fragments, we decided on the following: We will evaluate the performance of our classifiers, which were trained on the RiddleCoref train split, on both the RiddleCoref test split and on the seven remaining novels from the OpenBoek corpus (thus excluding *Eline Vere* and *Max Havelaar*). This way we can see whether the performance is better on a specific corpus, as well as analyze the potential differences.

We will report precision, recall and F1-scores, which were also used in earlier work (Muzny et al., 2017; van Cranenburgh, 2019). We report only scores indicating whether the quote was attributed to the correct speaker cluster. We do not report whether the quote was attributed to the same speaker mention as in the gold data, since this is a somewhat arbitrary annotation choice.

The evaluation can be further divided. During the training of our classifier and our initial experiments, we made use of gold standard coreference files that were already available for the RiddleCoref dataset. We will report the scores obtained by our classifier and the baseline systems when using these gold coreference files, meaning these systems have access to all the manually corrected mentions when making their predictions.

System	Threshold	P	R	F1
baselines:				
closest mention	N/A	40.7	40.7	40.7
embeddings only	0.20	53.9	53.6	53.7
dutchcoref	N/A	88.4	62.9	73.5
classifiers:				
neural +precision	0.20	91.5	58.8	71.6
neural +recall	0.20	85.8	67.9	75.8
neural +F1	0.20	87.6	67.9	76.5
classifiers w/ optimal thresholds:				
neural +precision	0.24	**92.9**	57.4	71.0
neural +recall	0.02	79.4	**77.2**	78.3
neural +F1	0.09	85.5	74.7	**79.8**

Table 1: Quote attribution on the RiddleCoref dev. set, using gold coreference, with classifiers optimizing precision, recall, or F1.

Additionally, we will implement the classifier into the existing dutchcoref system as an independent module. This way, we can compare its performance as a part of the dutchcoref system and compare whether it actually improves the rule-based approach in a realistic, end-to-end setting.

It must be noted that quotes that do not have a gold speaker are not taken into consideration during this evaluation, as this should be addressed as part of the quote extraction process, which is not the focus of this paper.

In the following subsections, we first report the results achieved in our experiments using gold standard coreference files. For these results, we also show which features contributed the most to each of our classifiers. Then, we report the results that our classifiers achieved when implemented into the dutchcoref system.

6.1 Results with gold coreference files

We first report the quote attribution results that were obtained when training the classifier on the RiddleCoref development set, using the available gold-standard coreference files. This way, we can see how well each system would perform in an ideal setting, where the quote attribution performance is not influenced by how well the dutchcoref system performs on other subtasks, as this evaluation setting will be discussed in Section 6.2.

Table 1 shows the performance of the baselines, as well as our neural classifiers, both with and without optimized thresholds. The simple baselines of always attributing a quote to the closest candidate mention or only using BERT embeddings as features are heavily outperformed by the rule-based dutchcoref module. However, we were able to train three different neural classifiers, each focused on outperforming the dutchcoref system on a specific evaluation metric.

We first apply the same probability threshold of 0.2 (below which no speaker will be assigned) to all classifiers in order to make an initial performance comparison. When looking at the speaker cluster scores, we see that the *+precision* classifier achieves an improvement of 3.1% on the precision metric over the dutchcoref system, although it performs worse in terms of recall and F1-score. Similarly, the *+recall* classifier outperforms the dutchcoref system by 5.0% on the recall metric, and the *+F1* classifier outperforms the dutchcoref system by 3.1% on the F1 metric. However, none of the classifiers outperforms the dutchcoref systems on all three metrics.

Then, we experimented with the probability thresholds in order to further improve the performance of our classifiers at their respective metrics. Increasing the threshold results in a higher precision score, while decreasing the thresholds results in a higher recall score. After optimizing these threshold values, the *+precision* classifier now achieves a precision score of 4.5% higher than the dutchcoref system. The *+recall* and *+F1* classifiers outperform the dutchcoref system on both recall and F1-score, with the *+recall* classifier achieving a recall score 14.3% higher and the *+F1* classifier achieving an F1-score 6.3% higher than the dutchcoref system.

In order to see which features contribute the most to each classifier's performance, we performed ablation experiments. Table 2 shows the performance of each classifier when removing one feature at a time. The *paragraph distance* feature seems to be by far the most important feature in all the three classifiers. Removing this feature would even mean that the *+precision* and *+F1* classifiers no longer outperform the dutchcoref system on their respective metrics. Interestingly, the *mention type* feature does not seem to contribute that much to the performance of each classifier. Removing this feature from the *+precision* classifier would result in slightly higher precision scores, however the F1-score would noticeably drop. Lastly, the *quote length* and *mention occurrence in previous quote* features that we introduced in Section 5.2 are not included in any of our three classifiers. While these features seemed to increase the scores in our initial experiments, they will unfortunately only decrease the performance when added to our final three classifiers.

Feature	P	R	F1
neural +precision:	92.9	57.4	71.0
- mention type	93.1	55.2	69.3
- mention attr. (excl. gender info)	88.6	55.5	68.2
- paragraph distance	**72.0**	50.8	59.6
- token distance	88.0	52.5	65.7
- quote distance	86.1	64.8	74.0
neural +recall:	79.4	77.2	78.3
- mention type	77.9	74.7	76.3
- mention attr. (excl. gender info)	76.6	74.7	75.7
- paragraph distance	69.8	**67.9**	68.8
- token distance	76.8	75.5	76.2
- subject of speech verb	76.8	74.7	75.8
neural +F1:	85.5	74.7	79.8
- mention type	84.1	72.5	77.9
- mention attributes	85.3	72.0	78.1
- paragraph distance	75.1	69.8	**72.4**
- token distance	83.9	73.1	78.1
- subject of speech verb	84.3	73.6	78.6
- quotes in between	81.3	73.1	77.0

Table 2: Ablation experiments for each classifier, removing one feature at a time.

QA module	Set	P	R	F1
rule-based	RC - dev	87.2	53.1	64.8
neural +precision	RC - dev	**94.6**	50.3	63.5
neural +recall	RC - dev	75.5	**71.4**	**73.3**
neural +F1	RC - dev	78.7	66.5	71.7
rule-based	RC - test	85.4	45.0	58.1
neural +precision	RC - test	**90.4**	43.4	58.2
neural +recall	RC - test	67.3	**65.0**	**66.1**
neural +F1	RC - test	72.9	58.8	64.7
rule-based	OpenBoek	**85.3**	64.0	72.8
neural +precision	OpenBoek	84.5	56.4	66.4
neural +recall	OpenBoek	76.0	**73.5**	**74.7**
neural +F1	OpenBoek	79.3	70.6	**74.7**

Table 3: End-to-end quote attribution results of different modules in the dutchcoref system.

6.2 Results with a coreference pipeline

For a more realistic evaluation of the performance of our classifiers, we compare the achieved scores again after implementing them as neural modules in the dutchcoref system. In Table 3, we report scores obtained on the RiddleCoref development and test sets, as well as on the selected seven OpenBoek novels. As expected, now that the quote attribution performance is dependent on the input received from earlier dutchcoref sieves, the scores achieved on the RiddleCoref development set are somewhat lower for all systems when compared to the scores from Table 1. Still, the neural classifiers each outperform the dutchcoref system on their respective metrics. It is interesting that this time, the *+recall* classifier obtains the highest recall **and** the highest F1-score of all four systems, both for the speaker mentions and for the speaker clusters.

For the RiddleCoref test set, all the scores are noticeably lower than they are for the development set. Again the *+recall* classifier achieves the the highest recall and F1-scores for the speaker clusters, although the *+F1* classifier does perform the best on the F1 metric if we look specifically at the speaker mentions performance. Seeing these relatively low scores on the test set inspired us to perform an error analysis, which we will discuss in Section 7.2.

Lastly, the quote attribution performance on the OpenBoek novels yields the highest F1-scores for all systems. This seems to be mostly due to all the recall scores being noticeably higher than they are for the RiddleCoref data splits. However, the *+precision* classifier does not outperform the rule-based approach on these seven novels. Furthermore, the rule-based approach achieves the highest F1 score looking purely at the speaker mentions and for the speaker clusters the difference in F1 scores between the rule-based approach and the best performing neural classifiers is noticeably smaller than on the RiddleCoref novels. For transparency, we included the results on each individual novel in Appendix A.3.

7 Analysis

To gain a better understanding of the challenges of literary quote attribution, we now take a closer look at the test data and model outputs. We first consider the distribution of quote types, and then perform an error analysis of the systems we evaluated.

7.1 Quote type distribution

In order to compare the RiddleCoref test novels to the OpenBoek novels, we consider the distribution of the quote types per novel (see Section A.4 for detailed statistics). As mentioned before, we distinguish between four different quote types: **explicit** (said Tom), **anaphoric pronoun** (said he), **anaphoric other** (said his friend) and **implicit**. Looking at the relative frequencies, we see that the percentage of anaphoric other quotes is roughly the same for both datasets. However, we see a big difference in the relative amount of implicit quotes: 57% for the RiddleCoref test novels vs only 32% for the OpenBoek novels. Whereas implicit quotes are by far the most prominent in the RiddleCoref test novels, anaphoric pronoun quotes are the most prominent in the OpenBoek novels, slightly surpassing the implicit quotes. The large dataset of classic English novels by Vishnubhotla et al. (2022) has about 36% implicit and 29% anaphoric quotes (based on Table 5). This figure is similar to that of OpenBoek and suggests that contemporary novels may contain more implicit quotes than classic novels, which makes the task of quote attribution harder for contemporary novels.

Furthermore, it is interesting to see that even within the datasets the quote type distribution can differ considerably per novel. For instance, in the novel *Gooische Vrouwen*, 67% of the quotes are explicit, whereas this percentage is only 4% for *Cobra* and 0% for *Mannentester*. Similar outliers can be seen for the OpenBoek novels, where *De Agra Schat* contains 61% quotes of type anaphoric pronoun, but *Reis Om De Wereld* contains only 12% quotes of the same type. Some of this variance could be attributed to genre, but also to author style.

This distribution helps us better understand the difference in performance of our classifiers on these datasets, which we discuss in the next subsection.

7.2 Error analysis

Looking at the speaker cluster F1-scores in Table 3, we see a large difference in performance on the RiddleCoref test novels and the OpenBoek novels. This difference is not only visible for our neural classifiers, but also for the rule-based approach, which achieved 14.7% F1 points higher on the OpenBoek novels. As the performance was the worst on the RiddleCoref test novels, we analyzed the mistakes that the different systems made on each novel. See Section A.4 for a breakdown of mistakes per quote type and novel.

We see that for each system the majority of the mistakes are made on implicit quotes. Even by our best classifier, these quotes are still incorrectly classified in 53% of the cases, with our worst performing classifier incorrectly classifying these quotes 76% of the time. The anaphoric pronoun quotes seem to be the easiest to classify for each system, especially for the *+recall* and *+F1* classifiers, which only make mistakes on 2% of these quotes.

Looking at these mistakes in combination with the quote distribution of Table 10 helps us understand the difference in performance on the aforementioned datasets. As can be seen from the quote distribution, the RiddleCoref test novels contain 57% implicit and 20% anaphoric pronoun quotes, whereas these percentages are 32% implicit and 35% anaphoric pronoun quotes for the OpenBoek novels. Seeing how by far the most mistakes are made on implicit quotes, it is only natural to see a worse performance on a dataset with novels that contain on average more of these implicit quotes.

It is also interesting to see how our neural *F1* classifier substantially outperforms the rule-based approach for explicit-, anaphoric other- and especially anaphoric pronoun quotes, but only slightly for the implicit quotes. The *+precision* classifier actually performs worse than the rule-based approach only for the implicit quotes. This shows us that even with the features we presented and implemented in our classifiers, we still have an especially hard time attributing implicit quotes to the right speaker.

Lastly, we see that for each system, anaphoric non-pronoun quotes are substantially harder to classify than anaphoric pronoun quotes, which is in line with the results presented in (Muzny et al., 2017).

8 Conclusion

In this paper, we focused on training a classifier to improve the task of quote attribution when compared to dutchcoref's rule-based approach. We trained three different feed-forward neural network classifiers, each one focused a different metric for speaker clusters: precision, recall and F1-score. For the task of quote attribution, we manage to improve on the rule-based approach by 8.0% F1 points on the RiddleCoref test novels and by 1.9% F1 points on the OpenBoek novels.

With our quote attribution error analysis we show that each system makes the most mistakes on implicit quotes. Moreover, anaphoric pronoun quotes prove to be harder than anaphoric non-pronoun quotes, as each of the systems performs the best on the anaphoric pronoun quote type. This also explains why the quote attribution performance on the OpenBoek novels is notably higher than on the RiddleCoref test novels, as the OpenBoek novels contain relatively more anaphoric pronoun quotes and less implicit quotes.

For future work, we think there is still a lot of improvement to be gained, especially on implicit quotes. As we have found features that reduce mistakes on anaphoric pronoun quotes by 91.7% with respect to the rule-based approach, future experiments can look specifically at how to decrease mistakes on implicit quotes. Furthermore, we did not consider the task of identifying addressees, thus having to rely on the rule-based approach to identify these after we first identify the speakers using our neural classifiers. Jointly identifying speakers and addressees may yield additional performance gains, since it would enable the classifier to pick up on turn-taking patterns in a data-driven manner. Reported speech verbs (also known as cue words) were not part of the annotations, but detected using a predefined list. Recall may be improved by detecting them using a classifier trained on annotated cue words. In terms of machine learning, fine-tuning BERT for the task of quote attribution (rather than simply using averaged token embeddings as features) and/or incorporating more context with for example an LSTM on top of the BERT embeddings can be expected to yield additional improvements.

Lastly, we think further improvements can also be made on quote extraction, as we saw that there were still a lot of mistakes made on the OpenBoek novels *Max Havelaar* and *Eline Vere*. As most of these mistakes were made on quotes starting with a dash sign, more elaborate rules targeting these kind of quotes could improve the overall performance of dutchcoref even more.

Acknowledgements

The authors are grateful to Khalid Al-Khatib and three anonymous reviewers for helpful comments.

References

Mariana S. C. Almeida, Miguel B. Almeida, and André F. T. Martins. 2014. A joint model for quotation attribution and coreference resolution. In *Proceedings of EACL*, pages 39–48.

David Bamman, Ted Underwood, and Noah A. Smith. 2014. A Bayesian mixed effects model of literary character. In *Proceedings of ACL*, pages 370–379.

Julian Brooke, Adam Hammond, and Graeme Hirst. 2017. Using models of lexical style to quantify free indirect discourse in modernist fiction. *Digital Scholarship in the Humanities*, 32(2):234–250.

Joanna Byszuk, Michał Woźniak, Mike Kestemont, Albert Leśniak, Wojciech Łukasik, Artjoms Šeļa, and Maciej Eder. 2020. Detecting direct speech in multilingual collection of 19th-century novels. In *Proceedings of LT4HALA*, pages 100–104.

Wietse de Vries, Andreas van Cranenburgh, Arianna Bisazza, Tommaso Caselli, Gertjan van Noord, and Malvina Nissim. 2019. BERTje: A Dutch BERT Model. arXiv:1912.09582.

David Elson, Nicholas Dames, and Kathleen McKeown. 2010. Extracting social networks from literary fiction. In *Proceedings of ACL*, pages 138–147.

David K. Elson and Kathleen R. McKeown. 2010. Automatic attribution of quoted speech in literary narrative. In *Twenty-Fourth AAAI Conference on Artificial Intelligence*.

Kevin Glass and Shaun Bangay. 2007. A naive salience-based method for speaker identification in fiction books. In *Proceedings of the 18th Annual Symposium of the Pattern Recognition Association of South Africa (PRASA'07)*, pages 1–6.

Hua He, Denilson Barbosa, and Grzegorz Kondrak. 2013. Identification of speakers in novels. In *Proceedings of ACL*, pages 1312–1320.

Armand Joulin, Edouard Grave, Piotr Bojanowski, and Tomas Mikolov. 2017. Bag of tricks for efficient text classification. In *Proceedings of EACL*, pages 427–431.

Corina Koolen, Karina van Dalen-Oskam, Andreas van Cranenburgh, and Erica Nagelhout. 2020. Literary quality in the eye of the Dutch reader: The national reader survey. *Poetics*.

Eve Kraicer and Andrew Piper. 2019. Social characters: The hierarchy of gender in contemporary English-language fiction. *Journal of Cultural Analytics*, 3(2).

Vincent Labatut and Xavier Bost. 2019. Extraction and analysis of fictional character networks: A survey. *ACM Computing Surveys*, 52(5).

Heeyoung Lee, Angel Chang, Yves Peirsman, Nathanael Chambers, Mihai Surdeanu, and Dan Jurafsky. 2013. Deterministic coreference resolution based on entity-centric, precision-ranked rules. *Computational Linguistics*, 39(4):885–916.

Grace Muzny, Michael Fang, Angel Chang, and Dan Jurafsky. 2017. A two-stage sieve approach for quote attribution. In *Proceedings of EACL*, pages 460–470.

Tim O'Keefe, Silvia Pareti, James R. Curran, Irena Koprinska, and Matthew Honnibal. 2012. A sequence labelling approach to quote attribution. In *Proceedings of EMNLP-CoNLL*, pages 790–799.

Tim O'Keefe, Kellie Webster, James R. Curran, and Irena Koprinska. 2013. Examining the impact of coreference resolution on quote attribution. In *Proceedings of ALTA*, pages 43–52.

Sean Papay and Sebastian Padó. 2020. RiQuA: A corpus of rich quotation annotation for English literary text. In *Proceedings of LREC*, pages 835–841.

Silvia Pareti. 2012. A database of attribution relations. In *Proceedings of LREC*, pages 3213–3217.

Silvia Pareti. 2016. PARC 3.0: A corpus of attribution relations. In *Proceedings of LREC*, pages 3914–3920.

Silvia Pareti, Tim O'Keefe, Ioannis Konstas, James R. Curran, and Irena Koprinska. 2013. Automatically detecting and attributing indirect quotations. In *Proceedings of EMNLP*, pages 989–999.

Corbèn Poot and Andreas van Cranenburgh. 2020. A benchmark of rule-based and neural coreference resolution in Dutch novels and news. In *Proceedings of CRAC*, pages 79–90.

Andrew Salway, Paul Meurer, Knut Hofland, and Øystein Reigem. 2017. Quote extraction and attribution from norwegian newspapers. In *Proceedings of the 21st Nordic Conference on Computational Linguistics*, pages 293–297.

Elena Semino and Mick Short. 2004. *Corpus Stylistics: Speech, writing and thought presentation in a corpus of English writing*. Routledge Advances In Corpus Linguistics. Routledge, London.

Matthew Sims and David Bamman. 2020. Measuring information propagation in literary social networks. In *Proceedings of EMNLP*, pages 642–652.

Ted Underwood, David Bamman, and Sabrina Lee. 2018. The transformation of gender in english-language fiction. *Journal of Cultural Analytics*, 3(2).

Andreas van Cranenburgh. 2019. A Dutch coreference resolution system with an evaluation on literary fiction. *Computational Linguistics in the Netherlands Journal*, 9:27–54.

Andreas van Cranenburgh, Esther Ploeger, Frank van den Berg, and Remi Thüss. 2021. A hybrid rule-based and neural coreference resolution system with an evaluation on Dutch literature. In *Proceedings of CRAC*, pages 47–56.

Andreas van Cranenburgh and Gertjan van Noord. 2022. Openboek: A corpus of literary coreference and entities with an exploration of historical spelling normalization. *Computational Linguistics in the Netherlands Journal*, 12:235–251.

Krishnapriya Vishnubhotla, Adam Hammond, and Graeme Hirst. 2022. The project dialogism novel corpus: A dataset for quotation attribution in literary texts. In *Proceedings of LREC*, pages 5838–5848.

Chak Yan Yeung and John Lee. 2017. Identifying speakers and listeners of quoted speech in literary works. In *Proceedings of IJCNLP*, pages 325–329.

Michael Yoder, Sopan Khosla, Qinlan Shen, Aakanksha Naik, Huiming Jin, Hariharan Muralidharan, and Carolyn Rosé. 2021. FanfictionNLP: A text processing pipeline for fanfiction. In *Proceedings of the Third Workshop on Narrative Understanding*, pages 13–23.

	RiddleCoref			OpenBoek
	train	dev	test	
documents	23	5	5	9
sentences	6,803	1,525	1,536	5,709
sentences per document	295.8	305.0	307.2	643.3
average sentence length	15.5	18.4	18.3	18.1
tokens	105,517	28,042	28,054	103,522
mentions	25,194	6,584	6,869	23,650
entities	9,041	2,643	3,008	8,875
mentions / entities	2.79	2.49	2.28	2.66
mentions / tokens	0.24	0.23	0.24	0.23
entities / tokens	0.09	0.09	0.11	0.09
% pronouns	40.4	35.7	38.1	40.9
% nominals	47.0	49.4	52.8	48.0
% names	12.6	14.9	9.1	11.1

Table 4: RiddleCoref and OpenBoek corpora statistics.

A Appendices

A.1 Corpus statistics

See Table 4 for various statistics of the two corpora used in this paper. Table 5 lists the number of annotated quotes for each text (fragment).

A.2 Inter-Annotator Agreement

For the RiddleCoref corpus, ten of the fragments were annotated by the first author at an earlier stage, allowing us to look at inter-annotator agreement. However, these annotations were made before the annotation guidelines were created, so some inconsistencies are to be expected. While this score is often calculated using Cohen's kappa, we found that this method was not applicable here, as there is not always a clear number of possible speaker mentions and speaker clusters to which a quote could be attributed. Instead, we evaluated our annotations against the other annotations to calculate the F1-scores for each fragment, which can be found in Table 6.

Looking at the F1-scores for the clusters, we see that we achieve an average F1-score of 83.7, indicating that we often attribute quotes to the same speaker cluster. This score is noticeably lower for the mentions, as the choice of which mention to pick is a rather arbitrary choice, which is best shown for the novel by Barnes. For the 23 quotes this novel contains, we tend to attribute the quotes to different mentions, achieving an F1-score of 9.3, while still often attributing these quotes to the same speaker cluster, as can be seen from the cluster F1-score of 73.4. Ultimately, it is the speaker cluster that should be correctly recognized by our final system, so getting these correct is what matters most.

Still, for the speaker cluster scores we see two especially low scores. For the novel *De begraafplaats van Praag*, we see an F1-score of 40.0. Here, the challenge is whether the detected quotes are meant to be attributed to a speaker or not, as we show for the following two detected quotes:

(5) *(...) je hoeft alleen maar af te geven op een ander volk, dus bijvoorbeeld ["wij Polen hebben dat en dat manco"]$_{quote}$, of ze zeggen meteen, omdat ze voor niemand onder willen doen, zelfs niet als het iets negatiefs betreft: ["O nee, hoor! Hier in Frankrijk zijn we veel erger"]$_{quote}$, waarna ze aan een anti-Franse tirade beginnen die pas eindigt als het tot ze doordringt dat ze erin zijn getuind.*
(...) you only have to speak ill of another people, for example ["we Poles have such and such a defect"]$_{\text{quote}}$, and since they do not want to be second to anyone, even in wrong, they react with: ["Oh no, here in France we are worse"]$_{\text{quote}}$, and they start running down the French until they realize they've been caught out.

Whereas the other annotator does not assign a speaker to either of these quotes, we argue that the second quote can be attributed to the underlined mention *ze* (they). This scenario is repeated for another quote in the novel, where the other annotator

Riddlecoref - train	# quotes	**Riddlecoref - dev**	# quotes
Abdolah, Koning	94	Gilbert, Eten Bidden Beminnen	9
Barnes, Alsof Voorbij Is	23	Kluun, Haantjes	16
Bernlef, Zijn Dood	104	Kooten, Verrekijker	57
Bezaz, Vinexvrouwen	11	Mitchell, Niet Verhoorde Gebeden	222
Binet, Hhhh	23	Springer, Quadriga	82
Carre, Ons Soort Verrader	9	***Total***	***386***
Collins, Hongerspelen	129		
Dewulf, Kleine Dagen	11	**Riddlecoref - test**	
Eco, Begraafplaats Van Praag	3	Forsyth, Cobra	46
Eggers, Wat Is Wat	19	Japin, Vaslav	114
Grunberg, Huid En Haar	19	Proper, Gooische Vrouwen	36
James, Vijftig Tinten Grijs	11	Royen, Mannentester	25
Kinsella, Shopaholic Baby	51	Verhulst, Laatste Liefde Van	48
Koch, Diner	12	***Total***	***269***
Mansell, Versier Me Dan	41		
Moor, Schilder En Meisje	5	**OpenBoek**	
Rowling, Harry Potter	468	Conan Doyle, De Agra Schat	186
Siebelink, Oscar	57	Couperus, Eline Vere	101
Vermeer, Cruise	23	Hugo, De Ellendigen	78
Voskuil, Buurman	54	Multatuli, Max Havelaar	31
Weisberger, Chanel Chic	7	Nescio, De Uitvreter	220
Worthy, James Worthy	15	Nescio, Dichtertje	150
Yalom, Raadsel Spinoza	20	Nescio, Titaantjes	91
Total	***1,209***	Tolstoy, Anna Karenina	182
		Verne, Reis Om De Wereld	153
		Total	***1,192***

Table 5: Number of quotes per text.

again does not assign a speaker, while we do. As the fragment of this novel contains very few quotes, each difference in our annotations heavily lowers the inter-annotator agreement score.

For the novel *Het diner*, the F1-score of 59.5 can also be explained by us assigning speakers to quotes more often than the other annotator does, as we show in example (6):

(6) *Maar ik noem haar zelden mijn vrouw — bij officiële gelegenheden af en toe, in zinnen als: ['Mijn vrouw kan op dit moment niet aan de telefoon komen']$_{quote}$, of: ['Mijn vrouw weet toch echt zeker dat zij een kamer met uitzicht op zee had gereserveerd.']$_{quote}$*
But I rarely refer to her as my wife — on official occasions sometimes, in sentences like ['My wife can't come to the phone right now']$_{\text{quote}}$, or: ['My wife is very sure she asked for a room with a sea view.']$_{\text{quote}}$

Again, both quotes are not assigned a speaker by the other annotator, whereas we attribute both quotes to the underlined mention *ik* (I). We notice that the quotes on which we disagree are often introduced by phrases like *bijvoorbeeld* (for example) or *zoals* (such as). These quotes can sometimes be interpreted as describing hypothetical dialogue, leaving the reader uncertain whether the dialogue has actually ever taken place. Still, we choose to assign these examples of dialogue to the intended speaker, causing our annotations to differ with the other annotator at times.

A.3 Quote attribution performance per novel

- RiddleCoref development set: cf. Table 7.
- RiddleCoref test set: cf. Table 8.
- OpenBoek novels: cf. Table 9.

Novel	Mentions F1	Clusters F1
Barnes, Alsof het voorbij is	9.3	73.4
Carre, Ons soort verrader	53.7	100
Eco, Begraafplaats van Praag	40.0	40.0
Eggers, Wat is de wat	52.6	100
Grunberg, Huid en haar	85.7	100
James, Vijftig tinten grijs	34.1	100
Koch, Diner	61.1	59.5
Moor, De schilder en het meisje	100	100
Voskuil, De buurman	76.3	97.7
Yalom, Het raadsel Spinoza	62.5	66.7
Average	***57.5***	***83.7***

Table 6: Annotator agreement on 10 RiddleCoref texts.

A.4 Analysis: detailed tables

Table 10 lists the number of quote types per annotated text. Table 11 lists the number of mistakes broken down by quote type in the texts of the RiddleCoref test set.

Novel	Mentions			Clusters		
	P	R	F1	P	R	F1
rule-based:						
Gilbert, Eten Bidden Beminnen	100	44.4	61.5	100	44.4	61.5
Kluun, Haantjes	85.7	37.5	52.2	85.7	37.5	52.2
Kooten, Verrekijker	78.6	64.7	71.0	81.0	66.7	73.1
Mitchell, Niet Verhoorde Gebeden	84.2	67.3	74.8	88.9	71.0	79.0
Springer, Quadriga	71.7	40.7	52.0	80.4	45.7	58.3
Average	***84.0***	***50.9***	***62.3***	***87.2***	***53.1***	***64.8***
neural +precision:						
Gilbert, Eten Bidden Beminnen	100	44.4	61.5	100	44.4	61.5
Kluun, Haantjes	100	25.0	40.0	100	25.0	40.0
Kooten, Verrekijker	90.7	76.5	83.0	95.3	80.4	87.2
Mitchell, Niet Verhoorde Gebeden	89.9	57.9	70.5	92.8	59.8	72.7
Springer, Quadriga	82.5	40.7	54.5	85.0	42.0	56.2
Average	***92.6***	***48.9***	***61.9***	***94.6***	***50.3***	***63.5***
neural +recall:						
Gilbert, Eten Bidden Beminnen	88.9	88.9	88.9	100	100	100
Kluun, Haantjes	53.8	43.8	48.3	61.5	50.0	55.2
Kooten, Verrekijker	84.3	84.3	84.3	88.2	88.2	88.2
Mitchell, Niet Verhoorde Gebeden	69.2	68.2	68.7	74.4	73.4	73.9
Springer, Quadriga	63.6	60.5	62.0	77.9	74.1	75.9
Average	***72.0***	***64.2***	***65.8***	***75.5***	***71.4***	***73.3***
neural +F1:						
Gilbert, Eten Bidden Beminnen	88.9	88.9	88.9	100	100	100
Kluun, Haantjes	50.0	31.2	38.5	60.0	37.5	46.2
Kooten, Verrekijker	86.0	84.3	85.1	90.0	88.2	89.1
Mitchell, Niet Verhoorde Gebeden	78.6	68.7	73.3	84.0	73.4	78.3
Springer, Quadriga	68.7	56.8	62.2	80.6	66.7	73.0
Average	***70.8***	***60.2***	***64.8***	***78.7***	***66.5***	***71.7***

Table 7: Quote attribution scores per novel on the RiddleCoref development set, when classifiers are implemented within the dutchcoref system.

Novel	Mentions			Clusters		
	P	R	F1	P	R	F1
rule-based:						
Forsyth, Cobra	84.2	34.8	49.2	84.2	34.8	49.2
Japin, Vaslav	90.3	57.5	70.3	95.8	61.1	74.6
Proper, Gooische Vrouwen	76.9	57.1	65.6	80.8	60.0	68.9
Royen, Mannentester	81.8	36.0	50.0	81.8	36.0	50.0
Verhulst, Laatste Liefde Van	78.9	31.2	44.8	84.2	33.3	47.8
Average	***82.4***	***42.3***	***56.0***	***85.4***	***45.0***	***58.1***
neural +precision:						
Forsyth, Cobra	85.0	37.0	51.5	85.0	37.0	51.5
Japin, Vaslav	87.3	42.5	57.1	89.1	43.4	58.3
Proper, Gooische Vrouwen	87.0	57.1	69.0	87.0	57.1	69.0
Royen, Mannentester	81.8	36.0	50.0	90.9	40.0	55.6
Verhulst, Laatste Liefde Van	100	39.6	56.7	100	39.6	56.7
Average	***88.2***	***42.4***	***56.9***	***90.4***	***43.4***	***58.2***
neural +recall:						
Forsyth, Cobra	57.6	41.3	48.1	57.6	41.3	48.1
Japin, Vaslav	64.3	63.7	64.0	73.2	72.6	72.9
Proper, Gooische Vrouwen	62.9	62.9	62.9	62.9	62.9	62.9
Royen, Mannentester	52.0	52.0	52.0	64.0	64.0	64.0
Verhulst, Laatste Liefde Van	59.5	52.1	55.6	69.0	60.4	64.4
Average	***59.3***	***57.7***	***58.6***	***67.3***	***65.0***	***66.1***
neural +F1:						
Forsyth, Cobra	67.9	41.3	51.4	71.4	43.5	54.1
Japin, Vaslav	70.4	61.1	65.4	81.6	70.8	75.8
Proper, Gooische Vrouwen	69.7	65.7	67.6	69.7	65.7	67.6
Royen, Mannentester	56.5	52.0	54.2	65.2	60.0	62.5
Verhulst, Laatste Liefde Van	70.6	50.0	58.5	76.5	54.2	63.4
Average	***67.0***	***54.0***	***59.4***	***72.9***	***58.8***	***64.7***

Table 8: Quote attribution scores per novel on the RiddleCoref test set, when classifiers are implemented within the dutchcoref system.

Novel	Mentions			Clusters		
	P	R	F1	P	R	F1
rule-based:						
Conan Doyle, De Agra Schat	92.8	76.2	83.7	94.7	77.8	85.5
Hugo, De Ellendigen	82.7	56.6	67.2	86.5	59.2	70.3
Nescio, De Uitvreter	89.5	70.0	78.6	91.4	71.5	80.2
Nescio, Dichtertje	66.2	35.3	46.1	75.0	40.0	52.2
Nescio, Titaantjes	71.4	49.5	58.4	77.8	53.8	63.6
Tolstoy, Anna Karenina	77.1	60.0	67.5	81.4	63.3	71.3
Verne, Reis Om De Wereld	86.2	78.3	82.1	90.6	82.2	86.2
Average	***80.8***	***60.8***	***69.1***	***85.3***	***64.0***	***72.8***
neural +precision:						
Conan Doyle, De Agra Schat	95.1	73.0	82.6	95.8	73.5	83.2
Hugo, De Ellendigen	80.7	60.5	69.2	86.0	64.5	73.7
Nescio, De Uitvreter	80.4	69.6	74.6	83.8	72.5	77.7
Nescio, Dichtertje	69.0	32.7	44.3	77.5	36.7	49.8
Nescio, Titaantjes	77.1	29.7	42.9	85.7	33.0	47.6
Tolstoy, Anna Karenina	81.5	61.1	69.8	85.9	64.4	73.7
Verne, Reis Om De Wereld	86.2	65.8	74.6	87.9	67.1	76.1
Average	***81.4***	***53.2***	***62.6***	***84.5***	***56.4***	***66.4***
neural +recall:						
Conan Doyle, De Agra Schat	77.7	75.1	76.4	79.3	76.8	78.0
Hugo, De Ellendigen	71.2	68.4	69.8	75.3	72.4	73.8
Nescio, De Uitvreter	76.3	76.3	76.3	84.5	84.5	84.5
Nescio, Dichtertje	53.5	50.7	52.1	66.9	63.3	65.1
Nescio, Titaantjes	50.6	49.5	50.0	67.4	65.9	66.7
Tolstoy, Anna Karenina	69.4	66.7	68.0	78.6	75.6	77.1
Verne, Reis Om De Wereld	75.7	71.7	73.6	79.9	75.7	77.7
Average	***67.8***	***65.5***	***66.6***	***76.0***	***73.5***	***74.7***
neural +F1:						
Conan Doyle, De Agra Schat	89.4	77.3	82.9	90.0	77.8	83.5
Hugo, De Ellendigen	80.0	68.4	73.8	83.1	71.1	76.6
Nescio, De Uitvreter	81.4	78.3	79.8	86.4	83.1	84.7
Nescio, Dichtertje	57.5	48.7	52.7	70.9	60.0	65.0
Nescio, Titaantjes	56.4	48.4	52.1	69.2	59.3	63.9
Tolstoy, Anna Karenina	70.8	66.1	68.4	79.2	73.9	76.4
Verne, Reis Om De Wereld	83.5	73.0	77.9	87.2	76.3	81.4
Average	***74.1***	***63.8***	***67.5***	***79.3***	***70.6***	***74.7***

Table 9: Quote attribution scores per novel on the selected OpenBoek novels, when classifiers are implemented within the dutchcoref system.

Novel	EXP	ANA-P	ANA-O	IMP
RiddleCoref - test:				
Forsyth, Cobra	2	5	9	30
Japin, Vaslav	5	39	1	69
Proper, Gooische Vrouwen	24	0	1	11
Royen, Mannentester	0	5	2	18
Verhulst, Laatste Liefde	12	4	7	25
Total	***43***	***53***	***20***	***153***
Relative total	***16%***	***20%***	***7%***	***57%***
OpenBoek:				
Conan Doyle, De Agra Schat	18	114	6	48
Hugo, De Ellendigen	8	31	22	17
Nescio, De Uitvreter	95	73	4	48
Nescio, Dichtertje	11	44	18	77
Nescio, Titaantjes	20	21	6	44
Tolstoy, Anna Karenina	43	70	12	57
Verne, Reis om de wereld	72	18	16	47
Total	***267***	***371***	***84***	***338***
Relative total	***25%***	***35%***	***8%***	***32%***

Table 10: Distribution of quote types in RiddleCoref test and OpenBoek texts. EXP: explicit; ANA-P: anaphoric pronoun; ANA-O: anaphoric other; IMP: implicit.

System	Novel	EXP	ANA-P	ANA-O	IMP
dutchcoref	Forsyth, Cobra	0	1	3	25
	Japin, Vaslav	1	6	0	37
	Proper, Gooische Vrouwen	7	0	0	7
	Royen, Mannentester	0	2	2	12
	Verhulst, Laatste Liefde Van	3	3	6	20
	Total	***11***	***12***	***11***	***101***
	mistakes / quotes	***0.26***	***0.23***	***0.55***	***0.66***
neural +precision	Forsyth, Cobra	0	1	3	25
	Japin, Vaslav	2	4	0	58
	Proper, Gooische Vrouwen	5	0	1	9
	Royen, Mannentester	0	1	1	13
	Verhulst, Laatste Liefde Van	0	2	5	22
	Total	***7***	***8***	***10***	***117***
	mistakes / quotes	***0.16***	***0.15***	***0.50***	***0.76***
neural +recall	Forsyth, Cobra	0	1	2	22
	Japin, Vaslav	2	0	0	28
	Proper, Gooische Vrouwen	5	0	1	7
	Royen, Mannentester	0	0	1	8
	Verhulst, Laatste Liefde Van	0	0	3	16
	Total	***7***	***1***	***7***	***81***
	mistakes / quotes	***0.16***	***0.02***	***0.35***	***0.53***
neural +F1	Forsyth, Cobra	0	0	2	23
	Japin, Vaslav	1	0	0	32
	Proper, Gooische Vrouwen	5	0	0	7
	Royen, Mannentester	0	1	1	8
	Verhulst, Laatste Liefde Van	0	0	3	19
	Total	***6***	***1***	***5***	***81***
	mistakes / quotes	***0.14***	***0.02***	***0.25***	***0.53***

Table 11: Mistakes per quote type on the RiddleCoref test novels.

Large Bibliographies as a Source of Data for the Humanities – NLP in the Analysis of Gender of Book Authors in German Countries and in Poland (1801-2021)

Adam Pawłowski
University of Wrocław
pl. Uniwersytecki 1
50-137 Wrocław, Poland
adam.pawlowski@uwr.edu.pl

Tomasz Walkowiak
Wrocław University of Science and Technology
27 Wybrzeże Wyspiańskiego St.
50-370 Wrocław, Poland
tomasz.walkowiak@pwr.edu.pl

Abstract

The subject of this article is the application of NLP and text-mining methods to the analysis of two large bibliographies: a Polish one, based on the catalogs of the National Library in Warsaw, and a German one, created by the Deutsche Nationalbibliothek. The data in both collections are stored in MARC 21 format, allowing the selection of relevant fields that are used for further processing (basically author, title, and date). The volume of the Polish corpus (after filtering out non-relevant or incomplete items) includes 1.4 mln of records, and that of the German corpus 7.5 mln records. The time span of both bibliographies extends from 1801 to 2021. The aim of the study is to compare the gender distribution of book authors in Polish and German databases over more than two centuries. The proportions of male and female authors since 1801 were calculated automatically, and NLP methods such as document vector embeddings based on deep BERT networks were used to extract topics from titles. The gender of the Polish authors was recognized based on the morphology of the first names, and that of the German authors based on a predefined list. The study found that the proportion of female authors has been steadily increasing both in Poland and in German countries (currently around 43%). However, the topics of women's and men's writings invariably remain different since 1801.

1 Introduction

The research conducted straddles two broad areas. One relates to the issue of the resources and methodologies (NLP and text-mining tools applied to **large bibliographies** – hereafter LB), and the other concerns a certain problem that belongs to the field of cultural anthropology and/or social sciences (equal gender participation in various social activities). We will first address the latter issue, while the former (data and methods) will be presented in the subsequent sections.

The complex and long-standing processes leading to a fairer participation of both genders in social, scientific, economic, and cultural life have been ongoing in Europe for at least two centuries. Their most visible public representation was for decades the feminist movement initiated in the USA in the mid-19th century (Women's Convention in Seneca Falls, USA, 1848). The actual gender status in European countries, however, is different in specific regions and largely independent of official policies and spectacular events publicized by the media. The real scope of the ongoing changes in this area can only be revealed by analyzing big data that consistently and synthetically reflect the state of affairs over a long period of time. In particular, a convincing analysis of this phenomenon should not highlight the most mediated, individual exponents of women's status (e.g. awards, prominent positions in politics or business). It should rather rely on information resources aggregating large amounts of data dispersed in various sources that we can consider the most objective possible.

Large bibliographies can be considered as sources that meet these conditions. They consist of data which represent a very important segment of intellectual life and are collected systematically according to the same principles. Also of significance is the fact that for decades, LB have remained insufficiently exploited by scientific methods. The present work is therefore of a pioneering nature. It should be noted that, so far, in empirical studies of complex processes related to gender equality, economic and legal measures have been used. However, they can hardly be trusted in the case of a politically fragile region with a turbulent history, such as Central Europe. Its multilingual diversity, the intensity of political change, different monetary systems, and border shifts over the past two centuries make publication stream analysis a more reliable approach that is highly resistant to the influence of random factors or systemic disruptions.

Proceedings of the 7th Joint SIGHUM Workshop on Computational Linguistics for Cultural Heritage, Social Sciences, Humanities and Literature (LaTeCH-CLfL2023), pages 63–71
May 5, 2023

Writing books is, among other things, the result of one's prosperity, exposure to knowledge, and education. In addition, social acceptance of the author's gender and social origin was necessary for the publication of a book. For example, medicine in the nineteenth century was almost entirely masculinized. Therefore, a female author of a work on, for example, surgery would not have been accepted by the readers, ergo no publisher would publish such a work.

2 Research Objective and Hypothesis

The first goal of this study is to show the proportions of women and men among the authors of books published from 1801 to 2021 in two European communities of communication, associated in various periods with the concept of a nation or of a state. For that purpose, we generated historical histograms showing the proportions of male, female, and unrecognized authors. A chronological (vertical) survey allowed us to show the dynamics of cultural change, occurring in the most populous and influential countries of Central Europe over a long period of time.

The second goal of the research was to extract topics specific to male and female authors from book titles. Its aim was to identify the main contents or topics that characterize the writing of both genders. We assumed that the authorship of a book aggregates a number of socially and psychologically salient variables that are difficult to capture, especially over a long period of time. Topics were generated from time sections, representing main historical periods. We hypothesized that in the 19th century (until ca 1910) there would be little, if any, similarity between the two sets both in Polish and in German data. We also expected to observe a growing overlap of topics generated from titles by male and female authors after the interwar period 1918-1945 for both Polish and German data.

The question as to whether this parameter is likely to become a universal and effective measure of gender equality remains open. Yet, it certainly provides a quantitative and possibly objective estimate of this phenomenon. Its advantage, from the point of view of methodology, is the use of big and "clean" data and the ensuing independence from random factors. Another issue was the choice of Poland and Germany as the objects of the study. These are countries geographically and culturally close but historically different in size and status. Despite the instability of borders and political systems, German culture maintained continuity in the 19th and 20th centuries based on various state organisms (including the Rhine Union, the Second Reich, the Weimar Republic, the Third Reich, and the Federal Republic of Germany). Additionally, in the 19th century German Countries (especially Prussia) were among the world leaders in science and culture. The situation of Poland was radically different. Poland lost its statehood at the end of the 18th century, and in effect existed until World War I only as an entity identified with its culture, history, religion, and, above all, its language. And even this status of an "imagined state" was constantly challenged by the occupation regimes. The country regained its independence in 1918, but then again was occupied between 1939 and 1945 by the Third Reich and the Soviet Union. After 1945, Poland became a vassal state subordinated to the Soviet Union; not regaining full sovereignty until 1989. Given the above circumstances, the discovery of similarities (or differences) related to the gender of book authors in both corpora will provide a result that seems objective, and scientifically relevant.

3 Related work

Much more research is now focused on the exploratory analysis of library catalogs around the world, for example, Lahti et al. (2019); Tolonen et al. (2019). However, surprisingly little research has been published on the use of artificial intelligence techniques in bibliography data (Wheatley and Hervieux, 2019; Pawłowski and Walkowiak, 2020; Pawłowski and Walkowiak, 2021). The problem of topic recognition from short texts is studied in the literature (Albalawi et al., 2020; Grootendorst, 2022), but application of such a method to a large number of book titles, that is, very short texts, is an original approach. Moreover, as discussed in Section 5 the applied method differs from methods known from literature (Grootendorst, 2022). Moreover, the paper deals with the problem of merging two bibliographies and deduplication of records (see Section 4). The problem is discussed in the literature (Wysota and Trzaska, 2021; Sitas and Kapidakis, 2008; Heron et al., 2013).

4 Research Material

The study was carried out on large bibliographies produced by the National Libraries of Poland[1]

[1] https://data.bn.org.pl/databases

and Germany (Deutsche Nationalbibliothek)[2]. Although these are not the official "national bibliographies", they functionally fulfill the conditions set for such monumental repositories. In particular, they have a predictable structure of data, the permanent care of a central institution, and the aspiration of covering the entire body of writings. It is worth mentioning that due to the lack of a Polish state in the 19th century (until 1918), there was no central institution to keep track of publications during this period. Records extracted from the Estreicher Polish Bibliography[3], which registers Polish works and Polonica from a period very poorly represented in the collection of the National Library, were therefore taken into account. For this purpose, the online part of the bibliography was used, which covers approximately 40% of the entire collection.

The records of the central libraries are stored in MARC format (Thomale, 2010) which allows for field searches and elimination of works that do not meet the analysis conditions. In the first iteration, records lacking authors or titles were filtered out. All nontext works (maps, notes, gramophone records, other sound recordings, etc.) were omitted. Periodical publications were also discarded. In the case of works extracted from the Estreicher Polish Bibliography, 5 pages were accepted as the lower limit of acceptable volume (this source includes very short documents too). In principle, most works in languages other than Polish or German were eliminated from both bibliographies. However, this criterion was problematic, as there is no easy way to automatically distinguish works by German (or Polish) authors writing in other languages from authors of other nationalities, but publishing in Germany or Poland (a frequent example from the 20th century are German doctorates in English). Several works by Polish authors from the 19th century that for political reasons were published in the languages of states that occupied Polish territory (mainly in German or Russian) or in some other other international language (e.g., Latin, French, and Ruthenian), were excerpted by hand and included.

The whole research material for German comprised 25.9 mln records, out of which 72% were rejected as nonrelevant, while for Polish a total of 2.3 mln records were processed (95% from the Polish National Library database, 5% from the Estreicher Bibliography), and 38% were rejected (38% among those from the National Library database, 50% from the Estreicher Bibliography). The distribution of data over time was not balanced, but this does not impede the results of our study (with incomplete representation, inductive inference is applicable).

The association of first names with gender is almost unambiguous and, in addition, the feminine gender in Polish is always indicated by the name ending *-a*. In the case of the Polish base, recognition was, therefore, based on this rule. The automatically generated database (mapping of name to gender) was then manually checked. Some names, especially foreign ones, are ambiguous, so they were marked as unknown. The German language, on the other hand, is not so consistent, as some Old High German names end in a consonant (e.g., Annetrud, Edeltraut, Gudrun etc.). An additional difficulty - especially after 1945 - in German, is the large number of borrowed names. For this reason, a reference catalog of German male and female names was prepared using open resources. It was manually verified again and completed manually for missing names that had an occurrence larger than 20. Finally, the gender of the authors was determined by automatically comparing their names with the list.

5 Methods of Data Processing

The MARC database is structured, but often requires additional procedures for information retrieval. For example, the publication date often contains additional characters that need to be removed. The author's first name is not a separate field and has to be automatically separated from the last name. Another problem was the use of umlaut character encoding (the umlaut was encoded as two characters) in German data that are not compliant with standard UTF-8. For processing MARC-21 files we have used a Python 3 PyMarc[4] library.

In the case of the Estreicher Polish Bibliography, the data are available as HTML tables, and the date of publication is an element of a single text containing the place of publication and the name of the publisher. This required the development of a set of heuristic rules to extract the publication data from the text. Another problem with the Estreicher Bibliography was the need for deduplication with the National Library of Poland. A special method

[2] https://data.dnb.de/DNB/

[3] https://www.estreicher.uj.edu.pl

[4] https://pymarc.readthedocs.io/

was developed that first splits data based on publication date and then uses Jaccard's token similarity between titles and authors to detect duplicates in a group of papers with the same publication date.

Detecting topics from short texts requires a dedicated procedure (Albalawi et al., 2020; Grootendorst, 2022), which differs from classic approaches to topic modeling, such as LDA (Blei et al., 2003). This is because titles are very short and we cannot rely on the co-occurrence of words in the same text and on the assumption that the text is a mixture of several topics. Therefore, the semantic analysis of titles (the second objective of the work) was based on a clustering procedure. This procedure requires a measure of similarity between titles. Therefore, each title was transformed into a vector space using deep BERT networks (Devlin et al., 2018). Since pre-trained BERT networks are not suitable for solving semantic similarity problems (Reimers and Gurevych, 2019), we used a Sentence-BERT approach (Reimers and Gurevych, 2019) based on metric learning (Bellet et al., 2015). It uses Siamese and triplet network structures to derive semantically meaningful sentence embeddings. In the case of Polish, we tuned the Sentence-BERT network on a publicly available corpus[5] of human-annotated sentence pairs in Polish for their semantic relatedness starting from the HerBERT (Mroczkowski et al., 2021) pretrained model. In the case of German, we used an already predeveloped Sentence-BERT model dedicated to English and German text[6]. Having embedded text, we applied classical K-Means (Hastie et al., 2013) clustering to obtain what we hoped were clusters of semantically distinct groups of titles. We then described the clusters using a set of words that identifies the content of the clusters. This is done using a modified TF-IDF (Salton G, 1988) procedure that takes into account class information (c-TF-IDF), which was proposed in Grootendorst (2022). This method yields list of words with their probabilities for each cluster; that is, topic as a concept used in topic modeling approaches (Blei et al., 2003). Our approach differs from BERTopic (Grootendorst, 2022) by omitting UMAP (McInnes et al., 2020) used for document vector reduction and replacing HDBSCAN (McInnes and Healy, 2017) clustering with K-Means. The authors tested BERTopic, but the results were not satisfactory because HDBSCAN's outlier detection function caused about 75% of the data to go off-topic, and UMAP's preservation of only local similarities caused semantically different titles to be mixed within a single topic.

Detected topics can be linked to gender by counting the number of titles assigned to a topic/cluster with authors of that gender. In the case of multiauthor books, we required that each author have the same gender. To express the relevance of a topic to a given gender, the importance index is defined as the ratio of books authored by women to men (or vice versa) about a given topic (cluster) normalized to the ratio of books for each gender. This allows the detection of a topic relevant to both men and women, irrelevant of the gender distribution among authors.

6 Results

6.1 The Volume of German and Polish Data

Analysis of the data volume has confirmed our expectations, but there were also some surprises. Namely, it turned out that the data coverage of the period roughly referred to as the 19th century, both in the case of Poland and Germany, is poor (until 1910). However, this did not significantly impede the analyses. We have assumed that data from the 19th century should be treated as a representative sample (consisting of the most significant works), while data from the period 1911-2021 are almost complete. Inspection of the histogram (time series) of the number of titles in successive years confirms that the German culture was and remains very productive (red plots in Figure 1). As a matter of fact each year the number of book titles published in Germany has exceeded the corresponding parameter in Poland by at least 5 times, and in some years even more (see Figure 1c). This is an unfavourable result from the Polish point of view because the difference in the size of the populations of the two countries would justify an advantage of only three times. This difference in volume can be explained, however, to some extent. Firstly, in Germany, all PhD dissertations must appear in print (with an ISBN code), whereas in Poland there is no such obligation. Secondly, the databases of the National Library of Germany include works belonging to the German Countries, including also those from Austria and Switzerland. Thirdly, in Poland during the communist period, due to paper shortages and the lack of a normal publishing market, multiple

[5]https://huggingface.co/datasets/allegro/klej-cdsc-r

[6]https://huggingface.co/T-Systems-onsite/cross-en-de-roberta-sentence-transformer

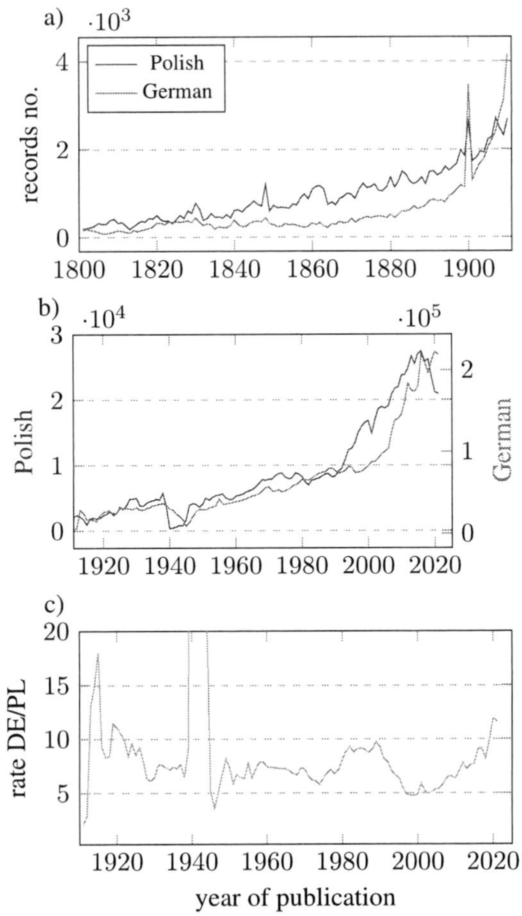

Figure 1: Number of records meeting the analysis criteria (non-empty field of title and authors, publication date between 1801 and 2021, and Polish/German language); a) Polish and German for years 1801-1910; b) 1911-2021 (notice that scale for German is 10 times larger then for Poland); c) Number of German records in relation to Polish records in 1911-2021 (in 1940 it goes over 80).

editions of the same work were very rare, while in Germany many books appeared at the same time as softcover and as hardcover.

A closer analysis of these contemporary data also reveals interesting fluctuations due to World War 2 or political changes. What is conspicuous is the period from 1980 to 1990 in Poland (martial law), marked by a general collapse in culture and economy (Figure 1b in blue), and the period after 1990. Events at that time in Poland and partly in Germany were a co-occurrence of three factors: the fall of the totalitarian system and the abolition of censorship that released the creative energy of the society, the technological revolution that lowered the costs of publishing, and the spread of the personal computer that increased the speed of writing texts by authors. During that period, the DE/PL ratio systematically decreased (Figure 1c). The reason for the reversal of this tendency after 2005 is a change in the long-term trend in the German data (Figure 1b in red). This is, however, not due to the sudden increase of the number of German books published (a stable trend observed since the 1920s cannot change from year to year) but to the change of book coding method. Most of the new titles started to be counted twice or three times despite being the same work: printed version, e-books in various formats, and audio-books had different ISBN codes. Digital editions were also frequent in Poland at that period but were not considered as separate books (see sharp falls of the curve in Figure 1b).

The material from the years 1801-1911, although incomplete, is of interest too (Figure 1a). It shows, for example, negative effects of catastrophic events (e.g., in the Polish data there are visible traces of national uprisings in 1830 and 1861). On the other hand, the "round date effect", i.e., the tendency of people to accumulate special interest around points on the time line that are deemed some sort of symbolic borderlines, should be considered very interesting. This is the explanation for a strong peak of the curve in 1900 (Germany and Poland), and a smaller one in 1850. The question arises why such a peak did not appear in the millennium year (2000). Most likely this anomaly can be explained by fundamental changes of the leading medium in public communication. The peak was observed in electronic media including TV, and not in printed books, which in 1900 covered a much larger scope of social life.

6.2 Gender Distribution in German and Polish Data

An impressive visual representation of the enormous historical changes that have taken place in the societies of Poland and German Countries, and probably also throughout Europe, revealed here as Figure 2, showing two symbolic lines: the share of male and female authors over the period of the last 220 years (upper and lower line, respectively). The percentage of unrecognized data, as can be seen, is small and stable - fluctuating at approximately 6%. On the contrary, the female and male share lines run similarly, showing a very slow increasing

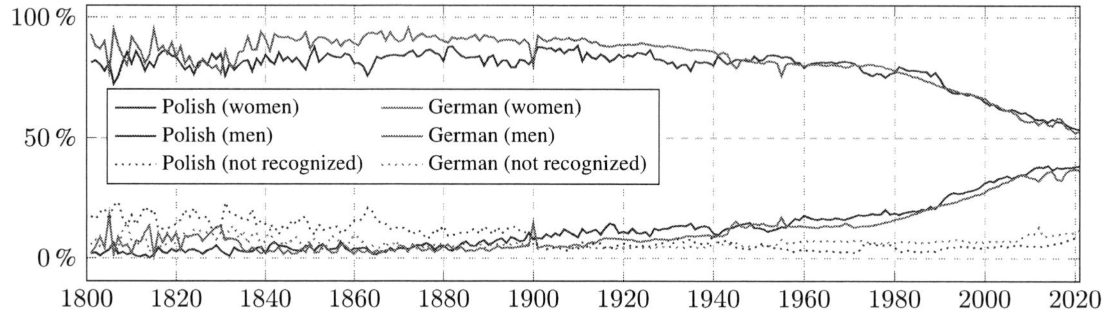

Figure 2: Gender breakdown of book authors over the years 1801-2021.

/ decreasing trend almost until the middle of the 20th century. In German Countries, the cut-off date indicating a change in the trend is around 1970 (one could hypothesize if this shift was related to the consequence of the mass unrest of 1968). In Poland, a strong acceleration in the development of women's writing occurs after 1990. Both curves react to one-off events (different for Poland and German Countries), but both have similar shapes. The disproportion in the number of records between Poland and Germany, as well as between different historical periods, is considerable (Figure 1). However, this does not affect the result presented here, as we are using proportions and not absolute values. The number of recognized male and female author names is high. In the German database, out of a total number of 8.1 mln individuals, the percentage of unrecognized items (or rejected for some other reason) was 7.7%, and in the Polish database the corresponding percentage was 5.3% out of a total number of 1.3 mln authors. All this makes the obtained result reliable. The process of the increasing participation of women writers is noticeable in the data (Figure 2). This indirectly indicates a growing gender equality, leading to a more balanced participation of men and women in intellectual and cultural life. Interestingly, despite the great differences between Poland and Germany in terms of culture, politics, and economy, both curves show virtually the same upward trend, which demonstrates the universality of the observed phenomenon, at least in this part of Europe. It is only on closer inspection that small differences are noticeable. Some of them seem long-lasting, while others are temporary disturbances in the overall trend.

The tools commonly applied in time series analysis (trend estimation, ACF function, etc.) were not used at this stage because there is no indication of periodic oscillations. However, the similarity between the two tendencies (PL, DE) was evaluated using a cross-correlation measure. The Pearson correlation coefficient of the Polish and German women's share series is equal to 0.93 with a p-value for testing for lack of correlation equal to $1e^{-97}$ thus verifying the hypothesis that the two processes are similar.

The shares of male and female authors were also compared separately for the Polish and German data. Overall, the average share of Polish female authors in the total publication stream is higher than that of German female authors (Figure 2). When the area under the curve is calculated over the entire period, the Polish data account for 12.1% and after 1900 it is 18.8%. For German data, it is, respectively, 11.1% and 16.1%. An exhaustive explanation of this result in terms of historical research and cultural anthropology would require a separate, comprehensive qualitative study that would take into account the following factors: the impact of the Polish struggle for the rebirth of a sovereign state between 1801 and 1918, the ideology of feminism and political struggle for equal rights for women throughout Europe, the influence of religion (Catholic, Protestant, Orthodox, Judaism) on women's status, and last but not least, specific social traditions in Polish and German culture.

6.3 Gender Specific Topics in German and Polish Titles

Table 1 shows the three most gender-differential topics (topics with the highest values of the importance ratio) for each gender in six time periods for Polish titles. The results for German titles are presented in Table 2. Topic detection was carried out independently for each period analyzed and each language. For the first time slot (1801-1910), we generated 20 topics for each language, for the next (1911-1945) 20 for Polish and 40 topics for Ger-

Period	Women		Men	
	Topic	C	Topic	C
1801-1910	woman	5.7	thesis defence	8.8
	youth	4.8	society report	5.6
	novel	2.8	academic	4.3
1911-1945	youth	4.9	judiciary	3.9
	romance	3.1	lecture	3.1
	novel	2.1	academic	2.2
1946-1980	child	4.7	electrics	4.7
	language	2.6	construction	4.1
	school	2.6	transport	4.0
1981-1999	school	4.2	transport	4.8
	child	3.8	electrics	4.4
	romance	3.3	construction	3.8
2000-2021	school	6.3	machine	4.8
	children	3.6	war	4.7
	woman	3.6	software	3.9

Table 1: The most gender specific topics detected in Polish titles in selected time periods. C denotes the importance ratio, calculated as the ratio of books by women to men (or vice versa) with a given theme (topic) normalized to the ratio of books for each gender.

Period	Women		Men	
	Topic	C	Topic	C
1801-1910	novel	4.6	Germany	3.3
	Rome	2.5	report, speech	3.1
	letter	1.9	religion	3.0
1911-1945	novel	3.5	tax	5.7
	story	3.3	economy	3.0
	child	3.2	judicary	2.9
1946-1980	romance	3.3	science	3.6
	woman	3.1	judicary	3.2
	child	2.8	electrics	2.8
1981-1999	child	2.8	software	3.2
	romance	2.3	mathematics	2.8
	medicine	2.0	applied science	2.8
2000-2021	romance	3.1	investigation	2.3
	child	2.8	finances	2.1
	cooking	2.1	religion	1.8

Table 2: The most gender specific topics detected in German titles.

Period	Polish		German	
	importance coefficient treshold			
	2	1.5	2	1.5
1801-1910	43.1%	55.7%	29.1%	71.9%
1911-1945	33.3%	57.4%	18.8%	49.6%
1946-1980	32.1%	50.8%	32.0%	49.5%
1981-1999	20.0%	41.5%	18.5%	41.9%
2000-2021	25.1%	42.6%	16.2%	42.8%

Table 3: Coverage (percentage of books) of gender-specific topics detected in Polish and German bibliographies. We count the ratio of books belonging to topics with a coefficient of importance above the given threshold (1.5, 2) to all books analyzed time periods.

man (since there are much more records) and 40 for the next time slots. For clarity of presentation, the topics were labelled by the authors on the basis of the list of key words generated by the c-TF-IDF algorithm. For example, the first four keywords (with highest probabilities) for topic "software" (for Polish data, male, years 2000-2021) are: programming (9.4%), windows (5.3%), excel (4.6%), and Microsoft (3.8%). And for topic "school" (in female group) they are: classroom (20.4%), school (18.5%), primary (9.3%), and textbook (7.8%). In the case of female authors, the topics are very stable over time and there is little difference between German and Polish titles. They mainly cover areas such as romance, novels, children, and women. In the group of male authors, the most gender-specific topics differ slightly between German and Polish texts, but there are many common elements, such as judiciary, science, and various technical fields. The limited volume of the article does not allow for more topics (and the corresponding keywords) to be presented, but their overtones are very similar: there are elements specific to male authors and others that are specific to female authors.

We have also used Fisher's exact test to analyze the topics shown in Tables 1 and 2. Technically, we built contingency tables for each topic and verified the null hypothesis that men and women are equally likely to write books on a particular topic. All the tests returned a p-value very close to 0, hence the listed topics are specific for gender. In addition, we analyze the volume of books covering gender-specific topics, that is, topics with an importance factor greater than a given threshold. The results for the Polish and German bibliographies and the thresholds equal to 1.5 and 2 are presented in Table 3. It shows that the share of books with gender-specific topics is slowly decreasing over time but is still very high (more than 40%).

All experiments can be replicated using standard workstations. We used an Nvidia GeForce GTX 1080/2080 Ti card to train Sentence-BERT and generate embeddings; all other analyses do not require a GPU. The only computational problem was the process of generating topics from German data for the period 2000-2021, which required about 100GB of memory.

7 Conclusions

The research presented here was developed by combining advanced NLP techniques, mathematical statistics, programming, and large bibliographic data. It has demonstrated that the ratio of male and female authors in book publishing, when measured over a long period of time, should be considered one of the most reliable indicators of women's empowerment in the society. In the context of politically unstable regions, it has two main advantages: it is relatively **time-proof** in the period of late modernity (i.e. approximately since 1800), and it is **synthetic**. The former characteristic implies that the data are comparable over a long period of time. They were created under similar conditions (open publishing market) and the object of measurement remains the same (books from the 19th and the 20th century do not differ in essence). The latter feature means that it includes some specific measures that economics, history, or cultural anthropology used to apply separately (access to education, financial standing, social status, etc.). It also showed to be sensitive to one-time events such as wars, political or technological breakthroughs.

The study confirmed the hypothesis that in German Countries and in Poland similar upward trend in gender equality may be observed (Figure 2). However, the question remains open as to whether this phenomenon would have a similar dynamics throughout Europe. The current share of the authors of the book is approximately 43% women and 57% men (note that these are values after deducting unrecognized items, so slightly different from those in Figure 2). The value of the cross-correlation coefficient, i.e., 0.93, confirmed that statistically the two processes (gender equality in German Countries and in Poland) may be observed are not identical, although very similar. An interesting issue is whether participation of women in public life was higher in Poland or in German Countries. The overall ratio of female authors in Poland and Germany is slightly higher in Poland (12.1%) than in German Countries (11.1%). Analyzing Figure 2, one can also ask whether there is a target state of optimal social balance between both genders. For example, would the ideal be an equal share of male and female authors? Perfect symmetries are a product of human imagination and expectations, rather than empirical observable phenomena (Fleck et al., 1981). Equal parities should be treated with distrust in the social sphere as well as attempts to realize new utopias, not different in essence from those once conceived by philosophers, e.g. Thomas Morus (*Utopia*) or Tommaso Campanella (*City of the Sun*). Differences in the psychological profiles and interests of men and women have always existed and – as we demonstrate in our study – translate into various types of book content published. Therefore, a balanced and socially favorable level of participation of both genders among book authors would have to be considered 50% with a large margin, even 10%. It seems that this point will soon be reached both in Germany and in Poland.

The result of the research on the topics confirms some of the above statements. Multiple analyses of the entire corpus, as well as of its horizontal sections (19th and 20th centuries, contemporary period), conducted on German and Polish data, confirmed that the areas of interest of male and female authors are different. Their thematic profiles, generated using machine learning methods (BERT language models), shows a wide number of almost non-shared topics. This result does not, of course, resolve the issue of gender, and thus whether it should be seen as a purely biological or culturally conditioned phenomenon. However, it is an important contribution to the discussion on this topic, as it is based on sound methodology and a massive factual resource from two languages and cultures. The concluding remark applies to all the research conducted here. It shows that the analysis of large bibliographies by methods of data science, text mining, corpus linguistics, and NLP is a new, fully-fledged, promising strand of research.

7.1 Limitations

The study raised some debatable methodological issues. The first was the comparison of sets with significantly different numbers (7.1 mln compared with 1.4 mln records). However, in the case of gender, we are analyzing proportions of numbers and not absolute values. This makes the results of comparison, despite the different volumes of the Polish and German corpus, fully reliable. Another difficult issue was the automatic identification of the gender of the authors. This information cannot be found in MARC records, so it is necessary either to retrieve it from another source (data linking) or to recognize the gender automatically. Automatic gender recognition by name is not 100% effective, but it has been proven practically feasible.

Acknowledgements

Financed by the European Regional Development Fund as a part of the 2014-2020 Smart Growth Operational Programme, CLARIN - Common Language Resources and Technology Infrastructure, project no. POIR.04.02.00-00C002/19.

References

Rania Albalawi, Tet Hin Yeap, and Morad Benyoucef. 2020. Using topic modeling methods for short-text data: A comparative analysis. *Frontiers in Artificial Intelligence*, 3.

Aurélien Bellet, Amaury Habrard, and Marc Sebban. 2015. *Metric Learning*. Synthesis Lectures on Artificial Intelligence and Machine Learning. Morgan & Claypool Publishers.

David M. Blei, Andrew Y. Ng, and Michael I. Jordan. 2003. Latent Dirichlet Allocation. *J. Mach. Learn. Res.*, 3:993–1022.

Jacob Devlin, Ming-Wei Chang, Kenton Lee, and Kristina Toutanova. 2018. BERT: Pre-training of deep bidirectional transformers for language understanding. *arXiv preprint arXiv:1810.04805*.

Ludwik Fleck, Thaddeus Joseph Trenn, R. Merton, Fred Bradley, and Thomas Kuhn. 1981. *Genesis and development of a scientific fact*. University of Chicago Press, Chicago.

Maarten Grootendorst. 2022. BERTopic: Neural topic modeling with a class-based TF-IDF procedure. *arXiv preprint arXiv:2203.05794*.

Trevor J. Hastie, Robert John Tibshirani, and Jerome H. Friedman. 2013. *The elements of statistical learning: data mining, inference, and prediction*. Springer Series in Statistics. Springer, New York.

Susan Jane Heron, Betsy Simpson, Amy K. Weiss, and Jean Phillips. 2013. Merging catalogs: Creating a shared bibliographic environment for the State University Libraries of Florida. *Cataloging & Classification Quarterly*, 51(1-3):139–155.

Leo Lahti, Jani Marjanen, Hege Roivainen, and Mikko Tolonen. 2019. Bibliographic data science and the history of the book (c. 1500–1800). *Cataloging & Classification Quarterly*, 57(1):5–23.

Leland McInnes and John Healy. 2017. Accelerated hierarchical density based clustering. In *Data Mining Workshops (ICDMW), 2017 IEEE International Conference on*, pages 33–42. IEEE.

Leland McInnes, John Healy, and James Melville. 2020. UMAP: Uniform manifold approximation and projection for dimension reduction. *arXiv preprint arXiv:1802.03426*.

Robert Mroczkowski, Piotr Rybak, Alina Wróblewska, and Ireneusz Gawlik. 2021. HerBERT: Efficiently pretrained transformer-based language model for Polish. In *Proceedings of the 8th Workshop on Balto-Slavic Natural Language Processing*, pages 1–10, Kiyv, Ukraine. Association for Computational Linguistics.

Adam Pawłowski and Tomasz Walkowiak. 2020. Automatic recognition of gender and genre in a corpus of microtexts. In *Theory and Applications of Dependable Computer Systems*, pages 472–481, Cham. Springer International Publishing.

Adam Pawłowski and Tomasz Walkowiak. 2021. Analysis of toponyms from the Polish National Bibliography. In *Proceedings of the 6th International Workshop on Computational History (HistoInformatics 2021) co-located with ACM/IEEE Joint Conference on Digital Libraries 2021 (JCDL 2021), Online event, September 30-October 1, 2021*, volume 2981 of *CEUR Workshop Proceedings*. CEUR-WS.org.

Nils Reimers and Iryna Gurevych. 2019. Sentence-BERT: Sentence embeddings using Siamese BERT-networks. In *Proceedings of the 2019 Conference on Empirical Methods in Natural Language Processing and the 9th International Joint Conference on Natural Language Processing (EMNLP-IJCNLP)*, pages 3982–3992, Hong Kong, China. Association for Computational Linguistics.

Buckley C. Salton G. 1988. Term-weighting approaches in automatic text retrieval. *Information Processing and Management*, 24(5):513–523.

Anestis Sitas and Sarantos Kapidakis. 2008. Duplicate detection algorithms of bibliographic descriptions. *Library Hi Tech*, 26.

Jason Thomale. 2010. Interpreting MARC: Where's the bibliographic data? *Code4Lib Journal*, 11.

Mikko Tolonen, Leo Lahti, Hege Roivainen, and Jani Marjanen. 2019. A quantitative approach to book-printing in Sweden and Finland, 1640–1828. *Historical Methods: A Journal of Quantitative and Interdisciplinary History*, 52(1):57–78.

Amanda Wheatley and Sandy Hervieux. 2019. Artificial intelligence in academic libraries: An environmental scan. *Information Services & Use*, 39:1–10.

Witold Wysota and Kacper Trzaska. 2021. Correlation of bibliographic records for OMNIS project. In *Theory and Engineering of Dependable Computer Systems and Networks*, pages 487–495, Cham. Springer International Publishing.

Emotion Recognition based on Psychological Components in Guided Narratives for Emotion Regulation

Gustave Cortal[1], **Alain Finkel**[1,4], **Patrick Paroubek**[2], **Lina Ye**[3]
[1]Univ. Paris-Saclay, CNRS, ENS Paris-Saclay, LMF, 91190, Gif-sur-Yvette, France
[2]Univ. Paris-Saclay, CNRS, LISN, 91400, Orsay, France
[3]Univ. Paris-Saclay, CNRS, ENS Paris-Saclay, CentraleSupélec, 91190, Gif-sur-Yvette, France
[4]Institut Universitaire de France, France
{gustave.cortal, alain.finkel}@ens-paris-saclay.fr,
pap@limsi.fr, lina.ye@centralesupelec.fr

Abstract

Emotion regulation is a crucial element in dealing with emotional events and has positive effects on mental health. This paper aims to provide a more comprehensive understanding of emotional events by introducing a new French corpus of emotional narratives collected using a questionnaire for emotion regulation. We follow the theoretical framework of the Component Process Model which considers emotions as dynamic processes composed of four interrelated components (BEHAVIOR, FEELING, THINKING and TERRITORY). Each narrative is related to a discrete emotion and is structured based on all emotion components by the writers. We study the interaction of components and their impact on emotion classification with machine learning methods and pre-trained language models. Our results show that each component improves prediction performance, and that the best results are achieved by jointly considering all components. Our results also show the effectiveness of pre-trained language models in predicting discrete emotion from certain components, which reveal differences in how emotion components are expressed.

1 Introduction

Emotion analysis in text consists of associating an emotion from a predefined set (e.g. *fear*, *joy*, *sadness*) to a textual unit (e.g. word, clause, sentence). Several psychological theories are used to define the emotion classes to be predicted. Basic emotion theories (Ekman, 1992) consider discrete emotions shared by all, as they may have innate neural substrates and universal behavioral phenotypes. Dimensional theories (Russell and Mehrabian, 1977) define emotions through affective dimensions, such as the degree of agreeableness (*valence*) and the degree of physiological activation (*arousal*).

Previous studies (Bostan and Klinger, 2018) have conducted analyses on various corpora for emotion classification in text. Most of them neglect the existing psychological knowledge about emotions, which can be used to clarify what an emotion is and how it can be caused. To the best of our knowledge, only a few approaches incorporate cognitive psychological theories to classify emotions in texts. These include a knowledge-base-oriented modeling of emotional events (Cambria et al., 2020), a corpus annotated according to dimensions of cognitive appraisal of events (Troiano et al., 2022), an annotation scheme for emotions inspired by psycholinguistics (Etienne et al., 2022), and the identification of emotion component classes (Casel et al., 2021) according to the Component Process Model (CPM) (Scherer, 2005) in cognitive psychology.

These papers, like ours, are based on the cognitive appraisal theory (Lazarus and Folkman, 1984), which posits that emotions arise from the evaluation of an event based on various cognitive criteria, such as *relevance*, *implication*, *coping*, and *normative significance*. The CPM is rooted in this theory and defines emotion as a set of cognitive appraisals that modulate the expression of five components in reaction to an event (*cognitive appraisal*, *physiological response*, *motor expression*, *action tendency*, and *subjective feeling*). Our chosen components are closely related to the components originally proposed in the CPM. In this paper, we follow the theoretical framework of the CPM by considering emotions as dynamic processes composed of four interrelated components: BEHAVIOR ("I'm giving a lecture"), FEELING ("My heart is beating fast"), THINKING ("I think he's disrupting my lecture") and TERRITORY ("He attacks my ability to be respected") proposed by Finkel (2022). In our corpus, each narrative is structured by the writers according to these components. Table 1 shows an example of a structured narrative.

Proceedings of the 7th Joint SIGHUM Workshop on Computational Linguistics for Cultural Heritage, Social Sciences, Humanities and Literature (LaTeCH-CLfL2023), pages 72–81

Component	Answer
BEHAVIOR	I'm giving a lecture on a Friday morning at 8:30. A student goes out and comes back a few moments later with a coffee in his hand.
FEELING	My heart is beating fast, and I freeze, waiting to know how to act.
THINKING	I think this student is disrupting my class.
TERRITORY	The student attacks my ability to be respected in class.

Table 1: Example of an emotional narrative structured according to emotion components. The writer identified that he was angry.

We rely on the same assumptions made by Casel et al. (2021), namely that emotions in a text are expressed in several ways. Emotion components are associated with different linguistic realizations. In this paper, we study how emotions are expressed through components by introducing a new French corpus composed of emotional narratives. Narratives were collected with a questionnaire following a new psychological method, called Cognitive Analysis of Emotions (Finkel, 2022), which aims to modify (negative) representations of an emotional event to help people better regulate their emotions. Our corpus is structured according to emotion components and contains 812 narratives, corresponding to 3082 answers. Each narrative contains several answers, and each answer corresponds to a single component.

In this paper, we describe the annotation of our corpus and evaluate traditional machine learning methods and pre-trained language models for discrete emotion classification based on emotion components. To the best of our knowledge, this work is the first to study the interaction between linguistic realizations of components for emotion classification. We aim to answer several questions: does a component influence emotion prediction and, if so, does it increase or decrease performance? Does each component contribute equally or unequally to the prediction? Does considering all components lead to the best performance?

Contributions We present a new French corpus composed of emotional narratives structured according to four components (BEHAVIOR, FEELING, THINKING and TERRITORY). Each narrative is related to a discrete emotion and is structured based on all emotion components by the writers, allowing us to study the interaction of components and their impact on emotion classification. We evaluate the influence of components on emotion classification using traditional machine learning methods and pre-trained language models (CamemBERT). Our results show that each component improves prediction performance, and that the best results are achieved by jointly considering all components. Our results also show that CamemBERT effectively predict discrete emotion from THINKING, but do not improve performance from FEELING compared to traditional machine learning approaches, which reveal differences in how emotion components are expressed. We believe that our analysis can provide a further insight into the semantic core of emotion expressions in text.

2 Background and Related Work

2.1 Psychological Theories of Emotion

Discrete and Continuous theories Among emotion theories, we can distinguish between those that suppose the existence of a finite number of distinct basic emotions and those considering that emotion has several dimensions. The basic emotion theories list several emotions common to human beings, such as Ekman's universal emotions (*sadness*, *joy*, *anger*, *fear*, *disgust*, and *surprise*) (Ekman, 1992) and Plutchik's wheel of emotions (Plutchik, 2001). Instead of categorizing an emotion according to a discrete set, dimensional theories consider emotion as a point in a multidimensional Euclidean space. For example, Russell and Mehrabian (1977) consider emotions along three dimensions: an emotion is identifiable according to its degree of agreeableness (*valence*), its degree of physiological activation (*arousal*), and its degree of felt control (*dominance*).

Appraisal theories The cognitive appraisal theory (Lazarus and Folkman, 1984) identifies cognitive dimensions of emotion, considered criteria for evaluating an event. For example, it considers that an individual evaluates how an event helps him or her in satisfying a need or accomplishing a goal. There are other appraisal criteria, such as the ability to cope with an event based on resources available to the individual. The type and intensity of an emotion provoked by an event depend on the result of cognitive appraisals.

Component Process Model Cognitive appraisals are integrated in the Component Process Model (CPM) (Scherer, 2005). It considers emotion as the expression of several components (*cognitive appraisal*, *physiological response*, *motor expression*, *action tendency*, and *subjective feeling*) that synchronize in reaction to an event. The cognitive appraisals of an event modulate the expression of components. For example, during an exam, I evaluate my ability to solve an exercise; I think I do not have the skills to solve it and will get a bad mark (*cognitive appraisal*). I panic (*subjective feeling*), I sweat (*physiological response*), my legs shake (*motor expression*), I feel like getting up and running away from the classroom (*action tendency*). In this text, we can infer that I am afraid (*fear*). Our corpus explores the interaction between linguistic realizations of components. Despite being closely related, our components proposed by the Cognitive Analysis of Emotion differ from the original ones presented by the CPM.

Cognitive Analysis of Emotion The Cognitive Analysis of Emotion (Finkel, 2022) is a cognitive appraisal theory that explores the basic emotions (*anger*, *fear*, *joy*, and *sadness*) with their corresponding behavioral (BEHAVIOR), physiological (FEELING), and cognitive (THINKING and TERRITORY) components. Like other psychological and neuroscientific theories, it assumes that the mind processes emotional information, in order to prepare for and take appropriate action. If the information is not processed satisfactorily according to an individual's values, beliefs, or goals, the mind may repress, block, or loop, leading to unsatisfactory outcomes. The Cognitive Analysis of Emotion uses the CPM to reorganize the narrative of experienced emotional events. This process helps individuals better understand and regulate their emotions, as well as prepare for necessary actions. It provides a method for understanding emotions that can modify negative representations of emotional events. The narratives are categorized using a questionnaire, presented in Section 3.1. Cortal et al. (2022) introduce the use of natural language processing to automate parts of the Cognitive Analysis of Emotion.

2.2 Emotion Analysis in Text

Most methods for analyzing emotions in text focus on either the classification of discrete emotional states (Bostan and Klinger, 2018) or the recognition of affective dimensions such as *valence*, *arousal*, and *dominance* (Buechel and Hahn, 2017).

Emotion Cause Extraction Recently, some new studies aim to not only recognize the emotional state present in the text, but also the span of text that serves as its underlying cause. Lee et al. (2010) introduce the Emotion Cause Extraction task and define it as the identification of word-level factors responsible for the elicitation of emotions within text. Chen et al. (2010) analyze the corpus presented by Lee et al. (2010) and suggest that clause-level detection may be a more suitable unit for detecting causes. Xia and Ding (2019) propose the Emotion-Cause Pair Extraction task, i.e., the simultaneous extraction of both emotions and their corresponding causes. Several extensional approaches have been proposed to address this task with better performance (Ding et al. (2020a), Wei et al. (2020), Ding et al. (2020b), Chen et al. (2020), Singh et al. (2021)).

Structured Emotion Analysis The goal of semantic role labelling (Gildea and Jurafsky, 2000) is to determine the participants involved in an action or event indicated by a predicate in a given sentence. For emotion analysis, the task shifts its focus from actions to emotional cues, which are words or expressions that trigger emotions. Emotion semantic role labelling consists of answering the question: "Who feels What, towards Whom, and Why?" (Campagnano et al., 2022). Mohammad et al. (2013) annotate tweets during the 2012 U.S. presidential elections, Bostan et al. (2020) annotate news headlines and Kim and Klinger (2018) annotate literary paragraphs. They identify emotion cues with the corresponding emotion experiencers, causes and targets. Campagnano et al. (2022) propose a unified annotation scheme for different emotion-related semantic role corpora, including those presented previously. To the best of our knowledge, the only French language studies that address the identification of emotion-related semantic roles are the corpus for recognizing emotions in children's books (Etienne et al., 2022), the corpus for extremist texts (Dragos et al., 2022), and the Défi Fouille de Textes campaign (Paroubek et al., 2018), which annotates tweets related to transportation in the Île-de-France region.

Appraisal Theories for Emotion Analysis A few approaches incorporate cognitive psychological theories to classify emotions in text. The ISEAR project (Scherer and Wallbott, 1994) compiles a textual corpus of event descriptions. However, they focus on the existence of emotion components, but not on the linguistic expression of emotion components. Cambria et al. (2020) identify event properties including people's goals for sentiment analysis using a knowledge-base-oriented approach. Troiano et al. (2022) compile a corpus that considers the cognitive appraisal of events from both the writer and reader perspectives. Very few studies focus on emotion component analysis. Kim and Klinger (2019) analyze the communication of emotions in fan fiction through some variables related to emotion components such as facial and body posture descriptions, subjective sensations, and spatial relations of characters. Casel et al. (2021) annotate existing literature and Twitter emotion corpora with emotion component classes based on the CPM. However, not all emotion components are expressed to characterize an emotional event. In our corpus, each narrative is structured based on all emotion components, allowing us to study the interaction of components and their impact on emotion classification.

Menétrey et al. (2022) represents the pioneering effort in examining the interaction of components for discrete emotion prediction. However, their annotation approach deviates from ours. They use a scale ranging from 1 to 7 to solicit annotators' agreement with predefined descriptions (e.g. "To what extent did you feel calm?"). This approach disregards the linguistic manifestation of emotion components. In contrast, our questionnaire employs open-ended questions to gather the linguistic expression of emotional events, enabling the application of natural language processing techniques.

3 Corpus Creation

3.1 Corpus Annotation

In a Cognitive Analysis session, the participants, who wish to manage their emotions better, write a narrative of an experienced emotional event with identified characters in a given place and time. The writer first identifies the basic emotion he/she has experienced, then he/she structures the narratives according to emotion components by filling in a questionnaire. The writer also describes the actions that could have been performed but that he/she had not considered or that he/she had forbidden himself/herself to do during the emotional event. We do not consider this last action part of the questionnaire in our study, as we are only interested in the emotion components.[1] Table 1 shows a structured narrative based on components described by Finkel (2022). We provide a summary below :

- BEHAVIOR: the writer describes the observable behaviors of himself/herself and others. They are identified by answering "Who did what?" and "Who said what?". The writer also provides the context of an emotional event, such as location and date.
- FEELING: the writer expresses his/her physical feelings during the emotional event.
- THINKING: the writer reports what he/she thought during the emotional event.
- TERRITORY: the writer describes whether his/her needs are satisfied or not by analyzing the different cognitive appraisals that he/she thinks he/she has made during the emotional event. The Cognitive Analysis of Emotion considers that an emotion arises when we evaluate an event that invalidates or confirms our model of the world, the latter containing territories associated with our needs. Territories are concrete objects such as an individual body or home, or abstract objects such as individual values, beliefs, or self-image.

Using the questionnaire, a writer categorizes an emotional narrative by considering four emotion components (BEHAVIOR, FEELING, THINKING, and TERRITORY) proposed by Finkel (2022), closely related to components originally proposed by the CPM. For example, FEELING may contain *physiological responses* ("My heart is beating fast") and *motor expressions* ("I feel I am smiling"). THINKING may contain *action tendencies* ("I felt like hitting him") and *subjective feelings* ("I was relaxed"). TERRITORY provides information on criteria involved in the *cognitive appraisal* of an event ("The student attacks my ability to be respected in class").

We point out that compared to previous studies on emotion component analysis (Casel et al., 2021;

[1]We point out that, in this paper, we only study the linguistic realizations of emotion components.

Component	$\#A$	$\overline{t_A}$	Emotion	%
BEHAVIOR	802	82	*Anger*	52
FEELING	799	27	*Fear*	36
THINKING	799	54	*Sadness*	14
TERRITORY	682	34	*Joy*	11

(a) Entire corpus (Total).

Component	$\#A$	$\overline{t_A}$	Emotion	%
BEHAVIOR	392	93	*Anger*	48
FEELING	392	26	*Fear*	32
THINKING	392	59	*Sadness*	10
TERRITORY	392	38	*Joy*	10

(b) Subset of Total for the emotion classification task (Emotion).

Table 2: Number of answers ($\#A$), average number of tokens for answers ($\overline{t_A}$) and distribution of emotion classes. For Total, a questionnaire can correspond to more than one emotion class.

	$\#N$	$\overline{t_N}$	$\#A$	% Completion
Total	812	190	3082	61
Emotion	392	216	1568	100

Table 3: Number of narratives ($\#N$), average number of tokens for narratives ($\overline{t_N}$), number of answers ($\#A$) and completion rate for questionnaires. Statistics for the entire corpus (Total) and the subset for the emotion classification task (Emotion).

Menétrey et al., 2022), our corpus contains linguistic realizations of all components for each emotional narrative, providing a more comprehensive understanding of emotional events. Menétrey et al. (2022) do not consider linguistic realizations of components, and Casel et al. (2021) do not consider all components for each emotional event, hence they cannot study the interaction of components. Moreover, our corpus is annotated by the writers of narratives themselves, rather than external annotators, as in Casel et al. (2021). An interesting direction for future research would involve the incorporation of external annotations into our corpus to conduct a comparative analysis between the writer's perspective and that of the reader.

3.2 Corpus Statistics

Practitioners trained in Cognitive Analysis of Emotion manually collected questionnaires from individuals who chose to participate in emotion regulation trainings between 2005 and 2022. During these years, the format of questionnaires has changed several times, as well as the instructions given. All questionnaires were converted into a standard format. Each questionnaire is completed by a single person and corresponds to a narrative related to a discrete emotion. We did not collect specific data on the writers. Most of them are master's students (20 to 22 years old), doctoral students (22 to 30 years old) and teachers (25 to 50 years old, with an average around 30) studying or working in France, and who have given their consent for the questionnaires to be collected and processed.

Narratives are disidentified using a named entity recognition model.[2] We then manually verify and correct the automatic disidentification. Specific tokens replace personal names, organizations, dates, and locations to preserve the privacy of writers. We delete empty answers containing less than 3 tokens.

Our corpus is composed of 812 unique questionnaires, for a total of 3082 answers (Total). Each answer is related to a single component. We introduce a subset (Emotion) of our entire corpus (Total) composed of questionnaires with all components filled in and corresponding to a single emotion class. For the emotion classification task, described in the next section, we use the Emotion subset.

Corpus statistics obtained with SpaCy (Honnibal and Montani, 2017) are illustrated for each component in Table 2. Although a questionnaire corresponds to one primary emotion class, sometimes writers indicate experiencing other secondary emotion classes. Table 2 also shows the distribution of emotion classes. The dominance of negative emotions is expected; writers usually fill in a questionnaire when they want to better deal with a distressing event. Table 3 shows general statistics for Total and Emotion.

4 Experiments and Results

4.1 Methods

In this study, we aim to examine the interaction between linguistic realizations of emotion components through traditional machine learning methods and pre-trained language models. Our corpus is unique in that it provides multiple components for each emotional event, enabling us to investigate the interaction of components and their impact on emotion classification. Our research questions include: does the presence of a component impact emotion prediction? Does considering all components result

[2] https://huggingface.co/Jean-Baptiste/camembert-ner

Component	Logistic Regression Precision	Recall	F_1	CamemBERT Precision	Recall	F_1
All	71.2 (2.6)	69.1 (2.2)	67.8 (2.3)	**85.1**	**84.8**	**84.7**
Without BEHAVIOR	77.4 (2.3)	75.8 (2.4)	74.5 (2.6)	80.3	79.8	79.7
Without FEELING	64.3 (1.9)	61.5 (1.2)	61.3 (2.2)	81.6	79.8	79.9
Without THINKING	70.9 (1.8)	69.1 (2.0)	68.3 (2.2)	79.6	78.5	78.7
Without TERRITORY	64.3 (4.1)	64.5 (2.4)	62.3 (2.8)	78.7	78.5	78.6
Only BEHAVIOR	52.1 (3.5)	54.6 (2.9)	51.7 (2.9)	68.4	67.1	66.6
Only FEELING	69.6 (1.5)	68.9 (2.1)	68.4 (2.0)	67.8	68.4	67.7
Only THINKING	50.1 (3.4)	53.8 (2.3)	50.6 (2.7)	70.5	70.1	70.1
Only TERRITORY	68.2 (1.8)	66.8 (2.2)	66.6 (2.3)	71.4	68.4	68.9

Table 4: Scores (± std) for discrete emotion classification based on components.

in the best prediction performance? We answer the same questions posed by Menétrey et al. (2022), but we focus on the linguistic expression of emotional events, instead of the existence of described event properties.

Traditional machine learning methods We train logistic regressions, support vector machines, and random forests on our corpus represented as a bag-of-words (unigrams), averaged using the TF-IDF method. The words are pre-processed through lemmatization using SpaCy. To prevent bias, we remove terms directly related to the emotion classes (e.g. "fear", "anger", "sad", "joy"). For model evaluation, we perform a five-fold cross-validation, and we calculate F_1 score, recall, and precision using a weighted mean.[3] For training our models, we use Scikit-learn (Pedregosa et al., 2011) with default hyperparameters.

Pre-trained language models We fine-tune a transformers-based model (Vaswani et al., 2017) using the distilled version (Delestre and Amar, 2022) of CamemBERT (Martin et al., 2020), a BERT model (Devlin et al., 2019) for the French language. We use the raw answers, but we also remove terms directly related to the emotion classes to prevent bias. The corpus is split into 80% for training and 20% for evaluation. We train models for 5 epochs using PyTorch (Paszke et al., 2019) and HuggingFace's Transformers (Wolf et al., 2020), with model parameters for each epoch saved. We select the model with the highest F_1 score on the evaluation data. Training hyperparameters and fine-tuned CamemBERT weights are publicly available on HuggingFace.[4]

4.2 Emotion Classification

In this study, we aim to investigate the impact of component interaction on discrete emotion classification. We train models on all components at once, on all but one component at once, and on a single component. To account for multiple components, we concatenate their respective answers. For example, "Only TERRITORY" models are trained on TERRITORY, "Without BEHAVIOR" models are trained on all components except BEHAVIOR and "All" models are trained on all components, which represent an entire narrative. Models are trained on the Emotion subset.

Results Results are shown in Table 4. We do not show the performance of support vector machines and random forests since they perform worse than logistic regressions. The best results are achieved when all components are considered simultaneously, as indicated by the highest F_1 (84.7) with CamemBERT "All". The results of CamemBERT models with the removal of individual components show a decrease in performance compared to CamemBERT "All", with a decrease in F_1 ranging from -4.8 for "Without FEELING" to -6.1 for "Without TERRITORY". Hence, each component is relevant for classifying discrete emotions. Our findings lend support to Scherer's hypothesis (Scherer, 2005) that an emotional event is characterized by the synchronization of emotion components. This result is not self-evident, as individual components may convey conflicting information regarding the emotion classification task. Our results, coming from a natural language processing perspective, are

[3] As the emotion class distribution is imbalanced.

[4] https://huggingface.co/gustavecortal/distilcamembert-cae-all

consistent with those of Menétrey et al. (2022), who studied the interaction of components for discrete emotion prediction from the existence of described event properties.

In general, CamemBERT models show improved performance relative to logistic regressions, which is in line with expectations. However, the improvement is inconsistent across the models that only considered a single component, ranging from -0.7 for "Only FEELING" to +19.5 for "Only THINKING". Our results show an important increase in F_1 for "Only BEHAVIOR" (+14.9) and "Only THINKING" (+19.5), whereas "Only TERRITORY" shows a slight increase (+2.3) and "Only FEELING" shows a slight decrease (-0.7). We discuss these results which reveal ways in which components are expressed in a text.

Discussions For emotions expressed through TERRITORY (+2.3 for "Only TERRITORY"), we believe that the way the question is asked to the writers influences strongly the way they answer, hence answers are biased due to the questionnaire format. For example, according to the Cognitive Analysis of Emotion, an attacked territory indicates that the corresponding emotion is *anger* or *fear*. Hence, the presence of only two unigrams, "territory" and "attack" can discriminate between *anger fear* and *joy sadness*, which can easily be performed by a logistic regression with TF-IDF features.

For emotions expressed through BEHAVIOR (+14.9 for "Only BEHAVIOR"), we believe that CamemBERT can discriminate the writer's behaviors from the behaviors of others characters in an emotional event, thus improving emotion prediction compared to logistic regressions.

CamemBERT improves performance for emotions expressed through THINKING (+19.5 for "Only THINKING"), while not having an important impact on performance for emotions expressed through FEELING (-0.7 for "Only FEELING"). Emotion expression modes (Micheli, 2014), studied in linguistics, could explain the differences in performance between logistic regressions and CamemBERT models trained on individual components. Micheli (2014) presents a comprehensive study of French emotion denotation, examining the diverse mechanisms used to convey emotions in text. The study categorizes a vast array of heterogeneous markers into three emotion expression modes: emotions directly labeled by emotional words (*labeled emotion*), emotions displayed through characteristics of utterances (*displayed emotion*), and emotions illustrated by the description of a situation socially associated with an emotion (*suggested emotion*).

We hypothesize that there is an important, yet unexplored, relationship between emotion expression modes and linguistic realizations of emotion components. For instance, THINKING may include *suggested emotions*, while FEELING may include *labeled emotions*. Classifying discrete emotions based on a *suggested emotion* (e.g. "I think this student is disrupting my class") would be more challenging compared to classifying discrete emotions from a *labeled emotion* (e.g. "I am upset"). Understanding a *suggested emotion* requires the understanding of the entire sentence and the sociocultural context of the emotional event, whereas understanding a *labeled emotion* only requires identifying the relevant emotional words ("upset"), which can easily be performed by a logistic regression. Therefore, CamemBERT models are likely to outperform logistic regressions in terms of performance for emotions expressed through the *suggested emotion* mode. This is due to CamemBERT's ability to encode the meaning of a sentence as a whole, as well as its pre-training that allows it to grasp the sociocultural context of an event, which logistic regression with TF-IDF features cannot do.

4.3 Component Classification

Model	Precision	Recall	F_1
RL	84.9 (0.3)	84.3 (0.3)	84.4 (0.3)
cBERT	**93.2**	**93.0**	**93.1**

Table 5: Scores (± std) for emotion component classification. cBERT = CamemBERT.

We train traditional machine learning models and fine-tune CamemBERT to predict the emotion component class, i.e., whether an answer is a BEHAVIOR, a FEELING, a THINKING, or a TERRITORY. Compared to the emotion classification task, models are trained on the entire corpus Total.

Table 5 show the results. We obtain great performances, logistic regression and CamemBERT can easily identify emotion component classes in our corpus. Training hyperparameters and fine-tuned CamemBERT weights are publicly available on HuggingFace.[5] We hope our corpus will benefit the

[5]https://huggingface.co/gustavecortal/

research community for classifying components in text, a recent task introduced by Casel et al. (2021).

5 Conclusion and Future Work

Emotion regulation is a critical aspect of emotional events and has noteworthy implications for psychological well-being. In this paper, we aimed to provide a more comprehensive understanding of emotional events by introducing a French corpus of 812 emotional narratives (3082 answers). Our corpus was annotated following the Component Process Model and was collected using a recent psychological method for emotion regulation, named the Cognitive Analysis of Emotion. Casel et al. (2021) were the first to annotate corpora with external annotators according to emotion components. Our corpus differs because each narrative is annotated by the writers and is structured according to all components (BEHAVIOR, FEELING, THINKING, and TERRITORY), which allows for the study of their interaction.

We employed traditional machine learning methods and pre-trained language models (CamemBERT) to investigate the interaction of components for discrete emotion classification. Our results show that each component is useful for classifying discrete emotions, and that the model with the best performance considers all components, supporting Scherer's hypothesis (Scherer, 2005) that components synchronize during an emotional event.

Our results also show that CamemBERT effectively predict discrete emotion from THINKING, but do not improve performance from FEELING compared to traditional machine learning approaches, which reveal differences in how emotion components are expressed. We hypothesize that this may be explained by emotion expression modes studied in linguistics (Micheli, 2014). To test this hypothesis, we plan to annotate emotion expression modes in our corpus using a recent annotation scheme proposed by Etienne et al. (2022).

Limitations

In our corpus, the distribution of emotion classes is imbalanced, which may bias the analyses, and notably impact the performance of trained models. Moreover, the data collected through a questionnaire may suffer from response bias, as the language used to describe an emotional narrative can be influenced by the questionnaire format and the elapsed time between the emotional event and its verbalization. We also point out that the linguistic expression of emotion does not necessarily capture the full extent of an emotional event, thus different from psychological or physiological studies on emotion (Gu et al., 2019).

distilcamembert-cae-component

Ethics Statement

In this paper, we collected data from individuals who attended emotion regulation trainings and provided consent for the collection and analysis of questionnaires. The corpus has not been published yet, as it is undergoing validation by the ethics committee of École Normale Supérieure Paris-Saclay.

By disidentifying our corpus, we have taken standard precautions to mitigate the introduction of biases into our models. Despite our efforts, it is possible that our models may still contain biases that we are not aware of. Our models are not intended for diagnostic purposes, and we do not provide automatic feedback to individuals for regulating their emotion, as we would need to be sure that such feedback does not have any adverse effects on individuals' mental health and, instead, facilitates improved emotion regulation.

References

Laura Ana Maria Bostan, Evgeny Kim, and Roman Klinger. 2020. GoodNewsEveryone: A corpus of news headlines annotated with emotions, semantic roles, and reader perception. In *Proceedings of the 12th Language Resources and Evaluation Conference*, pages 1554–1566, Marseille, France. European Language Resources Association.

Laura-Ana-Maria Bostan and Roman Klinger. 2018. An analysis of annotated corpora for emotion classification in text. In *Proceedings of the 27th International Conference on Computational Linguistics*, pages 2104–2119, Santa Fe, New Mexico, USA. Association for Computational Linguistics.

Sven Buechel and Udo Hahn. 2017. EmoBank: Studying the impact of annotation perspective and representation format on dimensional emotion analysis. In *Proceedings of the 15th Conference of the European Chapter of the Association for Computational Linguistics: Volume 2, Short Papers*, pages 578–585, Valencia, Spain. Association for Computational Linguistics.

Erik Cambria, Yang Li, Frank Z. Xing, Soujanya Poria, and Kenneth Kwok. 2020. Senticnet 6: Ensemble application of symbolic and subsymbolic AI for sentiment analysis. In *Proceedings of the 29th ACM International Conference on Information and Knowledge Management*, CIKM '20, page 105–114, New

York, NY, USA. Association for Computing Machinery.

Cesare Campagnano, Simone Conia, and Roberto Navigli. 2022. SRL4E – Semantic Role Labeling for Emotions: A unified evaluation framework. In *Proceedings of the 60th Annual Meeting of the Association for Computational Linguistics (Volume 1: Long Papers)*, pages 4586–4601, Dublin, Ireland. Association for Computational Linguistics.

Felix Casel, Amelie Heindl, and Roman Klinger. 2021. Emotion recognition under consideration of the emotion component process model. In *Proceedings of the 17th Conference on Natural Language Processing (KONVENS 2021)*, pages 49–61, Düsseldorf, Germany. KONVENS 2021 Organizers.

Xinhong Chen, Qing Li, and Jianping Wang. 2020. A unified sequence labeling model for emotion cause pair extraction. In *Proceedings of the 28th International Conference on Computational Linguistics*, pages 208–218, Barcelona, Spain (Online). International Committee on Computational Linguistics.

Ying Chen, Sophia Yat Mei Lee, Shoushan Li, and Chu-Ren Huang. 2010. Emotion cause detection with linguistic constructions. In *Proceedings of the 23rd International Conference on Computational Linguistics (Coling 2010)*, pages 179–187, Beijing, China. Coling 2010 Organizing Committee.

Gustave Cortal, Alain Finkel, Patrick Paroubek, and Lina Ye. 2022. Natural language processing for cognitive analysis of emotions. In *Semantics, Memory, and Emotion 2022*, Paris, France.

Cyrile Delestre and Abibatou Amar. 2022. DistilCamemBERT : Une distillation du modèle français CamemBERT. In *CAp (Conférence sur l'Apprentissage automatique)*, Vannes, France.

Jacob Devlin, Ming-Wei Chang, Kenton Lee, and Kristina Toutanova. 2019. BERT: Pre-training of deep bidirectional transformers for language understanding. In *Proceedings of the 2019 Conference of the North American Chapter of the Association for Computational Linguistics: Human Language Technologies, Volume 1 (Long and Short Papers)*, pages 4171–4186, Minneapolis, Minnesota. Association for Computational Linguistics.

Zixiang Ding, Rui Xia, and Jianfei Yu. 2020a. ECPE-2D: Emotion-cause pair extraction based on joint two-dimensional representation, interaction and prediction. In *Proceedings of the 58th Annual Meeting of the Association for Computational Linguistics*, pages 3161–3170, Online. Association for Computational Linguistics.

Zixiang Ding, Rui Xia, and Jianfei Yu. 2020b. End-to-end emotion-cause pair extraction based on sliding window multi-label learning. In *Proceedings of the 2020 Conference on Empirical Methods in Natural Language Processing (EMNLP)*, pages 3574–3583, Online. Association for Computational Linguistics.

Valentina Dragos, Delphine Battistelli, Aline Etienne, and Yolène Constable. 2022. Angry or sad ? emotion annotation for extremist content characterisation. In *Proceedings of the Thirteenth Language Resources and Evaluation Conference*, pages 193–201, Marseille, France. European Language Resources Association.

Paul Ekman. 1992. An argument for basic emotions. *Cognition and Emotion*, 6(3-4):169–200.

Aline Etienne, Delphine Battistelli, and Gwénolé Lecorvé. 2022. A (psycho-)linguistically motivated scheme for annotating and exploring emotions in a genre-diverse corpus. In *Proceedings of the Thirteenth Language Resources and Evaluation Conference*, pages 603–612, Marseille, France. European Language Resources Association.

Alain Finkel. 2022. *Manuel d'analyse cognitive des émotions: Théorie et applications*. Dunod, Paris.

Daniel Gildea and Daniel Jurafsky. 2000. Automatic labeling of semantic roles. In *Proceedings of the 38th Annual Meeting of the Association for Computational Linguistics*, pages 512–520, Hong Kong. Association for Computational Linguistics.

Simeng Gu, Fushun Wang, Nitesh P. Patel, James A. Bourgeois, and Jason H. Huang. 2019. A model for basic emotions using observations of behavior in drosophila. *Frontiers in Psychology*, 10.

Matthew Honnibal and Ines Montani. 2017. spaCy 2: Natural language understanding with Bloom embeddings, convolutional neural networks and incremental parsing. To appear.

Evgeny Kim and Roman Klinger. 2018. Who feels what and why? annotation of a literature corpus with semantic roles of emotions. In *Proceedings of COLING 2018, the 27th International Conference on Computational Linguistics*, Santa Fe, USA.

Evgeny Kim and Roman Klinger. 2019. An analysis of emotion communication channels in fan-fiction: Towards emotional storytelling. In *Proceedings of the Second Workshop on Storytelling*, pages 56–64, Florence, Italy. Association for Computational Linguistics.

Richard S. Lazarus and Susan. Folkman. 1984. *Stress, appraisal, and coping*. Springer Pub. Co New York.

Sophia Yat Mei Lee, Ying Chen, and Chu-Ren Huang. 2010. A text-driven rule-based system for emotion cause detection. In *Proceedings of the NAACL HLT 2010 Workshop on Computational Approaches to Analysis and Generation of Emotion in Text*, pages 45–53, Los Angeles, CA. Association for Computational Linguistics.

Louis Martin, Benjamin Muller, Pedro Javier Ortiz Suárez, Yoann Dupont, Laurent Romary, Éric de la Clergerie, Djamé Seddah, and Benoît Sagot. 2020. CamemBERT: a tasty French language model.

In *Proceedings of the 58th Annual Meeting of the Association for Computational Linguistics*, pages 7203–7219, Online. Association for Computational Linguistics.

Maëlan Q. Menétrey, Gelareh Mohammadi, Joana Leitão, and Patrik Vuilleumier. 2022. Emotion recognition in a multi-componential framework: The role of physiology. *Frontiers in Computer Science*, 4.

Raphaël Micheli. 2014. *Les émotions dans les discours*. De Boeck Supérieur.

Saif M. Mohammad, Svetlana Kiritchenko, and Joel Martin. 2013. Identifying purpose behind electoral tweets. In *Proceedings of the Second International Workshop on Issues of Sentiment Discovery and Opinion Mining*, WISDOM '13, New York, NY, USA. Association for Computing Machinery.

Patrick Paroubek, Cyril Grouin, Patrice Bellot, Vincent Claveau, Iris Eshkol-Taravella, Amel Fraisse, Agata Jackiewicz, Jihen Karoui, Laura Monceaux, and Juan-Manuel Torres-Moreno. 2018. DEFT2018 : recherche d'information et analyse de sentiments dans des tweets concernant les transports en Île de France (DEFT2018 : Information retrieval and sentiment analysis in tweets about public transportation in Île de France region). In *Actes de la Conférence TALN. Volume 2 - Démonstrations, articles des Rencontres Jeunes Chercheurs, ateliers DeFT*, pages 219–230, Rennes, France. ATALA.

Adam Paszke, Sam Gross, Francisco Massa, Adam Lerer, James Bradbury, Gregory Chanan, Trevor Killeen, Zeming Lin, Natalia Gimelshein, Luca Antiga, Alban Desmaison, Andreas Kopf, Edward Yang, Zachary DeVito, Martin Raison, Alykhan Tejani, Sasank Chilamkurthy, Benoit Steiner, Lu Fang, Junjie Bai, and Soumith Chintala. 2019. Pytorch: An imperative style, high-performance deep learning library. In *Advances in Neural Information Processing Systems 32*, pages 8024–8035. Curran Associates, Inc.

F. Pedregosa, G. Varoquaux, A. Gramfort, V. Michel, B. Thirion, O. Grisel, M. Blondel, P. Prettenhofer, R. Weiss, V. Dubourg, J. Vanderplas, A. Passos, D. Cournapeau, M. Brucher, M. Perrot, and E. Duchesnay. 2011. Scikit-learn: Machine learning in Python. *Journal of Machine Learning Research*, 12:2825–2830.

Robert Plutchik. 2001. The nature of emotions: Human emotions have deep evolutionary roots, a fact that may explain their complexity and provide tools for clinical practice. *American Scientist*, 89(4):344–350.

James A Russell and Albert Mehrabian. 1977. Evidence for a three-factor theory of emotions. *Journal of Research in Personality*, 11(3):273–294.

Klaus R. Scherer. 2005. What are emotions? and how can they be measured? *Social Science Information*, 44(4):695–729.

Klaus R. Scherer and Harald G. Wallbott. 1994. Evidence for universality and cultural variation of differential emotion response patterning. *Journal of Personality and Social Psychology*, 66(2):310–328.

Aaditya Singh, Shreeshail Hingane, Saim Wani, and Ashutosh Modi. 2021. An end-to-end network for emotion-cause pair extraction. In *Proceedings of the Eleventh Workshop on Computational Approaches to Subjectivity, Sentiment and Social Media Analysis, WASSA@EACL 2021, Online, April 19, 2021*, pages 84–91. Association for Computational Linguistics.

Enrica Troiano, Laura Oberländer*, and Roman Klinger. 2022. Dimensional modeling of emotions in text with appraisal theories: Corpus creation, annotation reliability, and prediction. *Computational Linguistics*, pages 1–72.

Ashish Vaswani, Noam Shazeer, Niki Parmar, Jakob Uszkoreit, Llion Jones, Aidan N. Gomez, Lukasz Kaiser, and Illia Polosukhin. 2017. Attention is all you need.

Penghui Wei, Jiahao Zhao, and Wenji Mao. 2020. Effective inter-clause modeling for end-to-end emotion-cause pair extraction. In *Proceedings of the 58th Annual Meeting of the Association for Computational Linguistics*, pages 3171–3181, Online. Association for Computational Linguistics.

Thomas Wolf, Lysandre Debut, Victor Sanh, Julien Chaumond, Clement Delangue, Anthony Moi, Pierric Cistac, Tim Rault, Remi Louf, Morgan Funtowicz, Joe Davison, Sam Shleifer, Patrick von Platen, Clara Ma, Yacine Jernite, Julien Plu, Canwen Xu, Teven Le Scao, Sylvain Gugger, Mariama Drame, Quentin Lhoest, and Alexander Rush. 2020. Transformers: State-of-the-art natural language processing. In *Proceedings of the 2020 Conference on Empirical Methods in Natural Language Processing: System Demonstrations*, pages 38–45, Online. Association for Computational Linguistics.

Rui Xia and Zixiang Ding. 2019. Emotion-cause pair extraction: A new task to emotion analysis in texts. In *Proceedings of the 57th Annual Meeting of the Association for Computational Linguistics*, pages 1003–1012, Florence, Italy. Association for Computational Linguistics.

Linking the *Neulateinische Wortliste* to the LiLa Knowledge Base of Interoperable Resources for Latin

Federica Iurescia, Eleonora Litta, Marco Passarotti,
Matteo Pellegrini, Giovanni Moretti, Paolo Ruffolo
Università Cattolica del Sacro Cuore, Milan
{federica.iurescia}{eleonoramaria.litta}{marco.passarotti}
{matteo.pellegrini}{giovanni.moretti}{paolo.ruffolo}@unicatt.it

Abstract

This paper describes the process of interlinking a lexical resource consisting of a list of more than 20,000 Neo-Latin words with other resources for Latin. The resources are made interoperable thanks to their linking to the LiLa Knowledge Base, which applies Linguistic Linked Open Data practices and data categories to describe and publish on the Web both textual and lexical resources for the Latin language.

1 Introduction

The Latin language shows a diachronic span covering more than two millennia, from the first literary texts in the 3rd century BC until today, when, for instance, Latin is the official language of the Vatican State. Moreover, having been for centuries the *lingua franca* of what is now referred to as the European area, Latin has been used in several different places by people with different cultural backgrounds, who produced texts of different typologies, thus resulting in a substantial degree of diatopic, diastratic and diaphasic variation.

Such a variation concerns every level of metalinguistic analysis, including morphology (Korkiakangas and Passarotti, 2011), syntax (Ponti and Passarotti, 2016), semantics (Perrone et al., 2021) and the lexicon.

As for the latter, despite the closed-corpus status of the Latin language (with a few exceptions of newly coined terms), there is not one fully comprehensive lexical resource that features the entire Latin lexicon. Yet, throughout the centuries, the lexicographic work on Latin has produced several dictionaries, lexica and glossaries covering specific eras (and/or areas) of the Latin language. For instance, the Latin-English dictionary by Lewis & Short (Lewis and Short, 1879) includes lexical entries about words from the Classical era, while the glossary by du Cange (du Cange et al., 1883–1887) and the Frankfurt Latin Lexicon (Mehler et al., 2020) concern Medieval Latin.

Over the last two decades, the research area dealing with linguistic resources for Latin has grown substantially, leading to the current availability of a large number of (annotated) corpora, including five treebanks available in the *Universal Dependencies* collection (de Marneffe et al., 2021) and several retro-digitised and newly built lexical resources. Such a situation raised the issue of the interoperability between the resources for Latin (like for many other languages), which are stored in separate silos and cannot interact. Starting in 2018, the *LiLa: Linking Latin* project[1] addressed this issue, by building a Linked Data Knowledge Base of interoperable resources for Latin. In the LiLa Knowledge Base, interoperability between resources is achieved by linking all those entries in lexical resources and tokens in corpora that point to the same lemma. As a consequence, the core of the LiLa Knowledge Base consists of a large collection of Latin lemmas (called Lemma Bank), published as Linked Data and following the vocabulary and categories of the OntoLex-Lemon model (McCrae et al., 2017; Passarotti et al., 2020).

Given the central role played by the Lemma Bank in the architecture of LiLa, its lexical coverage is of the utmost importance.[2] In order to enhance the Lemma Bank with lemmas belonging to the so-called Neo-Latin or Modern Latin variety, we have recently started the process of linking the lexical entries of the *Neulateinische Wortliste* (NLW) by J. Ramminger, a dictionary of Latin from Petrarch up to the 18th century (Ramminger, 2016).[3] The dictionary currently includes about 21k entries, promising to allow for a relevant

[1] https://lila-erc.eu.

[2] Before the work described in this paper, the LiLa Lemma Bank included about 200k lemmas for approximately 130k words. One word can have more than one lemma, like in the case of graphical variants: see Section 3.

[3] http://nlw.renaessancestudier.org.

Proceedings of the 7th Joint SIGHUM Workshop on Computational Linguistics for Cultural Heritage, Social Sciences, Humanities and Literature (LaTeCH-CLfL2023), pages 82–87
May 5, 2023

widening of the lexical coverage of the Lemma Bank. This paper describes the stages of this ongoing linking process, detailing the ones that we have already accomplished and outlining the future work.

2 Data

The NLW is a lexical resource that collects entries from the so-called Neo-Latin lexicon. These were retrieved mainly from literary sources and partly from secondary literature, such as scientific publications on Neo-Latin (Schoeck et al., 1990). The diachronic range covered by the resource spans between 1300 and 1700, on the basis of a decision taken by field experts, as explained by the author in the documentation available on the website.[4]

In the NLW, Neo-Latin is considered as the diachronic development of a specific diastratic variety of the language, namely Latin written production influenced by the linguistic ideals of Renaissance Humanists. These ideals may be subsumed under two general purposes: recovery of the language of Classical Antiquity, and enriching the lexicon with new entries that mirror contemporary changes in the society, e.g. *typographus* 'typographer'. However, the NLW does not feature the entire Neo-Latin lexicon according to these criteria, but it reflects its author's interests, as stated in the documentation.

The word list, consisting of 21,352 entries, was provided by the author in .docx format. The content of each entry is organised into a set of fields. The first one contains the citation form(s) of the lemma and all its graphical variants, followed by morphological information about its inflectional category, e.g. the endings of other forms of the word and a shortcut for the gender: for instance, "-a, -um" (the feminine and neuter of the nominative singular) for first class adjectives like *bizarrus* 'moody'; "-i, m." (the genitive singular and the gender) for second declension masculine nouns like *almirarchus* 'admiral'; "-ire, -ivi, -itum" (the present active infinitive, first-person singular of the perfect and supine) for fourth conjugation regular verbs like *semiambio* 'to half-circle'. The other fields feature a translation into German of the lemma and examples of its usage in textual sources, a set of administrative metadata (i.e. date of the creation), a numeric unique identifier for the entry, and philological and etymological information. Information about the presence of the lemma in a set of Classical and Medieval Latin dictionaries and lexicographic databases is provided as well.[5]

3 The *Neulateinische Wortliste* in LiLa

The LiLa Knowledge Base follows the principles of the Linguistic Linked Open Data paradigm. It adopts the RDF data model (Lassila and Swick, 1998), where information is coded in terms of triples that connect a subject to an object through a property. Each instance of an item ("individual") belongs to a specific class. The structure of the data is expressed by means of subclass relations and/or restrictions on the domain and range of properties – i.e., on the kinds of elements that they can have as subject and object, respectively. Classes and properties of existing ontologies are reused when possible, new ones are introduced if necessary.

As was hinted above, the core class of the LiLa Knowledge Base is `lila:Lemma`.[6] The lemmas of the Lemma Bank, to which the entries of lexical resources and the tokens of textual resources are linked, belong to this class. The lemma is simply defined as the citation form of a word, as it is recorded in dictionaries. Therefore, it is treated as a subclass of the class of forms in the OntoLex vocabulary (`ontolex:Form`).[7] This is the vocabulary that is used for the inclusion of lexical resources into the LiLa Knowledge Base: their entries belong to the class `ontolex:LexicalEntry`,[8] and they are connected to the corresponding `lila:Lemma` in the Lemma Bank by means of the property `ontolex:canonicalForm`;[9] entries of different resources that refer to the same word are linked to the same lemma in the Lemma Bank, thus achieving the desired interoperability.

As a consequence, the very first step of our procedure consisted in going through the entries of the

[4] `http://nlw.renaessancestudier.org/varia/einleit.htm`.

[5] *Thesaurus Linguae Latinae* (`https://tll.degruyter.com/about`), the *Ausführliches lateinisch-deutsches Handwörterbuch* (Georges, 1998), the *Lexicon totius latinitatis* by Forcellini (Forcellini, 1965), the *Dictionary of Medieval Latin from British Sources* (Latham et al., 2018), and the *Dictionary of Medieval Latin from Celtic Sources* (Devine et al., 1998).

[6] `http://lila-erc.eu/lodview/ontologies/lila/Lemma`. In this notation, a shorthand of the ontology where the class or property is defined precedes the colon, that is followed by the name of the class or property (in camel style with or without capitalisation of the first letter, respectively).

[7] `http://www.w3.org/ns/lemon/ontolex#Form`.

[8] `http://www.w3.org/ns/lemon/ontolex#LexicalEntry`.

[9] `http://www.w3.org/ns/lemon/ontolex#canonicalForm`.

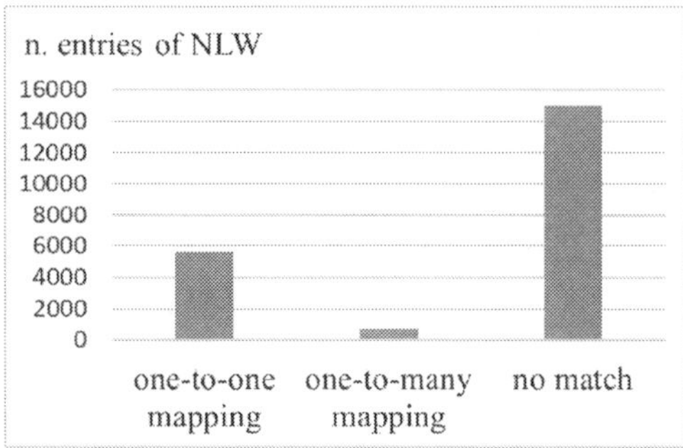

Figure 1: Mapping from NLW entries to LiLa lemmas

NLW and looking for the corresponding lemma(s) in the Lemma Bank. This was done by matching the string of the entry as it appears in the first field of the data that were delivered to us (see Section 2) with the different graphical variants of the lemmas in the Lemma Bank – coded as different `writtenRepresentations` using the OntoLex vocabulary.[10] This allowed us to unambiguously link 5,651 entries to their corresponding lemmas. In other cases (716 entries), however, more than one lemma matched the string of the NLW entry, so a disambiguation is needed to select which lemma is the correct one. Lastly, there are 14,985 entries of the NLW that are not found in the Lemma Bank: in these cases, we need to add a new lemma to be able to link those entries. Figure 1 shows this distribution visually.

In what follows, we describe our procedure i) to automatically generate new lemmas with all the relevant information (Section 3.1), and ii) to disambiguate between different homographic lemmas that match the string of a single NLW citation form (Section 3.2).

3.1 Automatic generation of new lemmas

In the Lemma Bank, several pieces of information are associated to each lemma by means of a set of dedicated properties. Among other things, each lemma is assigned a part of speech through the property `lila:hasPOS`;[11] information on the inflectional category – verbal conjugations, nominal declensions, adjectival classes – is provided through the property `lila:hasInflectionType`;[12] additionally, gender (masculine/feminine/neuter) is coded for nouns through the property `lila:hasGender`[13] and gradation (positive/comparative/superlative) for adjectives through the property `lila:hasDegree`.[14] When generating new lemmas for the entries of the NLW that have no match among the already existing lemmas of the Lemma Bank, to infer all these features we exploited the morphological information provided by the NLW entries.

Firstly, we isolated the information about the inflectional category (and, for nouns only, the gender) as a set of separate codes, e.g., the code "-i, m." identifying masculine 2nd declension nouns. This yielded a classification in almost a thousand (993) distinct codes. However, many of them (730) are attested in only one entry (*hapaxes*), and the overwhelming majority (920) are attested in less than 10 entries. At this stage, we focused on the 73 codes that are attested in more than 10 entries. Because of the frequency distribution of codes, this is sufficient to cover for most of the entries of the NLW (19,935 out of 21,352). Since the other codes often correspond to more marginal and not fully regular cases, they are best left for a successive stage of manual or semi-automatic insertion (when they are not already linked to existing lemmas of the Lemma Bank).

The 71 codes then underwent a process of normalisation, whereby some entries that are coded differently in the NLW data are attributed to the same class. In some cases, this is necessary because the coding of a single class is not uniform, due to inconsistencies in the way in which the original data have been compiled by hand. For instance, first class adjectives are coded sometimes as "-a, -um", sometimes as "-a -um", sometimes as "-a, .-um", sometimes with other minor variations, that are obviously not relevant to the morphological classification of the data. In other cases, the normalisation is motivated by the fact that different codes reflect a classification that is more fine-grained than the one of the Lemma Bank, so they can be conflated into a single class for our purposes. For instance, verbs of the first conjugation are coded in different ways in the NLW according to their strategy to form the perfect active indicative and the supine, e.g., by suffixation of *-avi* and *-atum* (see the verb *concentro* 'to concentrate', with code "-are, -avi, -atum") or by suffixation of *-ui* and *-tum* (see the

[10] `http://www.w3.org/ns/lemon/ontolex#writtenRep`.

[11] `http://lila-erc.eu/ontologies/lila/hasPOS`.

[12] `http://lila-erc.eu/ontologies/lila/hasInflectionType`.

[13] `http://lila-erc.eu/ontologies/lila/hasGender`.

[14] `http://lila-erc.eu/ontologies/lila/hasDegree`.

NLW code	regex match	POS	Infl. Type	Gender
-ei, f.		NOUN	n5	f
-i, m.	^[a-z]+(us|(eli)r)$	NOUN	n2	m
-i, m.	^[A-Z]+(us|(eli)r)$	PROPN	n2	m
-i, m.	^[a-z]+os$	NOUN	n2e	m
-i, m.	^[A-Z]+os$	PROPN	n2e	m

Table 1: Mapping from the NLW morphological codes to the LiLa vocabulary

verb *triseco* 'to trisect', "-are, -ui, -ctum"), respectively. However, this difference is not reflected in the inflectional classification adopted in the Lemma Bank, and both these words would simply be assigned to the first conjugation class. Therefore, the two codes – together with all the other variants for the same conjugation – were normalised to a single one (namely, "-are") at this stage.

Such normalised codes were then used to generate the morphological information according to the tagset adopted in the Lemma Bank, as illustrated in Table 1. In some cases, a direct mapping is possible. For instance, if a word is assigned the code "-ei, f." in the NLW, then it can be reliably inferred that it is a feminine noun of the 5th declension (n5) – e.g., *faceties* 'witticism'. In other cases, however, the code by itself does not allow for a direct mapping, and it needs to be complemented with information on the character string of the citation form. For such cases, we specified different regular expressions that the string of the NLW citation form needs to match for the corresponding lemma to be assigned a given part of speech, inflection type and gender in the LiLa Knowledge Base. For instance, the code "-i, m." is used for masculine nouns of the second declension in the NLW. However, such nouns are classified differently in the LiLa Knowledge Base according to their shape: as for their part of speech, they are considered to be proper nouns if they start with a capital letter, common nouns otherwise; as for their inflection type, they are grouped with regular second declension nouns (n2) if they end with "us", "er", or "ir" (e.g., *vicenuntius* 'deputy envoy', *cultrifer* 'knife man', *proseptemuir* 'deputy member of the consortium of The Seven Men'), with irregular ones (n2e) if they end with "os" (e.g., in Greek loanwords like *misanthropos* 'misanthropist'). By applying such mappings to the cases of entries of the NLW with no match in the Lemma Bank, we enhanced it with 13,477 new lemmas.[15]

[15]We excluded 976 entries of the NLW providing more than one citation form, as these cannot always be treated automatically (see also the discussion in Section 4).

3.2 Automatic disambiguation between homographic lemmas

In order to disambiguate automatically at least some of the cases where more than one lemma in the Lemma Bank matched the string of the entry of the NLW, we used the same mappings discussed in Section 3.1 and exemplified in Table 1. For instance, the string of the citation form of the NLW entry *formularius* 'compositor' matches two different lemmas of the Lemma Bank, one of them being a noun[16] and the other one an adjective.[17] However, since the NLW entry in question is assigned the code "-i, m.", we know that the entry is a second declension noun. Therefore, we can safely link it to the lemma with the corresponding part of speech and morphological features in the Lemma Bank.

This procedure was applied to all the cases of one-to-many mapping between the NLW and the Lemma Bank, again excluding the 214 cases with more than one citation form, that are left for manual disambiguation because they cannot be categorised automatically. Out of the 501 remaining ambiguous cases, 359 were automatically disambiguated, and each of them is consequently linked to a single lemma in the Lemma Bank at the end of the process.

4 Conclusion and Future Work

In this paper, we have described the ongoing process of linking a dictionary of Neo-Latin to the LiLa Knowledge Base.

Based on the lexical entries of the dictionary, the collection of lemmas that represents the core component of LiLa was enhanced with more than 13,000 new items.[18] Such an extension of the LiLa Lemma Bank promises to improve its lexical coverage of the Neo-Latin texts that we plan to link to the Knowledge Base in the near future. In particular, the texts will be taken from the CAMENA corpus, that counts about 50 million tokens.[19]

Besides the citation form (the lemma) and the translation(s) in German of the words (modelled as individuals belonging to the class

[16]`http://lila-erc.eu/data/id/lemma/103663`.

[17]`http://lila-erc.eu/data/id/lemma/103662`.

[18]The Lemma Bank can be queried at `https://lila-erc.eu/query/`.

[19]`http://mateo.uni-mannheim.de/camenahtdocs/camena_e.html`.

ontolex:LexicalSense),[20] the lexical entries of the NLW feature also a number of sample attestations of their use in Neo-Latin texts. We modelled and published this information as Linked Data, using the Frequency, Attestation and Corpus (FrAC) module of OntoLex-Lemon (Chiarcos et al., 2022a).

Furthermore, we have seen in Section 3.1 that the NLW provides a morphological classification of lemmas that is sometimes more fine-grained than the one adopted in the Lemma Bank, and was thus not exploited in our procedure to automatically generate new lemmas. However, this is a potentially useful piece of information, that we plan to model in Linked Data, using the Morphology module (morph) of OntoLex-Lemon (Chiarcos et al., 2022b).

Lastly, we have seen in Sections 3.1 and 3.2 that those entries of the NLW that have more than one citation form were left out from our automatic procedure. This is motivated by the fact that the nature of the different citation forms and the relation between them can be diverse, and consequently require a different modelling. In some cases (e.g., *typographicus/typograficus* 'typographic'), they are simply graphical variants, that should be treated as written representations of the same lemma. In other cases, they would be considered as different lemmas, connected to each other through the property lila:lemmaVariant,[21] according to the current practice of the LiLa Knowledge Base – e.g., because they have different genders, as in *cibulus*(M)/*cibulum*(N) 'morsel'. Since an ontolex:LexicalEntry cannot have more than one ontolex:canonicalForm relation, such cases require the introduction of different (sub-)entries, whose organisation can be modelled using classes and properties of the Lexicography module (lexicog)[22] of OntoLex-Lemon.

After converting the NLW into a RDF serialisation (Turtle), we published the resource as Linked Data in the LiLa Knowledge Base, so to make it interoperable with the other lexical and textual resources for Latin already included therein.[23]

[20] https://www.w3.org/ns/lemon/ontolex#LexicalSense.

[21] http://lila-erc.eu/ontologies/lila/lemmaVariant.

[22] https://www.w3.org/2019/09/lexicog/.

[23] The URI (Uniform Resource Identifier) of the NLW is http://lila-erc.eu/data/lexicalResources/NLW/Lexicon. The Turtle file is available at https://github.com/CIRCSE/NeulateinischeWortliste.

5 Acknowledgments

This project has received funding from the European Research Council (ERC) under the European Union's Horizon 2020 research and innovation programme – Grant Agreement No. 769994

References

Christian Chiarcos, Elena-Simona Apostol, Besim Kabashi, and Ciprian-Octavian Truică. 2022a. Modelling Frequency, Attestation, and Corpus-Based Information with OntoLex-FrAC. In *Proceedings of the 29th International Conference on Computational Linguistics*, pages 4018–4027.

Christian Chiarcos, Katerina Gkirtzou, Fahad Khan, Penny Labropoulou, Marco Passarotti, and Matteo Pellegrini. 2022b. Computational Morphology with OntoLex-Morph. In *Proceedings of the 8th Workshop on Linked Data in Linguistics within the 13th Language Resources and Evaluation Conference*, pages 78–86.

Marie-Catherine de Marneffe, Christopher D. Manning, Joakim Nivre, and Daniel Zeman. 2021. Universal Dependencies. *Computational Linguistics*, 47(2):255–308.

Kieran Devine, Francis J Smith, and Anthony Harvey. 1998. *Database of Medieval Latin from Celtic Sources*.

Charles du Fresne sieur du Cange, bénédictins de la congrégation de Saint-Maur, d. Pierre Carpentier, Johann Christoph Adelung, G. A. Louis Henschel, Lorenz Diefenbach, and Léopold Favre. 1883–1887. *Glossarium mediae et infimae latinitatis*. Favre, Niort, France.

Egidio Forcellini. 1965. *Lexicon totius latinitatis*. Arnaldo Forni, Bologna, Italy.

Karl Ernst Georges. 1998. *Ausführliches lateinisch-deutsches Handwörterbuch*. Wissenschaftliche Buchgesellschaft, Darmstadt, Germany. Reprint of first edition of 1913–1918, Hannover, Germany: Hahnsche Buchhandlung.

Timo Korkiakangas and Marco Passarotti. 2011. Challenges in Annotating Medieval Latin Charters. *Journal for Language Technology and Computational Linguistics*, 26(2):103–114.

Ora Lassila and Ralph R. Swick. 1998. Resource Description Framework (RDF) Model and Syntax Specification.

Ronald E. Latham, David R. Howlett, and Richard K. Ashdowne, editors. 2018. *Dictionary of Medieval Latin from British Sources*. British Academy (through Oxford University Press), Oxford, UK.

Charlton Thomas Lewis and Charles Short. 1879. *A Latin Dictionary*. Clarendon Press, Oxford, UK.

John P McCrae, Julia Bosque-Gil, Jorge Gracia, Paul Buitelaar, and Philipp Cimiano. 2017. The OntoLex-Lemon Model: Development and Applications. In *Electronic lexicography in the 21st century. Proceedings of eLex 2017 conference*, pages 587–597, Brno, Czech Republic. Lexical Computing CZ s.r.o.

Alexander Mehler, Bernhard Jussen, Tim Geelhaar, Alexander Henlein, Giuseppe Abrami, Daniel Baumartz, Tolga Uslu, and Wahed Hemati. 2020. The Frankfurt Latin Lexicon. From Morphological Expansion and Word Embeddings to SemioGraphs. *Studi e Saggi Linguistici*, LVIII(1):121–155.

Marco Passarotti, Francesco Mambrini, Greta Franzini, Flavio Massimiliano Cecchini, Eleonora Litta, Giovanni Moretti, Paolo Ruffolo, and Rachele Sprugnoli. 2020. Interlinking through Lemmas. The Lexical Collection of the LiLa Knowledge Base of Linguistic Resources for Latin. *Studi e Saggi Linguistici*, LVIII(1):177–212.

Valerio Perrone, Simon Hengchen, Marco Palma, Alessandro Vatri, Jim Q Smith, and Barbara McGillivray. 2021. Lexical semantic change for Ancient Greek and Latin. *Computational approaches to semantic change*, pages 287–310.

Edoardo Maria Ponti and Marco Passarotti. 2016. Differentia compositionem facit. A slower-paced and reliable parser for Latin. In *Proceedings of the Tenth International Conference on Language Resources and Evaluation (LREC'16)*, pages 683–688, Portorož, Slovenia. European Language Resources Association (ELRA).

Johann Ramminger. 2016. Ein Wörterbuch des Lateinischen von Petrarca bis 1700.

Richard J Schoeck, Martina Rütt, and H-W Bartz. 1990. A Step Towards a Neo-latin Lexicon: A First Wordlist Drawn from "Humanistica Lovaniensia". *Humanistica Lovaniensia*, 39:340–365.

What do Humor Classifiers Learn? An Attempt to Explain Humor Recognition Models

Marcio Lima Inácio and **Hugo Gonçalo Oliveira**
CISUC - University of Coimbra
Department of Informatics Engineering
Polo II, Pinhal de Marrocos, 3030-290
Coimbra, Portugal
{mlinacio, hroliv}@dei.uc.pt

Gabriela Wick-Pedro
Federal University of São Carlos
Departamento de Letras
Rod. Washington Luís, 235, 13965-905
São Carlos, Brazil
gwpedro@estudante.ufscar.br

Abstract

Towards computational systems capable of dealing with complex and general linguistic phenomena, it is essential to understand figurative language, which verbal humor is an instance of. This paper reports state-of-the-art results for Humor Recognition in Portuguese, specifically, an F1-score of 99.6% with a BERT-based classifier. However, following the surprising high performance in such a challenging task, we further analyzed what was actually learned by the classifiers. Our main conclusions were that classifiers based on content-features achieve the best performance, but rely mostly on stylistic aspects of the text, not necessarily related to humor, such as punctuation and question words. On the other hand, for humor-related features, we identified some important aspects, such as the presence of named entities, ambiguity and incongruity.

1 Introduction

As part of usual human language, dealing with complex deep linguistic knowledge, such as figurative language, is an important element of research on Natural Language Processing (NLP). Verbal humor is a large instance of figurative language, whose understanding and generation are crucial for language fluency and the comprehension of deeper nuances of language (Tagnin, 2005).

Additionally, computational systems capable of processing humor might give other fields of research (e.g. Linguistics, Psychology, Philosophy, to name a few) insights about how this phenomenon works and how it is conceived through language.

Regarding such computational models, we must always call in question their trustworthiness before drawing any conclusion that they are suitable to solve any specific problem, especially in tasks deemed as extremely complex, such as Humor Recognition, Fake News Detection, Irony Recognition, and the like (Ribeiro et al., 2016; Monteiro et al., 2018). Thus, it is essential to question if it is possible to really understand what the machine is learning and if it is actually capturing information relevant to the phenomenon being studied. In this way, we can find flaws with the methods or resources used, which drives to further research on the subject to develop better models.

Within this context, we present a study on Humor Recognition with a special focus on identifying which features and pieces of information are mostly used by supervised Machine Learning (ML) models for this task, including classical ML classification algorithms and deep learning Large Language Models (LLMs). We further highlight that the entirety of this work was made for the Portuguese Language, much more underdeveloped on this task when compared to languages like English.

Towards our goal, we first replicated the current state-of-the-art methods for Humor Recognition in Portuguese (Gonçalo Oliveira et al., 2020). In addition, we fine-tuned a BERT model pretrained for Portuguese (Souza et al., 2020) for the same task. Results were further analyzed with SHAP (Lundberg and Lee, 2017), a tool for Machine Learning explainability. SHAP provided scores for each feature, word, or sub-word used by the respective models, which, together with careful manual analysis, helped in understanding what exactly the models had learned from the provided data. All experiments were carried out on the corpus created by Gonçalo Oliveira et al. (2020), which is, to the best of our knowledge, the only corpus in Portuguese created for the task of Humor Recognition.

Our results show that the BERT model outperformed all other ML methods in terms of F1-score, achieving a score of 99.6%. However, through careful analysis, we discovered that this model, alongside other methods based on content-features, based their decisions primarily on stylistic aspects of the texts, such as punctuation, and other phenomena not necessarily related to humor, for instance the presence of questions.

Proceedings of the 7th Joint SIGHUM Workshop on Computational Linguistics for Cultural Heritage, Social Sciences, Humanities and Literature (LaTeCH-CLfL2023), pages 88–98
May 5, 2023

We also noted aspects of the set of humor-related features proposed by Gonçalo Oliveira et al. (2020) that might not have been expected by their original authors, such as the relation between concreteness and humor, and the association of people named entities with humorous texts. However, some of their interpretations were reinforced by the ML models, for example, the connection of ambiguity and incongruity to humorousness.

The remainder of this paper is organized as follows: some relevant related work about Humor Recognition and ML Explainability is presented in section 2, followed by an overall description of our methodology, in section 3. Later, the results are presented and discussed in section 4, with the final remarks and future work mentioned in section 5. In the end of the paper, we note some limitations of the current work, as well as ethical aspects that should be considered in the future.

2 Related Work

This paper has relations with two main areas of research: general Humor Recognition, usually interpreted as a ML classification task, and ML Explainability, which aims at creating explanations for computational models, in order to inspect what information the model actually uses for inference.

2.1 Humor Recognition

Humor Recognition research dates back to the 2000s, when Mihalcea and Strapparava (2005) used a hand-crafted feature set (including features like alliteration, slang usage, and antonymy presence) to train supervised ML algorithms for classifying texts in two categories: humorous and non-humorous. Since then, Humor Recognition has been approached with this supervised ML point-of-view, varying with different sets of attributes, including:

- Stylistic, e.g., keywords and text similarity with other jokes (Sjöbergh and Araki, 2007);
- Semantic information, e.g., presence of vocabulary focused on professional communities, sentiment polarity, and words related to negative human traits (Mihalcea and Pulman, 2007);
- Surface-level characteristics, e.g., punctuation and word frequency (Barbieri and Saggion, 2014).

More recently, following the general trends on many different NLP tasks, the current state-of-the-art in this task is achieved by Deep Learning (Ren et al., 2021; Kumar et al., 2022) and LLMs (Devlin et al., 2019; Weller and Seppi, 2019).

For languages other than English, the HAHA series of shared-tasks (Castro et al., 2018; Chiruzzo et al., 2021) has encouraged much advance for research on recognizing verbal humor in Spanish. In their latest event, Grover and Goel (2021), the winners, used an ensemble of LLMs to outperform other contestants. For Portuguese, however, there is still few research on the matter; to the best of our knowledge, current systems are still based on classical ML algorithms with a specific set of hand-crafted features (Gonçalo Oliveira et al., 2020), in a similar fashion to those methods from the early 2000s. Hence, there is still much to advance for this specific language.

On the other hand, also for Portuguese, we acknowledge research on Irony Detection (Carvalho et al., 2009; de Freitas et al., 2014; Wick-Pedro and Vale, 2020; Corrêa et al., 2021), a task that is to some extent related to humor, especially when dealing with satirical content (Wick-Pedro and Santos, 2021; Carvalho et al., 2020).

2.2 Machine Learning Explainability

As most ML models, Humor Recognition systems lack a qualitative understanding about how their prediction is obtained, i.e., what exactly the machine has learned from the provided examples. This brings up concerns regarding how trustful and understandable such models are, as well as questions if they are indeed basing their decision on meaningful parts of the data (Ribeiro et al., 2016).

Traditionally, ML explainability has been tackled simply through the usage of models that are inherently interpretable, such as linear classifiers (Ustun and Rudin, 2016) or rule-based methods (Wang and Rudin, 2015). Additionally, modern Neural Network models still have some degree of interpretability, through close inspection of their parameters, e.g., attention weights, especially for Computer Vision (Xu et al., 2015). However, such approaches are still limited to specific models; furthermore, they can get too overwhelming as the number of parameters increases.

There is, however, research on creating model-agnostic ML explanations, for example with tools like LIME (Ribeiro et al., 2016) and SHAP (Lundberg and Lee, 2017), which focus on approximating a simpler interpretable model by perturbing the inputs and measuring how each attribute (or token, pixel, subword, etc.) contribute to the original more complex one. These methods target local explainability, i.e., approximating models that work well on a vicinity of a given input, which is possible to be generalized for the whole data space through careful analysis of different instances.

3 Methodology

Our work has two main fronts of research: first, the implementation of Humor Recognition systems for the Portuguese language; then, a deeper analysis of their performance, to assess their weaknesses and stimulate further research. This includes a discussion on how to overcome some challenges, followed by what could be developed towards improved systems.

3.1 Humor Recognition Methods for Portuguese

Our first step was to re-implement the methods described by Gonçalo Oliveira et al. (2020) and Clemêncio (2019), as their source code is not publicly available and it is the only previous work for Humor Recognition in Portuguese. Their approach consists of testing different ML algorithms (i.e., SVM, Random Forest, and Naïve Bayes) with different sets of attributes: content and humor-related features. As content features, the original authors used a bag-of-words with TF-IDF counts for 1,000 tokens (or n-grams) selected via a χ^2 test. For humor-related features, they used different kinds of information, namely: alliteration through character n-grams, out-of-vocabulary words, average word embedding similarity, Named Entity Recognition (NER) counts, count of antonymy pairs, sentiment polarity, slang usage, concreteness, imageability, and ambiguity.

As we will see in subsection 4.1, our re-implementation outperformed the original reported values, leading us to reconsider our code and find some minor details, which might explain this difference in the evaluation metrics. In our implementation, we did not use the χ^2 test for selecting which attributes would comprise the final 1,000 content features, instead we used the most frequent ones. Additionally, we used the NLPyPort toolkit (Ferreira et al., 2019) for the content-features and not only for the humor-related ones, as shown in the original paper. In fact, comparing our feature analysis in subsection 4.2 to the one by Gonçalo Oliveira et al. (2020), we have strong evidence that their tokenizer discards punctuation, which NLPyPort does not. Differences between versions of the tools and resources used might also be an option, but we find the tokenization difference to be the most plausible reason for this difference in the results.

During our work, we decided to keep these changes as they resulted in a clearly higher performance. In all other aspects, we followed the same methodology as Gonçalo Oliveira et al. (2020), testing the same ML algorithms on the same corpus, with the same feature sets obtained from the same resources.

In addition, we fine-tuned BERTimbau, a pre-trained BERT model for Portuguese (Souza et al., 2020)[1], for Humor Recognition during 3 epochs with a learning rate of 5×10^{-5}. This was motivated by the broad utilization of LLMs for performing this and other tasks, leading to the current state-of-the-art in other languages (e.g., English and Spanish), as mentioned in subsection 2.1.

3.2 Corpus

We used the data set provided by Gonçalo Oliveira et al. (2020)[2], with short humorous texts in two main formats: satirical news headlines and one-line jokes. The authors were careful when including negative examples (non-humorous texts) into the corpus, trying to add only instances with a similar format to the humorous examples collected. For example, they included real news headlines as a counterpart to the satirical ones. For one-liners, as most of the jokes have a question-answer pattern, they used texts with this same composition from a trivia website and from MultiEight-04 (Magnini et al., 2005), a corpus for Question Answering. They also included proverbs to account for those one-liners not written in a question-answer fashion. We present some examples of instances from the corpus in Table 1.

Since the original corpus has different configurations available, we used the balanced one with texts from all sources, with a total of 2,800 texts, 1,400 humorous and 1,400 non-humorous instances. We should also note that, since we do not have access to the original train-test split used

[1]Available at: https://huggingface.co/neuralmind/bert-base-portuguese-cased.

[2]Available at: https://github.com/NLP-CISUC/Recognizing-Humor-in-Portuguese.

Original text in Portuguese	Translation	Comments
	Humor examples	
O que é uma fofoca? É um animal mamarítimo.	*What is a gossip? It is a mamarine animal.*	The humorous effect comes from the fact that the word "fofoca" (*gossip*) sounds like "foca" (*seal*) with a doubled initial syllable, so the answer says it is a marine animal, but also with a doubled initial syllable.
Patrões exigem vacinação obrigatória contra o bicho do sindicalismo	*Employers demand mandatory vaccination against the trade unionism bug*	The humor in this satirical headline arises from a semantic shift, as the association of vaccination is typically with disease rather than unionism. Furthermore, since satire employs humor as a means of criticism, this example serves as a critique of the bosses' opposition to unionism.
	Non-humor examples	
Onde fica Hyde Park? nos Estados Unidos.	*Where is Hyde Park? In the United States.*	–
Presidente promulga dia de luto nacional pelas vítimas de violência doméstica.	*President proclaims national day of mourning for victims of domestic violence.*	–

Table 1: Examples of instances present in the corpus

by Gonçalo Oliveira et al. (2020), we made a new split with the same reported ratio (80% train and 20% test).

3.3 Feature and Model Analysis

After the implementation, training, and testing of the models, we first used the SHAP explainability tool (Lundberg and Lee, 2017) to calculate importance values for each of the features proposed by Gonçalo Oliveira et al. (2020), both content and humor-related. Since SHAP was originally developed for explaining single instances of the data set, in order to measure the overall importance of each feature, we use the absolute mean value (over all examples in the test corpus); this is complemented with visualization techniques, such as beeswarm plots, to better understand how each feature behaves in general.

We also carried out an analysis of the fine-tuned BERT model, identifying which pieces of information were actually used by the system to distinguish humorous from non-humorous texts. For this, we used SHAP once again. However, as this kind of model does not consist of a pre-defined set of features, we were not able to use the absolute mean value, as it would have to comprise every single sub-word in the model. Therefore, we decided to perform such analysis manually, by examining specific instances that are representative of the corpus; to select such examples, we followed a simpler approach, using a clustering algorithm, namely K-Means with $k = 56$ (2% of the data set), on sentence embeddings obtained from BERTimbau fine-tuned for Semantic Textual Similarity[3], and selected the centroid instances as a sample of the whole corpus. Then, we carefully analyzed those sentences and their SHAP values, to finally identify some clear patterns that BERT learned for classification.

It is important to mention that Gonçalo Oliveira et al. (2020) also did a feature analysis procedure using a χ^2 test. However, this approach is not related to specific models and how they interpret the input, but rather focuses on finding relations between the features and the true labels.

4 Results

This work has two main results. First, a new fine-tuned BERT model for Humor Recognition in Portuguese, which outperforms the current state-of-the-art for this task in terms of automatic evaluation metrics. Secondly, a deeper analysis of such models, identifying how well they are suited for the task in general.

4.1 Humor Recognition

The results for each of the implemented approaches, alongside those reported by Gonçalo Oliveira et al.

[3]Available at: https://huggingface.co/rufimelo/bert-large-portuguese-cased-sts.

(2020), are presented in Table 2. Due to space limitations, we show only the results obtained by the best model for each set of features.

Feature Set	Model	F1
Content features	SVM	96.4%
Humor features	Random Forest	78.8%
All features	Random Forest	97.1%
—	Fine-tuned BERT	99.6%
Gonçalo Oliveira et al. (2020)		
Content features	SVM	75%
Humor features	Random Forest	64%
All features	SVM	78%

Table 2: Best results for Humor Recognition with different models and different feature sets

We note that our re-implementation produced better results than those by Gonçalo Oliveira et al. (2020); for example, while their best model using all features (content and humor-related) reportedly and F1 of 78%, our models reached up to 97.1%. The probable reasons for such a large gap have been discussed in subsection 3.1.

In addition, we found it surprising that our models had such positive results – BERT had a nearly perfect score of 99.6% – for a task that is usually mentioned in the literature as extremely difficult and subjective (Veale, 2004; Hempelmann, 2008; Reyes Pérez, 2013; Kumar et al., 2022). From this observation, we decided to do an explainability analysis to identify exactly which features and pieces of information our trained models were leveraging on when classifying their input.

4.2 Explainability Analysis

In the first analysis, we used SHAP to calculate the importance values of each feature for the best methods reported in the previous subsection 4.1. For the SVM model using exclusively content features, Figure 1 presents the most important (i.e., larger average absolute SHAP value) features for the humor class. In the plot, each feature is represented in the Y axis, with each point representing an instance of classification; their color expresses the relative value of the feature in that specific instance, while their placement along the X axis indicates their importance. For example, we can see that the most important feature used by the model is the presence of a full stop (a period followed by an end-of-sentence special token), and that they are most important for the humor class (positive SHAP values, right of the central vertical bar) when their TF-IDF counts are low (blue). This same behavior can be seen for the second most important feature (period), indicating that the model is interpreting the mere presence of periods as an indicative of non-humorousness. This is probably a fault from the corpus, as will be further discussed in subsection 4.3.

Another interesting observation that can be drawn from this analysis is that the model leverages question-related features as indicatives of humor, for example the usage of question marks, and wh-question words ("qual é", "o que", "qual", and "que"[4]). One can note that the model considers them important to identify humor when their TF-IDF counts are higher (red points), meaning that it is associating questions to humor despite the presence of similar texts as negative examples of humor, as mentioned in subsection 3.2.

Due to space and resource limitations, we cannot extensively analyze all 1,000 content-features. However, we report that the next features in the list are still wh-question words, such as "porque", "qual é o", and "como" [5], or punctuation marks (colons, double quotes, and exclamation marks). We highlight, however, that the explainability results for all features will be made publicly available alongside the code and results obtained by the models, so that the research community can observe this data in its entirety.

The second analysis refers to only humor-related features, presented in Figure 2. The most important feature is the number of out-of-vocabulary words, which is seen as a strong indicative of humor. Then, the average level of concreteness follows with a not so clear disparity of how its values interact with its importance; however, there seems to be a preference of higher values to be positive contributions to the humor class, which is contradictory to the interpretation by Gonçalo Oliveira et al. (2020) that non-humorous texts are more concrete, while humor is more related to mental images.

Another remarkable note is that higher NER counts for people ("PESSOA") is usually taken as evidence to favor the humor class, which is again the opposite speculated by Gonçalo Oliveira et al. (2020). The authors mention that real headlines would contain more names of people, but we argue that they are also present in satirical headlines and

[4]"Which is", "what", "which", and "what". Translated by the authors.

[5]"Why", "which is the", and "how". Translated by the authors.

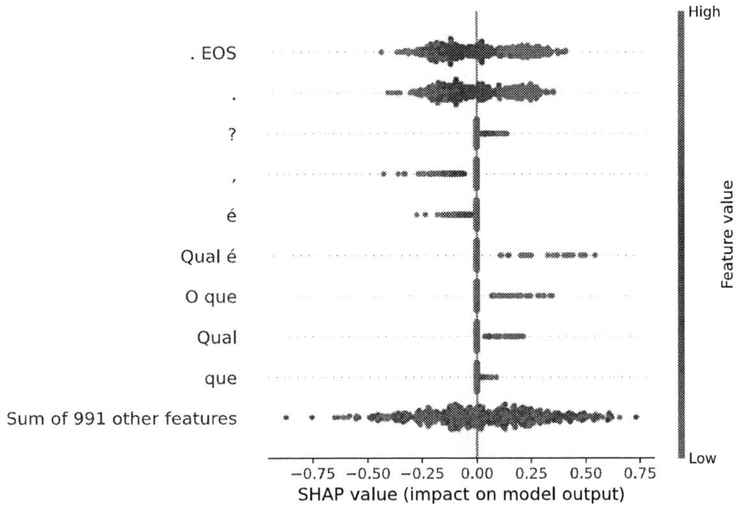

Figure 1: Beeswarm plot with the most important content features used by the SVM model

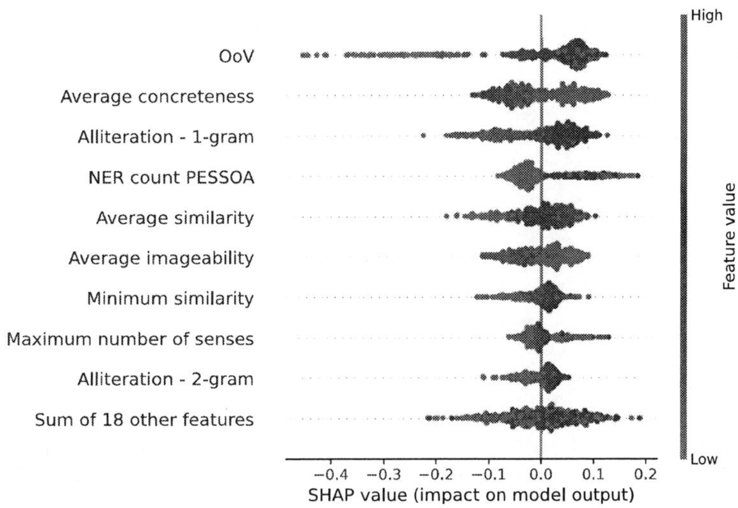

Figure 2: Beeswarm plot with the most important humor-related features used by the Random Forest model

one-liner jokes (e.g. "Por que a Angélica não mata baratas? Ela espera o Maurício Mattar."[6]), so that the model learned to link them to humor instead.

Finally, in accordance to the reasoning of Gonçalo Oliveira et al. (2020), the average and minimum similarity features are evidences of humor when they have lower values, which represents a higher incongruity among the words. Thus, it seems fruitful to model incongruity as word similarity. Also, the model favors high numbers of senses to classify an instance as humor, reaffirming the argument that humor resides in ambiguity.

When combining both kinds of features, the observations do not vary much: the Random Forest model relies mainly on punctuation (full stop, period, question mark), and wh-question words. It is, however, noticeable that humor-related features such as concreteness, imageability, person NER counts, and average similarity are considered more important than question words in this scenario. We highlight, once more, that an extensive display of these results will be made available.

4.3 Explainability Analysis of BERT

As mentioned in subsection 3.3, for the fine-tuned BERT model, we needed to do a careful manual

[6] "Why doesn't Angélica kill cockroaches? She waits for Maurício Mattar." Translated by the authors.

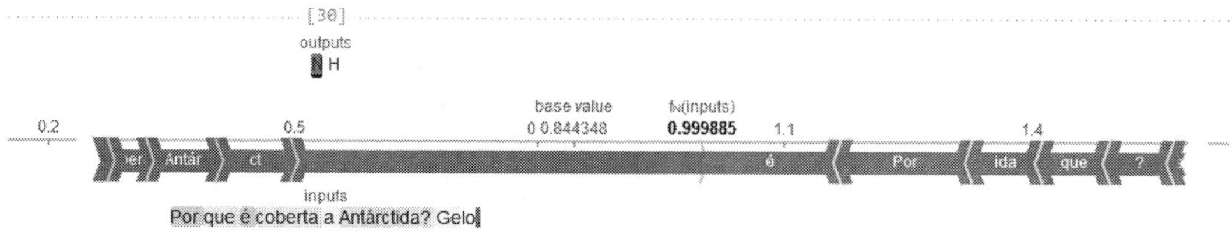

Figure 3: Example of BERT explanation obtained via SHAP

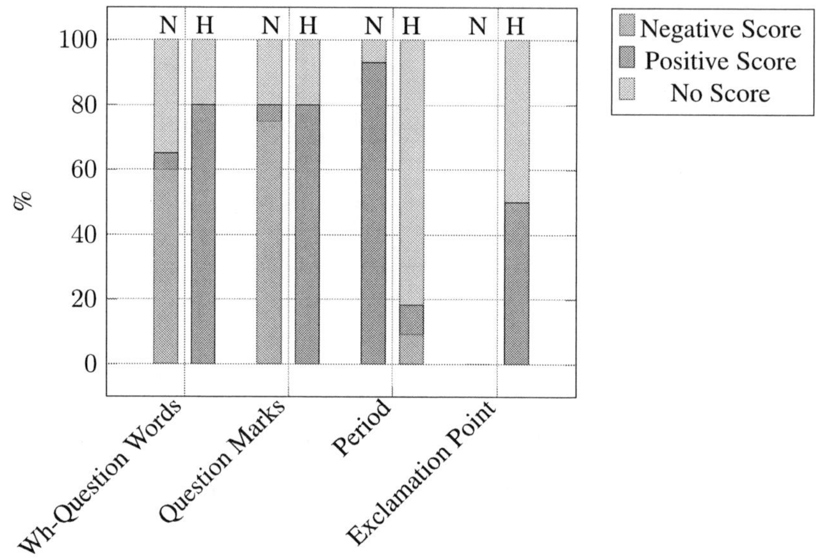

Figure 4: Results of the BERT explanation analysis

analysis of a subset of representative instances of the corpus obtained via clustering. All 56 examples were explained by SHAP and handed to a linguist with previous experience on analyzing humorous and figurative language. An example of a SHAP explanation can be seen in Figure 3.

In the figure, the text "Por que é coberta a Antárctida? Gelo."[7] was classified as non-humorous ("N" is highlighted) with a confidence score ($fx(\text{inputs})$) of 0.999885. For the analysis, the BERT model starts at a base value – for this specific case, 0.844348 – obtained by masking out all input subwords. Then, each subword contributes to this value positively (in red) or negatively (in blue) until it reaches the final confidence score; moreover, larger bars represent a larger absolute contribution.

From this analysis, we have drawn two main observations, which are related to the results reported in the previous subsection 4.2. First, the usage of wh-question words – such as "o que", "quais", and "como"[8] – are in general taken by the model as evidence to classify an instance as humor; from all 29 examples classified as non-humorous, 20 (69.97%) have wh-question words, from which they contributed negatively in 12 instances (60%), positively in only 1 instance (5%), and in the remaining 7 texts (35%) they did not get any scoring.

Another evidence for this association of wh-question words with humor in the model is that, in 25 instances classified as humor, from which 15 (60%) had such type of words, 12 (80%) occurrences contributed positively to the classification, while the remaining 3 (20%) did not contribute at all. There were no cases in which BERT considered the presence of wh-question words as negative evidences for this class.

The second result of this analysis is about punctuation, which was also observed in other models as being extremely important. For instances classi-

[7] "What is Antarctica covered by? Ice." Translated by the authors.

[8] "What", "which", and "how." Translated by the authors.

fied as non-humorous, 20 (69%) contained question marks, 15 (75%) of which were assigned with negative SHAP values, 4 (20%) were not scored at all, and only 1 (5%) received a positive score. Meanwhile, for examples classified as humor, 15 (60%) had question marks, from which 12 (80%) were considered as positive evidences for this class, and the remaining 3 (20%) had no score; similarly to wh-question words, no question mark was considered as negative for the humor class.

We argue that these observations contribute to the point-of-view that BERT, similarly to the models discussed in subsection 4.2, is focusing on the textual form rather than specific humor-related linguistic devices by connecting the mere existence of questions to humor. Nonetheless, as mentioned in subsection 3.2, the original authors of the corpus were careful to also include question-answer texts with no humor, and the model still reached more than 99% F1-Score (Table 2), meaning that it is very likely classifying such instances correctly. In this context, as illustrated by Figure 3, another punctuation mark comes into place: the period, specially a full stop, which was also highly scored in the other methods discussed before.

All 29 examples classified as non-humor end with a period, from which 27 (93.10%) received positive SHAP scores and the remaining 2 (6.90%) were not scored at all; no period was deemed as a negative evidence for the non-humor class. Meanwhile, for the sample of 25 instances classified as being humorous, only 9 (36%) had periods, sometimes with more than one resulting in 11 periods, from which 1 (9.09%) was positive, 1 (9.09%) was negative and the remaining 9 (81.82%) received no scoring, indicating that BERT tends to not even consider periods for the humor class.

We highlight that the difference in the occurrence of periods between the humor and non-humor classes in the analyzed sample may indicate that this discrepancy also exists in the corpus. Likely, this specific aspect of the text format was overlooked by the original authors, which may explain why the models primarily use this punctuation mark to distinguish humor from non-humor.

Additionally, exclamation points are present only in the examples classified as humorous, with 4 (50%) being positive and 4 (50%) not having attributed any value to this instance. All these results are summarized in Figure 4.

From all these observations, we point out how difficult it is to find negative examples when creating a corpus for Humor Classification – and arguably to any classification task. LLMs are so powerful in finding surface-level patterns that even slight details (such as punctuation) can and will be used in the task, even if they are not necessarily part of the linguistic mechanism that produces the humorous effect, such as ambiguity, incongruity, and surprise (Attardo and Raskin, 1991; Tagnin, 2005; Reyes Pérez, 2013; Kao et al., 2016; Wick-Pedro and Vale, 2020; Aleksandrova, 2022).

5 Conclusion

In this paper, we presented a re-implementation of the previous state-of-the-art method for Humor Recognition in the Portuguese language, alongside a novel fine-tuned BERT model for the same task, reaching a nearly-perfect F1 score of 99.64%.[9]

However, a deeper analysis of the models using a Machine Learning explainability method, SHAP, enabled us to understand which pieces of information the models were relying on to do such classification. We came into the conclusion that BERT and models based on TF-IDF counts did not learn specific mechanisms of humor, but were instead leveraging mainly stylistic characteristics of the texts, such as punctuation and the presence of wh-questions.

Furthermore, the analysis of how humor-related features were interpreted by the ML model led to interesting observations not considered by their proposers (Gonçalo Oliveira et al., 2020). For example, the association of humor with person named entities or higher levels of concreteness; however, some of their reasoning can also be reinforced by how the model used some of the knowledge provided, e.g. humor was considered related to higher levels of ambiguity and incongruity within the text, which is up to par with linguistic descriptions of verbal humor (Raskin and Attardo, 1994; Tagnin, 2005; Aleksandrova, 2022).

As a final conclusion, we emphasize how challenging it is to create a text classification corpus for supervised ML in such a way that the model actually learns about the linguistic phenomenon in question, rather than resorting to specific attributes and shortcuts not directly related to the problem being studied. We find that humor is a specially difficult task to create such a corpus, as it is a largely di-

[9]All the code, models, results, and analysis is available at: `https://github.com/Superar/HumorRecognitionPT`.

verse phenomenon (verbal humor can be conveyed in many different ways), with an equally large universe of negative examples (non-humorous texts also present themselves in various formats).

From these conclusions, we can draw some fruitful paths for future research. First, we mention the creation of a new corpus for Humor Recognition in Portuguese, taking into account some of the flaws found in the corpus by Gonçalo Oliveira et al. (2020). However, as it is – to the best of our knowledge – the only available corpus for this task, it can still be evaluated if it is fit after some process of normalization, starting with punctuation, e.g., by adding full stops to the humor examples, which would be a less expensive process; some early experiments in this sense show a decrease of 4 percentage points in F-Score obtained by the BERT model when discarding or normalizing punctuation. Another point to be considered for the creation of a new corpus is the responsibility of which texts to include; as we mention later in our Ethics Statement, the corpus used in this work contains texts annotated as jokes that contain rather problematic content, e.g. riddles that are openly racist.

Another possibility for future work is to change the models and how they work. One could use methods, such as the one proposed by Kao et al. (2016), that are not based on ML, but rather on formalizing linguistic theories of humor to a computational environment. We also find it appealing to explicitly include linguistic knowledge into the ML models, so that they are powered with some information beyond the textual surface, argued by other researchers as vital to deal with complex phenomena such as humor (Hempelmann, 2008; Amin and Burghardt, 2020). This goal could also be achieved by exploring further the humor-related features, which were proposed originally from a linguistic point-of-view; other extra-linguistic aspects of Humor could also be studied, for instance how different cultural backgrounds affect the perception and definition of humorousness.

Limitations

As main limitation of this work, we mention the lack of an extensive analysis of the explainability results, limiting our examination to the most highly-scored features; additionally, we not consider the interaction among the features themselves. We also think that the analysis of the BERT model could use a larger set of representative instances of the corpus; regarding this selection, we also mention that there are probably other methods rather than clustering to ensure that the analyzed subset is actually a good representation of the data set in its entirety. Finally, we agree that the classification models deserve a deeper analysis on their performance, for example, by carrying out K-fold cross validation tests.

Ethics Statement

We believe that humor is a positive and constructive form of human expression to unite and reduce tensions while respecting cultural differences, beliefs, and people's identities. However, we acknowledge that humor, when used in a Christian or offensive way to discriminate, ridicule, or disparage individuals or groups, especially those who have been historically marginalized or oppressed, can have negative consequences.

So if there are jokes that promote violence, hatred, or prejudice, including but not limited to racial, gender, and sexual stereotypes, xenophobia, and similar forms of discrimination, then they ought not to be deemed acceptable. In this context we find it crucial to report that the corpus used in this paper contains some texts (annotated as humor) that are openly racist, specially against black people. Other texts considered as jokes have different groups represented in a negative light, for example alentejanos (people from a region in Portugal), jeweish people, and blonde women. Some other sensitive subjects are also present in the corpus, for instance suicide, and pedophilia.

It is crucial to take into account the potential effects that computer models designed for mood detection could have on individuals and society, both during the development phase and when utilizing them. Ensuring that these models are impartial and free of undesired bias is of utmost importance to prevent the perpetuation of stereotypes that could ultimately result in negative outcomes.

In conclusion, we would like to emphasize that models used for the recognition of humor have inherent limitations due to their subjective nature, which may vary significantly depending on cultural, social, and individual contexts. Therefore, these models are constantly evolving and improving, and evaluating their efficacy is an ongoing process.

Acknowledgements

This work was funded by national funds through the FCT – Foundation for Science and Technology, I.P. (grant number UI/BD/153496/2022), within the scope of the project CISUC (UID/CEC/00326/2020) and by the European Social Fund, through the Regional Operational Program Centro 2020.

References

Elena Aleksandrova. 2022. Pun-based jokes and linguistic creativity: Designing 3R-module. The European Journal of Humour Research, 10(1):88–107.

Miriam Amin and Manuel Burghardt. 2020. A survey on approaches to computational humor generation. In Proceedings of the the 4th Joint SIGHUM Workshop on Computational Linguistics for Cultural Heritage, Social Sciences, Humanities and Literature, pages 29–41, Online. International Committee on Computational Linguistics.

Salvatore Attardo and Victor Raskin. 1991. Script theory revis(it)ed: Joke similarity and joke representation model. Humor - International Journal of Humor Research, 4(3-4).

Francesco Barbieri and Horacio Saggion. 2014. Automatic Detection of Irony and Humour in Twitter. In International Conference on Computational Creativity, Ljubljana. Association for Computational Creativity (ACC).

Paula Carvalho, Bruno Martins, Hugo Rosa, Silvio Amir, Jorge Baptista, and Mário J. Silva. 2020. Situational Irony in Farcical News Headlines. In Paulo Quaresma, Renata Vieira, Sandra Aluísio, Helena Moniz, Fernando Batista, and Teresa Gonçalves, editors, Computational Processing of the Portuguese Language, volume 12037, pages 65–75. Springer International Publishing, Cham.

Paula Carvalho, Luís Sarmento, Mário J. Silva, and Eugénio de Oliveira. 2009. Clues for detecting irony in user-generated contents: Oh...!! it's "so easy" ;-). In Proceeding of the 1st International CIKM Workshop on Topic-sentiment Analysis for Mass Opinion - TSA '09, page 53, Hong Kong, China. ACM Press.

Santiago Castro, Luis Chiruzzo, and Aiala Rosá. 2018. Overview of the HAHA Task: Humor Analysis based on Human Annotation at IberEval 2018. In Proceedings of the Third Workshop on Evaluation of Human Language Technologies for Iberian Languages (IberEval 2018), pages 187–194, Sevilla. CEUR-WS.org.

Luis Chiruzzo, Santiago Castro, Santiago Góngora, Aiala Rosá, J. A. Meaney, and Rada Mihalcea. 2021. Overview of HAHA at IberLEF 2021: Detecting, Rating and Analyzing Humor in Spanish. Procesamiento del Lenguaje Natural, 67:257–268.

André Clemêncio. 2019. Reconhecimento Automático de Humor Verbal. MSc, Universidade de Coimbra, Coimbra.

Ulisses B Corrêa, Leonardo Coelho, Leonardo Santos, and Larissa A de Freitas. 2021. Overview of the IDPT task on irony detection in portuguese at IberLEF 2021. Procesamiento del Lenguaje Natural, 67:269–276.

Larissa A. de Freitas, Aline A. Vanin, Denise N. Hogetop, Marco N. Bochernitsan, and Renata Vieira. 2014. Pathways for irony detection in tweets. In Proceedings of the 29th Annual ACM Symposium on Applied Computing, pages 628–633, Gyeongju Republic of Korea. ACM.

Jacob Devlin, Ming-Wei Chang, Kenton Lee, and Kristina Toutanova. 2019. BERT: Pre-training of deep bidirectional transformers for language understanding. In Proceedings of the 2019 Conference of the North American Chapter of the Association for Computational Linguistics: Human Language Technologies, Volume 1 (Long and Short Papers), pages 4171–4186, Minneapolis, Minnesota. Association for Computational Linguistics.

João Ferreira, Hugo Gonçalo Oliveira, and Ricardo Rodrigues. 2019. Improving NLTK for Processing Portuguese. page 9 pages.

Hugo Gonçalo Oliveira, André Clemêncio, and Ana Alves. 2020. Corpora and baselines for humour recognition in Portuguese. In Proceedings of the 12th Language Resources and Evaluation Conference, pages 1278–1285, Marseille, France. European Language Resources Association.

Karish Grover and Tanishq Goel. 2021. HAHA@IberLEF2021: Humor Analysis using Ensembles of Simple Transformers. In Proceedings of the Iberian Languages Evaluation Forum (IberLEF 2021), pages 883–890, Málaga. CEUR-WS.org.

Christian F. Hempelmann. 2008. Computational humor: Beyond the pun? In The Primer of Humor Research, number 8 in Humor Research, pages 333–360. Victor Raskin, Berlin, New York.

Justine T. Kao, Roger Levy, and Noah D. Goodman. 2016. A Computational Model of Linguistic Humor in Puns. Cognitive Science, 40(5):1270–1285.

Vijay Kumar, Ranjeet Walia, and Shivam Sharma. 2022. DeepHumor: A novel deep learning framework for humor detection. Multimedia Tools and Applications, 81(12):16797–16812.

Scott M Lundberg and Su-In Lee. 2017. A unified approach to interpreting model predictions. In Advances in Neural Information Processing Systems, volume 30. Curran Associates, Inc.

Bernardo Magnini, Alessandro Vallin, Christelle Ayache, Gregor Erbach, Anselmo Peñas, Maarten de

Rijke, Paulo Rocha, Kiril Simov, and Richard Sutcliffe. 2005. Overview of the CLEF 2004 Multilingual Question Answering Track. In David Hutchison, Takeo Kanade, Josef Kittler, Jon M. Kleinberg, Friedemann Mattern, John C. Mitchell, Moni Naor, Oscar Nierstrasz, C. Pandu Rangan, Bernhard Steffen, Madhu Sudan, Demetri Terzopoulos, Dough Tygar, Moshe Y. Vardi, Gerhard Weikum, Carol Peters, Paul Clough, Julio Gonzalo, Gareth J. F. Jones, Michael Kluck, and Bernardo Magnini, editors, Multilingual Information Access for Text, Speech and Images, volume 3491, pages 371–391. Springer Berlin Heidelberg, Berlin, Heidelberg.

Rada Mihalcea and Stephen Pulman. 2007. Characterizing Humour: An Exploration of Features in Humorous Texts. In Alexander Gelbukh, editor, Computational Linguistics and Intelligent Text Processing, volume 4394, pages 337–347. Springer Berlin Heidelberg, Berlin, Heidelberg.

Rada Mihalcea and Carlo Strapparava. 2005. Making computers laugh: Investigations in automatic humor recognition. In Proceedings of Human Language Technology Conference and Conference on Empirical Methods in Natural Language Processing, pages 531–538, Vancouver, British Columbia, Canada. Association for Computational Linguistics.

Rafael A. Monteiro, Roney L. S. Santos, Thiago A. S. Pardo, Tiago A. de Almeida, Evandro E. S. Ruiz, and Oto A. Vale. 2018. Contributions to the Study of Fake News in Portuguese: New Corpus and Automatic Detection Results. In Aline Villavicencio, Viviane Moreira, Alberto Abad, Helena Caseli, Pablo Gamallo, Carlos Ramisch, Hugo Gonçalo Oliveira, and Gustavo Henrique Paetzold, editors, Computational Processing of the Portuguese Language, volume 11122, pages 324–334. Springer International Publishing, Cham.

Jonathan D. Raskin and Salvatore Attardo. 1994. Nonliteralness and non-bona-fide in language: An approach to formal and computational treatments of humor. Pragmatics & Cognition, 2(1):31–69.

Lu Ren, Bo Xu, Hongfei Lin, and Liang Yang. 2021. ABML: Attention-based multi-task learning for jointly humor recognition and pun detection. Soft Computing, 25(22):14109–14118.

Antonio Reyes Pérez. 2013. Linguistic-based Patterns for Figurative Language Processing: The Case of Humor Recognition and Irony Detection. Procesamiento del Lenguaje Natural.

Marco Tulio Ribeiro, Sameer Singh, and Carlos Guestrin. 2016. "Why Should I Trust You?": Explaining the Predictions of Any Classifier. In Proceedings of the 22nd ACM SIGKDD International Conference on Knowledge Discovery and Data Mining, pages 1135–1144, San Francisco California USA. ACM.

Jonas Sjöbergh and Kenji Araki. 2007. Recognizing Humor Without Recognizing Meaning. In Francesco Masulli, Sushmita Mitra, and Gabriella Pasi, editors, Applications of Fuzzy Sets Theory, volume 4578, pages 469–476. Springer Berlin Heidelberg, Berlin, Heidelberg.

Fábio Souza, Rodrigo Nogueira, and Roberto Lotufo. 2020. BERTimbau: Pretrained BERT Models for Brazilian Portuguese. In Intelligent Systems: 9th Brazilian Conference, BRACIS 2020, Rio Grande, Brazil, October 20–23, 2020, Proceedings, Part I, pages 403–417, Berlin, Heidelberg. Springer-Verlag.

Stella E. O. Tagnin. 2005. O humor como quebra da convencionalidade. Revista Brasileira de Linguística Aplicada, 5(1):247–257.

Berk Ustun and Cynthia Rudin. 2016. Supersparse linear integer models for optimized medical scoring systems. Machine Learning, 102(3):349–391.

Tony Veale. 2004. Incongruity in humor: Root cause or epiphenomenon? Humor - International Journal of Humor Research, 17(4).

Fulton Wang and Cynthia Rudin. 2015. Falling Rule Lists. In Proceedings of the Eighteenth International Conference on Artificial Intelligence and Statistics, volume 38 of Proceedings of Machine Learning Research, pages 1013–1022, San Diego, California, USA. PMLR.

Orion Weller and Kevin Seppi. 2019. Humor Detection: A Transformer Gets the Last Laugh. In Proceedings of the 2019 Conference on Empirical Methods in Natural Language Processing and the 9th International Joint Conference on Natural Language Processing (EMNLP-IJCNLP), pages 3621–3625, Hong Kong, China. Association for Computational Linguistics.

Gabriela Wick-Pedro and Roney L. S. Santos. 2021. Complexidade textual em notícias satíricas: Uma análise para o português do Brasil. In Anais Do XIII Simpósio Brasileiro de Tecnologia Da Informação e Da Linguagem Humana (STIL 2021), pages 409–415, Brasil. Sociedade Brasileira de Computação.

Gabriela Wick-Pedro and Oto Araújo Vale. 2020. Comentcorpus: descrição e análise de ironia em um corpus de opinião para o português do Brasil. Cadernos de Linguística, 1(2):01–15.

Kelvin Xu, Jimmy Ba, Ryan Kiros, Kyunghyun Cho, Aaron Courville, Ruslan Salakhudinov, Rich Zemel, and Yoshua Bengio. 2015. Show, attend and tell: Neural image caption generation with visual attention. In Proceedings of the 32nd International Conference on Machine Learning, volume 37 of Proceedings of Machine Learning Research, pages 2048–2057, Lille, France. PMLR.

Estimating Overreporting in the Creditor Reporting System on Climate Adaptation Finance Using Text Classification and Bayesian Correction

Janos Borst
Leipzig University, Germany
janos.borst@uni-leipzig.de

Thomas Wencker
German Institute for Development Evaluation
Thomas.Wencker@deval.org

Andreas Niekler
Leipzig University, Germany
andreas.niekler@uni-leipzig.de

Abstract

Development funds are essential to finance climate change adaptation and are thus an important part of international climate policy. However, the absence of a common reporting practice makes it difficult to assess the amount and distribution of such funds. This problem has attracted attention in international affairs research and is increasingly being investigated using methods of the broader field of computational social science. Lately, the mentioned research field has questioned the credibility of reported figures, indicating that adaptation financing is in fact lower than published figures suggest. Projects claiming a greater relevance to climate change adaptation than they target are referred to as "overreported". To estimate realistic rates of overreporting in large data sets over time, we propose an approach based on state-of-the-art text classification. To date, assessments of credibility have relied on small, manually evaluated samples. We use such a sample data set to train a classifier with an accuracy of $89.81\% \pm 0.83\%$ (tenfold cross-validation) and extrapolate to larger data sets to identify overreporting. Additionally, we propose a method that incorporates evidence of smaller, higher-quality data to correct predicted rates using Bayes' theorem. This enables a comparison of different annotation schemes to estimate the degree of overreporting in climate change adaptation. Our results support findings that indicate extensive overreporting of 32.03% with a credible interval of [19.81%; 48.34%].

1 Introduction

The climate crisis is one of the greatest challenges of our time. Climate change is accelerating toward a catastrophe that will almost certainly become a humanitarian crisis as well. According to a United Nations committee, the next decade counts: The latest IPCC reports make it clear that limiting global warming to a relatively safe level still is possible, but it requires global cooperation and billions in financial support (Plumer, 2023; Mukherji et al., 2023). Failure of the global community to respond to the climate crisis will result in millions of people having to live with the consequences of extreme heat, food and water shortages, as well as the proliferation of pathogens, all of which add to the humanitarian crisis. Therefore, ensuring that populations are able to secure their livelihoods necessitates focus on both adaptation to the impacts and mitigation of the effects of climate change. Implementation of climate change adaptation measures is one of five targets set to reach the 13th Sustainable Development Goal (SDG): "Take urgent action to combat climate change and its impacts". There is international consensus on the need to respond to the global threat posed by climate change (Paris Accord, Article 2). Development funds are essential to finance climate change adaptation and are thus an important part of international climate policy. Specifically, Article 9.1 of the Paris Agreement states that "[d]eveloped country parties shall provide financial resources to assist developing country parties with respect to both mitigation and adaptation in continuation of their existing obligations under the Convention."[1]. Prior to that, the 2009 Copenhagen Accord had already declared a goal of mobilizing USD 100 billion by 2020. Based on these agreements, the Conference of the Parties (COP) meets annually to assess implementation efforts and to ensure effective implementation of the conventions. One basis for this activity is the Creditor Reporting System (CRS), which is administered by the OECD Development Assistance Committee (DAC). It monitors financial flows for adaptation and climate change mitigation activities that flow from OECD DAC member countries to developing countries. As such, it is the central system for monitoring and evaluating the efforts of the international community to address climate change. To

[1] https://unfccc.int/sites/default/files/english_paris_agreement.pdf

Proceedings of the 7th Joint SIGHUM Workshop on Computational Linguistics for Cultural Heritage, Social Sciences, Humanities and Literature (LaTeCH-CLfL2023), pages 99–109
May 5, 2023 ©2023 Association for Computational Linguistics

date, this dataset includes more than 1.5M aid activities. One of the challenges in ensuring valid reporting – or at least comparable figures – across reporting countries is that these agreements lack standardized indicators. These tasks and this area of activity of international politics can be classified as a field of research in international affairs, which is increasingly being researched using methods of the broader field of computational social science (Tavoni, 2023).

To this end, in 2009 the OECD DAC established the "Rio markers" for climate change adaptation (CCA) and mitigation (CCM). For each aid activity, donors self-report whether it contributes to CCA, i.e. reducing "the vulnerability of human or natural systems to the current and expected impacts of climate change, including climate variability, by maintaining or increasing resilience, through increased ability to adapt to, or absorb, climate change stresses, shocks and variability and/or by helping reduce exposure to them" (OECD DAC, 2022, 4). Activities are eligible for a marker if "a) the climate change adaptation objective is explicitly indicated in the activity documentation; and b) the activity contains specific measures targeting the definition above." (OECD DAC, 2022, 4). The Rio marker r can take three values: 2, if CCA is the principal objective; 1, if CCA is a significant objective; and 0, if CCA is neither a principal nor a significant objective. However, there is increasing evidence that the level of adaptation financing is in fact lower than public figures suggest (Weikmans et al., 2017; Junghans and Harmeling, 2012). The authors refer to this phenomenon as *overreporting*, which primarily indicates a discrepancy between the qualitative descriptions of the financing purposes and the specified Rio markers. One possible reason is that there is no common practice for reporting climate finance (Weikmans and Roberts, 2019; Weikmans et al., 2020) and reporting agencies thus follow different reporting rules. This makes it difficult to assess the total amount of CCA or CCM finance, to compare commitments between donors, and to assess the geographical and sectoral distribution of funding (Weikmans and Roberts, 2019).Moreover, CCA finance estimates vary among reporting agencies (Yeo, 2019). Hence, aggregate figures of adaptation finance are increasingly considered unreliable given that they comprise thousands of individual aid activity descriptions from the CRS data. Consequently, assessments of credibility have to date relied on analysis of small samples covering a limited period of time (Weikmans et al., 2017). Returning to the fact that the COP is utilizing these reports, among other things, as source of information the unreliable nature of these reports jeopardizes the well-being of the people who are affected by climate change. Regardless of whether this discrepancy is result of deliberate misreporting or due to the inconsistent nature of the reporting procedure, this system, with all its strengths and weaknesses, is part of global communication about the environment and environmental issues.

This study applies state-of-the-art machine learning methods for Natural Language Processing to estimate overreporting of CCA finance for all aid activities as reported in the OECD DAC CRS since the introduction of Rio markers. We model the information and knowledge contained in the reports using NLP methods to aid the requirement that the assessment of the reports is consistent, thorough and complete. This contributes to effective and targeted measures based on realistic assessments so that the necessary assistance can be provided to protect people's livelihoods and social structures.

Our main challenge in applying machine learning methodology is the quality and quantity of available annotated data. We have access to two data sets re-evaluated by experts and published in previous work: The first is small, but following a thorough re-evaluation process, we regard it as high-quality. One concern is that the current de facto standard of fine-tuning language models tends to be unstable with very small data sets and is hard to evaluate properly. The second set is much larger, but because it was re-evaluated with access to less information, we regard it as lower quality; nevertheless, its size makes it adequate for training. We propose to combine these two data sets, using the larger for training and extrapolation, and the smaller, higher-quality set to correct first estimates. The contribution of this paper is two-fold: 1. We propose and evaluate a machine learning model to detect overreporting in the CRS data and discuss extrapolation. 2. We propose and attempt to use a Bayesian Framework for correction of extrapolated overreporting rates.

2 Related Work

In recent years, several studies have estimated the level of overreporting in CCA finance (Michaelowa and Michaelowa, 2011; Weikmans et al., 2017;

Junghans and Harmeling, 2012; Schramek and Harmeling, 2021). These studies are distinguished, first, by the rigor of their methodology to assess overreporting and, second, by the number of aid activities they analyze. Some studies classify multiple aid activities but employ, rather simplistically, keyword searches only on short descriptions of aid activity (Michaelowa and Michaelowa, 2011; Roberts et al., 2008; Junghans and Harmeling, 2012). Other studies examine only a few aid activities by scrutinizing extant project documentation against in-country expert assessments (Schramek and Harmeling, 2021). Weikmans et al. (2017) strike a balance by manually assessing a large number of short project descriptions.

We are among the first to apply state-of-the-art machine learning - which allows us to code all aid activities reported in the OECD DAC CRS database - to fully automate the process of detecting overreporting of CCA finance. Moreover, our method can be easily applied to future data releases of the OECD DAC CRS data as well as comparable text data.

Machine learning approaches to classify official development assistance are still rare. Pincet et al. (2019) used machine learning to classify SDGs. More recently, Toetzke et al. (2022) developed a machine-learning classifier to identify climate finance based on the title and descriptions of bilateral aid activities in the OECD DAC CRS dataset. ClimateFinanceBERT first classifies the relevance of aid activities to adaptation, mitigation, or the environment. Subsequently, relevant activities are further differentiated into ten categories. In contrast, our classifier directly predicts Rio Markers for climate change adaptation. Moreover, we address possible shortcomings due to the limited information contained in the OECD DAC CRS descriptions by integrating evidence from a high-quality re-evaluation.

Here, we rely on textual resources to automatically assign Rio markers to CRS Reports. Project reports typically contain both short and long descriptions of the project goals, ranging from one to a few sentences. Currently, neural networks produce virtually every state-of-the-art result in text classification, either by training task-specific architectures, e.g. (Kim, 2014) or adapting pre-trained language models to a given task (Devlin et al., 2019; Liu et al., 2019; Yang et al., 2019; Aly et al., 2019; Pal et al., 2020). Also, recent works have achieved both higher overall performance (Devlin et al., 2019; Yang et al., 2019) and greater sample efficiency, achieving better results with less data (Halder et al., 2020). The typical problems of previous classical machine learning approaches in text classification, like out-of-vocabulary or ambiguity, are directly handled by the language model, which is especially important in this case, because not all of the texts we deal with are free of orthographic and syntactical anomalies. We experiment with these models in various combinations to find the best fit for the task at hand.

3 Automatic Classification of Climate Change Adaptation Markers

3.1 Data

The CRS tracks OECD DAC member countries' aid activities. This study works with the original CRS data and two re-evaluated data sets:

Creditor Reporting System (CRS): The publicly available CRS contains harmonized data on aid activities. We use CRS data from 2006 to 2019 containing 1,529,984 aid activities. It includes up to 91 fields of data for each aid activity. The most important information in our context is flagged by: donor, recipient, Rio marker, project title, and short and long description.

WK: Weikmans et al. (2017) sampled 4,757 aid activities from 2012 CRS data and manually re-evaluated the Rio markers based on the aid activity descriptions. The re-evaluation includes a new marker (99) to indicate insufficient information for determining the Rio marker. (Weikmans et al., 2017) argue that label 99 can be treated as 0 (not climate adaptation related) because the Rio marker methodology explicitly requires a CCA objective to be indicated in the aid activity documentation.

CARE: Schramek and Harmeling (2021) of the Cooperative for Assistance and Relief Everywhere (CARE) sampled 117 aid activities from the CRS. Each case was re-evaluated and assigned a new Rio marker by experts with access to detailed project-level information beyond the data contained in the CRS.

3.2 Approach

We consider CARE as a high-quality re-evaluation with very few samples. The WK data set has substantially more observations, but the re-evaluation had access only to CRS information. Since information from the CRS can be very limited, especially in cases where CCA is not the primary goal, this likely leads to a higher proportion of projects being considered overreported. However, the WK data set is substantially larger than the CARE data set and can be used to train a classifier, which is why we use WK for the training and CARE to estimate a correction factor to extrapolate the CARE annotations implicitly.

Our approach is as follows: First, we train a high-quality classification model on the WK data set using information only from the CRS meta fields and the re-evaluated Rio markers. We mark a project as overreported if the classifier predicts a lower Rio marker than reported. Second, we calculate the classifier's overreporting rate on the CARE data set. By comparing overreporting with the high-quality re-evaluation, we can estimate an error factor between the two annotation schemes in a Bayesian framework. Finally, we extrapolate to the complete CRS database and estimate overreporting rates for both annotation schemes.

3.3 Model Training and Model Selection

The WK data in the CRS provides us with text descriptions and the corresponding Rio markers (0, 1, 2 and 99), which we consider input and target of the classifier respectively. To find the best model, we test various language models with standard finetuning and in combination with a CNN architecture to find the best model. The CNN architecture follows (Kim, 2014) and comprises four 1D-convolutions with kernel sizes 3,4,5 and 6, with 100 filters each. The resulting vectors are max-pooled and projected by a linear layer onto the number of classes.

We conduct experiments with a RoBERTa (Liu et al., 2019) base model, a BERT (Devlin et al., 2019) base model and a distilled version of RoBERTa (Sanh et al., 2019) as published in the Hugging Face 'transformers' library (Wolf et al., 2020). We use the AdamW (Loshchilov and Hutter, 2019) optimizer with a learning rate of $5e$-6, a batch size of 32, 25 epochs, and check-pointing to restore the best model with regards to average macro F1 score. To ensure stability and quality, we test these hyper-parameters for all models with tenfold cross-validation to identify the best model. The results of the cross-validation experiments for all model combinations are shown in Table 1. We used one Tesla V100 32GB for these experiments, one tenfold cross-validation for one model combination (one row in Table 1) took around five hours to complete for BERT and RoBERTa, and around 2.5 h for the distilled RoBERTa. After ensuring an average performance, we randomly split the data 80/20 and train a model with the same parameters.[2]

As shown in Table 1, the combination of CNN and RoBERTa not only reaches the highest average scores in accuracy and macro F1, but also the lowest standard deviation in the tenfold cross-validation. This leads us to believe that this model will not only generalize well but also will less likely deviate from the performance, which is why we choose this model as our classifier. Table 2 shows detailed results for the final model per label. It shows that predicting the label 1 is most difficult. Label "99" can be predicted with an F1 value of around 83%. We follow the argumentation in Weikmans et al. (2017) and regard these predictions as Rio marker 0. The influence of these examples is negligible as, ultimately, 99 is predicted in only $< 0.04\%$ of the CRS in the end.

The Rio marker classification model is a proxy to identify overreported cases. We are interested in those cases where our classification algorithm differs from the reported Rio marker, specifically classifying lower than the reported value We define overreporting o of activity x as

$$\mathbf{o(x)} = \begin{cases} 1 & \text{if reported(x)} > \text{classifier(x)} \\ 0 & \text{otherwise} \end{cases} \tag{1}$$

This leads to three cases of overreporting: The classifier predicts 0 and the Rio marker reports 1 or 2, and the much harder case where Rio marker reports 2 and the classifier predicts 1.

3.4 CARE Data

We apply our classifier to the CARE data set and compare the findings to the manual CARE annotations. The set of examples in CARE data set are distinct from those in the WK data. We create an overreported flag for the CARE data by comparing the reported Rio marker to their re-evaluation markers using Equation (1). This marks 21.80% of the data as overreported. Our classifier predicts an overreporting rate of 54.14% on the same data, indicating a significant difference in the annotation schemes. WK annotations appear stricter, leading to higher rates of overreporting than the CARE re-evaluation.

[2]Code and final model will be made available upon publication to not jeopardize anonymity of the review.

		accuracy	macro P	R	F1
CNN	roBERTa-base	**89.81 ± 0.83**	**84.83 ± 2.0**	80.54 ± 2.03	**82.31 ± 1.8**
	BERT	88.89 ± 1.3	83.35 ± 2.13	79.64 ± 2.81	80.97 ± 2.28
	distilroberta	89.16 ± 1.3	83.47 ± 2.24	**81.28 ± 2.96**	82.12 ± 2.21
Transformer	RoBERTa-base	89.64 ± 1.61	84.1 ± 2.33	80.58 ± 3.74	82.0 ± 2.87
	BERT	89.27 ± 1.5	84.57 ± 3.39	79.59 ± 2.41	81.52 ± 2.36
	distilroberta	89.14 ± 1.19	83.93 ± 2.76	79.47 ± 1.98	81.35 ± 1.93

Table 1: Aggregated results of the tenfold cross-validation for all tested models. Best results for each metric are highlighted in bold.

	F1	P	R
0	94.17 ± 0.64	92.83 ± 1.13	95.57 ± 0.95
1	59.62 ± 7.28	64.68 ± 9.55	56.15 ± 8.38
2	86.74 ± 2.09	86.11 ± 4.2	87.52 ± 2.02
99	88.72 ± 3.09	95.69 ± 4.19	82.94 ± 5.04

Table 2: Detailed per-class results of the cross-validation for the chosen model (CNN + RoBERTa).

3.5 Extrapolation of CARE Annotation using the Bayesian Formula

Using the Bayesian formula, we estimate the difference in annotation scheme and extrapolate it. As discussed above, our training relies on the WK data set. The approach of training and classifying new data ultimately transfers their annotation scheme to other data sets. Given the high number of hand-coded aid activities, the WK data set is well suited for training purposes. However, comparing the resulting classification with CARE data, we find that this might overestimate overreporting. We estimate the probability that if the classifier would mark any sample as overreported according to the WK data annotations, CARE annotations would agree, and vice versa. Using the Bayesian formula, we update the estimation of our classification. In mathematical formulation we define two events: W (classifier marks sample as overreported) and C (CARE annotates sample as overreported). We further denote the data set from which we calculate the corresponding term as the parameter D. The Bayesian formula is then:

$$P(C; D{=}\text{CRS}) = \frac{P(C|W; D{=}\text{CARE})}{P(W|C; D{=}\text{CARE})} \cdot P(W; D{=}\text{CRS}) \tag{2}$$

We note that this Bayesian formulation makes implicit assumptions about the independence of annotation schemes and data samples. We argue that since the CRS data is the basis for all of these samples, that these simplifications are acceptable and lead to a simple model to show the potential and benefits of this approach. We plan to investigate and apply more complex models to these dependencies in future work.

We calculate $P(W|C)$, i.e. the probability that our classifier would agree with CARE, and $P(C|W)$, i.e. the probability that CARE would agree with our classifier, from the CARE data set. Since the calculation is based on a small sample, we consider the uncertainty of the estimate using the beta distribution to approximate the factors and simulate the propagation of these uncertainties:

$$P(W|C) \propto \text{beta}(1+n, 1+m), \tag{3}$$

where n is the number of positive examples and m the number of negative examples in the data. We then report the credible interval of 95%. This leads to the correction factor

$$\frac{P(C|W)}{P(W|C)} = 42.57\% \,([26.47\%; 64.39\%]) \quad . \tag{4}$$

We denote the credible interval of 95% in brackets behind the point estimate. Using the same procedure, we propagate the correction factor to adjust the overall overreporting rate using Equation (2).

3.6 Extrapolation and Exploration

We can now apply the classification algorithm to the CRS data. We restrict the CRS to projects that have a Rio marker higher than 0, otherwise, by definition, they cannot be overreported in Equation (1) and we consider only at the top five DAC donors: France, Germany, Japan, the United Kingdom and the United States. We use the fastText (Joulin et al., 2017) language detection to classify the language of the descriptions. While Germany, Japan, the United Kingdom and the United States report almost all their projects in English, France tends to report in French. The classifier was also trained on French descriptions from the WK set, however, we predict Rio markers for these projects using both the original French descriptions and also automated translations into English using Google Translate (the influence of which is discussed below). After that, the data set contains 46,280 projects from 2010 to 2019 with short and long textual descriptions and a reported Rio marker of 1 or 2. This also complies with how data was sampled in the WK and the CARE data sets.

Figure 1 shows the results of the extrapolation. Table 5 in Appendix A shows the underlying values and the number of observations. Extrapolation is done, again, by concatenating the project title and long description into a text string and feeding it into the network. The network assigns a Rio marker prediction to every project. After that we use Equation (1) to mark all activities with a flag for overreporting. The classifier detects an overall overreporting rate of **75.35 %** in the CRS in terms of WK annotations and an estimated $\mathbf{32.03}\%$ ($[\mathbf{19.81}\%; \mathbf{48.34}\%]$) in terms of CARE annotation.

3.7 The Influence of Input Length

Systematic variation of text length by donor or year might bias our results. Longer descriptions usually contain more information and thus improve the validity of the classification. Elaborating on the difficulty of classifying short texts is beyond the scope of this paper and is its own established field of research, e.g. (Chen et al., 2019; Wang et al., 2017). This should specifically pertain to cases where CCA is a 'significant' but not a 'principal' objective (i.e., $r = 1$). Here, descriptions might not mention CCA because it is not the main motivation of the aid activity. Moreover, it seems likely that very short descriptions are mostly classified as $r = 0$ for lack of information.

We find evidence that classification quality correlates with description length. As we do not know the true Rio marker for aid activities, we use the rate of agreement between our classification and the assigned Rio marker as an indicator of classification quality. We assume that very low rates of agreement indicate poor performance of classification. As Figure 2 shows, the share of cases where classification results and Rio marker are identical increases with description length.

Description lengths systematically differ by donor and year (for both: p < 0.00, Kruskal-Wallis rank sum test), although the distribution of description lengths across donors and years shows that, overall, absolute differences are not large. Regarding donors, Japan is an exception, with considerably shorter descriptions than the median of the other donors (78 vs. 315 characters, respectively). The time series shows an increasing trend where the median of description length increased from 231 to 345 characters between 2010 and 2019 (see also Appendix B, Figure 4). If classification quality depends on description lengths, and description lengths vary by donor and year, this could introduce confounding bias distorting the comparison of overreporting rates across years and donors. More specifically, an increase in description lengths could be interpreted erroneously as a decrease in overreporting. As an example, Japan's high rates of overreporting (see Figure 3) could be partly explained by the brevity of aid descriptions in the CRS.

To account for possible distortion of our results, we rerun our analysis excluding short descriptions from our estimation of overreporting. We used the interquartile range (IQR) method to identify outliers (Ilyas and Chu, 2019, p. 12), i.e. we excluded descriptions with lengths below the threshold of $Q1 - 1.5 \times IQR$ (in our case, 62 characters; logarithmic: 4.1). This seems appropriate as indicated by an increase in agreement between Rio marker and classifier (see Figure 2).

We rerun the analysis that created Table 5, but excluded all projects with fewer than 62 characters. We also excluded from the CARE data set data points shorter than 62 characters, when calculating the correction factor. A comparison of the results is presented in Figure 1. The overall overreporting rate per year drops slightly, while the estimation based on CARE increases. This stems from the fact that the classifier agrees with the high-quality CARE re-evaluation more often for longer texts. The correction factor and uncertainty in this case slightly increases from 42.57% ([26.47%; 64.39%]) to 44.32% ([27.55%; 66.62%]).Overall this leads to slightly lower overreporting rate according to WK but a slightly higher estimate for CARE-corrected overreporting.

In summary, we do find evidence that systematic variation of text length by donor or year can bias results. However, robustness tests indicate that the bias does not change overall conclusions.

3.8 Extrapolation Per Donor Per Year

The values in Table 3 show overreporting as identified by the classifier based on the WK data set from

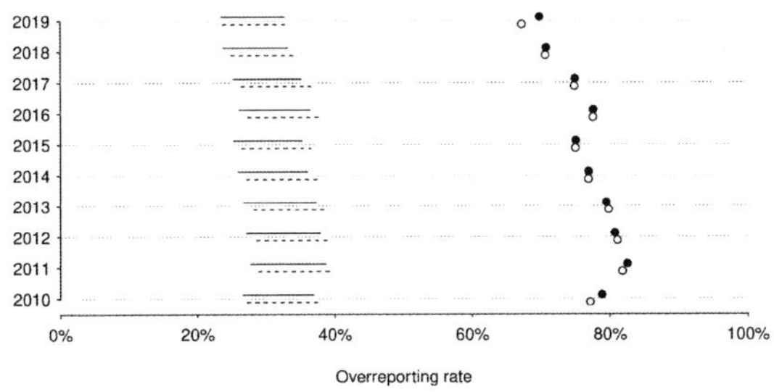

Figure 1: Estimated overreporting rate extrapolation of WK data by year (dots) and estimated correction based on CARE data (lines). Black dots and solid lines show estimates based on the full sample. Hollow circles and dashed lines show estimates based on samples excluding very short descriptions.

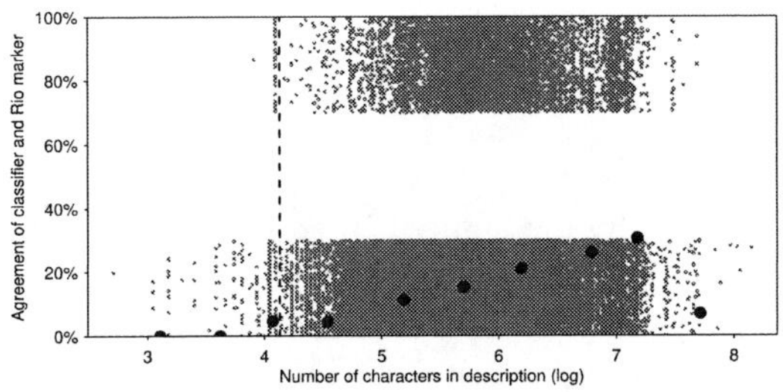

Figure 2: Agreement of classifier with Rio marker by lengths of activity description. Random noise is added to the point locations in the y-direction for better visibility. Circles show averages of binned data. The vertical dotted line indicates the cut-off for outliers based on the IQR method for outliers.

2010 to 2019. France had the lowest number of projects in CRS reported with at least Rio marker 1 in 2011 and 2012 with 84 and 114 projects respectively. The rates in Table 3 for 2012 coincide rather well with the findings in (Weikmans et al., 2017) for Germany (81%), Japan (92%) and the United Kingdom (82%). The United States was not part of the sample in (Weikmans et al., 2017).

The classifier detects significantly lower overreporting rates for France (76.32%) than in the original paper (92%) in 2012. We found that, of the 114 projects reported in 2012 by France, only 58 have unique descriptions, which produces very high uncertainty. Manual evaluation shows that there are cases of the same description occurring up to 11 times and is marked as not overreported. This alone can account for around a 10% difference in overreporting measure when classified differently. We therefore marked the fields where there are a fewer data points than 500 in orange in Table 3 to show

Year	France	Germany	Japan	U.K.	U.S.
2010	74.8%	74.66%	78.99%	73.11%	90.09%
2011	88.1%	84.16%	79.94%	71.95%	87.63%
2012	76.32%	77.52%	90.68%	74.47%	85.76%
2013	90.87%	74.57%	91.75%	69.9%	84.17%
2014	82.61%	75.3%	89.36%	56.46%	83.07%
2015	90.66%	74.78%	89.62%	58.52%	78.43%
2016	96.46%	74.41%	88.8%	55.26%	81.68%
2017	97.91%	72.92%	92.15%	49.76%	79.27%
2018	95.87%	72.04%	92.62%	41.12%	74.44%
2019	94.31%	69.23%	94.28%	45.61%	69.01%

Table 3: Overreporting rates - extrapolation of WK data split by donor country. Note that colored cells have fewer than 500 data points. Darker color corresponds to fewer data points.

where these effects could have larger impact.

Figure 3 also shows the classification results when translating the French descriptions to English (dotted line). There are significant differences in overreporting rates in the period 2013-2015, while the two lines are reasonably close between 2016 and 2019. The year 2014 in particular shows a difference of around 50%, from 33.7% in the translated case to 82.6% when using the original French descriptions. We argue that this happens for two reasons: First, the years with the biggest differences when translating descriptions coincide with the years when very few projects reported, thus the influence of a single misclassification is higher. Second, there is considerable noise in the data, which further increases variance in prediction when switching language.

In 2014, France reported 184 projects, but there are only 53 unique descriptions. The most frequent description was used 36 times, each of the occurrences having a unique ID in the CRS. Half of these 36 projects are reported with a Rio marker 1 and half with Rio marker 2. Every classifier predicting a Rio marker on the basis of these descriptions will therefore differ from the reported value at least half the time. This alone accounts for a difference in overreporting of 10% in that year. This argument also holds for the second and third most frequent project descriptions, which were used 19 and 18 times respectively. When considering only the unique descriptions, the predictions' detection of overreporting in English and French agree in 77% of cases, while only in 51% of cases overall. In general, the larger the number of projects, the smaller the influence of this phenomenon. However, of the projects that France reported, only around 40% of the descriptions are unique (see Table 4 for more details).

Year	Over-reported	Over-reported (translated)	Count	Unique	Unique (relative)
2010	74.80%	81.71%	246	133	54.07%
2011	88.10%	82.14%	84	80	95.24%
2012	76.32%	64.04%	114	57	50.00%
2013	90.87%	66.54%	263	186	70.72%
2014	82.61%	33.70%	184	53	28.80%
2015	90.66%	66.54%	257	89	34.63%
2016	96.46%	95.29%	594	171	28.79%
2017	97.91%	94.91%	1100	477	43.36%
2018	95.87%	93.74%	847	372	43.92%
2019	94.31%	86.91%	1054	669	63.47%

Table 4: Overreporting for France following the WK data set by years. The second and third columns denote the estimated overreporting rate for French descriptions and English translations, respectively. The following columns show: number of projects, number of unique descriptions, and the ratio of these two.

4 Discussion

Our re-evaluation of aid activities reported as contributing to CCA indicates a lack of quality in the self-reporting of donors. A substantial share of reported adaptation aid activities does not explicitly mention CCA in project descriptions. This is problematic because valid indicators are required to assess whether the international community is meeting its climate policy obligations as described in, for example the Paris Accord. Our finding indicates an overestimation of adaptation aid. Even after downward adjustment of our estimates to account for insufficient information from short project descriptions, our best estimate suggests that about every third activity categorized by donors as adaptation aid is not adaptation related. However, we cannot say whether this is due to a lack of clear reporting standards (Weikmans et al., 2020), a lack of compliance with reporting standards, or even incentives to report more than is actually delivered (Michaelowa and Michaelowa, 2011). Moreover, our estimates are subject to considerable uncertainty because an unambiguous classification of aid activities based on the Rio Marker methodology requires extensive knowledge of individual aid activities.

Although the estimates are somewhat uncertain, our results confirm earlier findings of a substantial discrepancy between the figures reported by donors and re-evaluations by independent researchers (Michaelowa and Michaelowa, 2011; Weikmans et al., 2017; Junghans and Harmeling, 2012; Schramek and Harmeling, 2021). This can be partly explained by the fact that our approach draws on earlier classifications as training data and is thus not completely independent. However, our study also goes well beyond existing research in temporal and geographical scope: We assess every adaptation aid activity reported by OECD DAC donors since the Rio marker on adaptation aid was introduced in 2010. If donors had changed their reporting practice, we would likely see this in our data, yet, overall, we find no indication that reporting practices have changed significantly since 2010. The share of overreporting remains at a high level between 2010 and 2019. Although the classifier indicates a slight decrease of overreporting, the fluctuations are within the range of uncertainty of our adjusted estimates. Nevertheless, the results are mainly driven by a significant decrease in overreporting by the United Kingdom. However, we are careful to infer from our data substantial differences in reporting standards between countries; Country-specific results should be examined more closely in future research. We have no reason to suspect that the classifier has particular problems with data reported by the UK based on the results of the cross-validation and given the fact that most project descriptions are in English.

5 Conclusion

In this paper we propose an automated way of detecting overreporting of climate adaptation finance based on CRS project descriptions. Our approach is based on state-of-the-art text classification using finetuning neural language models. We consider the quality of the annotations of our training data when estimating overall overreporting rates, and propose a Bayesian approach to estimate an extrapolation of high-quality annotations. Our approach indicates significant overreporting throughout the study period.

There are two key challenges with this approach: The quality and quantity of annotation scheme data, and the quality of the textual input. While, ultimately, the first challenge can be overcome by extending data with higher-quality annotations, the second proves trickier. Unfortunately, the CRS data does not have uniform quality built into its textual descriptions. We have discussed the influence of description length and language on the quality of our

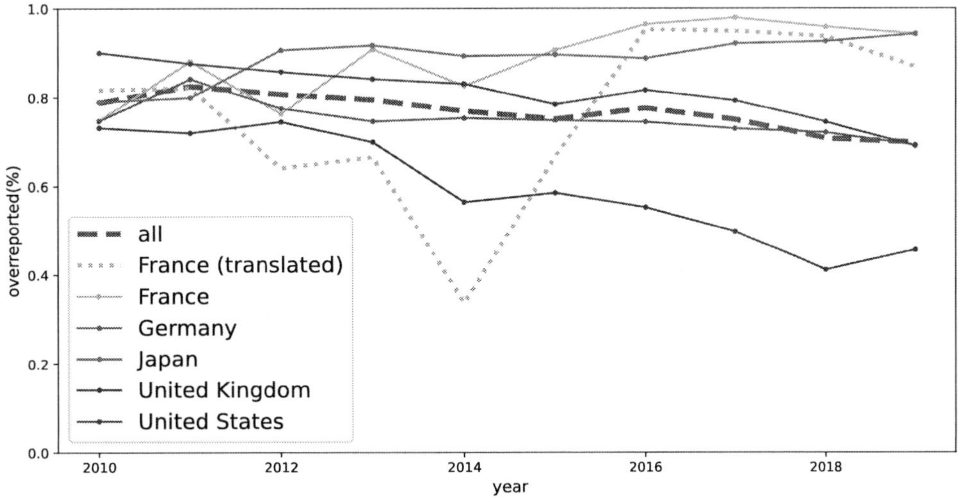

Figure 3: Rates of overreporting by donor country, 2010 to 2019

classifier, but while future work may incorporate techniques from short-text classification research, in many cases the information the CRS contains will likely not suffice to use techniques like augmentation or conceptualization. To improve on this, additional external data would be necessary, to which, at this point, we had no access. Especially deciding if the CCA aspects of a project comprises a "significant" or "principal" object should benefit from this. Another way to improve would be to pay more attention to multi lingual classification research and either incorporate techniques for multi lingual text classification or utilize a high-quality pipeline for translation.

References

Rami Aly, Steffen Remus, and Chris Biemann. 2019. Hierarchical Multi-label Classification of Text with Capsule Networks. In *Proceedings of the 57th Annual Meeting of the Association for Computational Linguistics: Student Research Workshop*, pages 323–330, Florence, Italy. Association of Computational Linguistics.

Jindong Chen, Yizhou Hu, Jingping Liu, Yanghua Xiao, and Haiyun Jiang. 2019. Deep short text classification with knowledge powered attention. *Computing Research Repository*, arxiv:1902.08050.

Jacob Devlin, Ming-Wei Chang, Kenton Lee, and Kristina Toutanova. 2019. BERT: Pre-training of deep bidirectional transformers for language understanding. In *Proceedings of the 2019 Conference of the North American Chapter of the Association for Computational Linguistics: Human Language Technologies, Volume 1 (Long and Short Papers)*, pages 4171–4186. Association for Computational Linguistics.

Kishaloy Halder, Alan Akbik, Josip Krapac, and Roland Vollgraf. 2020. Task-aware representation of sentences for generic text classification. In *Proceedings of the 28th International Conference on Computational Linguistics*, pages 3202–3213, Barcelona, Spain (Online). International Committee on Computational Linguistics.

Ihab F. Ilyas and Xu Chu. 2019. *Data cleaning*, 1st edition. Number 28 in ACM Books. Association for Computing Machinery.

Armand Joulin, Edouard Grave, Piotr Bojanowski, and Tomas Mikolov. 2017. Bag of tricks for efficient text classification. In *Proceedings of the 15th Conference of the European Chapter of the Association for Computational Linguistics: Short Papers*, volume 2, pages 427–431, Valencia, Spain. Association for Computational Linguistics.

Lisa Junghans and Sven Harmeling. 2012. Different tales from different countries: A first assessment of the oecd 'adaptation marker'. *Germanwatch Briefing Paper*. (Accessed 2022-01-07).

Yoon Kim. 2014. Convolutional Neural Networks for Sentence Classification. In *Proceedings of the 2014 Conference on Empirical Methods in Natural Language Processing (EMNLP)*, pages 1746–1751, Doha, Qatar. Association for Computational Linguistics.

Yinhan Liu, Myle Ott, Naman Goyal, Jingfei Du, Mandar Joshi, Danqi Chen, Omer Levy, M. Lewis, Luke Zettlemoyer, and Veselin Stoyanov. 2019. Roberta:

A robustly optimized bert pretraining approach. *Computing Research Repository*, arxiv:1907.11692.

Ilya Loshchilov and Frank Hutter. 2019. Decoupled weight decay regularization. In *International Conference on Learning Representations (ICLR)*.

Axel Michaelowa and Katharina Michaelowa. 2011. Coding error or statistical embellishment? the political economy of reporting climate aid. *World Development*, 39.

Aditi Mukherji, Peter Thorne, William W L Cheung, Sarah L Connors, Matthias Garschagen, Oliver Geden, Bronwyn Hayward, Nicholas P Simpson, Edmond Totin, Kornelis Blok, Siri Eriksen, Erich Fischer, Gregory Garner, Céline Guivarch, Marjolijn Haasnoot, Tim Hermans, Debora Ley, Jared Lewis, Zebedee Nicholls, Leila Niamir, Sophie Szopa, Blair Trewin, Mark Howden, Carlos Méndez, Joy Pereira, Ramón Pichs, Steven K Rose, Yamina Saheb, Roberto Sánchez, Cunde Xiao, and Noureddine Yassaa. 2023. SYNTHESIS REPORT OF THE IPCC SIXTH ASSESSMENT REPORT (AR6). SYNTHESIS REPORT (AR6), The Intergovernmental Panel on Climate Change (IPCC).

OECD DAC. 2022. OECD DAC Rio Markers for Climate: Handbook. (Accessed 2022-01-07).

Ankit Pal, Muru Selvakumar, and Malaikannan Sankarasubbu. 2020. Magnet: Multi-label text classification using attention-based graph neural network. *Proceedings of the 12th International Conference on Agents and Artificial Intelligence*.

Arnaud Pincet, Shu Okabe, and Martin Pawelczyk. 2019. Linking Aid to the Sustainable Development Goals – a machine learning approach. OECD Development Co-operation Working Papers 52, OECD Publishing.

Brad Plumer. 2023. Climate change is speeding toward catastrophe. the next decade is crucial, u.n. panel says. New york times (accessed 2023-03-23). Section: Climate.

J. Timmons Roberts, Kara Starr, Thomas Jones, and Dinah Abdel-Fattah. 2008. The Reality of Official Climate Aid. (Accessed 2022-07-01).

Victor Sanh, Lysandre Debut, Julien Chaumond, and Thomas Wolf. 2019. Distilbert, a distilled version of bert: smaller, faster, cheaper and lighter. In *The 5th Workshop on Energy Efficient Machine Learning and Cognitive Computing (NeurIPS)*.

Camilla Schramek and Sven Harmeling. 2021. Adaptation finance : Fact or fiction ? (Accessed 2022-01-07).

Massimo Tavoni. 2023. Computational climate change: How data science and numerical models can help build good climate policies and practices. In Eleonora Bertoni, Matteo Fontana, Lorenzo Gabrielli, Serena Signorelli, and Michele Vespe, editors, *Handbook of Computational Social Science for Policy*, pages 261–277. Springer International Publishing.

Malte Toetzke, Anna Stünzi, and Florian Egli. 2022. Consistent and replicable estimation of bilateral climate finance. *Nature Climate Change*, 12(10):897–900. Number: 10 Publisher: Nature Publishing Group.

Jin Wang, Zhongyuan Wang, Dawei Zhang, and Jun Yan. 2017. Combining knowledge with deep convolutional neural networks for short text classification. In *International Joint Conference on Artificial Intelligence (IJCAI)*.

Romain Weikmans and J. Timmons Roberts. 2019. The International Climate Finance Accounting Muddle: Is There Hope on the Horizon? *Climate and Development*, 11(2):97–111.

Romain Weikmans, J. Timmons Roberts, J. Baum, María Camila Bustos, and Alexis Durand. 2017. Assessing the credibility of how climate adaptation aid projects are categorised. *Development in Practice*, 27:458 – 471.

Romain Weikmans, J. Timmons Roberts, and Stacy-Ann Robinson. 2020. What counts as climate finance? Define urgently. *Nature*, 588(7837).

Thomas Wolf, Lysandre Debut, Victor Sanh, Julien Chaumond, Clement Delangue, Anthony Moi, Pierric Cistac, Tim Rault, Rémi Louf, Morgan Funtowicz, Joe Davison, Sam Shleifer, Patrick von Platen, Clara Ma, Yacine Jernite, Julien Plu, Canwen Xu, Teven Le Scao, Sylvain Gugger, Mariama Drame, Quentin Lhoest, and Alexander M. Rush. 2020. Transformers: State-of-the-art natural language processing. In *Proceedings of the 2020 Conference on Empirical Methods in Natural Language Processing: System Demonstrations*, pages 38–45. Association for Computational Linguistics.

Zhilin Yang, Zihang Dai, Yiming Yang, Jaime G. Carbonell, Ruslan Salakhutdinov, and Quoc V. Le. 2019. XLNet: Generalized Autoregressive Pretraining for Language Understanding. In *Advances in Neural Information Processing Systems 32: Annual Conference on Neural Information Processing Systems (NeurIPS)*, pages 5754–5764.

Sophie Yeo. 2019. Climate Finance: The Money Trail. *Nature*, 573:328–331.

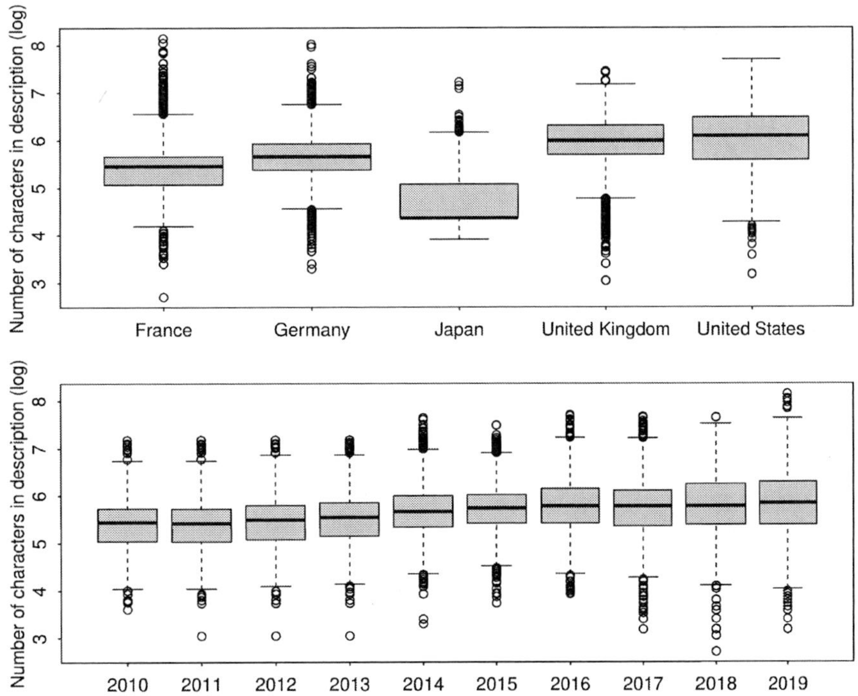

Figure 4: Activity description lengths (logarithmic) by donor (top figure) and by years (bottom figure).

year	Classifier	CARE Estimated	count
2010	77.06%	20.31 – 49.46%	1683%
2011	81.76%	21.55 – 52.48%	3076%
2012	81.0%	21.35 – 51.99%	2858%
2013	79.75%	21.02 – 51.18%	3698%
2014	76.79%	20.24 – 49.28%	3739%
2015	74.91%	19.75 – 48.08%	4308%
2016	77.49%	20.43 – 49.73%	5300%
2017	74.78%	19.71 – 48.0%	7284%
2018	70.5%	18.58 – 45.25%	6631%
2019	66.99%	17.66 – 43.0%	7111%

Table 5: Overreporting rates - extrapolation of WK data and the estimated correction of CARE data.

year	Classifier	CARE Estimated	count
2010	77.12%	27.22 – 37.61%	1683
2011	81.83%	28.88 – 39.9%	3076
2012	81.11%	28.62 – 39.55%	2858
2013	79.83%	28.17 – 38.93%	3698
2014	76.89%	27.14 – 37.5%	3739
2015	75.0%	26.47 – 36.57%	4308
2016	77.55%	27.37 – 37.82%	5300
2017	74.86%	26.42 – 36.51%	7284
2018	70.65%	24.93 – 34.46%	6631
2019	67.22%	23.72 – 32.78%	7111

Table 6: Overreporting rates - extrapolation of WK data and the estimated correction of CARE data after eliminating all inputs with fewer than 62 characters.

A Overreporting per Year

Tables 5 and 6 show detailed numerical results on estimating overreporting split by year. These two tables were summarized in Figure 3, comparing the resulting rates.

B Analysis of Text Length

Figure 4 illustrates increasing average descriptions lengths over the study period in a standard box plot, for the argument in section 3.7. Also, Japan tends to use fewer characters in descriptions compared to the other donors. This supplements Figure 2 and informs the decision to use the *IQR* range to quantify the lower limit for the number of characters. This also checks that cutting off at 62 characters (logarithmic: 4.1) does not introduce a bias for a particular year or donor.

"Who is the Madonna of Italian-American Literature?": Extracting and Analyzing Target Entities of Vossian Antonomasia

Michel Schwab[1], **Robert Jäschke**[1,2] **and Frank Fischer**[3]
[1]Humboldt-Universität zu Berlin, Germany
[2]L3S Research Center, Hannover, Germany
[3]Freie Universität Berlin, Germany
{michel.schwab,robert.jaeschke}@hu-berlin.de
fr.fischer@fu-berlin.de

Abstract

In this paper, we present approaches for the automated extraction and disambiguation of a part of the stylistic device Vossian Antonomasia (VA), namely the target entity described by the expression. We model the problem as a coreference resolution and a question answering task and also combine both. To tackle the tasks at hand, we utilize state-of-the-art models in these areas. In addition, we visualize the connection between source and target entities of VA in a web demo to provide a deeper understanding of their mutual relationship.

1 Introduction

Vossian Antonomasia (or *VA* for short) is a popular stylistic device used to describe an entity by refering to another entity, typically in a witty and resourceful way. Structure-wise, a VA expression consists of three parts: target (trg), source (src), and modifier (mod). The combination of source and modifier is used to describe the target. Take, for instance, the sentence "It is the Madonna of Italian-American literature in that it shows the transition from the Italian immigrant to American citizen like no other book of its genre." (NYT 1991/08/07/1128838).[1] The author uses "Madonna", the popular American singer, as source and transfers a set of characteristics of Madonna to the target, Helen Barolini's novel "Umbertina". The modifier "Italian-American literature" projects these characteristics onto the target.

In general, the source consists of a universally known, famous named entity, from which one or more typical traits or characteristics are to be invoked. The target, on the other hand, does not necessarily have to be a named entity (e.g., "Rally$_{\mathtt{trg}}$ car$_{\mathtt{trg}}$ racing$_{\mathtt{trg}}$ is the David$_{\mathtt{src}}$ Hasselhoff$_{\mathtt{src}}$ of motor$_{\mathtt{mod}}$ sports$_{\mathtt{mod}}$" (NYT 2006/08/02/1780256)). It is also possible that no specific target is meant, in which case the VA expression would be hypothetical, for instance, "We're waiting for the Raffi$_{\mathtt{src}}$ of our$_{\mathtt{mod}}$ industry$_{\mathtt{mod}}$." (NYT 1989/06/11/0257799), or there is a target, but it is not explicitly mentioned in the article content.

The task of extracting VA expressions focusing on source and modifier has already been covered (Fischer and Jäschke, 2019; Schwab et al., 2019, 2022). The models are also able to identify a reference of the target inside a sentence where source and modifier appear, but in most cases, these references are in the form of pronouns or other mentions of the entity that cannot be linked to a knowledge base for disambiguation. To the best of our knowledge, there exists no method for extracting the target entity from texts. As the phrase consisting of source and modifier, such as "the Madonna of Italian-American literature", is a specific mention of the target entity ("Umbertina"), it should appear in the reference chain of the target when using coreference resolution. However, as we will later show, coreference resolution often fails to detect these complex mentions.

For a deeper understanding of VA expressions and their meaning, the target entity is an essential part. We need to identify it to comprehend the transferred characteristics. After its identification, we can compute VA chains where the source of one VA expression is the target of another to track the transfer of characteristics across multiple entities and also analyze the assignments of characteristics to entities. Thus, in this paper, we tackle two tasks:

Target extraction: The automatic extraction of the full name of the target entity inside a text.

Target Linking: Disambiguation and linking to Wikidata.

In addition, we visualize the results in a web demo for exploration and visualization.[2]

[1]To avoid an excessively long reference list, all examples taken from the New York Times corpus (Sandhaus, 2008) are cited using the pattern "NYT year/month/day/article-id".

[2]`https://vossanto.weltliteratur.net/sighum2023/`

Proceedings of the 7th Joint SIGHUM Workshop on Computational Linguistics for Cultural Heritage, Social Sciences, Humanities and Literature (LaTeCH-CLfL2023), pages 110–115

Our annotated data (Schwab et al., 2023) and code are freely available.[2]

2 Related work

The detection and extraction of VA has recently been worked on. While Jäschke et al. (2017); Fischer and Jäschke (2019) used semi-automated approaches to detect VA expressions, Schwab et al. (2019) developed the first automated approach for the detection of VA expressions on the sentence-level. They developed a finer extraction approach on the word-level (Schwab et al., 2022). In particular, they employed pre-trained contextual language models, for instance, BERT (Devlin et al., 2019), and fine-tuned them on an annotated dataset modeling the problem as a sequence tagging task. However, all models lack the ability to identify the target entity within the article.

The automated detection and extraction of other stylistic devices, such as metaphors, has been covered widely. The extraction of VA expressions consisting of source and modifier is closely related to metaphor detection. However, our focus is on the extraction of the target entity, so we do not consider such related work.

3 Annotation and Methods

3.1 Dataset and Annotation

We use the dataset from Schwab et al. (2022), which is an annotated VA dataset on the word-level. The dataset consists of 5,995 sentences, of which 3,066 contain VA expressions and 2,929 do not. In this paper, we focus only on sentences containing VA expressions. The dataset originally emerged from Schwab et al. (2019) who used nine syntactic patterns to identify VA candidates focusing on the syntax around the source entity. Those candidates were extracted from The New York Times Annotated Corpus (Sandhaus, 2008) which contains more than 1.8 million newspaper articles from the years 1987 to 2007. Thus, the syntax around the source of each VA expression in the dataset consist of one of the nine following variations: "a/an/the SOURCE of/for/among MODIFIER" (e.g., "the Madonna$_{\mathsf{src}}$of Italian-American$_{\mathsf{mod}}$literature$_{\mathsf{mod}}$"), which we refer to as "VA phrase" in the sequel.

The target annotation in this dataset is limited to a reference within the sentence where the VA phrase appears, which mostly does not include the target's name but pronouns (e.g., "she"), other denotations (e.g., "the president"), or which does not exist at all.

Sentences in the dataset may include multiple VA expressions. In order to separate them, we created copies of such sentences for each VA expression with just one annotation resulting in 3,115 sentences. Two trained students annotated all target names inside each NYT article containing a VA expression from the dataset by Schwab et al. (2022). Specifically, the annotators took a closer look at the article in which the sentence occurred and extracted the name of the entity to which the VA expression referred. In other words, they conducted coreference resolution modeling the VA expression as one reference of the target. In addition, they linked the marked entity to the corresponding Wikidata entity, if available, and extracted the Wikidata ID. This resulted in an inter-annotator agreement calculated by Cohen's Kappa of 0.96 (annotation) and 1.0 (linking), measured on a sample of 500 randomly selected sentences in the dataset. Disagreements were discussed and then re-annotated. In 2,853 (91.6%) of the cases, there existed a target name. In all other examples, there was no mention of the target and therefore we omit these cases for our study. In 2,354 (75.6%) of the cases, the annotators were able to link the name to the corresponding Wikidata entity. The absence of Wikidata entries for the remaining target entities could be due to a lack of prominence or relevance.

3.2 Coreference Resolution (COREF)

In our annotated dataset, there exist two references to the target entity: The first is the VA phrase itself (e.g., "the Madonna of Italian-American Literature") as explained previously. The second is the mention of the target inside the same sentence as the VA phrase. Schwab et al. (2022) annotated the mention (e.g., "It", "Mr. Woods"), if it existed and their models are able to identify this reference together with the source and modifier within a sentence. Both expressions should be part of the reference chain of the target entity.

Thus, the obvious choice to tackle the problem of extracting the target entity is coreference resolution as it is already well-studied. Because of this, we will use the coreference resolution model as baseline.

Modern coreference resolution systems show strong results but lack the size of the input document. To tackle this problem, Beltagy et al. (2020) introduced Longformer, pre-trained language models that are able to handle input documents with up to 4,096 tokens. Toshniwal et al. (2021) picked up this idea and used the Longformer model as a base for their coreference resolution model which showed state-of-the-art results for a variety of datasets. Therefore, we will use this model to perform coreference resolution on the entire article text and create two baselines. In the first one, we select the reference chain that includes the VA phrase, whereas in the second, we choose the chain of the annotated target mention. As our task is to find the full target name rather than the reference chain including the name, we need to choose a mention from the chain as output. To do this, we utilize a named entity tagger, specifically the NER model from Akbik et al. (2018). The tagger identifies all named entities that appear in the reference chain. We then select the first named entity that emerges in the chain, based on the assumption that authors usually introduce named entities with their complete names in article texts.

$\mathbf{LF}_{\{p,t\}}$: We use the joint model from Toshniwal et al. (2021), which is fine-tuned for coreference resolution over a mixture of datasets (OntoNotes, LitBank, and PreCo). LF_p refers to the model that focuses on the reference chain of the VA phrase, LF_t concentrates on the chain that includes the target mention.

3.3 Question Answering (QA)

Coreference resolution is one way to tackle the problem. However, as we do not look for the complete reference chain but only for the name of the entity, coreference resolution is not needed after all. Another way to solve the problem is to re-formulate the task as an extractive question answering problem by using the advantage of the annotated VA phrase within the sentence. Since the VA phrases are syntactically similar (see Sec. 3.1), we use them to formulate the query: "Who is the/a/an SOURCE of/for/among MODIFIER?". For the task of extractive question answering, we need to give the model a context text to extract the answer from.

In one scenario, we use the complete article content the VA expression appears in as context. In another scenario, we only use the content before the sentence that includes the VA expression together with the sentence itself and the subsequent 200 characters. In a preliminary analysis, we found that the target entity is typically mentioned earlier in the article, thus the noise of the rest of the article may decrease the performance of the model. Still, in some cases, the target entity is mentioned shortly after the VA expression. Thus, we include 200 characters after the sentence with the VA phrase which covers more than 98% of all cases.

Similar to coreference resolution, QA is a widely studied task. Therefore, instead of training a new model, we use a state-of-the-art fine-tuned language model, namely the one from Clark et al. (2020). The problem of the length of our documents (articles) is tackled by a sliding window approach.

$\mathbf{ELE}_{\{c,\,s\}}$: We employ the ELECTRA large model that is fine-tuned on the SQuAD2.0 dataset using both context scenarios. ELE_c refers to the complete context, ELE_s to the short context scenario.

3.4 Hybrid Approach

In a third approach, we combine both methods, using QA first and coreference resolution on top of it. In some cases, the QA models return an answer which is not the full target name but only another reference of the target entity, for instance, "Mrs. Merkel" instead of "Angela Merkel". This is not a correct output for our task. Thus, we apply coreference resolution on the QA output to get the entire reference chain. As in the baselines, we identify all named entities in the selected chain. Then, we leverage the QA output and choose the longest named entity (in terms of characters) that shares at least one word with the QA output. For instance, if the QA output is "Mr. McCaw" and the named entities in the reference chain include "McCaw", "Craig O. McCaw" and "Mr. McCaw" (in this order), we select "Craig O. McCaw" as the output. This is because it shares a word ("McCaw") with the QA output and is longer than the other candidates that share at least one word ("McCaw", "Mr. McCaw"). In the baseline scenarios, "McCaw" would have been selected. This heuristic approach surpasses the performance of multiple fuzzy string matching algorithms, such as the Levenshtein distance (Levenshtein et al., 1966) and Jaro-Winkler similarity (Winkler, 1999).

ELE+LF: We concatenate both methods using ELE and LF.

3.5 Entity Linking (EL)

In a second step, we aim to disambiguate the entities found with the previous methods and link them to their corresponding Wikidata entries. For this, we employ GENRE (De Cao et al., 2021), a state-of-the-art entity linking approach. GENRE is a sequence-to-sequence model that is based on a fine-tuned BART architecture (Lewis et al., 2020) which links the given input entity to a Wikipedia entity using the surrounding context. In particular, it is a generation model that generates the output using constrained beam search. As each Wikipedia entry has a unique Wikidata entry, we can get the Wikidata ID of the Wikipedia entry using the MediaWiki Action API.[3] If the output of the extraction method is a reference chain, we conduct entity linking on each mention in the chain separately, skipping all pronouns. For the baselines, we select the prediction that appeared most frequently. For ELE_s+LF, we choose the prediction that shares the largest word overlap with the QA output. If predictions are equally frequent or share an equal number of overlapping tokens, we choose the prediction that is closest to the beginning of the text. Consider, for instance, the reference chain consisting of "Lomax", "Alan Lomax, the musicologist who evangelized folk music for most of the 20th century", "the Johnny Appleseed of folk revivalists", "Alan Lomax" and "Lomax" and the QA output "Alan Lomax". The EL predictions for the chain are "Alan Lomax", "Alan Lomax", "Johnny Appleseed", "Alan Lomax" and "John Lomax". The highest share of words between the QA output and the predictions is "Alan Lomax' which we take as output.

GEN: We use the entity disambiguation GENRE model that is pre-trained on the BLINK dataset and fine-tuned on the AIDA CoNLL-YAGO dataset.

4 Results

4.1 Evaluation

We use two different evaluation metrics in order to evaluate the target extraction models. The first metrics, namely precision, recall and F_1, are based on the overlapping tokens of prediction and ground truth. The second metric, exact match (em), measures the percentage of predictions that fully match the ground truth.

Additionally, we evaluate the entity linking model. For that, we use InKB micro precision (mp). Micro precision describes the share of correctly linked entities and InKB, which is introduced in Röder et al. (2018), means that we only consider entities that have a valid Wikidata entry.

[3] https://www.mediawiki.org/wiki/API:Main_page

	Extraction				Linking
model	prec	rec	f1	em	mp
LF_p	.29	.28	.29	.25	.21
LF_t	.58	.54	.56	.47	.46
ELE_c	.66	.62	.64	.52	.55
ELE_s	.74	.71	.72	.61	.62
ELE_s+LF	.78	.77	.78	.71	.64

Table 1: Performance of the three proposed approaches in comparison with the baselines ($LF_{\{p,t\}}$).

The results, presented in Table 1, demonstrate that the baselines are unable to solve this task effectively. In particular, LF_p shows that coreference resolution on the VA phrase does not work as expected. ELE_c has a significant gap in comparison to ELE_s, where we used our trick of truncating the context, across all metrics. The combined model, ELE_s+LF, outperforms all other models, especially in the em score by, a large margin.

While GEN has an upper limit of .84 (mp) on the annotated target names, a score of .64 is not necessarily poor. However, it does suggest that there is room for improvement and underscores the overall complexity of entity linking in general.

4.2 Error Analysis

$LF_{\{p,t\}}$: Most errors in the baselines occured because the selected reference chains did not include the full target name. In particular, only in 887 (31.0%) and 1,687 (58.4%) of the cases for LF_p and LF_t, respectively, the reference chain include the full target name. That shows the difficulty for the baseline models to achieve a better result. Additionally, finding the correct mention in the chain was challenging. Only in around 80% of all instances, the correct mention was chosen when the correct reference chain had been select before. This is because the first named entity in the reference chain is not always the full target name, e.g., when the VA phrase appeared in the reference chain before the full target name in the article.

ELE_s+LF: In our best approach, the correct reference chain was found in 72%. Choosing the correct mention in the reference chain worked well. Only in around 1% of all instances, our approach did not select the correct mention. Interestingly, ELE_s provided the correct answer in 1746 (61%) of the cases. In around 20% of all instances, it found a mention of the target entity where the correct name was in-

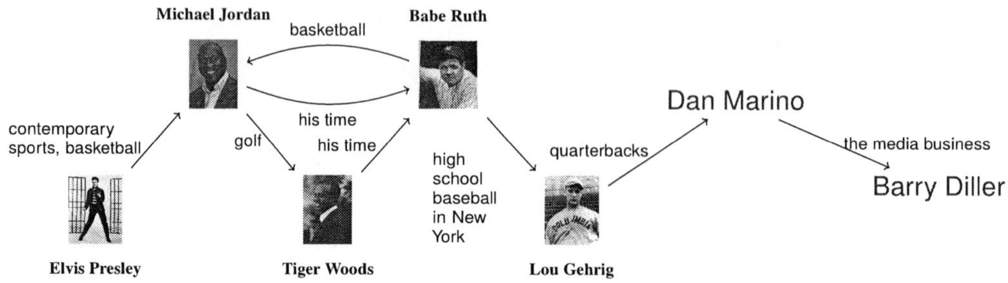

Figure 1: The longest VA chain in the dataset.

cluded, e.g. "Mr./Ms./Mrs./Dr. surname" or first names in direct speech, i.e. another reference of the target entity. Most of the other false predictions consisted of incorrect chosen entities.

In addition, we tested two hypotheses regarding the impact on the performance (em score) of the model using the Point-Biserial Correlation Coefficient as the em score is a binary label. The first hypothesis is whether there exists a negative correlation between the character-wise distance of the full target name and the VA phrase in the article text and the performance. The results show a weak negative correlation between the two variables (-0.131), and, with a p-value of 0.00, it is statistically significant. This result can be interpreted that the distance does have a slight negative effect on the model's performance. The second hypothesis examines whether the size of the reference chain that includes the full target name is important for the model's performance. We assumed that it might be easier for the model to predict the correct cluster if the target entity is an important figure in the article and thus, which normally results in a larger cluster size. However, the r-value of 0.035 indicates almost no correlation between the two variables and as the p-value is 0.088, the assumption is not statistically significant and should be withdrawn.

4.3 Application Scenario

From the point of view of stylistics, VA is a powerful device because it can not only "spice up" a text, but can also set a decisive accent through its often surprising suggestiveness, which is why it is also well suited for headings or subheadings. So far, due to a lack of available data, the phenomenon has not been analyzed on a large scale, specifically, the relationships between source and target entities. In this paper, we lay the groundwork for such analysis, which enables the exploration of the transfer of characteristics between different entities. To accomplish this, we visualize the results in a web demo.[4] In particular, we model the source and target entities as nodes in a network and connect them with edges when they co-occur in a VA expression. The web demo displays the annotated dataset. It helps to explore chains between entities and can provide new insights in the use of VA and the choice of entities, see Figure 1.

5 Conclusion

We have shown that the extraction of the target name and its linking is not a trivial task, and that state-of-the-art coreference resolution models, which should cover this task, do not perform as well as they do on common datasets in their domain. However, our idea of modeling the problem as a question-answering task by employing the annotation of source and modifier shows better results and the concatenation of both models, first ELE_s followed by LF shows promising results. Notably, re-formulating the VA expression into a QA problem works on all syntactic forms of VA expressions and is not limited to the syntax in the dataset. These findings also show that the annotated VA dataset that emerged from the target annotations, even though it is a specific device, can be used as an out-of-domain evaluation dataset for QA and COREF models in general.

With the disambiguation of the target entity we are able to deepen the understanding of VA. The ability to track VA chains is a completely new field that can lead to many interesting insights into the function and use of VA, for example, regarding the transfer of characteristics. Our web demo greatly simplifies the exploration of connections between source and target entities.

[4] https://vossanto.weltliteratur.net/sighum2023/graph.html

References

Iz Beltagy, Matthew E. Peters, and Arman Cohan. 2020. Longformer: The long-document transformer. *arXiv:2004.05150*.

Kevin Clark, Minh-Thang Luong, Quoc V. Le, and Christopher D. Manning. 2020. ELECTRA: Pre-training text encoders as discriminators rather than generators. In *ICLR*.

Nicola De Cao, Gautier Izacard, Sebastian Riedel, and Fabio Petroni. 2021. Autoregressive entity retrieval. In *9th International Conference on Learning Representations, ICLR 2021, Virtual Event, Austria, May 3-7, 2021*. OpenReview.net.

Jacob Devlin, Ming-Wei Chang, Kenton Lee, and Kristina Toutanova. 2019. BERT: Pre-training of deep bidirectional transformers for language understanding. In *Proceedings of the 2019 Conference of the North American Chapter of the Association for Computational Linguistics: Human Language Technologies, Volume 1 (Long and Short Papers)*, pages 4171–4186, Minneapolis, Minnesota. Association for Computational Linguistics.

Frank Fischer and Robert Jäschke. 2019. 'The Michael Jordan of greatness'—Extracting Vossian antonomasia from two decades of The New York Times, 1987–2007. *Digital Scholarship in the Humanities*, 35.

Robert Jäschke, Jannik Strötgen, Elena Krotova, and Frank Fischer. 2017. "Der Helmut Kohl unter den Brotaufstrichen". Zur Extraktion Vossianischer Antonomasien aus großen Zeitungskorpora. In *Proceedings of the DHd 2017*, DHd '17, pages 120–124. Digital Humanities im deutschsprachigen Raum.

Vladimir I Levenshtein et al. 1966. Binary codes capable of correcting deletions, insertions, and reversals. In *Soviet physics doklady*, volume 10, pages 707–710. Soviet Union.

Mike Lewis, Yinhan Liu, Naman Goyal, Marjan Ghazvininejad, Abdelrahman Mohamed, Omer Levy, Veselin Stoyanov, and Luke Zettlemoyer. 2020. BART: Denoising sequence-to-sequence pre-training for natural language generation, translation, and comprehension. In *Proceedings of the 58th Annual Meeting of the Association for Computational Linguistics*, pages 7871–7880, Online. Association for Computational Linguistics.

Michael Röder, Ricardo Usbeck, and Axel-Cyrille Ngonga Ngomo. 2018. Gerbil–benchmarking named entity recognition and linking consistently. *Semantic Web*, 9(5):605–625.

Evan Sandhaus. 2008. The New York Times Annotated Corpus LDC2008T19. DVD, Linguistic Data Consortium, Philadelphia.

Michel Schwab, Robert Jäschke, and Frank Fischer. 2022. "The Rodney Dangerfield of Stylistic Devices": End-to-end detection and extraction of vossian antonomasia using neural networks. *Frontiers in artificial intelligence*, 5.

Michel Schwab, Robert Jäschke, and Frank Fischer. 2023. Annotated vossian antonomasia dataset.

Michel Schwab, Robert Jäschke, Frank Fischer, and Jannik Strötgen. 2019. 'A Buster Keaton of Linguistics': First automated approaches for the extraction of Vossian Antonomasia. In *Proceedings of the 2019 Conference on Empirical Methods in Natural Language Processing and the 9th International Joint Conference on Natural Language Processing*, EMNLP '19, pages 6239–6244. Association for Computational Linguistics.

Shubham Toshniwal, Patrick Xia, Sam Wiseman, Karen Livescu, and Kevin Gimpel. 2021. On generalization in coreference resolution. In *Proceedings of the Fourth Workshop on Computational Models of Reference, Anaphora and Coreference*, pages 111–120, Punta Cana, Dominican Republic. Association for Computational Linguistics.

William E Winkler. 1999. The state of record linkage and current research problems. *Statistical Research Division, US Bureau of the Census, Washington, DC.*

Detecting intersectionality in NER models: A data-driven approach

Ida Marie S. Lassen
Mina Almasi
Kenneth Enevoldsen
Ross Deans Kristensen-McLachlan
Center for Humanities Computing
Aarhus University, Denmark
idamarie@cas.au.dk, mina.almasi@post.au.dk,
kenneth.enevoldsen@cas.au.dk, rdkm@cc.au.dk

Abstract

The presence of bias is a clear and pressing concern for both engineers and users of language technology. What is less clear is how exactly bias can be measured, so as to rank models relative to the biases they display. Using an innovative experimental method involving data augmentation, we measure the effect of intersectional biases in Danish models used for Named Entity Recognition (NER). We quantify differences in *representational biases*, understood as a systematic difference in error or what is called *error disparity*. Our analysis includes both gender and ethnicity to illustrate the effect of multiple dimensions of bias, as well as experiments which look to move beyond a narrowly binary analysis of gender. We show that all contemporary Danish NER models perform systematically worse on non-binary and minority ethnic names, while not showing significant differences for typically Danish names. Our data augmentation technique can be applied on other languages to test for biases which might be relevant for researchers applying NER models to the study of textual cultural heritage data.

1 Introduction

Issues of bias and discrimination are essential in contemporary Natural Language Processing (NLP). Research has consistently pointed to bias in word embeddings (Kurita et al., 2019; Manzini et al., 2019), and for downstream tasks such as coreference resolution (Zhao et al., 2018), and language generation (Sheng et al., 2021). Several survey papers have also mapped out the landscape of bias research in the field of NLP, showing a lack of clear definitions of bias and normative motivation in NLP bias research (Blodgett et al., 2020); and further emphasising the lack of explicit theorising over the concept of "gender" even when gender biases are the primary concern of a paper (Devinney et al., 2022); and pointing to lack of considerations about the ethical implications of biases in NLP frameworks (Stanczak and Augenstein, 2021).

In this paper, we build on these findings and contribute to ongoing work measuring and quantifying the effects of biases in NLP. We focus on one specific downstream task, namely Named Entity Recognition (NER), and we focus only on the Danish language. We examine error disparities as a function of sensitive features (Borkan et al., 2019; Shah et al., 2020), where earlier work has shown differences across different demographic groups, namely gender and ethnicity (Enevoldsen et al., 2021; Kristensen-McLachlan et al., 2022).

Existing work has highlighted how unintended bias in NLP systems leads to systematic differences in performance for different demographic groups (Borkan et al., 2019; Gaut et al., 2020; Zhao et al., 2018). In response to these results, various frameworks, fairness metrics, and recommendations for the field have been developed to quantify and mitigate bias (Shah et al., 2020; Borkan et al., 2019; Czarnowska et al., 2021; Gaut et al., 2020; Blodgett et al., 2020). Additionally, a growing body of work has demonstrated how *Counterfactual Data Augmentation* (CDA) of training data can be used to mitigate biases in NLP frameworks. This approach has been used for coreference resolution (Zhao et al., 2018), and its applicability has been shown for a broader set of NLP tasks (Lu et al., 2020). We propose another use of data augmentation, namely as a method to *test* the robustness of NLP models and uncover potential social biases in the models.

Informed by intersectional feminism (Crenshaw, 2013), we expand on earlier analysis to investigate the effect of different dimensions of bias and prejudice. The fundamental idea in intersectional feminism relates to how multiple dimensions of inequality result in complex, intersected inequality that cannot be accounted for through an isolated analysis of the single inequalities. For example, minority women might experience other types of discrimination than majority women and still others

Proceedings of the 7th Joint SIGHUM Workshop on Computational Linguistics for Cultural Heritage, Social Sciences, Humanities and Literature (LaTeCH-CLfL2023), pages 116–127
May 5, 2023

than those experienced by minority men.

As the discussion and investigation of bias require more than a narrow focus on the overall performance score, adding nuances to bias tests opens up new findings and further reflections. In this paper, we examine how names mainly used by minority communities *and* names used by different genders affect the performance of NER models *together*. Including non-gendered names in our experiment, we furthermore look to challenge the binary understanding of gender dominating the field of bias research.

Our experiments are limited to Danish, a relatively high-resource language from a fairly homogeneous society with a restrictive gendered name law. Our results demonstrate that for contemporary Danish NER, error disparity is *not* evenly distributed across social groups and genders. This result adds significant nuances to the discussion of bias outlined in earlier iterations of this study (Enevoldsen et al., 2021; Kristensen-McLachlan et al., 2022) by highlighting the importance of nuanced perspectives on performance scores (Birhane et al., 2022) and encouraging awareness of who is affected by NLP pipelines.

In drawing attention to differences in performance across sensitive attributes, our focus is on biases as *representational harms* (Crawford, 2017). The harmful aspects derive from the consequences of being excluded from the functionalities of automated systems employed in specific contexts. Communities and individuals who are unrecognised risk falling into the *residual space* of being unseen and treated as irrelevant (Star and Bowker, 2007). In the case of textual cultural heritage, this manifests itself as *archival silence*, the absence of certain voices, stories, and histories (Carter, 2006). We argue that it is vital for those studying textual cultural heritage data with language technology to be able to measure the kinds of bias we outline, in order to avoid reproducing this silence.

2 Bias in NLP

According to one influential definition, bias in computer systems can be defined as systems which 'systematically and unfairly discriminate against certain individuals or groups of individuals in favour of others' (Friedman and Nissenbaum, 1996). This can be further broken down to distinguish between *preexisting biases* with roots in institutions, practices, and attitudes; *technical biases* arising from the resolution of issues in the technical specifications; and *emergent bias* which occurs in a use-context after the implementation of a given system. It has furthermore been suggested to include 'freedom of bias' in the criteria for good computer systems.

Blodgett et al. (2020) provide a survey of bias research in NLP specifically and present a conceptual framework to characterize and compare biases. Drawing on earlier work (Crawford, 2017), they distinguish between *allocation bias* and *representational bias*. The former is a difference in the allocation of resources and opportunities; while the latter is differences in representations, such as stereotyping and negative generalisation of social groups. Representational bias furthermore includes differences in system performance, such as how well an automated system performs for different demographic groups.

We focus on *representational bias* as differences in system performance, measured as differences in error on a particular task. Crawford (2017) emphasise representational bias as *harmful* in itself, mirroring the ideas of an *emergent bias* in Friedman and Nissenbaum (1996). Further bias emerges when systems whose performance differs systematically across different demographic groups are implemented.

In social science and humanities, researchers who apply NLP tools in their work need to consider such performance differences when deciding which framework to use. For example, a researcher working in the field of gender history might need their models to be particularly robust with respect to gender; a scholar of social media might have a specific reason to require that their model is particularly robust to different ethnicities represented in their data. For those who work with cultural heritage data, there may therefore need to be a necessary trade-off between the overall accuracy of a particular framework and the bias that it exhibits relative to different groups.

In the following section, we outline how existing societal biases in Denmark make it crucial to test NLP frameworks for technical biases.

2.1 Intersections of discrimination

Injustices encountered by social groups can rarely be accounted for through a single variable (such as either gender or race) but interacts with other systems of oppression (such as race, age, class,

$$\begin{array}{r} \\ \textit{women} \\ \textit{men} \end{array} \begin{array}{cc} \textit{majority} & \textit{minority} \\ \left[\begin{array}{cc} \mathcal{A} & \mathcal{B} \\ \mathcal{C} & \mathcal{D} \end{array}\right] \end{array}$$

Figure 1: The intersectional subgroups $\mathcal{A}$ = majority women, $\mathcal{B}$ = minority women, $\mathcal{C}$ = majority men, $\mathcal{D}$ = minority men, are defined by combinations of senstive attributes – in this case gender and ethnicity (Subramanian et al., 2021).

disabilities, education level, etc.). This has been termed *intersectionality* as different dimensions of oppression intersect and affect the encountered injustice (Crenshaw, 2013).

Nevertheless, most research on bias in machine learning - and in NLP specifically - focuses on a single dimension of discrimination, most often either race (Field et al., 2021; Manzini et al., 2019) or gender (Kurita et al., 2019; Basta et al., 2019). If multiple bias markers are examined, the combined effect is often left out of the picture (Garg et al., 2018; Czarnowska et al., 2021; Nadeem et al., 2021). However, recent work has shed light upon intersectional biases in NLP. In particular, Lalor et al. (2022) benchmark multiple NLP models on fairness and predictive performance across various NLP tasks. They deploy multiple demographic dimensions and evaluate various downstream NLP tasks for *allocation biases*. Furthermore, Subramanian et al. (2021) evaluate different debiasing techniques and suggest a post-hoc debiasing method particularly useful for intersectional biases. In a more analytical line of work, Herbelot et al. (2012) provide a quantitative analysis of concepts from gender studies and presents a methodological approach to the investigation of intersectional bias at the level of word representations.

In this paper, we examine *representational bias* in named entity recognition in Danish NLP frameworks. We define bias as a difference in system performance measured by error rate as a function of sensitive features – gender and ethnicity. To test the error disparities for NER across different demographic groups, we divide our data set into subgroups functioning as proxies for the demographic subgroups in question. To do so, we use gender-divided name lists with minority and majority names, which allow us to conduct an intersectional analysis of the effect of different oppressive dimensions. We furthermore include unisex names in our experiments in an attempt to move beyond binary conceptions of gender.

2.2 Muslim names as a proxy for ethnic minority

With names come strong connotations to both ethnicity and religion, and a name often reveals group affiliation for individuals (Khosravi, 2012). In Denmark, the largest immigrant community has members descended from Middle Eastern and Muslim countries (Statistics Denmark, 2022). Research has pointed out how people in this group experience various types of discrimination spanning from harsh rhetoric in political discourse over ministerial administration (Vinding, 2020) to hate crimes (Mannov, 2021) and exclusion of labour market (Dahl and Krog, 2018).

Given the sociological evidence, it is clearly worth considering the impact of machine learning technologies for a large part of the Danish population who is vulnerable to discrimination (Jørgensen, 2023, Ranchordás and Scarcella, 2021). A list of Muslim first names used in Denmark was retrieved from Meldgaard (2005), which presented the names of Muslim origin used in Denmark in 2005, together with an explanation of the meaning of each name. As most immigrants in Denmark come from predominantly Muslim countries, we apply this list of names as a proxy for minority ethnicity. The list is furthermore divided into women's and men's names.

Of course, not all minority people in Denmark will be represented on this list of names, which represents a known limitation of our work. Instead, we infer only ethnicity on a group level, and as research has shown that Middle Eastern immigrants are being subjected to discrimination on the basis of their names (Dahl and Krog, 2018), we argue that testing performance for this group is a necessary step for quantifying bias in NLP frameworks.

A name of Muslim origin might, however, not be the only source of discrimination. Experiments in which fictitious job applications were randomly assigned either a Danish or Middle Eastern-sounding name and sent to actual job openings showed that minority men are consistently subject to a much larger degree of discrimination than minority women (Dahl and Krog, 2018). Similarly, experiments on commercial automated facial analysis systems for gender classification showed that women with darker skin are the most misclassified group (Buolamwini and Gebru, 2018). Hence, the protected and privileged group might vary across contexts, and to examine the intersection between ethnicity and gender discrimination, a proxy for gender is needed.

2.3 Names as a proxy for gender

Denmark has a high level of formal equality, with anti-discrimination laws ensuring constitutional equality and discrimination protection. However, structural oppression still exists and can be shown in studies on the gender pay gap (Gallen et al., 2019) as well as in statistics on violence against women (European Union Agency For Fundamental Rights, 2014). The work by Dahl and Krog (2018) furthermore showed that in a labour market context, women were subject to discrimination except in the women-dominated fields, where men experienced a slightly lower call-back rate.

Using a gendered name list as a proxy has advantages and disadvantages. On the one hand, demarcating our results on proxies for gender *and* ethnicity allows us to conduct an intersectional analysis of the relative effect of gender and ethnicity on the error disparities. Denmark has strict name laws relative to many other European countries, restricting which names a person can be assigned according to their gender (something which has been actively criticised by citizen activist groups[1]). Hence we are not only relying on a majority count of the usage of a name but on a legal context determining the 'gender' of a name – highly dominated by a binary understanding of gender.

On the other hand, the disadvantages of augmenting on gendered name lists are the risk of reinforcing a folk conception of gender (Keyes, 2018), where gender is understood as binary and static, and ruling out other gender identities (Dev et al., 2021). Danish names are neither inherently nor definitively gendered, and the implementation of laws restricting the choice of name based on sex assigned at birth emphasises how ideology is present both in Danish name laws and in the language in general (Blodgett et al., 2020).

Instead of a bio-essential binary understanding, gender can be conceptualised as both performative and constituted by discursive practices (Butler, 2006). With such an understanding of gender, biological sex and cultural gender are separated, and neither can be inferred from a name or physiological appearance. Introducing ourselves with certain names and pronouns can be one way of performing a gender but is not the only way. It may, therefore, still be problematic to use gendered name lists to infer the gender of an individual. However, as mentioned above, we only infer at the group level to assess the potential biases for different demographic groups when subjected to NLP frameworks. Furthermore, we do not link names to pronounces and do not draw conclusions about individual *gender identity*.

In an attempt to go beyond a solely binary understanding of gender, we include unisex names which are culturally understood as being used by both men and women. However, it should go without saying that non-binary people do not specifically use these names, and it might be an insufficient way of challenging the binary concept of gender.

We do not claim that these proxies for either gender or ethnicity are perfect. However, as we do not infer values of sensitive attributes at the level of individuals but examine structural differences at the group level, we find these proxies highly productive for examining differences in system performance for different demographic groups and to expand earlier analysis by considering the intersection of oppressive dimensions.

Given these qualifications, our experiment in data augmentation is motivated by the following research questions:

- **RQ1** Does system performance differ across the subgroups shown in Figure 1?
- **RQ2** Does system performance differ for unisex names compared to majority names?
- **RQ3** Does system performance for the different groups differ across the selected NLP frameworks?

In order to answer these questions, we test the system performance on all known systems for performing Danish NER.

3 Method

We define bias as the systematic difference in error, *error disparity*, as a function of a given sensitive feature (Shah et al., 2020). We deploy *Counterfactual Data Augmentation* (CDA) (Lu et al., 2020), not as a way of debiasing the framework, but as a test method for examining *error disparity* across different sensitive features. In other words, bias in the model is measured through the difference

[1] See Ligebehandling for alle (2021) for citizen proposal for abolishing of the gender-separated name lists including critique and explanations (is available in Danish).

in performance accuracy when data is augmented with different gender and ethnicity features.

In Enevoldsen et al. (2021), a range of contemporary Danish NLP frameworks was subjected to a series of data augmentation strategies to test their robustness during training. These augmentations included random keystroke augmentation to simulate spelling errors; and spelling variations specific to the Danish language. Additionally, among the augmentation strategies were the following name augmentations:

1. Substitute all names (PER entities) with randomly sampled majority names, respecting first and last names.

2. Substitute all names with randomly sampled minority names (Meldgaard, 2005), respecting first and last names.

3. Substitute all names with sampled majority men's names, respecting first and last names.

4. Substitute all names with sampled majority women's names, respecting first and last names.

These augmentations specifically tested the robustness of named entity recognition in each Danish NLP framework, given data augmented relative to gender and ethnicity. If a framework performed just as well (or better) with these augmentations as without, this was interpreted as an indicator of robustness. Conversely, if a framework performed worse, our approach makes it possible to quantify exactly where the model is failing and, hence, where potential biases reside.

We expand on this analysis by testing the disparities in performance across different dimensions of sensitive attributes, namely gender and ethnicity. This is done by dividing minority names into gender. Instead of relying on a solely binary conception of gender, we furthermore test the robustness of named entity recognition in each Danish NLP framework for names on the unisex name list.

Hence, adding to the above list:

5. Substitute all names with sampled minority women's names, respecting first and last names.

6. Substitute all names with sampled minority men's names, respecting first and last names.

7. Substitute all names with sampled unisex names, respecting first and last names.

3.1 Danish NLP frameworks

We have attempted in this experiment to draw on all existing frameworks which can be used to perform NER on Danish language data. Each framework uses different architectures and training data.

spaCy uses pre-trained word-embedding initialised using a tok2vec component[2]. For the purposes of this experiment, we have not included spaCy's Transformer-based model, *da_core_news_trf*, since it corresponds to the DaCy-medium outlined below.

DaCy (Enevoldsen et al., 2021) is a unified state-of-the-art framework for Danish NLP built on spaCy. DaCy-small is based on a Danish Electra (14M parameters); DaCy-medium is based on the Danish BERT (110M parameters)[3]; and DaCy-large is based on the multilingual XLM-Roberta (550M parameters).

ScandiNER[4] is a model trained for NER across many Scandinavian languages including Danish. The model itself is a finetuned BERT-base model trained on the digitised collections of the Norwegian national library[5]. While explicitly referred to as a Norwegian model, it has been trained on a wide range of data and has proven to be highly performant on Danish text data [6].

Flair (Akbik et al., 2019) is a BiLSTM-based model which has demonstrated high levels of performance on Danish as well as similar languages, such as English and German. BiLSTM models tend to be computationally more expensive to train than Transformers due to their use of recurrence. However, BiLSTM models like Flair continue to be popular and are hence included in our experiment.

Polyglot employs a static word embedding model using word embeddings trained on Wikipedia (Al-Rfou' et al., 2013). While not as widely used as it once was, we have included this model to illustrate differences in performance between older models and more state-of-the-art Transformer-based models.

Many of these models are built on top of BERT-style architectures. In the case of English, models from this family have been shown to encode spe-

[2]https://explosion.ai/blog/deep-learning-formula-nlp

[3]https://huggingface.co/Maltehb/danish-bert-botxo

[4]https://huggingface.co/saattrupdan/nbailab-base-ner-scandi

[5]https://huggingface.co/NbAiLab/nb-bert-base

[6]https://scandeval.github.io/

Data set overview	All	Filtered
Nr. of unisex first names	500	500
Nr. of majority first names	1,000	943
women's names	500	485
men's names	500	458
Nr. of majority last names	500	500
Nr. of minority first names	1,134	1,121
women's names	452	443
men's names	625	621
Nr. of minority last names	526	526

Table 1: The number of names used in the data augmentation: The left column is the number of names; 500 majority names for men, women, and unisex are chosen to match the number of minority names. The right columns show the number after the overlap between majority and minority lists is filtered away. The number of minority women's and men's names do not amount to the total number of minority names due to an overlap of names, which is not filtered out.

cific biases across multiple axes of discrimination (Bender et al., 2021). It has also been demonstrated that BERT-style models have a tendency to learn stereotypical representations (Kurita et al., 2019). Previous work has shown that all Danish models exhibit statistical significant bias in terms of ethnicity, while only Polyglot shows a gender bias (Enevoldsen et al., 2021). As such, we expect to see similar results when testing Danish NER models, with poorer performance for the subgroups marginalised among more than one dimension.

All models are fine-tuned on the DaNE dataset (Hvingelby et al., 2020) with the exception of Polyglot, which is trained using the Wikipedia data.

3.2 Data

As described in Section 2 the list of minority names is retrieved from Meldgaard (2005) containing $\sim 1,000$ names. For minority last names, a list of Muslim last names are retrieved from FamilyEducation[7]. The majority and last names lists are retrieved from Statistics Denmark[8], filtered on the 500 most used names for men, women, and last names to approximately match the number of minority names. Finally, the list of unisex names is retrieved from The Agency of Family Law[9] we have filtered on the 500 most popular unisex names according to the data from Statistics Denmark.

As the list of Danish names consists of popular names in Denmark, there is an overlap of 75 names also classified as minority names according to the list from Meldgaard (2005). To report the true effect of the minority names, we have filtered out those such that they only appear in the list of minority names - resulting in 458 majority men's names and 485 majority women's names.

For example, as Mohammed is a common name in Denmark with Islamic origin, it occurs in both the majority and minority name lists. However, Mohammed is most likely a name being subjected to discrimination in line with the work by Dahl and Krog (2018). Therefore, we have filtered it out to only occur on the list of minority names. However, we found some names impossible to classify as *either* majority or minority names, and we included them in both lists. This includes names like Sara, Sarah, Laila, and Ben. A similar sorting of the overlap between the gendered name lists and the unisex name lists is not meaningful, as it is the very definition of the unisex names that they can be used by all genders. Table 1 provides an overview of the number of names for each category[10].

The experimental pipeline is set up as follows. For each sentence in the DaNE dataset, we augment the dataset by replacing each "PERSON" entity with a name randomly sampled from one of the given lists. To avoid nonsensical sentences, we ensure that within one document, a specific name is always replaced by the same name. Following this, the NER performance for all models is tested on the augmented data, estimated by calculating F1 scores across all tags. As the random choice of name influences the performance, we repeat this process 20 times for each model to estimate a mean F1 score. Finally, we used a t-test to compare whether the F1 scores obtained on the augmented data varied significantly from the baseline. For the baseline, we used the majority names for both genders (see Table 2. As we perform multiple comparisons, we make sure to adjust the p-values using a Bonferroni correction.

The name augmentation was performed using Augmenty (Enevoldsen, 2022) and the model evaluation was performed using DaCy framework. All code is publicly available and open source, shared

[7] https://www.familyeducation.com/baby-names/surname/origin/muslim

[8] https://www.dst.dk/da/Statistik/emner/borgere/navne/navne-i-hele-befolkningen

[9] https://familieretshuset.dk/navne/navne/godkendte-fornavne

[10] See https://github.com/centre-for-humanities-computing/Danish-NER-bias/tree/main/name_lists for complete name lists

using an Apache 2.0 license[11].

4 Results

In Table 2, we see the results of the name augmentation experiments. We see that larger, transformer-based models consistently outperform other models on NER tasks. These results underline three well-known trends in deep learning and NLP: 1) larger models tend to perform better than smaller models; 2) higher quality pre-training data leads to better models; and 3) multilingual models perform competitively with monolingual models (Brown et al., 2020; Raffel et al., 2020; Xue et al., 2021).

More pertinently, our results show that the NER performance of every model is affected by the data augmentations. It is immediately apparent, though, that not all models are affected equally, and not all augmentations cause pronounced effects. Our results seem to demonstrate that Danish language models are relatively more robust to the impact of randomly changing women and men's names *at the majority level*. However, this is not the case for unisex names, where our results show that *all* Danish NLP models are significantly worse at recognising these compared to gender-conforming names.

Similarly, randomly replacing names with minority names results in significantly worse performance for all models. This suggests that Danish NLP models contain a greater relative bias regarding ethnicity than the binary gender division, emphasised by the results showing that all models performed consistently better for majority women's names than for minority men's names. For **ScandiNER**, all **DaCy** models, **DaNLP BERT**, **Flair**, and **NERDA**, the performance for minority women's names and minority men's names are similar - but still significantly lower than names from 'majority all'. For **Polyglot** and the **spaCy** models, the performance for minority women is worse than those for minority men. Especially interesting are the results from **DaCy Large**, where there is no apparent bias for minority names if intersectionality is left out of the picture. However, a bias towards minority women is shown when minority names are divided into men's and women's names. **ScandiNER** performs overall best of all models, and even though it shows bias towards 'minority all' and 'minority men', it still outperforms **DaCy Large**, which do not show the same bias in error rate for these groups.

One could argue that for the best performing models, **ScandiNER**, and the **DaCy** models, the differences in F1 scores are overall negligible. However, as small differences accumulate when used on large corpora we argue that even seemingly small differences (which are statistically significant) should be taken into consideration in an NLP pipeline. This becomes more pronounced when one considers the *increase in error rate.* The best performing model is **ScandiNER** shows a 7% increase in error from 'majority all' to 'minority women'. Similarly, for **DaCy medium** this amounts to an increase in error rate of 17%. For the poorest performing **Polyglot** model, we calculate a 72% increase in error rate.

Hence, according to Figure 1, we conclude that Danish NLP frameworks perform best for subgroups $\mathcal{A}$ and $\mathcal{C}$ (majority people). On the other hand, the models perform significantly worse for subgroups $\mathcal{B}$ and $\mathcal{D}$ (minority people), and some models are worst for subgroup $\mathcal{B}$ (minority women) specifically. Adding unisex names and the gendered demarcation of the minority lists (see 5-7 in the list in Section 3) to our tests shows that the error disparity is *not* evenly distributed across the social groups in Figure 1. These results open up the narrow focus on the overall performance scores and are significant contributions to the examination of bias started in earlier iterations of this study (Enevoldsen et al., 2021; Kristensen-McLachlan et al., 2022).

5 Discussion

Much of the work on representational bias focus on system performance and the concrete impact on individuals and groups as a result of biased models. However, we argue that similar considerations should underlie research applications of NLP, such as the use of language technology to study cultural heritage data. By ignoring the disparate performance of NLP frameworks on downstream tasks, we risk overlooking the testimony of marginalised voices in our corpora and archives.

Previous work has outlined how, in classification systems, residual categories are those that are left out when categories are established (Star and Bowker, 2007; Scheuerman et al., 2019). By not complying with the agreed-upon categories, the 'other' fall between the cracks of the categorisation

[11] See `https://github.com/centre-for-humanities-computing/Danish-NER-bias` for code for the experimental pipeline

Model	All		Men		Women		Unisex
	Majority	Minority	Majority	Minority	Majority	Minority	Majority
ScandiNER	89.1(0.4)	**88.3(0.6)***	89.0(0.5)	**88.4(0.4)***	89.0(0.4)	**88.3(0.6)***	**88.6(0.4)***
DaCy large	86.7(0.5)	86.4(0.6)	86.6(0.4)	86.3(0.4)	86.5(0.3)	**86.0(0.6)***	**86.2(0.5)***
DaCy medium	79.9(0.6)	**77.0(0.8)***	79.6(0.5)	**76.4(1.1)***	79.9(0.5)	**76.6(0.7)***	**78.2(0.8)***
DaCy small	77.8(1.0)	**74.8(1.0)***	77.8(0.8)	**74.6(1.2)***	77.6(0.8)	**74.9(1.1)***	**76.0(1.0)***
DaNLP BERT	83.4(0.5)	**81.1(1.0)***	83.4(0.4)	**81.1(0.7)***	83.6(0.5)	**80.8(0.9)***	**81.9(0.8)***
Flair	81.8(0.4)	**79.9(0.8)***	82.1(0.5)	**79.9(0.8)***	81.6(0.4)	**80.0(0.7)***	**79.8(0.8)***
NERDA	80.6(0.8)	**78.5(1.1)***	81.1(0.8)	**78.7(0.8)***	80.8(0.4)	**78.5(0.7)***	**79.8(0.9)***
SpaCy large	79.0(0.5)	**68.7(1.3)***	79.3(0.6)	**71.2(0.9)***	78.8(0.6)	**66.4(1.7)***	**75.8(0.8)***
SpaCy medium	78.2(0.8)	**64.6(1.4)***	78.7(0.5)	**66.7(1.8)***	78.3(0.5)	**61.0(1.2)***	**71.9(1.3)***
SpaCy small	64.8(0.7)	**57.5(1.4)***	64.6(1.3)	**57.5(1.5)***	65.1(1.4)	**56.3(1.5)***	**61.5(1.4)***
Polyglot	64.9(0.9)	**41.7(1.3)***	**66.1(0.7)***	**42.1(1.2)***	**63.3(1.4)***	**39.5(1.0)***	**57.4(1.5)***

Table 2: Named Entity Recognition (NER) performance of Danish Natural Language Processing (NLP) pipelines reported as average F1 scores excluding the MISC category on the test set. The column 'Majority All' names is considered the baseline for the augmentation of minority, women's, men's and unisex names. Bold and * denotes that the result is significantly different from the baseline using a significance threshold of 0.05 with Bonferroni correction for multiple comparisons. Values in parentheses denote the standard deviation.

schema. This can happen if the object is too complicated to classify in the often taken-for-granted categories or if the residual is unknown to the system. Falling into a residual space can result in people's experience being disregarded or overlooked, consciously or otherwise. In the context of named entity recognition, the classification performed is either recognised or unrecognised, and we argue that people whose names are unrecognised by automated systems reside in the *residual* spaces.

Our results show that, for contemporary Danish NER, there are differences in performance along different demographic lines – differences that may not have been obvious without testing performance for the different subgroups. This, first and foremost, highlights the importance of challenging the narrow focus on overall performance score (Birhane et al., 2022) and sheds light upon the existence of diversity in who is affected. Furthermore, these results also show a difference in the risk of residing into the residual space and potentially being disregarded and mistreated. The technical biases in these NLP frameworks risk reinforcing the existing structural biases if put into use. Therefore, we recommend NLP practitioners to take accountability (Buolamwini and Gebru, 2018) and consider these subgroup-specific performance results. The responsibility of measuring and mitigating such biases should be placed on those developing and implementing the tools – not on the marginalised group who are unfairly treated by the systems (Bender et al., 2021).

In this work, we defined bias as the difference in error rate across different demographic subgroups. This bias is only tested for one specific task. For our data augmentation, we used the DaNE corpus, which consists of a diverse set of written and spoken Danish from 1983–1992. However, minority names might occur more frequently in contexts which differ substantially from this corpus. If this is the case, our reported performances might vary according to how well Danish NLP frameworks perform on NER for minority names 'in the wild'. Hence, assessing the potential bias towards minority people might be even more complex.

A similar issue arises when approximating ethnicity for social groups through the use of name lists. This approach leaves out minority people who take names typical for the majority group. However, when it comes to the performance of NER tools, minority people with majority names are not at the same risk of being unfairly treated by NER tools as people with minority names. The reverse is also the case: a person from the ethnic majority with a name typical for the minority is at greater risk of not being recognised by NER tools than people with majority names. Nevertheless, this is not central to our analysis, insofar as we are only inferring at *group level* when examining the distribution of error rates across different social groups.

Further complexities in the use of names are the effect of rare names. For unisex names, we included the 500 most used names, which are approved unisex names in Denmark. In this list, there are names that are common gendered names, such as 'Anne', which in Denmark is primarily used by women. If we filtered out common and primarily gendered names, the performance might be even poorer, but then it might be an effect of rare names rather than unisex names.

Nevertheless, this paper presents an innovative experimental method which adds nuanced perspectives to the overall performance evaluation for these models. Based on data augmentation and the use of name lists as proxies for multiple dimensions of inequality, the method allows for an intersectional analysis of biases in Danish NLP models used for named entity recognition. Such findings are important to incorporate into scholarly pipelines in order to avoid enforcing *archival silence*.

6 Conclusions

In this paper, we have shown the importance of intersectional analysis of biases in Natural Language Processing (NLP) frameworks by testing Danish NLP frameworks' robustness to data augmentation in Named Entity Recognition (NER).

By augmenting test data on gender-divided name lists for both majority and minority names, we have shown that Danish NLP frameworks are relatively robust to the impact of women's and men's names *at the majority level*. However, *all* Danish NLP models are significantly worse at recognising unisex names compared to gender-conforming names. Furthermore, minority names cause significantly worse performance for all models. This suggests that Danish NLP models contain a greater relative bias regarding ethnicity than the binary gender division.

In the context of textual cultural heritage data, researchers regularly and increasingly incorporate language technology into their scholarly workflow. The most appropriate tool for a given task such as NER is usually chosen based on some pre-calculated metric score for how the technology performs for that task. However, based on the results presented here, we argue that a raw performance measure should not be the only criterion for deciding which NLP model to use. Instead, we emphasise that, in the case of textual cultural heritage data, *accuracy is not all you need*. We encourage researchers to take these sub-group-specific performance measures into account when setting up their research pipeline.

7 Limitations

The current study has some limitations. Firstly, our minority-majority categorisation is rather restricted, and a large group of the population will not be represented in this division insofar as we only include names of primarily Muslim backgrounds, excluding other minority ethnic communities in Denmark. In addition, our approach of manually sorting names which occur in both the majority and minority name lists is potentially problematic as our sorting is based on our (perhaps stereotyped) ideas of these names and not on any shared methodology.

Furthermore, gendered name lists corresponding to Danish name laws rely on, and so reinforce, a binary understanding of gender. We argue that these demarcations in our data are useful for understanding the societal biases which can be embedded in NLP frameworks but are not comprehensive.

Further work is needed to conclude the overall bias level of Danish NLP frameworks. In particular, bias tests for coreference resolution and word embeddings should be conducted. In addition, our work presented experimental results for a single, comparatively small Indo-European language. We would like to see similar experiments conducted on different languages, given an appropriate change of experimental conditions, to see if results are reproduced in different cultural contexts.

8 Ethics Statement

In this work, we have actively engaged with the fact that the actions of machine learning and NLP engineering can change the world and affect both society and individuals. The use of computer technologies may produce new or reproduce existing discrimination, and we, therefore, strive towards being as inclusive as possible. Not only do we wish to draw attention to social biases inherent in contemporary Danish language technology but we hope that our work can be used directly by other researchers when deciding on tools usages in their scholarly pipeline, particularly for those working with cultural heritage data.

9 Online Resources

See `https://github.com/centre-for-humanities-computing/Danish-NER-bias` for code for the experimental pipeline and complete name lists used in data augmentation.

References

Alan Akbik, Tanja Bergmann, Duncan Blythe, Kashif Rasul, Stefan Schweter, and Roland Vollgraf. 2019. FLAIR: An easy-to-use framework for state-of-the-art NLP. In *Proceedings of the 2019 Conference of the North American Chapter of the Association for Computational Linguistics (Demonstrations)*, pages 54–59. Association for Computational Linguistics.

Rami Al-Rfou', Bryan Perozzi, and Steven Skiena. 2013. Polyglot: Distributed word representations for multilingual NLP. In *Proceedings of the Seventeenth Conference on Computational Natural Language Learning*, pages 183–192. Association for Computational Linguistics.

Christine Basta, Marta R. Costa-jussà, and Noe Casas. 2019. Evaluating the underlying gender bias in contextualized word embeddings. In *Proceedings of the First Workshop on Gender Bias in Natural Language Processing*, pages 33–39, Florence, Italy. Association for Computational Linguistics.

Emily M. Bender, Timnit Gebru, Angelina McMillan-Major, and Shmargaret Shmitchell. 2021. On the dangers of stochastic parrots: Can language models be too big? In *Proceedings of the 2021 ACM Conference on Fairness, Accountability, and Transparency*, FAccT '21, page 610–623. Association for Computing Machinery.

Abeba Birhane, Pratyusha Kalluri, Dallas Card, William Agnew, Ravit Dotan, and Michelle Bao. 2022. The values encoded in machine learning research. In *2022 ACM Conference on Fairness, Accountability, and Transparency*, pages 173–184.

Su Lin Blodgett, Solon Barocas, Hal Daumé III, and Hanna Wallach. 2020. Language (technology) is power: A critical survey of "bias" in NLP. In *Proceedings of the 58th Annual Meeting of the Association for Computational Linguistics*, pages 5454–5476, Online. Association for Computational Linguistics.

Daniel Borkan, Lucas Dixon, Jeffrey Sorensen, Nithum Thain, and Lucy Vasserman. 2019. Nuanced metrics for measuring unintended bias with real data for text classification. In *Companion proceedings of the 2019 world wide web conference*, pages 491–500.

Tom Brown, Benjamin Mann, Nick Ryder, Melanie Subbiah, Jared D Kaplan, Prafulla Dhariwal, Arvind Neelakantan, Pranav Shyam, Girish Sastry, Amanda Askell, et al. 2020. Language models are few-shot learners. *Advances in neural information processing systems*, 33:1877–1901.

Joy Buolamwini and Timnit Gebru. 2018. Gender shades: Intersectional accuracy disparities in commercial gender classification. In *Conference on fairness, accountability and transparency*, pages 77–91. PMLR.

Judith Butler. 2006. *Gender Trouble: Feminism and the Subversion of Identity*. Routledge.

Rodney G.S. Carter. 2006. Of things said and unsaid: Power, archival silences, and power in silence. *Archivaria*, 61:215–233.

Kate Crawford. 2017. The trouble with bias - nips 2017 keynote - kate crawford #nips2017. [Online; accessed 18-February-2023], published by *The Artificial Intelligence Channel*.

Kimberlé Williams Crenshaw. 2013. Mapping the margins: Intersectionality, identity politics, and violence against women of color. In *The public nature of private violence*, pages 93–118. Routledge.

Paula Czarnowska, Yogarshi Vyas, and Kashif Shah. 2021. Quantifying social biases in nlp: A generalization and empirical comparison of extrinsic fairness metrics. *Transactions of the Association for Computational Linguistics*, 9:1249–1267.

Malte Dahl and Niels Krog. 2018. Experimental evidence of discrimination in the labour market: intersections between ethnicity, gender, and socio-economic status. *European Sociological Review*, 34(4):402–417.

Sunipa Dev, Masoud Monajatipoor, Anaelia Ovalle, Arjun Subramonian, Jeff Phillips, and Kai-Wei Chang. 2021. Harms of gender exclusivity and challenges in non-binary representation in language technologies. In *Proceedings of the 2021 Conference on Empirical Methods in Natural Language Processing*, pages 1968–1994, Online and Punta Cana, Dominican Republic. Association for Computational Linguistics.

Hannah Devinney, Jenny Björklund, and Henrik Björklund. 2022. Theories of "gender" in nlp bias research. In *2022 ACM Conference on Fairness, Accountability, and Transparency*, pages 2083–2102.

Kenneth Enevoldsen. 2022. Augmenty: The cherry on top of your NLP pipeline.

Kenneth Enevoldsen, Lasse Hansen, and Kristoffer Nielbo. 2021. Dacy: A unified framework for danish nlp. In *CEUR Workshop Proceedings*, pages 206–216, Amsterdam, The Netherlands. CHR 2021: Computational Humanities Research Conference.

European Union Agency For Fundamental Rights. 2014. Violence against women: an eu-wide survey. Technical report, European Union Agency For Fundamental Rights.

Anjalie Field, Su Lin Blodgett, Zeerak Waseem, and Yulia Tsvetkov. 2021. A survey of race, racism, and anti-racism in NLP. In *Proceedings of the 59th Annual Meeting of the Association for Computational Linguistics and the 11th International Joint Conference on Natural Language Processing (Volume 1: Long Papers)*, pages 1905–1925, Online. Association for Computational Linguistics.

Batya Friedman and Helen Nissenbaum. 1996. Bias in computer systems. *ACM Transactions on Information Systems (TOIS)*, 14(3):330–347.

Yana Gallen, Rune V Lesner, and Rune Vejlin. 2019. The labor market gender gap in denmark: Sorting out the past 30 years. *Labour Economics*, 56:58–67.

Nikhil Garg, Londa Schiebinger, Dan Jurafsky, and James Zou. 2018. Word embeddings quantify 100 years of gender and ethnic stereotypes. *Proceedings of the National Academy of Sciences*, 115(16):E3635–E3644.

Andrew Gaut, Tony Sun, Shirlyn Tang, Yuxin Huang, Jing Qian, Mai ElSherief, Jieyu Zhao, Diba Mirza, Elizabeth Belding, Kai-Wei Chang, and William Yang Wang. 2020. Towards understanding gender bias in relation extraction. In *Proceedings of the 58th Annual Meeting of the Association for Computational Linguistics*, pages 2943–2953, Online. Association for Computational Linguistics.

Aurélie Herbelot, Eva von Redecker, and Johanna Müller. 2012. Distributional techniques for philosophical enquiry. In *Proceedings of the 6th Workshop on Language Technology for Cultural Heritage, Social Sciences, and Humanities*, pages 45–54, Avignon, France. Association for Computational Linguistics.

Rasmus Hvingelby, Amalie Brogaard Pauli, Maria Barrett, Christina Rosted, Lasse Malm Lidegaard, and Anders Søgaard. 2020. DaNE: A named entity resource for danish. In *Proceedings of the 12th Language Resources and Evaluation Conference*, LREC '20, pages 4597–4604.

Rikke Frank Jørgensen. 2023. Data and rights in the digital welfare state: the case of denmark. *Information, Communication & Society*, 26(1):123–138.

Os Keyes. 2018. The misgendering machines: Trans/hci implications of automatic gender recognition. *Proceedings of the ACM on human-computer interaction*, 2(CSCW):1–22.

Shahram Khosravi. 2012. White masks/muslim names: immigrants and name-changing in sweden. *Race & class*, 53(3):65–80.

Ross Deans Kristensen-McLachlan, Ida Marie S. Lassen, Kenneth Enevoldsen, Lasse Hansen, and Kristoffer Laigaard Nielbo. 2022. Accuracy is not all you need. In *DH2022 Tokyo Book of Abstracts*, pages 281–284.

Keita Kurita, Nidhi Vyas, Ayush Pareek, Alan W Black, and Yulia Tsvetkov. 2019. Measuring bias in contextualized word representations. In *Proceedings of the First Workshop on Gender Bias in Natural Language Processing*, pages 166–172, Florence, Italy. Association for Computational Linguistics.

John P Lalor, Yi Yang, Kendall Smith, Nicole Forsgren, and Ahmed Abbasi. 2022. Benchmarking intersectional biases in nlp. In *Proceedings of the 2022 Conference of the North American Chapter of the Association for Computational Linguistics: Human Language Technologies*, pages 3598–3609.

Ligebehandling for alle. 2021. Ligebehandling for alle: Afskaf de kønsopdelte navnelister. [Online; accessed 18-February-2023], published by borgerforslag.dk.

Kaiji Lu, Piotr Mardziel, Fangjing Wu, Preetam Amancharla, and Anupam Datta. 2020. Gender bias in neural natural language processing. *Logic, Language, and Security: Essays Dedicated to Andre Scedrov on the Occasion of His 65th Birthday*, pages 189–202.

Jonas Mannov. 2021. Fakta om hadforbrydelser. [Online; accessed 31-January-2023], published by *The Danish Crime Prevention Council*.

Thomas Manzini, Lim Yao Chong, Alan W Black, and Yulia Tsvetkov. 2019. Black is to criminal as caucasian is to police: Detecting and removing multiclass bias in word embeddings. In *Proceedings of the 2019 Conference of the North American Chapter of the Association for Computational Linguistics: Human Language Technologies, Volume 1 (Long and Short Papers)*, pages 615–621, Minneapolis, Minnesota. Association for Computational Linguistics.

Eva Villarsen Meldgaard. 2005. Muslimske fornavne i danmark. Publisher: Københavns Universitet.

Moin Nadeem, Anna Bethke, and Siva Reddy. 2021. StereoSet: Measuring stereotypical bias in pretrained language models. In *Proceedings of the 59th Annual Meeting of the Association for Computational Linguistics and the 11th International Joint Conference on Natural Language Processing (Volume 1: Long Papers)*, pages 5356–5371, Online. Association for Computational Linguistics.

Colin Raffel, Noam Shazeer, Adam Roberts, Katherine Lee, Sharan Narang, Michael Matena, Yanqi Zhou, Wei Li, and Peter J. Liu. 2020. Exploring the limits of transfer learning with a unified text-to-text transformer. *J. Mach. Learn. Res.*, 21(1).

Sofia Ranchordás and Luisa Scarcella. 2021. Automated government for vulnerable citizens: intermediating rights. *Wm. & Mary Bill Rts. J.*, 30:373.

Morgan Klaus Scheuerman, Jacob M Paul, and Jed R Brubaker. 2019. How computers see gender: An evaluation of gender classification in commercial facial analysis services. *Proceedings of the ACM on Human-Computer Interaction*, 3(CSCW):1–33.

Deven Santosh Shah, H. Andrew Schwartz, and Dirk Hovy. 2020. Predictive biases in natural language processing models: A conceptual framework and overview. In *Proceedings of the 58th Annual Meeting of the Association for Computational Linguistics*, pages 5248–5264, Online. Association for Computational Linguistics.

Emily Sheng, Kai-Wei Chang, Prem Natarajan, and Nanyun Peng. 2021. Societal biases in language generation: Progress and challenges. In *Proceedings of the 59th Annual Meeting of the Association for Computational Linguistics and the 11th International Joint Conference on Natural Language Processing (Volume 1: Long Papers)*, pages 4275–4293, Online. Association for Computational Linguistics.

Karolina Stanczak and Isabelle Augenstein. 2021. A survey on gender bias in natural language processing. *arXiv preprint arXiv:2112.14168*.

Susan Leigh Star and Geoffrey C Bowker. 2007. Enacting silence: Residual categories as a challenge for ethics, information systems, and communication. *Ethics and Information Technology*, 9:273–280.

Statistics Denmark. 2022. Fakta om indvandrere og efterkommere i danmark. [Online; accessed 31-January-2023].

Shivashankar Subramanian, Xudong Han, Timothy Baldwin, Trevor Cohn, and Lea Frermann. 2021. Evaluating debiasing techniques for intersectional biases. In *Proceedings of the 2021 Conference on Empirical Methods in Natural Language Processing*, pages 2492–2498, Online and Punta Cana, Dominican Republic. Association for Computational Linguistics.

Niels Valdemar Vinding. 2020. Discrimination of muslims in denmark. In *State, Religion and Muslims*, pages 144–196. Brill.

Linting Xue, Noah Constant, Adam Roberts, Mihir Kale, Rami Al-Rfou, Aditya Siddhant, Aditya Barua, and Colin Raffel. 2021. mT5: A massively multilingual pre-trained text-to-text transformer. In *Proceedings of the 2021 Conference of the North American Chapter of the Association for Computational Linguistics: Human Language Technologies*, pages 483–498, Online. Association for Computational Linguistics.

Jieyu Zhao, Tianlu Wang, Mark Yatskar, Vicente Ordonez, and Kai-Wei Chang. 2018. Gender bias in coreference resolution: Evaluation and debiasing methods. In *Proceedings of the 2018 Conference of the North American Chapter of the Association for Computational Linguistics: Human Language Technologies, Volume 2 (Short Papers)*, pages 15–20, New Orleans, Louisiana. Association for Computational Linguistics.

OdyCy – A general-purpose NLP pipeline for Ancient Greek

Jan Kostkan[1] and **Márton Kardos**[1] and **Jacob P.B. Mortensen**[2] and **Kristoffer L. Nielbo**[1]
[1]Center for Humanities Computing, Aarhus University, Denmark
[2]School of Culture and Society – Biblical Studies, Aarhus University, Denmark
{jan.kostkan, teojmo, kln}@cas.au.dk

Abstract

This paper presents a general-purpose NLP pipeline for Ancient or early forms of Greek (Classical, Koine, and Medieval) that achieves a slight state-of-art improvement by training on several Universal Dependencies treebanks jointly. We measure the performance of the model against other comparable tools. We show that the selected Greek language models tend not to generalize well to out-of-training set samples. More work is necessary to ensure interoperability between the existing datasets. We identify the main issues and list suggestions for improvements.

1 Introduction

The impact of digitization on literature research in contemporary English and other languages cannot be exaggerated. Computational linguistics and Natural Language Processing (NLP) have developed numerous tools that automate annotation and analysis that would otherwise have taken lifetimes of manual labor. Similar advances have not been made for historical and low-resource language areas, for instance, classical literature in Greek, Latin, and Hebrew. Computational studies of classical literature are limited not only by fewer tools but also paywalls and licensed access (ex. *Loeb Classical Library* and *Thesaurus Linguae Graecae*), altogether complicating the training of neural-based language technology. To remedy this and to contribute to a relatively small number of existing NLP resources in this domain, we present a general-purpose NLP pipeline for early forms of Greek that will enable a computationally assisted analysis of, among other things, early forms of Greek literature.

1.1 Related work

Most existing work on Ancient Greek NLP has focused on individual tasks such as lemmatization (Bary et al., 2017; de Graaf et al., 2022; Vatri and McGillivray, 2020) or morphological analysis and part of-speech-tagging (Celano et al., 2016; Singh et al., 2021). This work has primarily been conducted by subject-matter experts that incorporate their domain knowledge, making the model results more interpretable but less general.

There exists a few examples of full language pipelines for Ancient Greek. One notable example is The Classical Language Toolkit (CLTK) (Johnson et al., 2021), which has been the go-to option for classicists needing NLP tools. CLTK, however relies heavily on domain-specific knowledge. Other pipelines have been trained using well-known NLP frameworks, usually relying on neural components for individual tasks. These include Stanza's (Qi et al., 2020), UDPipe's (Straka, 2018), and Trankit's (Van Nguyen et al., 2021) pipelines. These neural models are language agnostic and hence general-purpose. One additional spaCy pipeline should be mentioned, greCy[1], that has been developed for the Diogenet project[2].

The pipelines mentioned have opted for training separate models for each UD Treebank in Ancient Greek. Raw accuracies generally tend to be higher for models trained and evaluated on *UD Proiel*, compared to *UD Perseus* models. However, due to Ancient Greek being a highly fragmented and low-resource language, high performance on one data set may not generalize for corpora of substantially different quality or nature.

The model presented here, *odyCy* relies on spaCy, which offers a fully modular framework in which individual components can be modified with relative ease. The goal is to allow researchers to integrate this model into their particular use case easily; for example, by fine-tuning the model for a downstream task such as document classification or using it to normalize raw texts for topic modeling. The model also easily integrates with other tools in the spaCy ecosystem, such as TextDescriptives

[1]https://github.com/jmyerston/greCy
[2]https://diogenet.ucsd.edu/

Proceedings of the 7th Joint SIGHUM Workshop on Computational Linguistics for Cultural Heritage, Social Sciences, Humanities and Literature (LaTeCH-CLfL2023), pages 128–134

(Hansen and Enevoldsen, 2023) for calculating metrics from text.

2 Methods

2.1 Treebanks

For training the pipeline, both UD Treebanks, *UD Perseus* and *UD Proiel*, available for Ancient Greek, were used in order to increase the robustness of the model. The *UD Perseus* Treebank (Bamman and Crane, 2011) contains 13,919 sentences. This dataset contains texts in Ancient and Koine Greek distributed over various genres (e.g. tragedies by Aeschylus and Sophocles, biographies by Plutarch, or the Iliad) and various dialects. The *UD Proiel* Treebank (Haug and Jøhndal, 2008) contains 17,081 sentences. The content is mostly New Testament (in Koine Greek), with chapters from Herodotus' Histories. Notably, unlike the main branch of the Proiel Treebank, the UD version does not contain Sphrantzes' Chronicles, written in Medieval (Byzantine) Greek (Singh et al., 2021).

Both treebanks are included in the Universal Dependencies framework (de Marneffe et al., 2021), which specifies annotation standards for multiple languages. Still, the two treebanks differ in some important aspects:

- Punctuation is absent from *UD Proiel* (except for elisions, e.g. ἀλλ'), making it a difficult resource to train a model for sentence segmentation.

- Proper nouns (PROPN) are only annotated in *UD Proiel*. For example, Ἑλλάς is labeled as a noun in *UD Perseus*, but as a proper noun in *UD Proiel*.

- Annotation standards for morphological features differ slightly between the two treebanks, even though the labels overlap for the most part. *UD Proiel* has richer annotations compared to *UD Perseus*, recognizing five additional morphological features (e.g. polarity, reflex or pronoun types) and 14 additional feature-value pairs[3].

- Ambiguous lemmas are handled differently between the two treebanks. *UD Perseus* contains lemmas of compound words in which the two stems are separated by a dash character (e.g., περί-κάθημαι). Furthermore, lemmas in *UD Proiel* may contain optional letters inside parentheses (e.g. Ἰωάν(ν)ης).

- The *UD Perseus* Treebank misrepresents some Ancient Greek characters, likely due to a problematic conversion of the annotations from beta code to Unicode. For example, the trailing apostrophe in the correct form ἀλλ' has been misinterpreted as a smooth breathing mark (̓) above λ.

- *UD Perseus* has been 'semi-automatically annotated'[4]. This means texts were manually annotated and then corrected with the help of Morpheus (morphologizer of the Perseus project).

2.2 Model architecture

The pipeline uses Ancient-Greek-BERT (Singh et al., 2021) as the base model for acquiring the context-rich vector representation of tokens. Subsequent components in the pipeline use the representations as input features to generate predictions. The transformer component has been fine-tuned during training for all downstream tasks simultaneously. These vector representations can be directly accessed on every token for semantic analyses.

Single softmax-activated dense layer models in the pipeline are responsible for morphological analysis and part-of-speech tagging. Tags get assigned on a token level. The models' inputs are the contextual representations obtained from the transformer. We used the default transition-based dependency parser component of spaCy. The component learns both to parse dependency trees in the text as well as to segment sentences.

Lemmatization seems to be the most challenging task for Ancient Greek NLP software. Vatri and McGillivray (2020) provides an overview of different lemmatizers for Ancient Greek, where other approaches were evaluated manually by multiple annotators instead of being benchmarked automatically, which in the case of languages without a canonical orthography is particularly desirable. The paper also shows that, on average, multi-layer lemmatization strategies perform better than single-layer and that large lookup lexicons should have higher priority than machine learning-based layers.

[3] https://universaldependencies.org/treebanks/grc-comparison.html

[4] https://github.com/PerseusDL/treebank_data/tree/master/v2.1/Greek

In addition, the study found that lemmatizers sensitive to part of speech are better than lemmatizers that solely rely on lemma frequency as a heuristic.

In order to incorporate these findings in the odyCy pipeline, we employ a multi-layer strategy for lemmatization. Similar to the approach of GLEM (Bary et al., 2017), we produced a lexicon from the training set containing information about token-lemma pairs and morphological features part-of-speech tags. The lemmatization process searches for tokens in the lexicon and matches them with part-of-speech tags and morphological information. If at any point this process fails, the most frequent lemma will be returned from the last successful match. If the token cannot be found in the lexicon, the tokenizer returns to a default lookup table in spaCy that does not contain morphological or part-of-speech information. If a lemma cannot be identified for the token, a context-sensitive neural edit-tree lemmatizer (Müller et al., 2015) will try to produce a prediction for the given token. If all else fails, it will return the original form of the token. For a schematic overview see Figure 1.

Due to the modular nature of spaCy either the lookup or the neural component may be removed or disabled with a single line of code. Our experiments show that for unseen data, the entire pipeline and the neural component's performance are comparable (see Table 3).

3 Results

When evaluated on the UD Perseus Treebank, our model achieves state-of-the-art performance in POS Tagging, Morphological Analysis, and Dependency Parsing (see Table 1). We achieve close to state-of-art in Sentence Segmentation and Lemmatization. On the UD Proiel Treebank, we achieve the second-best performance across all measures except for Lemmatization (see Table 2). The odyCy joint model, which was trained on both UD treebanks, scores higher than odyCy versions trained on individual treebanks (see Table 1 and 2). Notably, models trained on a single treebank systematically underperform on the other.

3.1 Tokenization and Lemmatization Error Analysis

To investigate errors that occurred during lemmatization and tokenization, we conducted a qualitative error analysis of randomly selected batches from

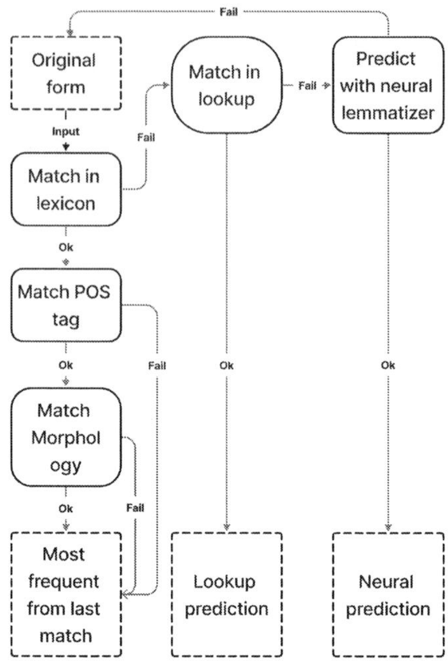

Figure 1: Schematic Overview of the Lemmatization Process.

the treebanks. This investigation revealed the following causes for the mismatch between the gold standard and predicted lemmas. The causes may overlap.

- *Tokenization mistakes.* In some cases, a form that should correspond to a single lemma splits into two lemmas. This causes token misalignment and renders every following lemma in the sentence incorrect.

- *Incorrect or Ignored POS-tags or Morphological Features.* Incorrect predictions of a token's morphological features, especially of the POS-tag can cause lemmatization errors. This is because the lemmatizer relies on predictions from the preceding pipeline components. Proper nouns, for example, get frequently misinterpreted as regular nouns due to the disagreement between the two annotation schemes, which can result in incorrect inflection. When the component falls back to the lookup table, there is a possibility of ignoring morphological information, as the lookup table only contains form-lemma pairs without context or morphology.

	Token	POS	Morphology	Sentence Segmentation			Dependency Parsing		Lemma
Model	Accuracy	Accuracy	Accuracy	Precision	Recall	F-1 Score	UAS	LAS	Accuracy
CLTK	NA*	80.50	61.49	0.00	0.00	0.00	33.05	24.25	79.46
odyCy$_{perseus}$	99.98	<u>95.00</u>	<u>91.98</u>	<u>97.86</u>	98.16	<u>98.01</u>	76.71	70.31	82.56
odyCy$_{proiel}$	99.98	73.14	60.59	3.85	6.66	4.88	66.35	50.26	81.00
odyCy$_{joint}$	99.98	**95.39**	**92.56**	97.57	<u>98.32</u>	97.94	**78.80**	**73.09**	<u>83.20</u>
greCy$_{perseus}$	99.89	93.50	90.59	90.76	94.79	92.73	76.34	70.20	75.10
greCy$_{proiel}$	99.89	81.97	61.26	10.21	17.38	12.86	69.30	53.14	68.92
Stanza$_{perseus}$	100.00	91.05	91.03	**99.31**	**98.93**	**99.12**	<u>78.69</u>	<u>71.82</u>	**87.58**
Stanza$_{proiel}$	87.68	68.73	50.14	40.88	34.84	37.62	46.75	35.73	70.55
UDPipe$_{perseus}$	99.99	80.95	85.70	**99.31**	**98.93**	**99.12**	63.97	55.81	82.73
UDPipe$_{proiel}$	87.33	65.23	45.85	37.46	48.01	42.08	35.16	26.73	65.91

Table 1: Model performances on the test fold of *UD Perseus* Treebank. Highest performance in bold, second highest underlined.

*CLTK's tokenization had to be manually fixed as it routinely added punctuation to tokens, and spaCy's evaluation scripts could not align them against the gold standard.

	Token	POS	Morphology	Sentence Segmentation			Dependency Parsing		Lemma
Model	Accuracy	Accuracy	Accuracy	Precision	Recall	F-1 Score	UAS	LAS	Accuracy
CLTK	NA*	96.95	90.76	50.00	33.33	40.00	57.61	54.57	96.50
odyCy$_{perseus}$	100.00	84.88	57.44	2.08	0.29	0.50	64.55	48.72	91.36
odyCy$_{proiel}$	100.00	97.61	92.84	62.91	64.47	63.68	81.42	77.07	94.42
odyCy$_{joint}$	100.00	<u>97.81</u>	<u>93.46</u>	<u>64.03</u>	<u>65.81</u>	<u>64.91</u>	<u>83.17</u>	<u>79.03</u>	94.41
greCy$_{perseus}$	100.00	80.42	56.11	0.78	0.10	0.17	63.03	47.58	89.13
greCy$_{proiel}$	100.00	**98.23**	**94.05**	**71.76**	**71.82**	**71.79**	**85.74**	**82.28**	**98.06**
Stanza$_{perseus}$	99.99	80.93	56.00	0.93	0.10	0.17	59.00	43.79	87.14
Stanza$_{proiel}$	100.00	97.39	92.20	55.34	52.44	53.85	81.51	77.48	<u>97.21</u>
UDPipe$_{perseus}$	100.00	74.19	53.17	0.00	0.00	0.00	51.29	37.94	81.69
UDPipe$_{proiel}$	100.00	95.97	88.62	52.97	49.38	51.11	72.40	67.48	93.17

Table 2: Model performances on the test fold of *UD Proiel* Treebank. Highest performance in bold, second highest underlined.

*CLTK's tokenization had to be manually fixed as it routinely added punctuation to tokens, and spaCy's evaluation scripts could not align them against the gold standard.

	UD Perseus		UD Proiel	
Lemmatizer	With Diacritics	Ignored Diacritics	With Diacritics	Ignored Diacritics
Lookup	75.27	76.52	89.13	90.69
Neural	84.16	85.54	93.5	94.58
Lexicon	76.79	78.4	94.4	94.53
Full	83.2	85.55	94.4	94.53

Table 3: Performances of individual lemmatizer components and the full lemmatization process of the odyCy$_{joint}$ model. Scores are accuracies.

- *Mismatch in diacritics.* Different Ancient Greek dialects and styles may employ diacritics in different ways. This leads to a mismatch in lemma annotations on multiple occasions; Consider ἐρῆμος versus ἔρημος. This problem can be alleviated by ignoring diacritics, which leads to higher lemmatization accuracies (see Table 3). However, diacritics are needed in the other components of the pipeline, for example, to distinguish between the nominative form πατήρ and the vocative πάτηρ.

- *Lemmas in neuter vs. masculine form.* Ancient Greek lacks a canonical lemmatization scheme, resulting in situations where both masculine and neuter forms of a word can function as a lemma in some instances, e.g. σίδηρος or σίδηρον.

- *Compound words.* Compound lemmas in Perseus are marked with dashes between the two words, sometimes leading to mismatches. This is either because the predicted lemma is missing a dash on Perseus data or it contains one when evaluating against the Proiel gold standard (see Section 2.1 for an example).

4 Conclusion

Comparing the performance of our model and several other comparable tools suggests there is a considerable amount of transferable information between *UD Perseus* and *UD Proiel* – the two most commonly used datasets for modeling linguistic features in Ancient Greek. We improved the state-of-art on some tasks, but more work is necessary to enhance the interoperability between the two datasets. We identify the main issues and list suggestions for improvement. Resolving these issues is a good way of addressing the low generalizability of Ancient Greek language models on out-of-training set samples (e.g., the bad performance of Proiel models on Perseus data).

Our best-performing model, $\text{odyCy}_{\text{joint}}$, comes with its own set of problems (see Limitations), but comparing its performance to similar tools suggests it generalizes better across the two datasets. This is advantageous when analyzing mixed corpora, where it is unclear whether the corpus to be analyzed is more Perseus-like or Proiel-like. However, it should be noted that a better solution exists for Proiel-like corpora, namely the $\text{greCy}_{\text{proiel}}$ model.

Finally, the model and its source code have been made open source[5], together with the source code for evaluating the performance of Ancient Greek NLP tools[6].

Limitations

Training on Both Treebanks

Since the two UD treebanks for Ancient Greek have different annotation schemes we are severely limiting the model's performance on certain corpora and tasks. Our model, for example is particularly bad at recognizing proper nouns as they are not included in Perseus at all. In our future work we intend to address these issues.

Low Variety in Training Data

Even though we are training odyCy on both available treebanks, the temporal, cultural, and literary variety of the data is relatively low. One perspective direction is to train and evaluate the model's performance on more datasets. This also poses some problems, because they have not been annotated following UD guidelines. An interesting data source that comes to mind are the Dependency Treebanks of Ancient Greek Authors (Gorman, 2020), which consists of Ancient Greek prose. As to texts picked for annotation, the treebank overlaps with *UD Perseus* to some extent. The partially annotated Collection of Greek Ritual Norms used by de Graaf et al. (2022) is also a good candidate for further annotation and usage.

Lemmatization Performance

On the *UD Perseus* testing data odyCy is outperformed by Stanza's Perseus model. We suspect that this difference might be attributed to the fact that Stanza uses full sequence-to-sequence lemmatizer models, which are much more flexible than the tree-based and lookup solutions we are using. We plan on addressing this issue either by implementing a sequence-to-sequence lemmatizer in our pipeline or by increasing the quality and quantity of the training data. Based on the results of the error analysis we have reasons to suspect that the latter might be sufficient.

Sentencization Performance

odyCy is outperformed by other neural pipelines trained on the *UD Perseus* Treebank in sentencization-

[5] odyCy (Github)

[6] greevaluation (Github)

tion. This might be due to the fact that both Stanza and UDPipe use recurrent neural networks for sentencization and tokenization as well as the fact the sentences end with punctuation and the pipelines don't have to rely as much on dependency parsing. Our models learn dependency parsing and sentence segmentation jointly. This approach might not work best with text containing clear sentence boundaries but clearly outperforms both UDPipe and Stanza on *UD Proiel*, where sentence boundaries are missing. greCy performs exceptionally on *UD Proiel*, as it ships with its own sentence recognizer component. However, since it is only trained on one treebank, it performs worse on *UD Perseus*. This issue might be addressed by adding a separate sentence recognizer to odyCy. Still, odyCy seems to already provide a robust solution for sentencization.

Variants of Greek

Furthermore, the model can benefit from additional error analysis comparing the regional and temporal variants of Greek. We have not investigated how well the pipeline handles e.g. Doric morphology. In order to evaluate and possibly enhance the performance of our pipeline on other dialects of Ancient Greek or other literary genres we will need newly annotated texts. The already existing pipeline might be of substantial help here, as annotation would only consist of fixing the model's errors.

Acknowledgements

The study was supported by The Carlsberg Foundation's Semper Ardens instrument ('Computing Antiquity: Computational Research in Ancient Text Corpora', grant holder Jacob P.B. Mortensen). We would also like to thank Ross Deans Kristensen-McLachlan, Yuri Bizzoni and Jacobo Myerston for their helpful comments.

References

David Bamman and Gregory Crane. 2011. The ancient greek and latin dependency treebanks. In *Language Technology for Cultural Heritage*, pages 79–98. Springer Berlin Heidelberg.

Corien Bary, Peter Berck, and Iris Hendrickx. 2017. A memory-based lemmatizer for ancient greek. In *Proceedings of the 2nd International Conference on Digital Access to Textual Cultural Heritage*, DATeCH2017, page 91–95, New York, NY, USA. Association for Computing Machinery.

Giuseppe G. A. Celano, Gregory Crane, and Saeed Majidi. 2016. Part of speech tagging for ancient greek. *Open Linguistics*, 2(1). Publisher: De Gruyter Open Access.

Evelien de Graaf, Silvia Stopponi, Jasper Bos, Saskia Peels-Matthey, and Malvina Nissim. 2022. Agile: The first lemmatizer for ancient greek inscriptions. In *Proceedings of the 13th Conference on Language Resources and Evaluation (LREC 2022)*, pages 5334–5344. European Language Resources Association (ELRA). The 13th Conference on Language Resources and Evaluation, LREC 2022 ; Conference date: 20-06-2022 Through 25-06-2022.

Marie-Catherine de Marneffe, Christopher D. Manning, Joakim Nivre, and Daniel Zeman. 2021. Universal dependencies. *Computational Linguistics*, pages 1–54.

Vanessa B. Gorman. 2020. Dependency treebanks of ancient greek prose. *Journal of Open Humanities Data*, 6(1). Publisher: Ubiquity Press.

Lasse Hansen and Kenneth Enevoldsen. 2023. Textdescriptives: A python package for calculating a large variety of metrics from text. *arXiv preprint arXiv:1503.06733*.

Dag TT Haug and Marius Jøhndal. 2008. Creating a parallel treebank of the old indo-european bible translations. In *Proceedings of the second workshop on language technology for cultural heritage data (LaTeCH 2008)*, pages 27–34.

Kyle P. Johnson, Patrick J. Burns, John Stewart, Todd Cook, Clément Besnier, and William J. B. Mattingly. 2021. The classical language toolkit: An NLP framework for pre-modern languages. In *Proceedings of the 59th Annual Meeting of the Association for Computational Linguistics and the 11th International Joint Conference on Natural Language Processing: System Demonstrations*, pages 20–29. Association for Computational Linguistics.

Thomas Müller, Ryan Cotterell, Alexander Fraser, and Hinrich Schütze. 2015. Joint lemmatization and morphological tagging with lemming. In *Proceedings of the 2015 Conference on Empirical Methods in Natural Language Processing*, pages 2268–2274, Lisbon, Portugal. Association for Computational Linguistics.

Peng Qi, Yuhao Zhang, Yuhui Zhang, Jason Bolton, and Christopher D. Manning. 2020. Stanza: A python natural language processing toolkit for many human languages. In *Proceedings of the 58th Annual Meeting of the Association for Computational Linguistics: System Demonstrations*, pages 101–108. Association for Computational Linguistics.

Pranaydeep Singh, Gorik Rutten, and Els Lefever. 2021. A pilot study for BERT language modelling and morphological analysis for ancient and medieval Greek. In *Proceedings of the 5th Joint SIGHUM Workshop on Computational Linguistics for Cultural Heritage,*

Social Sciences, Humanities and Literature, pages 128–137, Punta Cana, Dominican Republic (online). Association for Computational Linguistics.

Milan Straka. 2018. UDPipe 2.0 prototype at CoNLL 2018 UD shared task. In *Proceedings of the CoNLL 2018 Shared Task: Multilingual Parsing from Raw Text to Universal Dependencies*, pages 197–207, Brussels, Belgium. Association for Computational Linguistics.

Minh Van Nguyen, Viet Dac Lai, Amir Pouran Ben Veyseh, and Thien Huu Nguyen. 2021. Trankit: A light-weight transformer-based toolkit for multilingual natural language processing. *arXiv preprint arXiv:2101.03289*.

Alessandro Vatri and Barbara McGillivray. 2020. Lemmatization for ancient greek: An experimental assessment of the state of the art. *Journal of Greek Linguistics*, 20(2):179–196. Publisher: Brill.

Scent Mining: Extracting Olfactory Events, Smell Sources and Qualities

Stefano Menini[†], **Teresa Paccosi**[†‡], **Serra Sinem Tekiroğlu**[†] **Sara Tonelli**[†]
[†]Fondazione Bruno Kessler, Trento, Italy,
[‡]University of Trento, Italy
{menini,tpaccosi,tekiroglu,satonelli}@fbk.eu

Abstract

Olfaction is a rather understudied sense compared to the other human senses. In NLP, however, there have been recent attempts to develop taxonomies and benchmarks specifically designed to capture smell-related information. In this work, we further extend this research line by presenting a supervised system for olfactory information extraction in English. We cast this problem as a token classification task and build a system that identifies smell words, smell sources and qualities. The classifier is then applied to a set of English historical corpora, covering different domains and written in a time period between the 15th and the 20th Century. A qualitative analysis of the extracted data shows that they can be used to infer interesting information about smelly items such as tea and tobacco from a diachronical perspective, supporting historical investigation with corpus-based evidence.

1 Introduction

In recent years, research on sensory-related analysis of texts has become more and more relevant within the NLP community. Indeed, studies in linguistics, primarily aimed at assessing how sensory language differs across languages and how the different senses are described and compared (Majid and Burenhult, 2014; Strik Lievers and Winter, 2018; Winter et al., 2018; Winter, 2019), have then paved the way for more computationally-oriented analyses, aimed for example at structuring the sensory vocabulary in machine-readable taxonomies (Tekiroğlu et al., 2014a,b; McGregor and McGillivray, 2018; Menini et al., 2022a), using distributional semantics to explore sensory blending (Girju and Lambert, 2021), or extracting sensory information about cities using data from social media (Quercia et al., 2015).

Several works have dealt with olfaction, which is a sense that is traditionally less represented in the vocabulary of Western European languages and in texts (Winter et al., 2018), making it a very interesting domain to investigate with computational means. The first work trying to capture smelly experiences using two semi-supervised approaches was presented in Brate et al. (2020), while annotation guidelines and a multilingual benchmark for olfactory information have been recently released (Tonelli and Menini, 2021; Menini et al., 2022b). Along this research line, we present a supervised system for olfactory information extraction in English trained on the above benchmark. We cast this task as a token-classification problem, labelling smell words that evoke olfactory events and two related semantic roles: smell sources and qualities. We present not only a standard evaluation by measuring F1 on each element, but also a qualitative analysis, by applying our system to four historical corpora in English and manually interpreting the extracted information.

The code and the model used to extract olfactory information from texts are available at https://github.com/dhfbk/scent-mining.

2 Dataset

In order to train a system for olfactory information extraction, we use the English benchmark presented in Menini et al. (2022b).[1] The benchmark contains 85 documents, distributed evenly over a time period between 1620 and 1920 and covering 10 domains: *Household & Recipes*, *Law*, *Literature*, *Medicine & Botany*, *Perfumes & Fashion*, *Public health*, *Religion*, *Science & Philosophy*, *Theatre*, *Travel & Ethnography*.

The benchmark was annotated with olfactory information following the guidelines presented in Tonelli and Menini (2021). This scheme is inspired by frame semantics (Fillmore and Baker, 2001) and the FrameNet annotation project (Ruppenhofer

[1]Available at https://github.com/Odeuropa/benchmarks_and_corpora

Proceedings of the 7th Joint SIGHUM Workshop on Computational Linguistics for Cultural Heritage, Social Sciences, Humanities and Literature (LaTeCH-CLfL2023), pages 135–140
May 5, 2023 ©2023 Association for Computational Linguistics

et al., 2006),[2] whose goal is to capture situations and events present in texts. In the benchmark that we use for our experiments, only one event type was considered, i.e. *Olfactory event*, which according to the guidelines can be evoked by a *smell word*, or Lexical Unit (LU). Such smell word may be connected to one or more *Semantic roles* (so-called Frame Elements, FEs) participating in such event. English smell words include nouns such as 'stink', 'odour','stench','whiff', verbs such as 'to smell','to reek','to sniff', adjectives such as 'scented','odorous','reeking', and adverbs such as 'pungently'.

The benchmark contains 1,530 olfactory events. Concerning semantic roles, the annotation scheme foresees nine of them, namely *Smell source*, *Quality*, *Evoked odorant*, *Odour carrier*, *Perceiver*, *Time*, *Location*, *Effect* and *Circumstances*. The most frequent ones are *Smell source* and *Quality*, which are both represented by respectively 1,313 and 1,084 instances in the benchmark, while all the others are much more sparse. For this reason, we include in our first system for olfactory information extraction only the recognition of smell words, *Smell source* and *Quality*, leaving the other roles to future extensions.

We report in Table 1 the definition of these two FEs. According to these guidelines, if we consider the sentence below, we would annotate '[The coffee]' as *Smell source* and '[pungent]' as *Quality*, while 'smell' would be the lexical unit evoking the olfactory event.

[The coffee] had a [pungent] smell.

3 System for Olfactory Information Extraction

The model for olfactory information extraction has been designed as a token classification task, i.e. a natural language understanding task in which a label is assigned to each token in a given text. While past works in semantic frame parsing usually treated lexical unit detection and frame element annotation as two separate tasks (Das et al., 2014), we consider them both at the same level and build a single classification model. We use the IOB labeling data format, in which tokens in a span are marked with Inside–Outside–Beginning of smell-related elements. The model labels each token as O (outside), B-FRAME_ELEMENT (beginning of a span of an olfactory element) or I-FRAME_ELEMENT (inside of a span of an olfactory element) given an input sentence. As introduced above, we label both smell words and the two most frequent frame elements, namely *Smell Source* and *Quality*.

Frame Element	Definition and Example
Smell Source	The person, object or place that has a specific smell. It can also refer to (non)human/object that produces an odour (e.g. plant, animal, perfume, human). The entity or phenomenon that the perceiver experiences through his or her senses.
Quality	A quality associated with a smell and used to describe it. This is typically expressed by qualitative adjectives and it is often preceded by an intensifier such as 'very, really'. Qualities include intensity ('weak', 'distinct'), volume/reach ('far reaching'), duration ('lasting', 'permanent'), state ('old', 'deteriorated'), character ('dry', 'garlicky'), hedonic characteristics ('malodorous', 'aromatic').

Table 1: Definition of Smell Source and Quality from the benchmark annotation guidelines.

Considering the advantages of pre-trained language models (LM) based on the Transformer architecture for downstream NLP tasks (Vaswani et al., 2017), we use the pre-trained BERT models (Devlin et al., 2019) in our experiments. Each model has been fine-tuned with a token classification head on top.[3] We experiment both with a monolingual language model (bert-base-uncased)[4] and its multilingual variant (bert-base-multilingual-uncased)[5] and fine-tune these models for the token classification task.

We perform five-fold cross-validation, using 80% of the data for training, 10% for validation and 10% for testing. During training, a hyperparameter search is applied to Fold-0 with the model under investigation over the search space: learning rate $[1e-5, 2e-5, 3e-5, 4e-5, 5e-5]$, batch size $[4, 8]$, number of training epochs $range(1, 10)$. Warmup for 10% of the training steps was applied. After determining the hyperparameters for each model, it is fine-tuned 5 times, each time with a different data fold, and average scores are computed.

Table 2 shows the classification results obtained

[2] https://framenet.icsi.berkeley.edu

[3] The Huggingface Transformers library was used to implement the token classification task. https://huggingface.co/docs/transformers/tasks/token_classification

[4] https://huggingface.co/bert-base-uncased

[5] https://huggingface.co/bert-base-multilingual-uncased

	F1			
	Smell Word	Source	Quality	Overall
BERT	0.877	**0.503**	**0.686**	**0.689**
mBERT	**0.885**	0.490	0.672	0.682

Table 2: Classification results (macro F1) on English. We distinguish between using monolingual BERT and mBERT.

on *Smell Words*, *Smell Sources* and *Qualities*, as well as the overall score obtained by averaging the system performance on these three elements. Our evaluation is based on "exact match", i.e. the smell words and the other roles are considered correctly identified only if they match completely with the annotation in the gold standard. If there is a partial overlap of the tokens, the labelling is considered not correct.

We compare the results obtained with monolingual BERT and its multilingual version (mBERT). Note that performance on smell words is better than on the other frame elements because the former are mostly single words, while *Smell Source* and *Quality* are typically expressed by phrases and also the identification of the correct span can be very challenging. Overall, there is only a slight difference between BERT and mBERT, with BERT performing better. Therefore, we adopt this model for our next analysis.

4 Olfactory Information Extraction

We launch the BERT-based model on a set of historical corpora of English. Our goal is to analyse the smell-related information extracted by our system and to perform some qualitative study of the results. We focus on four freely available corpora:

Project Gutenberg:[6] A volunteer effort to digitize and archive cultural works, it contains different repositories, mainly in the literary domain (4,943 books, 366M tokens).

The Royal Society Corpus:[7] A repository of scientific periodicals issued between 1665 and 1869 (9,782 documents for a total of 31M tokens);

A pre-processed subset of *the Old Bailey Papers* dataset,[8] containing the court proceedings published between 1720 and 1913 (638 books 3.1M tokens).

Early English Books Online (EEBO),[9] containing documents published between 1475 and 1700 in different domains such as literature, philosophy, politics, religion, geography, history, politics, mathematics (60,329 documents for a total of 1.4B tokens)

In Table 3 we provide an overview of the olfactory information extracted from the above set of corpora. The data are divided into two groups based on their publication date, which will be used for the analysis presented in Section 5:

	1500-1799	1800-1930	Total
Smell Sentences	91,018	32,442	123,460
Smell Sources	66,070	27,776	93,846
Qualities	49,275	19,039	68,314

Table 3: Sentences containing at least a smell word and the number of associated *Smell Sources* and *Qualities*.

5 Case study: Perception shift

Inspired by past approaches to semantic shift detection, we examine potential changes in the way a specific smell source is described in texts. We argue that these variations may reflect a shift in the perception of specific smells, as already highlighted in historical research using qualitative approaches (Tullett, 2019b).

In our analysis we compare the meaning of the smell sources before and after 1800. We select this period because it represents a significant turning point in the cultural attitudes towards scent, especially in England. The sense of smell acquired an increasingly social significance and played a role in shaping both individual identities and those of specific places (Tullett, 2019a). For this purpose we split the extracted data in two parts, the first one covering the period from 1500 to 1799 and the second one from 1800 to 1930.

To identify perception shifts in the olfactory information extracted from our data, we follow the work by El-Ebshihy et al. (2018) on semantic shifts. First, we reduce the vocabulary of the text extracted by lemmatizing it with Stanza (Qi et al., 2020). Then, for each time period, we create an embedding space with FastText, using the skip-gram model and an embedding size of 100 (Bojanowski et al., 2016). To be able to compare the embeddings from the two time periods, we align the 1800-1930 space

[6]https://www.gutenberg.org/

[7]http://fedora.clarin-d.uni-saarland.de/rsc_v4/

[8]http://fedora.clarin-d.uni-saarland.de/oldbailey/downloads.html

[9]https://textcreationpartnership.org/tcp-texts/eebo-tcp-early-english-books-online/

Smell Source	Cosine Similarity	Smell Source	Cosine Similarity
tea	0.4627	fat	0.5233
vomit	0.4801	blood	0.5251
lead	0.4894	eau	0.5367
bullock	0.4930	dung	0.5421
corps	0.4934	liquid	0.5471
dust	0.5098	manure	0.5509
refuse	0.5131	**snuff**	0.5569
sick	0.5183	stomach	0.5622
sage	0.5187	beer	0.5627
bone	0.5211	**tobacco**	0.5658

Table 4: List of smell sources with cosine similarity lower than the threshold. The lower the similarity, the higher the perception shift of the smell source.

to the 1500-1799 one using a shared vocabulary. Shifts in the olfactory perception are then detected by computing the cosine similarity between the two embeddings of the same *Smell Source* in the two time periods. We focus on smell sources because we aim at analysing which items have undergone a significant change in the way their smell was perceived over time. In particular, we first compute the average similarity between all the smell sources in the two time spans and then we set as threshold for possible semantic shift the average similarity minus the standard deviation.

Table 4 shows the smell sources in the two time spans that have undergone the highest change in olfactory perception. As displayed in Table 2, the performance of the classifier is still rather law on smell sources, probably due to the evaluation strategy based on the exact match of the spans. For this reason, we performed a manual check of the smell sources detected by the shift analysis and their surrounding text. Interestingly, some items in the list were also analysed in previous historical research and were identified as key elements involved in olfactory change. We report few examples below.

Tea: The variation in the context related to this smell can be imputed to the great change in the perception of this beverage from a very exotic one when it first entered Europe (around 1630s-1640s) to a central role in the daily domestic life for the majority of Europeans (especially Dutch and English) in the nineteenth century (Webster and Parkes, 1844). Therefore, in the first period it is possible to find references to the flavor of tea as something new and not really pleasant to the European taste (see Example 1 below, extracted from our corpus), while by the early 19th Century the smell of tea becomes very common in European houses (Example 2).

(1) *Nor can it be drunk so strong without tasting an unpleasant bitterness, which the milk partly hides (1773)*

(2) *Benjamin led his mother on into the dining-room [...] the tea-table already spread, and a delicate, home-like aroma of toast and tea pervading it. (1879)*

Tobacco: Prior to the end of the 1700s, the odor of tobacco is regarded as a symbol of manliness and prevalent in most male settings. The adjectives linked to tobacco were mainly confined to the realm of male authority, with "strong" being a commonly used term to describe the scent of tobacco (Example 3). However, it isn't until the 1800s that unflattering descriptors like "disgusting", "nauseating" or "unpleasant" were linked to the scent of tobacco (Example 4).

(3) *I heard my brother say "you smell strong of tobacco". (1760)*

(4) *He had thick boorish hands, and he smelt unpleasantly of tobacco smoke. (1843)*

As smoking fell out of favor, *Snuff* emerged as the favored method of consuming tobacco (Tullett, 2019b; Goodman, 2005). Indeed, by the late eighteenth century, *Snuff* became the fashionable choice over smoking due to the prevailing manner of the period focused on the need to please others (Tullett, 2019b). Snuff's growing popularity provided in fact a more discreet form of tobacco consumption, which significantly reduced the likelihood of offending others with the pungent odor of smoke. This trend is reflected in the data through the frequent references to "pinch of snuff" and "snuff boxes" after 1800.

Even if the performance of the classifier is not very good in detecting smell sources, we consider these results promising. We plan to improve the system and to increase the amount of training data in the future to further refine our analysis.

6 Conclusions

In this paper we present the first information extraction system able to capture smell events, including smell words, smell sources and qualities. We then apply the system to four English corpora, covering a time period between 15th and 20th century.

Then, starting from the extracted data, we adapt an existing approach to semantic shift detection to capture which smell sources underwent a change in the way their odour was perceived before and after 1800. We find correspondences between the extracted items and the output of historical research concerning the smell of tobacco and tea.

Despite the limited amount of data, the results are promising and indicate that this research can yield valuable insights in the area of diachronical sensory analysis. In the future, we intend to broaden the scope of our data and conduct more comprehensive analyses on a greater variety of smell sources.

Acknowledgements

This research has been supported by the European Union's Horizon 2020 program project ODEUROPA under grant agreement number 101004469.

References

Piotr Bojanowski, Edouard Grave, Armand Joulin, and Tomás Mikolov. 2016. Enriching word vectors with subword information. *CoRR*, abs/1607.04606.

Ryan Brate, Paul Groth, and Marieke van Erp. 2020. Towards olfactory information extraction from text: A case study on detecting smell experiences in novels. In *Proceedings of the The 4th Joint SIGHUM Workshop on Computational Linguistics for Cultural Heritage, Social Sciences, Humanities and Literature*, pages 147–155, Online. International Committee on Computational Linguistics.

Dipanjan Das, Desai Chen, André FT Martins, Nathan Schneider, and Noah A Smith. 2014. Frame-semantic parsing. *Computational linguistics*, 40(1):9–56.

Jacob Devlin, Ming-Wei Chang, Kenton Lee, and Kristina Toutanova. 2019. BERT: Pre-training of deep bidirectional transformers for language understanding. In *Proceedings of the 2019 Conference of the North American Chapter of the Association for Computational Linguistics: Human Language Technologies, Volume 1 (Long and Short Papers)*, pages 4171–4186, Minneapolis, Minnesota. Association for Computational Linguistics.

Alaa El-Ebshihy, Nagwa M El-Makky, and Khaled Nagi. 2018. Using google books ngram in detecting linguistic shifts over time. In *KDIR*, pages 330–337.

Charles J. Fillmore and Collin F. Baker. 2001. Frame semantics for text understanding. In *In Proceedings of WordNet and Other Lexical Resources Workshop*.

Roxana Girju and Charlotte Lambert. 2021. Inter-sense: An investigation of sensory blending in fiction. In *Proceedings of the 1st International Workshop on Multisensory Data Knowledge*, volume 3064. CEUR-WS.

Jordan Goodman. 2005. *"To live by smoke" in Tobacco in history: The cultures of dependence*. Routledge, pp. 212-235.

Asifa Majid and Niclas Burenhult. 2014. Odors are expressible in language, as long as you speak the right language. *Cognition*, 130(2):266–270.

Stephen McGregor and Barbara McGillivray. 2018. A distributional semantic methodology for enhanced search in historical records: A case study on smell. In *Proceedings of the 14th Conference on Natural Language Processing, KONVENS 2018, Vienna, Austria, September 19-21, 2018*, pages 1–11. Österreichische Akademie der Wissenschaften.

Stefano Menini, Teresa Paccosi, Serra Sinem Tekiroğlu, and Sara Tonelli. 2022a. Building a multilingual taxonomy of olfactory terms with timestamps. In *Proceedings of the Thirteenth Language Resources and Evaluation Conference*, pages 4030–4039, Marseille, France. European Language Resources Association.

Stefano Menini, Teresa Paccosi, Sara Tonelli, Marieke Van Erp, Inger Leemans, Pasquale Lisena, Raphael Troncy, William Tullett, Ali Hürriyetoğlu, Ger Dijkstra, Femke Gordijn, Elias Jürgens, Josephine Koopman, Aron Ouwerkerk, Sanne Steen, Inna Novalija, Janez Brank, Dunja Mladenic, and Anja Zidar. 2022b. A multilingual benchmark to capture olfactory situations over time. In *Proceedings of the 3rd Workshop on Computational Approaches to Historical Language Change*, pages 1–10, Dublin, Ireland. Association for Computational Linguistics.

Peng Qi, Yuhao Zhang, Yuhui Zhang, Jason Bolton, and Christopher D. Manning. 2020. Stanza: A Python natural language processing toolkit for many human languages. In *Proceedings of the 58th Annual Meeting of the Association for Computational Linguistics: System Demonstrations*.

D. Quercia, R. Schifanella, L. Aiello, and K. McLean. 2015. Smelly maps: The digital life of urban smellscapes. In *Proceedings of ICWSM*.

Josef Ruppenhofer, Michael Ellsworth, Myriam Schwarzer-Petruck, Christopher R. Johnson, and Jan Scheffczyk. 2006. Framenet ii: Extended theory and practice. Working paper, International Computer Science Institute, Berkeley, CA.

Strik Strik Lievers and Bodo Winter. 2018. Sensory language across lexical categories. *Lingua*, 204:45–61.

Serra Sinem Tekiroğlu, Gözde Özbal, and Carlo Strapparava. 2014a. A computational approach to generate a sensorial lexicon. In *Proceedings of the 4th Workshop on Cognitive Aspects of the Lexicon (CogALex)*, pages 114–125, Dublin, Ireland. Association for Computational Linguistics and Dublin City University.

Serra Sinem Tekiroğlu, Gözde Özbal, and Carlo Strapparava. 2014b. Sensicon: An automatically constructed sensorial lexicon. In *Proceedings of the 2014 Conference on Empirical Methods in Natural Language Processing (EMNLP)*, pages 1511–1521, Doha, Qatar. Association for Computational Linguistics.

Sara Tonelli and Stefano Menini. 2021. FrameNet-like annotation of olfactory information in texts. In *Proceedings of the 5th Joint SIGHUM Workshop on Computational Linguistics for Cultural Heritage, Social Sciences, Humanities and Literature*, pages 11–20, Punta Cana, Dominican Republic (online). Association for Computational Linguistics.

William Tullett. 2019a. Re-odorization, disease, and emotion in mid-nineteenth-century england. *The Historical Journal*, 62(3):765–788.

William Tullett. 2019b. *Smell in Eighteenth-Century England: A Social Sense*. Oxford University Press.

Ashish Vaswani, Noam Shazeer, Niki Parmar, Jakob Uszkoreit, Llion Jones, Aidan N Gomez, Ł ukasz Kaiser, and Illia Polosukhin. 2017. Attention is all you need. In *Advances in Neural Information Processing Systems*, volume 30. Curran Associates, Inc.

Thomas Webster and Mrs William Parkes. 1844. *An Encyclopaedia of Domestic Economy: Comprising Such Subjects as are Most Immediately Connected with Housekeeping...* Longman, Brown, Green, and Longmans.

Bodo Winter. 2019. *Sensory linguistics: Language, perception and metaphor*, volume 20. John Benjamins Publishing Company.

Bodo Winter, Marcus Perlman, and Asifa Majid. 2018. Vision dominates in perceptual language: English sensory vocabulary is optimized for usage. *Cognition*, 179:213–220.

Exploring Social Sciences Archives with Explainable Document Linkage through Question Generation

Elie Antoine[1], **Hyun Jung Kang**[2], **Ismaël Rousseau**[2], **Ghislaine Azémard**[3]
Frederic Bechet[1], **Géraldine Damnati**[2]
(1) Aix Marseille Univ, CNRS, LIS, France {first.last}@lis-lab.fr
(2) Orange Innovation, DATA&AI, Lannion {first.last}@orange.com
(3) FMSH/Univ Paris 8 Chaire UNESCO ITEN azemard@msh-paris.fr

Abstract

This paper introduces the question answering paradigm as a way to explore digitized archive collections for Social Science studies. Question generation can be used as a way to create explainable links between documents. Question generation for document linking is validated on a new corpus of digitized archive collection of a French Social Science journal.

1 Introduction

From an information and communication science perspective, two steps are essential to bring together computer technology and human and social science objectives. The first essential step is the availability of annotated data in order to train and evaluate with objective metrics the model deployed to ensure their relevance and scientific interest. The second essential step is the creation of an interface adapted to the objectives of the device and respectful of the user by putting forward the explainability of the results provided.

This methodology was followed in the context of the *Archival* project[1]: firstly existing annotated data have been used to train and evaluate deep neural network question generation models; secondly we applied these models to a corpus of social science archives for evaluating their relevance in a real archive exploration application. This paper describes this second step, which study if recent advances in Natural Language Processing thanks to deep learning models translate into novel mediation interfaces for social science researchers.

This paper is structured as follows: section 2 presents our methodology for generating explainable links among documents based on question-generation models; section 3 presents the archive corpus used in this study; section 4 presents our question generation and filtering method; section 5 describes how generated questions can be used to create explainable links within documents; finally sections 6, 7 and 8 presents an experimental study on our archive corpus with quantitative, descriptive and qualitative evaluations of the method proposed.

[1] https://anr.fr/Projet-ANR-19-CE38-0011

2 Exploration through questions generation

When exploring a thematic archive collection, links can be made between documents or parts of documents according to various criteria such as co-occurence of entities (person, location, organisation, date, ...), keywords related to a knowledge base or a thesaurus (Tsatsaronis et al., 2014), or directly by a statistical similarity measure between documents or parts of documents such as sentences (Wang et al., 2016) or paragraphs (Dai et al., 2015).

Furthermore, some methods produce links directly between the embedding of the whole documents (Ginzburg et al., 2021), (Jiang et al., 2019), the sum of the word embeddings of the document (Landthaler et al., 2018) or by representing them with word-graphs and using shortest-path algorithms for linking (Nikolentzos et al., 2017). The graph structure obtained can then be used to design navigation interfaces such as maps representing linked documents or directly by inserting hypertext links (Mihalcea and Csomai, 2007; Brochier and Béchet, 2021).

The weaknesses of keywork/entity links are on the one hand the amount of links generated that can be very big if large sets of keywords or entities are considered and on the other hand the fact that the simple occurrence of relevant terms does not mean that their contexts of occurrence are relevant or interesting to users. On the contrary, similarity-based links take words in context into consideration, but the use of statistical similarity metrics make the links often difficult to interpret.

Recently, advances in Question Answering (QA) models from text have enabled the use of asking

Proceedings of the 7th Joint SIGHUM Workshop on Computational Linguistics for Cultural Heritage, Social Sciences, Humanities and Literature (LaTeCH-CLfL2023), pages 141–151
May 5, 2023

direct natural language questions in order to access to electronic documents. Impressive results have been obtained with current deep learning language models on benchmark corpora such as SQuAD (Rajpurkar et al., 2016), however it has been shown that the kind of questions that these models handle best are simple literal questions for which a factual answer can be found in the text and that performance drops when dealing with more abstract questions or questions needing a larger context than a sentence in order to be addressed. Moreover, most of these studies have been applied only on Wikipedia text. A recent study (Bechet et al., 2022) have shown that *realistic* questions, like those that can be asked by a professional reader analyzing social science archives are quite far from the simple benchmark questions used to evaluate QA systems, leading to poor performance.

However, even if current QA models might be too simplistic for use in a real archive exploration setting, we believe that Question Generation models can still be useful in order to characterize documents. Such models can be trained on the same corpora as QA models: while QA models are trained to generate a response given a question and a text document, Question Generation models are trained to predict a question given an *answer* and a text document. By selecting potential answers on text segments and generating questions from these answers and their context of occurrence, we obtain an abstraction of a text segment which contains the set of questions that can be asked on it. By estimating similarities between questions and answers belonging to different documents, we can predict links between them that can be explained by the two QA pairs, adding an explainability layer to the process. We believe that this is an efficient way of presenting links to a user: by looking only at the linked QA pairs, readers can decide if it is worth or not to follow this link, saving time compared to the standard solution consisting of following every link to decide if the similarity between two text segments is interesting or not.

In this study, we developed a question generation and filtering process which is used to obtain links between documents of a collection of social science archive corpus. This study presents the first quantitative and qualitative evaluation done of this method on this archive corpus.

3 The *self-management* archive corpus

In order to assess the previously described "exploration through questions generation" paradigm, we have chosen to focus on a particular type of Social Science archive source: a full collection of the *Autogestion* ("self-management") journal published for 20 years between 1966 and 1986. The originality of our work is hence to propose a way to access this rich source through explainable links.

The "self-management" notion falls within the large spectrum of social sciences. It concerns daily social environment, economic life, as well as political life, education, ecology, culture, architecture ... Nowadays, “self-management” supports in an underlying way the concepts of radical democracy, confederalism, social and solidarity economy and sustainable development. As a source of social innovation, self-management has variations all over the world and questions societal and economic models of development. It is a particularly transversal and interdisciplinary notion which can feed research in sociology, political science, economy, law, political anthropology and social history. The *Autogestion* journal [2] is distributed in its digitized form by the French Persée organization. It is part of a larger pluridisciplinary multilingual mixed collection (archives and documents) that has been gathered since the 1960’s by the FMSH[3] foundation’s library. The full collection has been granted the Collex label (*Collection d’Excellence* or Excellency Collection) from the CollEx-Persée[4] network under the supervision of higher education and research for the preservation of corpus of digitized or natively digital documents. (Weill, 1999) describes the journal as an observatory of liberation movements and states that it « *accompanied — preceeding and following — the liberation movement which called for workers’ self-management. Through analysis of its precursors, contemporary practices and historical precedents, the journal was a conceptual tool capable of inspiring action. Its disappearance coincided with the abandonment of the reference to workers’ self- management in socio-political movements, although the aspiration it represented continues to exist.*»

We are using an OCRized version of the corpus. The structure of the journal is rather standard

[2]https://www.persee.fr/collection/autog

[3]Fondation Maison des Sciences de l’Homme, https://www.fmsh.fr/

[4]https://www.collexpersee.eu/le-reseau/

(mono-column, few figures) and the quality of the OCR provided by Tesseract is sufficient to be exploited as is without manual corrections. Studying the impact of OCR errors is outside the scope of this study and should be investigated in further research work.

The resulting corpus is composed of 46 issues of the journal, ranging over 20 years, for an overall amount of 6298 pages and 1.98M tokens.

4 Question generation

The Question-Generation (QG) task is a classical NLP task that has been revisited thanks to the development of efficient deep learning sequence-to-sequence models (Du et al., 2017; Shakeri et al., 2020; Murakhovs'ka et al., 2022) and Large Language Models (Agrawal et al., 2022). It can be modeled as a neural generation task, where a sequence-to-sequence model is trained to *translate* a sequence of words representing a text segment (the *context*) containing an *answer* (a sub-sequence of words belonging to the *context*) into another sequence of words representing a question on the input. The task is then to generate a question given a *(context, answer)* pair. The availability of large databases of question/answer/context triplets such as SQUAD can be used to directly fine-tune sequence-to-sequence generation models such as *BART*.

One of the key decision that has to be made before generating a question is the choice of the *answers* on which questions will be generated. Choosing all noun phrases as answers can lead to an over generation of questions, most of them being not very relevant if the contexts of occurrence of answers is not informative. That is why we chose to use semantic annotations in order to select answer candidates in order to generate more informative questions. As proposed in (Pyatkin et al., 2021) and (Bechet et al., 2022), we use a Semantic Role Labelling (SRL) model following the PropBank formalism (Palmer et al., 2005) in order to select answers candidates among the semantic roles detected.

In our study, we train the question generation model by fine-tuning the BARThez (Kamal Eddine et al., 2021) language model on a French corpus of question-answer-context triplets called *FQuAD* (d'Hoffschmidt et al., 2020). This is a three steps process:

1. Annotation of the text corpus with Semantic Role Labelling (SRL) labels following the PropBank formalism
2. For each question-answer-context triplet:
   (a) Identification of the semantic role that corresponds to the answer of the given question through the alignment of gold answer spans and semantic role spans, selecting the one with maximum overlap
   (b) Generation of a training example, with the selected answer, current sentence as the context, additional semantic information derived from the semantic role analysis as the input sequence, and the question as the output sequence
3. Fine-tuning of the pre-trained generation model on the collected corpus.

At inference time, generating questions on a given sentence involves performing semantic analysis on the sentence, generating an input sequence for each detected semantic role, and using the fine-tuned seq-to-seq model to generate a question for each input sequence.

The following translated example is from the *FQuAD* training set with ANS being the *answer*, LU the lexical unit that triggers the semantic relation, and CTX the context:

source : `[ANS:ARG2] Héra (Hera)[LU] appelé (called) [CTX] Cérès fut également appelé Héra en Allemagne pendant une brève période. (Cérès was also called Hera in a brief period in Germany.)`
target : `What name did Ceres have for a short time in Germany ?`

The application of the question generation model on a sentence from the *self-management* corpus processed by an SRL parser is illustrated in the following example:

source : `[ANS:ARG0] une bonne partie du C.N.R.S. (a good part of the C.N.R.S.)[LU] évolue (is evolving) [CTX] progressivement une bonne partie du C.N.R.S. évolue vers une structure pour ainsi dire autogérée (gradually a good part of the C.N.R.S. is evolving towards a self-managed structure)`
generation : `Quel organisme évolue vers une structure autogérée ? (Which organization is moving towards a self-managed structure ?)`

We apply a series of filters to enhance the quality and reduce the quantity of generated examples. The first step (**F1**) is to restrict the SRL analysis to only include frames with a strictly verbal trigger (rejecting auxiliary verbs), as these are deemed to be of higher quality due to their ease of detection.

To further improve the quality of the generated examples, we apply a filter (**F2**) on the queries to remove those with non-informative answers or contexts. This includes answers that are less than 5 characters, or belonging to the NLTK (Bird et al., 2009) stopwords list in order to eliminate answers containing only pronominal coreferences. Queries with a context of fewer than 5 words are also filtered out.

The generated questions are also subjected to a filter (**F3**) based on the "roundtrip consistency" methodology proposed by (Alberti et al., 2019). This filter involves retaining only the synthetic examples where a QA model [5] is able to retrieve a portion of the target answer from the generated question. We consider that the model has successfully retrieved the answer if there is a minimum overlap of 30% between the predicted answer and the answer of the query.

Finally, we apply a final filter (**F4**) to eliminate duplicate questions, which are a frequent phenomenon due to slight variations in some queries, often resulting in very similar or identical questions.

5 Generating explainable links

The main originality of our approach is the use of our synthetic questions/answers to establish links between documents in our corpus. While traditional methods involve computing similarity via document embeddings at a chosen level of granularity (sentence, paragraph or textblock, page), our approach involves computing a similarity measure between question+answer (Q+A) embeddings. We consider a *source* and a *target* Q+A embeddings obtained by the concatenation of questions and answers produced by our method described in Section 4.

For example, this is the "`<question> | <answer>`" structure obtained on the example of the generated question given in the previous section:

`Quel organisme évolue vers une structure autogérée ? (Which organization is moving towards a self-managed structure?) | une bonne partie du C.N.R.S. (a good part of the C.N.R.S.)`

[5]in our case, a *CamemBert-large* (Martin et al., 2020) model trained on *FQuAD*

Our embedding projection for each Q+A pair use the SentenceTransformer (Reimers and Gurevych, 2019) library [6]. A cosine similarity measure is then employed between all pairwise combinations of these embeddings, resulting in the computation of a similarity matrix.

For each Q+A pair in our corpus, we extract the 49 most similar pairs across three granularities:

1. The entire collection, including the same page/sentence **(ALL)**
2. All documents within the same issue but in a different article **(OUT_ARTICLE)**
3. All documents outside the current issue **(OUT_NUM)**.

This method allows us to enrich the documents in our archive corpus with many links at different levels with an *explanation* for each link, represented by the two question/answer structures kept after filtering by means of the similarity metric.

In the archive exploration prototype developed for the *Archival* project, these links appear when a user highlight a portion of text in the original document: a window appears with a list of links to other documents from the same archive collection. Each link is *explained* by showing the source and the target questions used to produce the link, as well as a snippet of the target document containing the answer to the target question. The metadata (title, author, date) of the target documents are also displayed. This list of links is sorted according to the similarity metrics between source and target Q+A as well as several heuristics: Q+A containing named entities and terms from a thesaurus attached to the archive collection receive a positive score while Q+A containing coreference mentions receive negative score.

Thesaurus and coreference detection are presented in the next section as well as the analysis of the corpus of questions and links generated, both at a quantitative and qualitative level.

6 Quantitative and qualitative description of the generated questions

In this section, we analyze the application of our generation and filtering method to our *self-management* corpus. We provide first a quantitative study of the set of generated questions followed

[6]we use the multilingual model *distiluse-base-multilingual-cased-v1* (Reimers and Gurevych, 2020)

Filter	F1	F2	F3	F4
Nb. questions	247,907	193,685	129,119	79,869

Table 1: Summary of the different filters: F2 (remove non-informative answers), F3 (round-trip consistency), F4 (remove duplicates).

by a more in-depth descriptive study according to three criteria: question types, question themes and coreference chains.

6.1 Quantitative description

We applied our question generation method on a subset of 24 journal issues of the *Autogestion* collection ranging from 1966 to 1979. Each issue contains several short or long articles, for a total of 448 articles. Since the electronic version of this corpus is obtained through OCR, we have two additional level of segmentation: *page* (corresponding to the OCR of each image of a given page of the collection) and *textblock* (the minimal unit of coherent text output by the OCR system). We consider here a subset of the whole corpus presented in section 3. This subset contains 4786 pages, 33551 textblocks for a total of 1,5M tokens. Initially the Semantic Role Labeling process yields 143,317 Frame detections which is reduced to 124,925 detections when focusing on non-auxiliary verbs as of the **F1** filtering process. Each Frame detection yields an average of 1.7 Frame Elements, meaning that the first set is made of 247,907 questions. Table 1 provides the number of generated questions following the filtering processes described in 4.

As we can see, the total number of questions kept after the four-stage filtering process is 79,869. The average number of questions for each granularity level are given in table 2 as well as the percentage of elements containing at least one question for each level. We can see that about 8% of the articles do not contain any question, this corresponds to the summaries or bibliography where we could not detect Frames and therefore generate questions. More than half the textblocks contain at least one question, with an average of 6.2 questions per textblock. The 48.2% of textblocks that doesn't contain any question consists of very short ones such as end notes, titles and all micro-textblocks detected by the OCR.

6.2 Qualitative description

In this section, we analyze the structure and the content of the automatically generated questions.

measure	article	page	TextBlock
avg. nb. Q. per element	258	25.2	6.2
% elements with Q.	91.7%	95.2%	51.8%

Table 2: Average number of questions generated at each level of granularity (item, page, and textblock) and percentage of items with at least one question

6.2.1 Question types

First, we analyze which type of interrogative pronouns is most often used in the synthetic questions.

We can see in figure 1 that the most used interrogative pronoun is the pronoun "What", with a combined 45% of questions using it. This may be due to several things, the first being that many French words correspond to What (or Which), directly increasing the proportion of this class. The second is based on our training corpus, used twice in our process: in the training of our question generation model and in our roundtrip consistency filtering step. Indeed, in the latter, the proportion of "What" questions is very similar to ours (47.8%). We can assume that our question generation model is biased in this direction and that our filtering method, based on the same dataset and having seen more examples of this type, performs better in the MRQA task on questions of this type, and thus amplify this bias. However, this is also consistent with the distribution of ARG0 and ARG1 arguments predicted by the semantic role labeler.

In second place, a quarter of the generated questions are about a person or a group of persons with the pronoun "Who". This seems consistent with the fact that these types of entities are generally best detected by language models. This may also be related to the fact that our corpus contains many accounts of historical events, of positions taken on various influential characters or movements, thus mechanically increasing the number of questions of this type. To support this possibility, we can see that the *FQuAD* dataset contains only 12.2% of such questions, allowing us to rule out a bias similar to that of the "What" questions.

6.2.2 Question themes

We qualify the themes of the question generated with respect to a specific thesaurus which has been created on the *self-management* domain. Starting from prior knowledge of the domain, a first list of notions has been built. It has then been enriched by a list of keywords and keyphrases extracted from the articles of the *Autogestion* journal. These terms

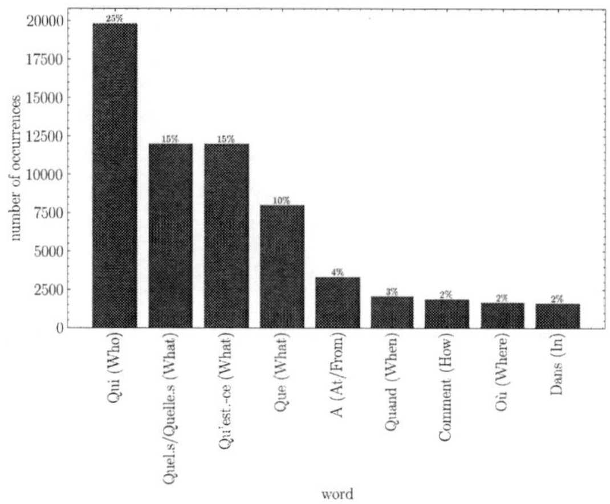

Figure 1: Number and percentage of total number of the interrogative pronoun

are mostly nominal phrases extracted thanks to a morphosyntactic analysis of the documents. When flexional variants of a locution are encountered, the form which has the largest number of occurrences is chosen (majority form). From all the extracted keyphrases, the experts have selected a list of additional thesaurus entries, by choosing terms that refer to general notions that can be relevant to index documents. The thesaurus is then sorted hierarchically in order to form a tree structure of maximum of 4 levels depth. The tree has 437 leaves and is organized in 8 general notions at the root of the tree (*Organisations, Social Classes, Economic Development, Exercice of Power, Justice, Political Models, Psycho-sociology, Social Values*).

We analyzed our corpus of synthetic question/answer pairs to investigate the usage of thesaurus entries. Our results show that **30.6%** of the generated questions and **25.1%** of the answers contain at least one term from the thesaurus. Furthermore, we found that **45.3%** of the question-answer pairs included at least one thesaurus word in either the question or the answer, and **10.4%** contained a thesaurus word in both.

A more detailed description of the distribution of the number of entries detected in the questions and answers can be found in Table 3 and the 10 most frequent entries in Table 4.

The pair with the most thesaurus terms is the following :

Q : Qu'est ce qui rendra possible le **développement** de la **participation** des **travailleurs** et de leurs **organisations** à la direction et à la gestion des entreprises nationales ? (What will make it possible to **develop** the **participation** of **workers** and their **organizations** in the direction and management of national enterprises?)

A : le **changement** – en **droit** et dans les faits – des formes de la **propriété** (the **change** - in **law** and in fact - of the forms of **ownership**)

$\lvert w \in T \rvert$	0	1	2	3	4	5
$\lvert Q + A \rvert$	43693	25159	8472	2129	355	58

Table 3: Distribution of the number of words (w) belonging to thesaurus T among questions+answers ($Q + A$)

entry (Fr)	**entry**	**occurrences**
travailleurs	workers	3247
travail	work	2668
pouvoir	authority	2214
société	society	1947
révolution	revolution	1834
production	production	1742
contrôle	control	1470
système	system	1426
ouvrier	laborer	1387
mouvement	movement	1362

Table 4: The ten most frequent thesaurus entries

This analysis suggests that apart from allowing the creation of links to explore the collection, generated questions could also be a way to illustrate the main notions that are addressed in the journal. Dedicated interfaces could be developed for this purpose in future work. Additionally, we aim to explore the potential of using those results to filter generated questions and weight links to favor those containing key notions of the corpus as we consider that these questions are more likely to refer to a meaningful concept with respect to the theme of the archive collection explored.

6.2.3 Coreference chains

We are also interested in the impact of coreference chains in our question generation process. Indeed, if a question or an answer contains a sub-specified element of a coreference chains, this can affect the quality of the questions generated and furthermore the relevance of the proposed links. Therefore, we applied a coreference resolution system to our corpus in order to qualify this phenomenon in our set of generated questions.

Modern coreference resolution systems adopt an end-to-end architecture, which integrates mention detection and coreference resolution into a single system. (Lee et al., 2017, 2018) were the first to propose such an architecture by considering all possible spans of text in the document and assigning coreference links based on the mention score between a pair of spans. There are also end-to-end coreference resolution systems for French, such as DeCOFre (Grobol, 2020) and coFR (Wilkens et al., 2020). DeCOFre[7] is trained primarily on spontaneous spoken language (ANCOR corpus, (Muzerelle et al., 2013)), while coFR[8] is trained on both spoken (ANCOR corpus) and written language (Democrat corpus, (Landragin, 2016)). For this study, we use coFR, as it is better suited for our corpus (i.e., archives and documents).

coFR produced coreference chains, each consisting of a set of mentions that refer to the same discourse entity, for instance: {*la participation au régime capitaliste, elle, La participation, elle*}. For the purpose of the study, we further detect the targets (*i.e.* the most representative mention) in the coreference chains. The longest mention of a coreference chain is chosen as the TARGET of the entity (or the first in case of two equally long mentions). An example for the chain mentioned above is that the TARGET is '*la participation au régime capitaliste*'. In cases where all mentions in a chain are pronouns or determiners (e.g. {*elle, son, sa*}), then the TARGET is considered to be "NONE". When there are multiple longest mentions of equal length, the first one is selected as the TARGET, e.g. the TARGET for {*Parti communiste, PCF, PCF, du Parti*} will be '*Parti communiste*'.

We analyze here the presence of mentions and targets in the question/answer pairs. Over half of the answers (51.3%) contain a mention, with 12.6% of the responses being entirely a co-reference, as for the questions, 16.6% of them contain mentions. These results suggest that performing co-reference resolution could enhance the similarity calculation and lead to more contextually grounded link suggestions.

7 Qualitative evaluation of the generated questions

In addition to the quantitative and descriptive evaluation of the generated questions on the *self-management* corpus, we performed a first qualitative evaluation on a subset of the collection.

In order to evaluate the quality and relevance of the generated questions, we annotate the generated questions according to two dimensions. The first dimension focuses on the quality of the question form, with questions being categorized as "Valid", "Incoherent question", or "Ungrammatical question". In the second dimension, we assess the relevance of the question after it has been validated in the previous dimension. This evaluation involves three 5-Point Likert scales:

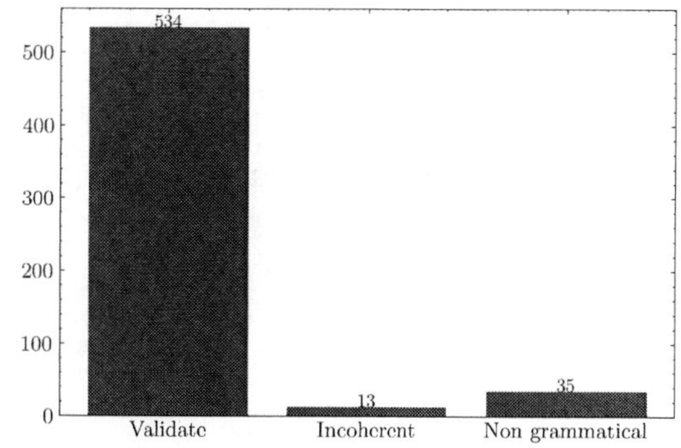

Figure 2: Evaluation of the quality of the form of the generated questions

1. "The highlighted segment corresponds well to an answer to the question"
2. "The question is relevant in the context of the sentence"
3. "The question is relevant in the overall context of the reading"

Professional annotators were hired for this task, they annotated a total of 582 questions. As shown in Figure 2, about 92% of the questions were validated on their surface form, which confirms the syntactic quality of our question generation system.

For the relevance annotations, the results are also promising. In terms of answer adequacy (Figure 3(a)), the majority of questions (67%) received a score that indicates a high level of adequacy [9]. The two Likert scales measuring question relevance are more subjective, but a large proportion of questions (over 68%) were rated as relevant in the local context (Figure 3(b)). In the global context (Figure 3(c)) of the reading, the percentage of questions rated as relevant drops, with just over half of the questions meeting the same score criterion.

To check inter-annotator agreement, a subset of 129 questions were annotated by two annotators.

[7]https://github.com/LoicGrobol/decofre
[8]https://github.com/boberle/cofr

[9]In this paragraph, the notion of high level of adequacy corresponds to likert scores > 3

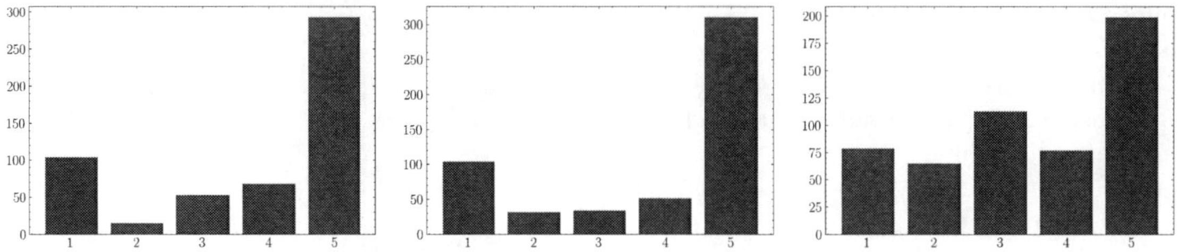

(a) Likert (1) (b) Likert (2) (c) Likert (3)

Figure 3: Evaluation on the relevance of the generated questions

On the first dimension (surface form) we noticed only 11 disagreements between the two annotators. On the second dimension, concerning the first Likert with a simplified 3 category evaluation by grouping the 1 and 2 choices and the 4 and 5 ones, we measured 25 disagreements out of 115 annotations. With the same grouping, we obtain 43 disagreements out of 115 annotations for Likert 2 and 65 out of 115 annotations for Likert 3. These higher numbers of disagreement were expected, as this last evaluation is highly subjective.

8 Document linking evaluation

We quantitatively evaluate the difference in the links generated by the question embeddings compared to two conventional embedding similarity methods. We create a link between two sentences or two paragraphs (textblock) if the similarity between their embeddings is below a threshold (or the top n links are kept).

The comparison results in three "similarity sets":

1. Sentence similarity set **[SENTENCE]**
2. TextBlock similarity set **[TEXTBLOCK]**
3. Question-Answer similarity set **[QA]**

We aim to evaluate the effectiveness of our question-based embedding approach in generating links between documents compared to more traditional embeddings. To quantify the difference, we consider the set of links produced by a question as a unique entity and compute the intersection with the set of links generated by other methods. To ensure that links are compared at the same level of granularity, we consider links identical if they point to the same page. To tackle the fact that one set of links is generated per question for a sentence or paragraph, we aggregate the sets of links for all questions in a sentence or paragraph through a union operation. Finally, the overlap percentage is calculated as the intersection between this union and the corresponding set of links from the sentence or paragraph embeddings.

	Percent of intersection		
Similarity sets	(ALL)	(OUT_ART)	(OUT_NUM)
[QA] // [SENTENCE]	21 %	17 %	19 %
[QA] // [TEXTBLOCK]	23 %	12 %	20 %

Table 5: % of intersection between the similarity sets

This evaluation alone does not allow us to measure the quality of our links. However, it does show (Table 5) that our system produces "original" links through QA embeddings, with nearly 80% of the 49 most similar pages being different from those produced by using similarity methods directly on text segments.

A subjective evaluation which will check the feedback of professional readers to the links and explanation proposed by our method will carried on within the *Archival* project.

9 Conclusion

This paper proposes a new approach for exploring digitized humanities and social sciences collections based on explainable links built from questions. Our experiments show the quality of our automatically generated questions and their relevance in a local context as well as the originality of the links produced by embeddings based on these questions. Analyses have also been performed to understand the types of questions generated on our corpus, and the related uses that can enrich the exploration. Additionally, we discussed the relationships between co-references, generated questions, and extracted answers from the text, which opens a path for future improvements for our system in their resolution. Experiments are still to be conducted to study more qualitatively the generated links, as well as to enrich and filter in a finer way the large quantity of questions on the corpus.

Limitations

A potential limitation of our method is the use of an SRL semantic framework parser, which can be quite costly to deploy for a very large collection. It would thus be interesting to compare other methods for extracting answers in the test, and for enriching or constraining the question generation.

Our study uses only French monolingual models and corpora, so language does not seem to be a limitation for languages with similar or superior resources.

Additionaly, our study should be pursued to further assess the relevance of links, which necessitates a dedicated evaluation protocole. However we believe that assessing in the first place the quality of generated questions is important for the rest of our work.

Acknowledgements

We would like to thank the reviewers for their insightful comments and suggestions. This work has been partially funded by the Agence Nationale pour la Recherche (ANR) through the following program: *ARCHIVAL* ANR-19-CE38-0011. This work was performed using HPC resources from GENCI–IDRIS (Grant 2022-AD011012688R1).

References

Priyanka Agrawal, Chris Alberti, Fantine Huot, Joshua Maynez, Ji Ma, Sebastian Ruder, Kuzman Ganchev, Dipanjan Das, and Mirella Lapata. 2022. Qameleon: Multilingual qa with only 5 examples.

Chris Alberti, Daniel Andor, Emily Pitler, Jacob Devlin, and Michael Collins. 2019. Synthetic QA corpora generation with roundtrip consistency. In *Proceedings of the 57th Annual Meeting of the Association for Computational Linguistics*, pages 6168–6173, Florence, Italy. Association for Computational Linguistics.

Frederic Bechet, Elie Antoine, Jérémy Auguste, and Géraldine Damnati. 2022. Question generation and answering for exploring digital humanities collections. In *Proceedings of the Thirteenth Language Resources and Evaluation Conference*, pages 4561–4568, Marseille, France. European Language Resources Association.

Steven Bird, Ewan Klein, and Edward Loper. 2009. *Natural language processing with Python: analyzing text with the natural language toolkit.* " O'Reilly Media, Inc.".

Robin Brochier and Frédéric Béchet. 2021. Predicting links on wikipedia with anchor text information. In *Proceedings of the 44th International ACM SIGIR Conference on Research and Development in Information Retrieval*, SIGIR '21, page 1758–1762, New York, NY, USA. Association for Computing Machinery.

Andrew M. Dai, Christopher Olah, and Quoc V. Le. 2015. Document embedding with paragraph vectors. *CoRR*, abs/1507.07998.

Martin d'Hoffschmidt, Wacim Belblidia, Quentin Heinrich, Tom Brendlé, and Maxime Vidal. 2020. FQuAD: French question answering dataset. In *Findings of the Association for Computational Linguistics: EMNLP 2020*, pages 1193–1208, Online. Association for Computational Linguistics.

Xinya Du, Junru Shao, and Claire Cardie. 2017. Learning to ask: Neural question generation for reading comprehension. In *Proceedings of the 55th Annual Meeting of the Association for Computational Linguistics (Volume 1: Long Papers)*, pages 1342–1352, Vancouver, Canada. Association for Computational Linguistics.

Dvir Ginzburg, Itzik Malkiel, Oren Barkan, Avi Caciularu, and Noam Koenigstein. 2021. Self-supervised document similarity ranking via contextualized language models and hierarchical inference. In *Findings of the Association for Computational Linguistics: ACL-IJCNLP 2021*, pages 3088–3098, Online. Association for Computational Linguistics.

Loïc Grobol. 2020. *Coreference resolution for spoken French*. Theses, Université Sorbonne Nouvelle - Paris 3.

Jyun-Yu Jiang, Mingyang Zhang, Cheng Li, Michael Bendersky, Nadav Golbandi, and Marc Najork. 2019. Semantic text matching for long-form documents. In *The World Wide Web Conference*, WWW '19, page 795–806, New York, NY, USA. Association for Computing Machinery.

Moussa Kamal Eddine, Antoine Tixier, and Michalis Vazirgiannis. 2021. BARThez: a skilled pretrained French sequence-to-sequence model. In *Proceedings of the 2021 Conference on Empirical Methods in Natural Language Processing*, pages 9369–9390, Online and Punta Cana, Dominican Republic. Association for Computational Linguistics.

Frédéric Landragin. 2016. Description, modélisation et détection automatique des chaînes de référence (DEMOCRAT). *Bulletin de l'Association Française pour l'Intelligence Artificielle*, (92):11–15.

Jörg Landthaler, Ingo Glaser, and Florian Matthes. 2018. Towards explainable semantic text matching. In *Legal Knowledge and Information Systems*, pages 200–204. IOS Press.

Kenton Lee, Luheng He, Mike Lewis, and Luke Zettlemoyer. 2017. End-to-end neural coreference resolution. In *Proceedings of the 2017 Conference on Empirical Methods in Natural Language Processing*, pages 188–197, Copenhagen, Denmark. Association for Computational Linguistics.

Kenton Lee, Luheng He, and Luke Zettlemoyer. 2018. Higher-order coreference resolution with coarse-to-fine inference. In *Proceedings of the 2018 Conference of the North American Chapter of the Association for Computational Linguistics: Human Language Technologies, Volume 2 (Short Papers)*, pages 687–692, New Orleans, Louisiana. Association for Computational Linguistics.

Louis Martin, Benjamin Muller, Pedro Javier Ortiz Suárez, Yoann Dupont, Laurent Romary, Éric de la Clergerie, Djamé Seddah, and Benoît Sagot. 2020. CamemBERT: a tasty French language model. In *Proceedings of the 58th Annual Meeting of the Association for Computational Linguistics*, pages 7203–7219, Online. Association for Computational Linguistics.

Rada Mihalcea and Andras Csomai. 2007. Wikify! linking documents to encyclopedic knowledge. In *Proceedings of the Sixteenth ACM Conference on Conference on Information and Knowledge Management*, CIKM '07, page 233–242, New York, NY, USA. Association for Computing Machinery.

Lidiya Murakhovs'ka, Chien-Sheng Wu, Philippe Laban, Tong Niu, Wenhao Liu, and Caiming Xiong. 2022. MixQG: Neural question generation with mixed answer types. In *Findings of the Association for Computational Linguistics: NAACL 2022*, pages 1486–1497, Seattle, United States. Association for Computational Linguistics.

Judith Muzerelle, Anaïs Lefeuvre, Jean-Yves Antoine, Emmanuel Schang, Denis Maurel, Jeanne Villaneau, and Iris Eshkol. 2013. ANCOR, premier corpus de français parlé d'envergure annoté en coréférence et distribué librement. In *TALN'2013, 20e conférence sur le Traitement Automatique des Langues Naturelles*, pages 555–563, Les Sable d'Olonne, France.

Giannis Nikolentzos, Polykarpos Meladianos, François Rousseau, Yannis Stavrakas, and Michalis Vazirgiannis. 2017. Shortest-path graph kernels for document similarity. In *Proceedings of the 2017 Conference on Empirical Methods in Natural Language Processing*, pages 1890–1900, Copenhagen, Denmark. Association for Computational Linguistics.

Martha Palmer, Daniel Gildea, and Paul Kingsbury. 2005. The proposition bank: An annotated corpus of semantic roles. *Comput. Linguist.*, 31(1):71–106.

Valentina Pyatkin, Paul Roit, Julian Michael, Yoav Goldberg, Reut Tsarfaty, and Ido Dagan. 2021. Asking it all: Generating contextualized questions for any semantic role. In *Proceedings of the 2021 Conference on Empirical Methods in Natural Language Processing*, pages 1429–1441, Online and Punta Cana, Dominican Republic. Association for Computational Linguistics.

Pranav Rajpurkar, Jian Zhang, Konstantin Lopyrev, and Percy Liang. 2016. Squad: 100,000+ questions for machine comprehension of text. In *Proceedings of the 2016 Conference on Empirical Methods in Natural Language Processing*, pages 2383–2392. Association for Computational Linguistics.

Nils Reimers and Iryna Gurevych. 2019. Sentence-bert: Sentence embeddings using siamese bert-networks. In *Proceedings of the 2019 Conference on Empirical Methods in Natural Language Processing*. Association for Computational Linguistics.

Nils Reimers and Iryna Gurevych. 2020. Making monolingual sentence embeddings multilingual using knowledge distillation. In *Proceedings of the 2020 Conference on Empirical Methods in Natural Language Processing (EMNLP)*, pages 4512–4525, Online. Association for Computational Linguistics.

Siamak Shakeri, Cicero Nogueira dos Santos, Henghui Zhu, Patrick Ng, Feng Nan, Zhiguo Wang, Ramesh Nallapati, and Bing Xiang. 2020. End-to-end synthetic data generation for domain adaptation of question answering systems. In *Proceedings of the 2020 Conference on Empirical Methods in Natural Language Processing (EMNLP)*, pages 5445–5460, Online. Association for Computational Linguistics.

George Tsatsaronis, Iraklis Varlamis, and Michalis Vazirgiannis. 2014. Text relatedness based on a word thesaurus. *CoRR*, abs/1401.5699.

Zhiguo Wang, Haitao Mi, and Abraham Ittycheriah. 2016. Sentence similarity learning by lexical decomposition and composition. In *Proceedings of COLING 2016, the 26th International Conference on Computational Linguistics: Technical Papers*, pages 1340–1349, Osaka, Japan. The COLING 2016 Organizing Committee.

Claudie Weill. 1999. La revue autogestion comme observatoire des mouvements d'émancipation. *L'Homme et la société*, 132(2):29–36. Included in a thematic issue : Figures de l' « auto-émancipation » sociale.

Rodrigo Wilkens, Bruno Oberle, Frédéric Landragin, and Amalia Todirascu. 2020. French coreference for spoken and written language. In *Proceedings of the Twelfth Language Resources and Evaluation Conference*, pages 80–89, Marseille, France. European Language Resources Association.

A Examples of generated questions

Examples of generated question kept after the filtering process:
Q : Quel organisme évolue vers une structure autogérée ? (*Which organization is moving towards a self-managed structure ?*)
A : une bonne partie du C.N.R.S. (*a good part of the C.N.R.S.*)
CTX : Mais je crois que progressivement une bonne partie du C.N.R.S. évolue vers une structure pour ainsi dire autogérée, bien que le terme, à ma connaissance, soit rarement avancé. (*But I believe that gradually a good part of the C.N.R.S. is evolving towards a self-managed structure, so to speak, although the term, to my knowledge, is rarely used.*)

Q : Quelle était la conséquence de l'autogestion ? (*What was the consequence of self-management ?*)
A : l'autogestion, si elle limitait leurs droits théoriques en transférant la gestion de l'entreprise à l'assemblée des travailleurs, ne leur offrait pas moins davantage de droits réels de direction de l'entreprise qu'ils n'en avaient jamais eu jusqu'à présent (*self-management, although it limited their theoretical rights by transferring the management of the enterprise to the workers' assembly, did not give them any less real rights to direct the enterprise than they had ever had before.*)
CTX : Les « managers » s'aperçurent que l'autogestion, si elle limitait leurs droits théoriques en transférant la gestion de l'entreprise à l'assemblée des travailleurs, ne leur offrait pas moins davantage de droits réels de direction de l'entreprise qu'ils n'en avaient jamais eu jusqu'à présent. (*The "managers" realized that self-management, although it limited their theoretical rights by transferring the management of the enterprise to the workers' assembly, did not give them any less real rights to direct the enterprise than they had ever had before.*)

Example of queston filtered by (F3) :
Q : Quelle est la nationalité de la Yougoslavie ? (*What is the nationality of Yugoslavia?*)
A : la Yougoslavie (*Yugoslavia*)
CTX : Yougoslavie ait été introduite et se développe pour des causes qui ne seraient pas purement économiques .... (*Yugoslavia was introduced and is developing for reasons that are not purely economic ...*)

B Examples of explainable links

Q_1 : Quel progrès a été réalisé dans l'agriculture avec un capital relativement faible ? (*What progress has been made in agriculture with relatively little capital?*)
A_1 : un progrès très rapide dans la technique et la technologie (*a very rapid progress in technique and technology*)
Q_2 : Qu'est ce qui permet d'augmenter la production agricole ? (*What makes it possible to increase agricultural production?*)
A_2 : méthodes agronomiques modernes (*modern agronomic methods*)

Q_1 : Quel est le but des questions administratives incompréhensibles ? (*What is the purpose of incomprehensible administrative questions?*)
A_1 : à créer leur dépendance (*to create their dependence*)
Q_2 : Quel est le but de la bureaucratie ? (*What is the purpose of bureaucracy?*)
A_2 : ses prétentions à la domination sociale (*its claims to social dominance*)

Q_1 : Qu'est ce qui permet à l'ouvrier gestionnaire d'augmenter son revenu personnel ? (*What allows workers-managers to increase their personal income?*)
A_1 : la productivité du travail (*labour productivity*)
Q_2 : Qu'est ce qui pousse les travailleurs à augmenter la productivité ? (*What drives workers to increase productivity?*)
A_2 : le revenu (*income*)

Q_1 : Quelles entreprises sont en train de se transformer en coopératives de production ? (*Which companies are transforming into production cooperatives?*)
A_1 : les entreprises autogérées et celles qui sont en train de le devenir (*self-managed companies and those in the process of becoming self-managed*)
Q_2 : Quelles entreprises ont eu tendance à perdre leur caractère de coopérative ? (*Which companies have tended to lose their cooperative character?*)
A_2 : Les coopératives ouvrières du XXème siècle (*Workers' cooperatives of the 20th century*)

Wartime Media Monitor (WarMM-2022): A Study of Information Manipulation on Russian Social Media during the Russia-Ukraine War

Maxim Alyukov
King's College London
maxim.alyukov@kcl.ac.uk

Maria Kunilovskaya
University of Saarland
maria.kunilovskaya@uni-saarland.de

Andrei Semenov
Higher School of Economics
andrey.semenov@hse.ru

Abstract

This study relies on natural language processing to explore the nature of online communication in Russia during the war on Ukraine in 2022. The analysis of a large corpus of publications in traditional media and on social media identifies massive state interventions aimed at manipulating public opinion. The study relies on expertise in media studies and political science to trace the major themes and strategies of propagandist narratives on three major Russian social media platforms over several months as well as their perception by the users. Distributions of several keyworded pro-war and anti-war topics are examined to reveal the cross-platform specificity of social media audiences. We release WarMM-2022, a 1.7M posts corpus. This corpus includes publications related to the Russia-Ukraine war, which appeared in Russian mass media (February to September 2022) and on social networks (July to September 2022). The corpus can be useful for the development of NLP approaches to propaganda detection and subsequent studies of propaganda campaigns in social sciences in addition to traditional methods, such as content analysis, focus groups, surveys, and experiments.

1 Introduction

Contemporary autocracies rely on media manipulation more than violent dictatorships of the past (Guriev and Treisman, 2020). As citizens might recognise manipulative intent (Roberts, 2018), authoritarian governments attempt to veneer the propaganda messages via state-sponsored social networks. These online "astroturfing" campaigns (Zerback and Töpfl, 2022) appear as a genuine grassroots support for the regime and artificially inflate the visibility of pro-regime messages. In this paper, we document the presence of such a campaign in Russia in 2022 and explore its key characteristics, using a large corpus of online messages from Russian social media about the Russian-Ukrainian war (WarMM-2022).

Our data-driven approach can provide a more realistic picture of audience response to political information in the context of war than traditional methods of communication research, such as surveys. An important outcome of this media monitoring project is a corpus of online publications on the Russian-Ukrainian war which appeared the websites of Russian newspapers and TV channels between February and September 2022 and on a number of social media platforms between July and September 2022. The corpus includes temporal, spatial, and some socio-demographic metadata, which can be used to develop NLP approaches to the detection of various forms of propaganda.

To the best of our knowledge, there is only one published dataset, *VoynaSlov* (Park et al., 2022), which is specifically designed to capture media coverage of, and public reaction to, content related to the Russia-Ukraine war. *VoynaSlov* includes posts from a limited pre-defined number of news outlets (42 in total) published on either *VKontakte* or *Twitter*. The data from these platforms have been sampled following dissimilar approaches: the *Twitter* subset includes posts with war-related hashtags while there is no such filter for *VKontakte*. In terms of the amount of textual data, *VoynaSlov* includes 597K documents published on *VKontakte* and 219K on *Twitter*. Our dataset has a much broader coverage with regard to the sources of information and includes only the publications about the war, although our time frame is more limited. Our dataset presents a realistic snapshot of the online information environment experienced by Russian internet users in real-time during the war, and we hope that this resource can be useful not only for the NLP community but also for communication scholars and political scientists.

2 Corpus Description

The WarMM-2022 corpus represents online political discourse produced in Russia for and by do-

Proceedings of the 7th Joint SIGHUM Workshop on Computational Linguistics for Cultural Heritage, Social Sciences, Humanities and Literature (LaTeCH-CLfL2023), pages 152–161
May 5, 2023

mestic audiences. The corpus is composed of two parts: a subcorpus of publications by traditional mass media (press and TV) and public posts from social networks. The full list of sources includes 415 websites of media outlets, 25 websites of TV channels, and 85 social media platforms. The distribution of publications is very uneven across the sources of each type. Most active media websites are by *gazeta.ru, ura.news, ren.tv, vz.ru, russian.rt.com, iz.ru*. The content of TV programmes related the Russian-Ukrainian war is captured by the respective transcripts published by TV channels on their websites. In our collection, the transcripts most often come from *Channel One, REN TV, Channel 5*, and *Russia 24*. Importantly, WarMM-2022 includes the regional affiliations of information sources allowing one to trace the specifics of Ukraine-related news coverage across Russia. By the number of collected documents, the most represented social media platforms are *VKontakte, Odnoklassniki, Telegram, Twitter, Facebook, LiveJournal, YouTube* (in decreasing order). The full list of mass-media, TV and social-media sources is released with the corpus. The textual data and associated metadata, including public reactions, such as the number of views, likes, re-posts and comments, were obtained with the technical support of *Scan Interfax* and *Brand Analytics* media monitoring systems. The parameters of data collection were configured to meet the requirements of the current project. Media sources were limited by their availability to Russian audiences, i.e. the crawled webpages were directly accessible in Russia at the time of collection. Social media sources were limited to posts from accounts that were registered in Russia and published in Russian, where possible.

We aim to produce a realistic snapshot of the online information environment regarding the war and during the war. The data collection began in July 2022 in a monitoring mode. We were aggregating publications that appeared on mass media websites and on social media daily until the end of September 2022. A separate subcorpus of publications on mass media and TV websites for the preceding months (February to June) was collected in a one-time retrospective crawling effort in mid-July 2022. The corpus was built using a list of eight general context keywords to filter in publications related to the war in Ukraine. These eight terms were *war, special operation, military operation, SVO (special military operation), special operation, military operation, denazification, and demilitarization* (in Russian). This list was developed as a result of iterative filter-setting experiments and manual analysis of daily crawls in the first two weeks preceding the start of the data collection.

The basic statistics for the WarMM-2022 corpus are presented in Table 1.

period	Press+TV	Social Media
February	12.7 K	–
March	27.3 K	–
April	19.9 K	–
May	21.4 K	–
June	15.9 K	–
July	18.2 K	602 K
August	28.7 K	546 K
September	38.3 K	558 K
Total	182 K	1,706 K

Table 1: Number of posts by month and media type

Table 1 shows that traditional media (Press+TV) and social media subcorpora are not well balanced by the number of included documents. Only about 10% of texts come from traditional media websites. The disbalance between subcorpora persists in terms of the overall word counts (not shown in Table 1): the overall size of the press subcorpus is 24.4 M tokens, TV transcripts - 1.7 M tokens, and social media subcorpus includes 268.4 M tokens. The analysis presented in this paper is based on the data from three months (July to September) - the period present in both press+TV and social media subcorpora.

Section 5 reports a cross-platform study focusing on the three most popular social media platforms in Russia (at the backdrop of traditional media content): *Odnoklassniki* (OK), *Telegram* (TG) and *VKontakte* (VK). Table 2 displays the parameters of the underlying subcorpus.

After Facebook and Instagram were banned in March 2022, OK, TG and VK became the dominant platforms in Russia alongside WhatsApp and YouTube. According to April 2022 data, 62% of Russians used VK, 55% used TG, and 42% used OK[1]. OK is often considered a space of Putin's electorate. Its audience is much older than the audience

[1]WCIOM (2022) Rossiyskaya Auditoriya Socialnih Setey: Izmeneniya Na Fone Specoperatsii. Avaliable at: https://wciom.ru/analytical-reviews/analiticheskii-obzor/rossiiskaja-auditorija-socialnykh-setei-i- messendzherov-izmenenija-na-fone-specoperacii

period	network	docs	words
July	ok.ru	153.8 K	26.6 M
	telegram.org	18.2K	2.7 M
	vk.com	334.4 K	87.1 M
August	ok.ru	169.5 K	33.7 M
	telegram.org	14.4 K	2.3 M
	vk.com	278.9 K	69.8 M
September	ok.ru	250.8 K	51.3 M
	telegram.org	15.0 K	2.4 M
	vk.com	309.9 K	76.2 M
Total		1,545 K	352.0 M

Table 2: Social media subcorpus size by network in tokens (the counts are given after pre-processing and annotation)

of other platforms. According to 2021 data, 7.4% of OK users were under 24, 25.2% were between 34-44, and the dominant 49.5% were older than 45 [2]. Public groups on OK are often anti-Western and pro-Kremlin and constitute the regime's 'Virtual Russian World' not only in Russia but in other countries with significant Russian-speaking populations (Teperik et al., 2018). VK has a much younger audience than OK: according to 2021 data, a dominant 31.3% of VK users were under 24 and only 18% were older than 45. Finally, the audience of a relative newcomer, TG, is slightly older than the audience of VK. The 2021 data reveals that 29.6% of TG users were under 24, dominant 30.6% were 24-34, and 18.5% were older than 45 [3].

In what follows, we describe the social and political context of the study, introduce theoretical concepts from media and communications research necessary to interpret our data (Section 3), present methodology (Section 4), and report analytical results and their interpretation (Section 5). We conclude with a summary (Section 7) and reflections on the limitations and ethical aspects of our project.

3 Background

3.1 Russia's Networked Authoritarianism

The rapid development of digital media in the early 2000s led some analysts to praise it as a "liberation technology" (Diamond and Plattner, 2012). Responding to this threat, authoritarian governments have been investing significant resources in creating various forms of "networked authoritarianism" (MacKinnon, 2011). Different models of control over online media emerged over time from largely hands-off policies to nurturing sophisticated digital environments conducive to authoritarian messaging (Greitens, 2013). More recently, *online astroturfing* – the strategy of giving online conversations seemingly genuine pro-governmental spin – emerged as "a novel form of disinformation that relies on the imitation of citizen voices to create the false impression that a particular view or idea has widespread support in society" (Zerback and Töpfl, 2022).

In Russia, the initial Kremlin's position not to disrupt online communications changed after the 2011-12 post-electoral protest (Sanovich et al., 2018). As a part of the "third generation controls" (Deibert et al., 2010), in the past ten years, Putin's government has been actively using automated bots and trolls (paid humans who rely on scripts to produce content) to shape online discussions (Sanovich et al., 2018). The Kremlin has been extensively using bots to create information noise, to promote pro-governmental messages in search engine results and in news aggregators, and to manufacture popularity of autocratic agents (Stukal et al., 2017, 2022). Research also shows that the Kremlin-linked agencies have conducted multiple information campaigns attempting to influence public opinion abroad (Linvill and Warren, 2020; Elshehawy et al., 2021).

After the full-scale invasion of Ukraine, the Kremlin shut down many remaining independent media and introduced repressive laws effectively imposing wartime censorship, hammering any public expression of discontent with the war. In addition, it started to use paid commentators and *"voenkors"* (military reporters on the battlefront) to shape citizens' perceptions of the invasion[4]. In our study, we attempt to document and explore the astroturfing campaign related to war using the WarMM-2022 corpus.

[2]Statista (2021). Gender and age distribution of Odnoklassniki. Available at: https://www.statista.com/statistics/1065018/russia-odnoklassniki-users-share-by-age/

[3]Brand Analytics (2021). Socialniye Seti v Rossii: Trendi i Tsifri, Osen' 2021. Available at: https://br-analytics.ru/blog/social-media-russia-2021/

[4]Fontanka (2022). «Vy ved' ne verite, chto jeto nastojashhie otzyvy?» Kak «Fontanka» zagljanula na peredovuju informacionnyh frontov Z. Available at: https://www.fontanka.ru/2022/03/21/70522490/

3.2 NLP for Communication Research and Political Science

The NLP community developed multiple methods for the analysis of mass media communications - in particular, for detecting various forms of information manipulation online. Most NLP research on propaganda uses supervised methods that require manual annotation, sometimes very fine-grained (see, for example, Da et al., 2020). These projects are focused primarily on solving NLP tasks rather than obtaining results requested by social sciences with regard to unfolding events. Park et al. (2022) pursued a task similar to what we face: they explored the proportion of topics in social media publications to reveal such information manipulation strategies as agenda-setting, framing, and priming. They employ state-of-the-art *unsupervised* methods for topic modeling (a structured topic model and a contextualized neural topic model) and frame analysis (using a zero-shot learning scenario and ignoring the differences in language, style, and cultural context between the available training data and intended end-use domain). However, they admitted that the results were contradictory, obscure, and difficult to interpret in both cases. Interestingly, they fall back on word statistics as a more reliable yardstick to evaluate their models. Elshehawy et al. (2021) relied on constructed lexicons to provide evidence that the Kremlin promoted refugee stories in the German media sphere in an attempt to influence the outcome of the elections. Following the principles of transparency of analysis and interpretability of its outcomes, we opted for the keyword frequency analysis approach as our main method for this preliminary study.

4 Methodology

The analysis of news topics includes statistical and unsupervised methods. The findings are interpreted in the context of external unfolding events. In this project, we constructed expert-curated lists of topical keywords, and their normalised frequencies were used to compare messaging across social media platforms (OK, VK, TG) in a time series fashion.

General frequency analysis setup. We focused on frequency of individual keywords and aggregated frequencies of pre-defined terms that marked a particular topic. In total, we explored 20 thematic aspects of the publications and extracted the frequencies of over 250 words and phrases.

The full list of search items in their non-lemmatised version in Russian for each topic is available in the corpus documentation. It is designed to include topics that are typical for pro-war and anti-war discourses as well as shared between the two. Appendix A lists the topics and subtopics. For example, we traced "dehumanisation", the topic marked by the use of derogatory names for the Ukrainians (e.g. *ukrop*) and numerous derivatives with *ukro-* and *nazi-* prefixes (e.g. *ukronazist, ukrofascist, banderovetz, nazbat*) as well as loaded ideological terms used to describe Ukraine (e.g. *Kyiv regime, sneaky, guileful, hypocrite*). The frequency of each item was based on a lemmatised version of the corpus to account for possible grammatical forms, which is important for morphologically-rich languages like Russian. The raw texts went through minimum preprocessing before lemmatisation, including symbol unification, discarding .png/.jpg and url to reduce noise. The lemmatised version of the corpus was obtained from morpho-syntactic annotation produced using UDPipe (v1, Straka and Straková, 2017), a parser within the Universal Dependencies framework. All frequencies were normalised to the size of the respective subcorpora within a given time series and subcorpus, with the normalisation base of 100,000 words. This made possible the comparison of frequencies across subcorpora of various sizes directly, including using them in graphs based on the same scale.

Time series. As we were interested in fluctuations of topical content, we constructed time series using three-day intervals as our default setting, i.e. most results in this study reflect the frequencies of search items in the documents published within successive 3-day periods. Whenever we wanted to explore a specific timespan in more detail or have a more aerial perspective, we analysed daily or monthly frequencies, respectively.

Unique publications vs repetitive content. Taking into account the anticipated repetitiveness of publications, we compared the frequencies of selected keywords before and after deleting duplicate posts. Duplicate posts were identified by matching the first 20 words in the raw text. The ratio of repeated texts (excluding the first occurrence) amounts to 47.98% on social media, with about 23.4% being exact unmodified copies of the original publication, often repeated many times.

User attitude studies. Several analytical approaches were employed in an attempt to reveal the users' attitudes to the topics discussed online. It is a challenging task as Russia's information environment is heavily censored and populated with bots and trolls masquerading as real citizens; risks of legal prosecution make it difficult for users to state their positions publicly. In an attempt to overcome these limitations, we analysed (i) publications by users with different levels of publication activity and (ii) publications with the highest engagement scores.

User groups by publication activity. This analysis was based on social media subcorpus only. The total number of unique users in this subcorpus is 263,665. Users produced 1,544,918 posts in three months. In particular, we distinguish between professional users (more likely accounts of established information agencies) who publish more than 20 posts about Ukraine a week (over 260 in three months) and the general public, i.e. users with one or fewer posts a week across 13 weeks. Other users include an intermediate group of active users with over 13 but less than 260 posts per week. The parameters of each group and their contribution to the production of content on the analysed social networks can be found in Table 3.

user group	users	% users	% posts
professional	710	0.27	22.62
active users	17,630	6.69	44.59
general public	245,325	93.04	32.78

Table 3: Activity of media outlets and ordinary users on social media

Activity patterns varied across the groups, with the professional users capable of generating surplus texts during some periods of time and being less active during others. These groups also demonstrated different patterns in the use of keywords from a range of analysed topics (see Section 5).

Engagement scores. The posts on social media were analysed from the point of view of public reactions they generated. We calculated the engagement index as a sum of likes, re-posts, and comments to each post and built a subcorpus of the most popular posts, which included 5% of all posts sorted by the involvement score. This subcorpus included 85,317 posts (out of 1,706,343 in the entire social media corpus across three months). The engagement scores in this subcorpus ranged from 110,528 to 39, with a mean of 444.1. Furthermore, to estimate the level of support for the pro- and anti-war messages and assess their visibility and influence in public discussion, we selected the top-1000 posts with the highest engagement score reactions and identified their sources. Using external knowledge, we classified these 215 authors as pro-war, anti-war, or neutral. Finally, we counted the number of posts by these authors and their overall engagement scores.

5 Results: Cross-platform Analysis

This section applies the described methodology to explore users' participation in online discussions, their attitudes and reactions to media content.

To capture the astroturfing campaign, we use a range of selected topics (pro-war and anti-war), which also help us to reveal political attitudes prevailing on the selected social media platforms. Generally, we noticed that social media had deviated from the press and TV in the frequency patterns of pro-war topics. The usage of keywords was very volatile with several regular peaks. We identified these peaks as massive infusions of almost identical messages. In Figure 1 these peaks are smoothed out by removing duplicate publications. In combination with observations for other topics, this can be a sign of information manipulation.

As discussed above, the major Russian social media platforms (Odnolassniki, VKontakte, Telegram) vary according to socio-demographic parameters. To disentangle the effect of repetitive publications observed in the entire social media subcorpus, shown in Figure 1, we looked at the frequencies of each topic by network.

First, the frequencies of *denazification* and *demilitarisation* – the key terms justifying Russian invasion – on TG and VK are both steady and low in comparison to abnormal spiky patterns registered in OK publications (the extreme frequencies ranging between 45 and 60 per 100K words vs over 140 on OK). Note that *demilitarisation*, which disappeared from state-controlled media accounts towards the end of summer 2022, fell into disuse on OK, too. Removing identical posts levels off the spikes in the use of justifications on OK. With duplicates removed, the three platforms demonstrate similar frequencies.

The same pattern across platforms is observed for *dehumanising language*. There is a significant amount of anti-Ukrainian derogatory terms on all

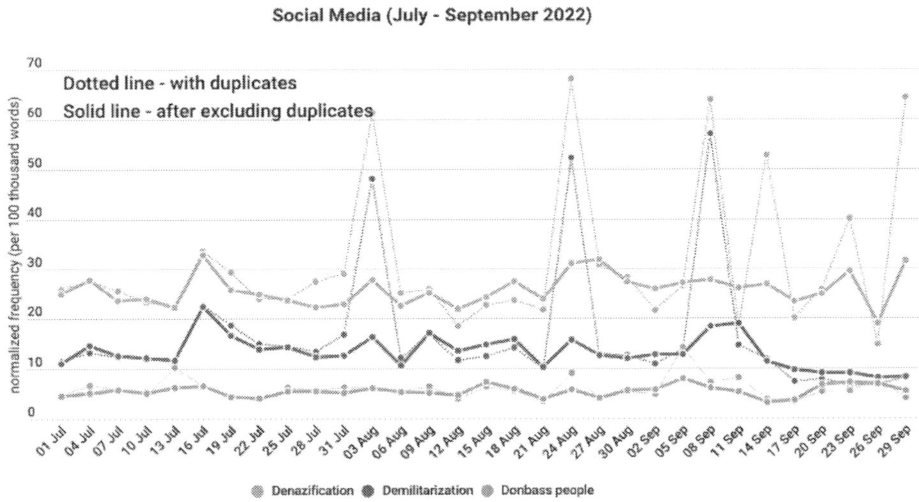

Figure 1: Impact of repeated publications: key concepts used to justify Russian actions in Ukraine (3-day aggregates)

three platforms. Markers of this language are more frequent on OK, where every month there are significant spikes that exceed the volume of VK and TG by the factors from two (late July and late August) to four (early September), and six (early August). The patterns on VK and TG are stable and do not suggest any artificial inflation. Nevertheless, all social media platforms remain plagued with hate speech toward Ukrainians.

To double-check that the observed peaks are artificial, aggregated frequencies based on the entire corpus after removing duplicates were compared. The amount of dehumanising vocabulary decreased manifold. Nonetheless, even without identical messages, OK remains the most pro-war platform followed by VK and TG. These observations suggest that the Kremlin disproportionately targets OK with pro-war online astroturfing.

The function of state-controlled trolls cannot be reduced to producing identical content. Paid users are often instructed to improvise and can produce original messages different from each other. Hence, identical messages alone do not represent the scale of online astroturfing accurately. However, as identical messages are unlikely to be attributed to anything else but artificial content, removing it can make us underestimate the scale of online astroturfing, not to overestimate it. In other words, identical messages are a conservative estimate of the scale of Kremlin-related astroturfing.

One might argue that the messages we identified as astroturf were viral and resonated with the online public. While we cannot exclude such a possibility, the short life-span of these messages (they disappeared completely from communications in 1-2 days) and a poor quality of its content (we found nothing sensational or novel in terms of production for several manually selected entries) indicate that the traction with the general public was limited at best.

To further investigate differences in ideological spin and the scale of online astroturfing, we focus on anti-war vocabulary. Figure 2 (on the left) shows the aggregated frequencies of keywords typical for Kremlin opponents, such as *Russian aggression, annexation, occupation of Ukrainian territories, Russian invasion, occupation of Donbas/Crimea, Russian occupants*, etc.

The graphs reflect the fluctuations in the use of anti-war language across platforms from July to September. It shows that TG is the most anti-war platform among the three. Despite the presence of many pro-Kremlin channels, the independent media flourish, too. Anti-war vocabulary is the least present on OK. Removing duplicates (the right panel in Figure 2) does not change the observed pattern significantly. If anything, the absence of repetitive content makes anti-war stance on VK more visible (notice the upward shift of the orange line in the right-hand panel). This might suggest that spamming the information space with duplicates makes sense as it creates additional noise and makes it more difficult for users to hear other voices. With identical messages removed, TG remains the most anti-war platform. Patterns on VK and OK resemble each other implying that they are

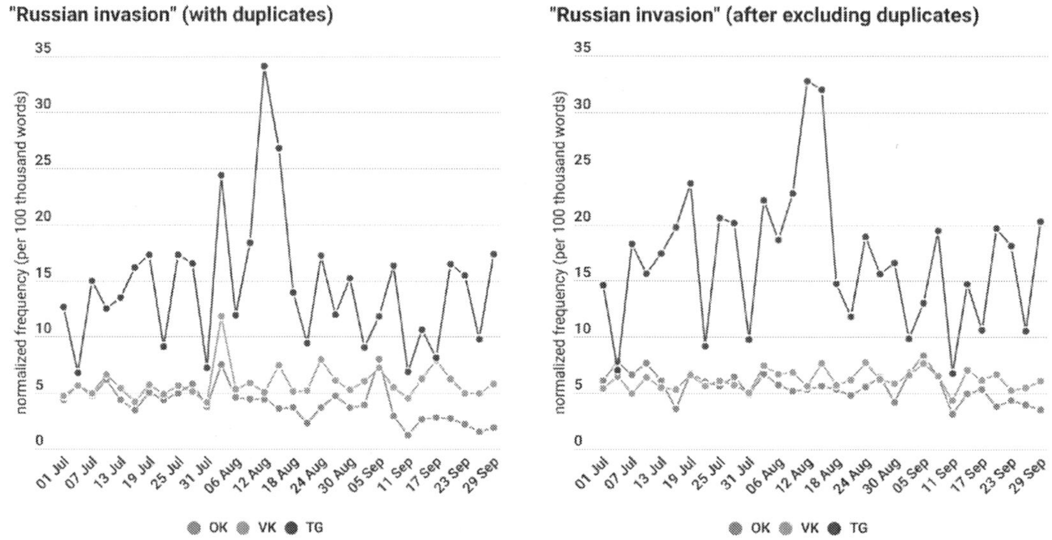

Figure 2: Anti-war language across platforms (weekly aggregates)

more similar in terms of ideological spin.

Additionally, we explored topics related to time-specific external events, such as the Ukraine's advances on the battlefield in late August - early September (e.g. *advances of Ukrainian army, Ukraine's military success, retreat of Russian troops, successful counterattack of Ukrainian forces, Russian defeat*, etc). Despite censorship on official press and TV, the news about the failures of the Russian military percolated to social media, especially TG. The frequencies capturing this topic were very low but genuine: removing duplicates did not affect the counts.

We conclude that OK was disproportionately targeted by the regime. The presence of astroturfing can also be confirmed by looking at the phrases from the *temniki* – the guidelines issued by the Kremlin to cover politically sensitive topics in the media. Unlike the other two platforms, OK demonstrated a growing scale of occurrences for this vocabulary from early August onwards suggesting that this platform was the primary target.

Public perception. The analysis of publications by professional users, who produce over 20 publications a week about Ukraine, and regular users, who might represent the general public, showed that the latter were less eager to portray Ukrainians as the enemy. In Figure 3, the flat orange line represents relatively low and stable frequencies for dehumanising vocabulary (which are still very high in comparison with visible anti-war stance in other graphs).

In a subcorpus built from the top 5% of publications based on engagement scores, anti-war topics (e.g. Ukrainian military success, framing Russian actions in Ukraine as war, occupation or invasion) are more frequent, while pro-war rhetoric is noticeably less dense than in the entire corpus.

Out of 215 authors who produced the publications with the highest engagement score, 80 were classified as anti-war (479 out of 1000 most popular posts), 24 authors as neutral with (27 posts), 111 authors were classified as pro-war (494 posts). However, in the top 50 most popular posts, we found only two posts by pro-war authors. The first 38 posts by the level of engagement and 48 posts in total (out of 50) were written by anti-war authors. As a result, the level of involvement for anti-war posts is 1.5 times higher than pro-war posts (8.5 mln reactions vs 5.7 mln reactions).

6 Discussion and consolidation

By tracing the frequencies of pro-war and anti-war topics across social media platforms over time, linking them to external events and checking for repetitive content, we were able to reveal signs of information manipulation aimed at shaping public opinion by controlling the agenda and framing the concepts to fit the current ideology.

As we demonstrate, some of the major themes artificially promoted by the state include: (i) the ideas of denazification and demilitarisaion and (ii) dehu-

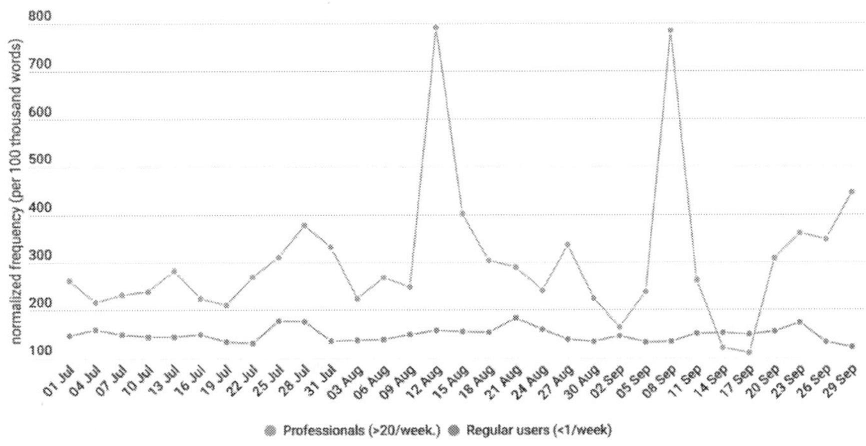

Figure 3: Anti-Ukrainian hate speech is publications by most prolific accounts and regular users

manization of Ukrainians. Based on this dataset, we also identify several other promoted ideas, such as (iii) the existential threat posed by NATO and (iv) framing Ukraine as controlled by the hostile 'collective West'. However, we do not include them in the analysis due to limited space.

The strategies of public opinion manipulation can include the attempts to undermine trust in mass media, frame any source of information except state-controlled as spreading 'fakes', and appropriate opponents' vocabulary and diluting its meaning. In this analysis, we demonstrate one of these strategies: imitation of popular support for promoted ideas on social media.

Our findings point at possible mechanisms behind the Kremlin's digital war propaganda. Instead of attempting to reach war opponents or users without clear preferences, the regime's astroturf communication seems to flourish in a predominantly pro-war environment. In line with both classical research on media effects (Lazarsfeld et al., 1960) and contemporary research on the effects of propaganda in authoritarian Russia (Shirikov, 2022), these findings suggest that the main strategy of the regime's astroturf online communication might be similar to the one of authoritarian propaganda: to reinforce beliefs of those who are already pro-regime rather than to win new supporters.

Our cross-platform analysis indicates that discussions on OK are largely influenced by astroturfing. TG remains a relatively free space devoid of official rhetoric, while VK users exhibit a mild tendency to re-produce official narratives about the war.

Aiming at revealing the level of support for promoted ideas and the effectiveness of the said strategies, our analyses based on user group activity and reactions on social media demonstrated that many of these narratives fall flat on domestic audiences. Modest numbers of Russians participating in public discussions show that a lot of communication online is one-way, with people withdrawing from the public space. The public reactions that are available in WarMM-2022 demonstrate that the extent of support for the promoted ideas is rather limited.

7 Conclusion

This study reports details of textual data collection and analysis in the interests of social sciences. We release WarMM-2022, a corpus of public online communications collected from a large number of mass media websites and social media platforms, which was used to obtain the results reported in this paper.

Our analysis relies on expert-curated lists of words and phrases which are used to cross-examine topical content in posts from a wide range of Russian mass media and most popular social media, published in July-September 2022. Informed by the previous work on data-driven propaganda detection, we aimed to assess the scale and societal impact of media manipulation in wartime Russia. In particular, we were interested in the distribution of, and support for, selected topics reflecting opposite viewpoints on the events in Ukraine. We revealed that the distribution of topics in social media (unlike traditional media, including TV) was largely affected by state-controlled interventions that varied in scale across the three social media compared in this work. The patterned nature of these interventions and their alignment with the Kremlin's intentions expressed in recommendations for the press suggest that these are signs of "networked authoritarianism", a system of measures to exert control over the internet. The study was focused on the pro-war and anti-war themes in social networks and revealed a considerable amount of "astroturfing" (imitation of public support online). Our results support the idea that the Kremlin employs a digital propaganda ecosystem including networks of state-controlled accounts – bots and paid influencers – across Russia's main social media platforms. This ecosystem is engaged in an organised manner to shape public opinion on current or forthcoming events. The frequency patterns of topics related to the Russia-Ukraine war reveal the artificial nature of online communication on Russian social media in July-September 2022 and help us to identify the key messages infused by the astroturfing campaigns, such as the existential threat posed by NATO, the need for patriotic unity against the hostile West and dehumanisation of the Ukrainians. Although anti-war voices are largely silenced by censorship and the threat of persecution, these opinions are heard and get more public attention than any propagandist content. At the same time, the number of Russians who get publicly involved in online participation as authors is ridiculously small. As users, Russians have to navigate an increasingly volatile, noisy, and restrictive environment infused with highly repetitive pro-war content.

Limitations

By construction, our corpus is not representative in any sense of the general population of messages related to the war on RuNet. Platforms blocked in March 2022 (notably, Facebook and Instagram) remained largely absent. Also, we restricted our analysis to Russian-based users while many Russian-speaking digital communities remained active from outside the country. Lexicon-based approaches are necessarily limited by the scope of topics that they are able to cover. Similarly, data collection decisions reduce the claims that can be made in the findings to the observations relevant to the given dataset. We admit that the explored topics do not exhaust the ideas that circulated online within the given time frame, and it is likely that we missed other important themes. Besides, despite care was taken to avoid including ambiguous keywords, and unexpected frequencies were checked in manual analysis at the stage of constructing the lexicons, simple word statistics cannot identify contexts. In fact, elements of pro-war narratives can occur in essentially anti-war publications as examples or mockery of the opponents' discourse. Keywords can generate high frequencies from a few repetitive documents in a time series, too. A better approach would be to operate at the level of documents and report results for complete statements rather than words. The manual analysis and annotation attempts demonstrated that social media content is very dependent on multimedia. However, we focused on the textual content and discarded linked images or videos. Finally, given the large number of comparisons that we carried out, we did not see it feasible to perform a proper statistical analysis of the differences between various subcorpora.

Ethics Statement

In considering the ethical aspects of this study, we strive to avoid any potential harm to individual Internet users or publishing outlets, to protect their privacy, and to respect their right to the created texts. These considerations motivated the following practical decisions. First, we used the publications that were publicly available at the time of collection. Second, the corpus is made available only as a list of links augmented with non-revealing attributes, such as date, media type, source (website or platform), region and engagement score (for social networks subcorpus) [5], with the actual textual content deleted from this version of the corpus. It is done to protect the users' right to take down their content and to avoid violating their copyright. While these restrictions imply reduced replicability of our results and additional efforts for researchers associated with the necessity to recollect the data, they were considered ethical to avoid potential harm to individuals. Third, we do not distribute any metadata or publish any considerable parts of the collected texts that can be used to identify individuals with particular political beliefs at the moment or in the future. This is particularly important, given the current scale of prosecution for anti-war publications and reactions expressed online in Russia. Finally, while we admit that research on propaganda strategies can be used to improve ways of information manipulation, we think that uncovering and describing these practices serves

[5] https://github.com/kunilovskaya/WarMM-2022

the greater social good of raising the awareness of the public about types of disinformation and potentially delusive environments that can be created online. When presenting the results of the analyses, care was taken to avoid any wording that can be interpreted as promoting particular political beliefs, where possible.

References

Giovanni Da, San Martino, Shaden Shaar, Yifan Zhang, Seunghak Yu, Alberto Barrón-Cedeño, Cede~ Cedeño, and Preslav Nakov. 2020. Prta: A System to Support the Analysis of Propaganda Techniques in the News. In *ACL 2020*.

RJ Deibert, John Palfrey, Rafal Rohozinski, and Jonathan Zittrain. 2010. *Access Controlled: The Shaping of Power, Rights, and Rule in Cyberspace*. The MIT Press.

Larry Diamond and Marc F Plattner. 2012. *Liberation technology: Social media and the struggle for democracy*. JHU Press.

Ashrakat Elshehawy, Konstantin Gavras, Nikolay Marinov, Federico Nanni, and Harald Schoen. 2021. Illiberal Communication and Election Intervention during the Refugee Crisis in Germany. *Perspectives on Politics*, pages 1–19.

Sheena Chestnut Greitens. 2013. Authoritarianism online: What can we learn from internet data in nondemocracies? *PS: Political Science & Politics*, 46(2):262–270.

Sergei Guriev and Daniel Treisman. 2020. A theory of informational autocracy. *Journal of public economics*, 186:104158.

Paul F Lazarsfeld, Bernard Berelson, and Hazel Gaudet. 1960. How the voter makes up his mind in a presidential campaign. *The people's choice*.

Darren L Linvill and Patrick L Warren. 2020. Troll factories: Manufacturing specialized disinformation on twitter. *Political Communication*, 37(4):447–467.

Rebecca MacKinnon. 2011. Liberation technology: China's "networked authoritarianism". *Journal of democracy*, 22(2):32–46.

Chan Young Park, Julia Mendelsohn, Anjalie Field, and Yulia Tsvetkov. 2022. Voynaslov: a data set of russian social media activity during the 2022 ukraine-russia war. *arXiv preprint arXiv:2205.12382*.

Margaret E Roberts. 2018. Censored. In *Censored*. Princeton University Press.

Sergey Sanovich, Denis Stukal, and Joshua A Tucker. 2018. Turning the virtual tables: Government strategies for addressing online opposition with an application to russia. *Comparative Politics*, 50(3):435–482.

Anton Shirikov. 2022. *How Propaganda Works: Political Biases and News Credibility in Autocracies*. Ph.D. thesis, The University of Wisconsin-Madison.

Milan Straka and Jana Straková. 2017. Tokenizing, POS Tagging, Lemmatizing and Parsing UD 2.0 with UDPipe. In *Proceedings of the CoNLL 2017 Shared Task: Multilingual Parsing from Raw Text to Universal Dependencies*, pages 88–99.

Denis Stukal, Sergey Sanovich, Richard Bonneau, and Joshua A Tucker. 2017. Detecting bots on russian political twitter. *Big data*, 5(4):310–324.

Denis Stukal, Sergey Sanovich, Richard Bonneau, and Joshua A Tucker. 2022. Why botter: how pro-government bots fight opposition in russia. *American political science review*, 116(3):843–857.

Dmitri Teperik, Grigori Senkiv, Giorgio Bertolin, Kateryna Kononova, and Anton Dek. 2018. Virtual russian world in the baltics. *NATO StratCom COE*, 21.

Thomas Zerback and Florian Töpfl. 2022. Forged examples as disinformation: The biasing effects of political astroturfing comments on public opinion perceptions and how to prevent them. *Political Psychology*, 43(3):399–418.

A Appendix

Individual search items and topics

- Context
  - war with/on Ukraine, etc
  - special/military operation, etc
- Aims and Explanations
- War with NATO
- Economic worries
- Isolation from world
- Nuclear threat
- Society Polarisation
- Fake (фейк as a noun)
- Undermining trust in media
- Spoiler Crisis
  - Ukrainian crisis
  - other (gas, food, economic crisis)
- Spoiler Wars
- Phrases from Circulated Recommendations
- Dehumanisation
- Lack of Ukraine independence
- #nopanic
- Annexation
- Russian invasion
- Against mobilisation
- Evading the draft
  - fleeing the country
  - dodging call-up
- Ukraine military success

Towards a More In-Depth Detection of Political Framing

Qi Yu
Cluster of Excellence "The Politics of Inequality" & Department of Linguistics
University of Konstanz
qi.yu@uni-konstanz.de

Abstract

In social sciences, recent years have witnessed a growing interest in applying NLP approaches to automatically detect framing in political discourse. However, most NLP studies by now focus heavily on framing effect arising from topic coverage, whereas framing effect arising from subtle usage of linguistic devices remains understudied.

In a collaboration with political science researchers, we intend to investigate framing strategies in German newspaper articles on the "European Refugee Crisis". With the goal of a more in-depth framing analysis, we not only incorporate lexical cues for shallow topic-related framing, but also propose and operationalize a variety of framing-relevant semantic and pragmatic devices, which are theoretically derived from linguistics and political science research. We demonstrate the influential role of these linguistic devices with a large-scale quantitative analysis, bringing novel insights into the linguistic properties of framing.

1 Introduction

Framing is a ubiquitous strategy to promote certain views, values or ideologies in political discourse: the information sender selectively makes certain aspects of an issue more salient in the discourse while excluding or denying the others, with the aim of ultimately influencing the public's opinions and behaviors (Gamson, 1985; Entman, 1993). In recent years, automated framing detection has received increasing attention in both NLP and social sciences. In an interdisciplinary project, we are interested in identifying framing strategies employed by different German newspapers in the discourse of the event "European Refugee Crisis" between 2014–2018, where a large amount of asylum seekers from war-torn countries in the Middle East and North Africa flooded into Europe.

By now, most of the NLP studies on automated framing detection have been focusing on *topical framing*, e.g, whether the topic of economic impact or cultural value is more dominant in the discourse of migration (see, inter alia, Khanehzar et al., 2021; Mendelsohn et al., 2021; Huguet Cabot et al., 2020). However, little is known about the linguistic properties of framing: in the existing NLP work, there is very few in-depth investigations on the effects of individual linguistic components in framing, which is mainly because many studies use neural networks (NNs) that lack explainability and do not allow a drilling down into the effects of linguistically meaningful components (see Section 2 for a detailed review). Moreover, the majority of the earlier studies apply supervised approaches which rely on intense manual annotation effort. This has led to a bias towards English in the research of framing detection: whereas several English datasets with annotations of framing have been released (see Section 2), for any language other than English, to our best knowledge, there is still no annotated dataset to date.

Addressing the lack of investigation on the linguistic aspects of framing, we bring together both shallow topical cues and in-depth linguistic devices to detect framing strategies in German newspaper articles on European Refugee Crisis. The novelty of our work is the investigation of how subtle semantic and pragmatic features contribute to framing a message: in theoretical linguistics, researchers have discovered a variety of subtle linguistic devices that play a fundamental role in expressing the speaker's attitude or leading the addressees to integrate information into their belief systems in a certain way. Consider the highlighted expressions in Example (1): the expression *nicht einmal* 'not even' reinforces the author's critical attitude to the ruling parties by conveying that the meaning of family in asylum cases should be the most basic knowledge they ought to have, but actually they do not. Besides, by using the modal particle *ja*, which does not have an English equivalence but can be loosely paraphrased to 'as we

Proceedings of the 7th Joint SIGHUM Workshop on Computational Linguistics for Cultural Heritage, Social Sciences, Humanities and Literature (LaTeCH-CLfL2023), pages 162–174
May 5, 2023 ©2023 Association for Computational Linguistics

all know', the author subtly renders his opinion as already being a consensus of all people (even if this might not be true), covertly increasing its credibility.

(1) *Die drei Parteien wissen ja nicht einmal, was im Falle der Flüchtlinge* [...] *unter Familie zu verstehen ist.*
'The three (ruling) parties do not even understand what family means in the case of the refugees - as we all know.'
(source: *Frankfurter Allgemeine Zeitung*)

Linguistic devices of such kind do not contribute to the topical content of the text, but frame the utterance by adding rhetorical flavors that reinforces specific stances of the author. In what follows, we refer to such framing effect as *rhetorical framing*. Building upon linguistic theories and insights from political science research on framing, we operationalize a set of deep semantic and pragmatic features that are relevant to rhetorical framing, and apply them to data-driven framing detection in a large-scale dataset with 8 million tokens. Our study makes the following contributions: **(a)** at the theoretical level, we propose a variety of deep semantic and pragmatic features relevant to framing, and illustrate their subtle yet powerful role in framing with a quantitative study. Our proposed linguistic features provide novel insights towards a deeper understanding of framing, and can also inform future work on creating annotation schemata for framing. **(b)** At the methodological level, we release a heuristic-based automated annotation pipeline for the proposed linguistic features.[1]

2 Related Work

The release of *The Policy Frames Codebook* (PFC; Boydstun et al., 2014) has facilitated the task of creating datasets and building models for automated framing detection. PFC proposes 14 topic-oriented frame categories that can be applied to any policy issue, e.g., *economic frames*, *morality frames*, or *security and defense frames*. This has provided a convenient basis for building annotation and classification. Since then, researchers have published several English-language datasets with manual annotation of frames using the taxonomy of PFC or a similar topic-oriented fashion (e.g., Card et al., 2015; Liu et al., 2019; Mendelsohn et al., 2021).

Owing to the PFC and these publicly available datasets, previous NLP work on framing has mainly focused on identifying *topical framing*. The recent SemEval 2023 Shared Task on framing detection[2] also adopts this topic-oriented setting. The approaches applied in previous studies range from fully unsupervised to fully supervised methods: Tsur et al. (2015) and Nguyen et al. (2015) rely on unsupervised topic models. Field et al. (2018) and Yu and Fliethmann (2022) compile framing vocabularies to measure the prevalence of different frames. Using a fully supervised fashion, Baumer et al. (2015) build Naïve Bayes classifier using theoretically derived linguistic features. More recent work has been leveraging powers of NNs, e.g., Naderi and Hirst (2017) (LSTM) and Ji and Smith (2017) (RNN). Especially, Transformer-based language models have been widely used in the last years (Hartmann et al., 2019; Akyürek et al., 2020; Huguet Cabot et al., 2020; Khanehzar et al., 2021; Mendelsohn et al., 2021; Bhatia et al., 2021; Hofmann et al., 2022).

However, studies using topic-oriented taxonomies of framing tend to oversimplify the concept of framing as a mere matter of topic coverage. This is insufficient for a deep understanding of framing. In political science, it is widely pointed out that framing is a multi-faceted phenomenon: it includes not only the information sender's intention of reinforcing specific topics, but also the facet of how the frames in a communication process affect the individual's thought (Chong and Druckman, 2007; Druckman, 2011). For the second facet, the usage of subtle linguistic devices can play a crucial role. Especially, certain pragmatic markers have an effect in manipulating mutual assumptions or facilitate processes of pragmatic inferences (Furko, 2017). In NLP, the impact of individual linguistic components in framing remains understudied with only a few exceptions: Baumer et al. (2015) utilize various semantic cues (*factive verb*, *assertive word*, *entailment* and *hedging*) to classify framing, but the authors do not provide discussion on what textual or rhetorical effect these cues have in framing a message. Demszky et al. (2019) and Ziems and Yang (2021) inspect the usage of deon-

[1]The dataset used in our study was purchased from the publishers. Due to their copyright regulations, the dataset is restricted to project-internal usage and unfortunately cannot be distributed to third parties. But all code and lexical resources resulting from this paper are publicly available at: `https://github.com/qi-yu/topical-and-rhetorical-framing`

[2]`https://propaganda.math.unipd.it/semeval2023task3/`

tic modal verbs (e.g., 'should', 'need') in calling for actions, assigning blames and making moral arguments. However, their argued importance of modal verbs only applies to texts with a primary function of calling to actions, but does not necessarily generate to all text types. Ziems and Yang (2021) investigate the usage of agentless passives (e.g. using 'He was killed' instead of 'He was killed *by police*') in removing blames. Yu (2022) shows that iterative adverbs such as 'again' can compose systematic framing strategies by evoking attitudinal subtexts via presuppositions. We follow this strand of work on linguistically informed framing detection, and quantitatively investigate the effect of a wider variety of semantic and pragmatic cues. We aim at extending the existing knowledge on the linguistic composition of framing.

3 Data

We focus on a dataset comprising of articles about the "European Refugee Crisis" published between 2014 to 2018 by the three most circulated newspapers in Germany: *BILD*, *Frankfurter Allgemeine Zeitung* (FAZ), and *Süddeutsche Zeitung* (SZ). All three are nationwide daily newspapers, and they build a balanced sample of different styles (tabloid vs. quality) and political orientations.

From each newspaper, we first collected articles with at least one match of the following quasi-synonyms of 'refugee' (including their inflected forms): {*Flüchtling*, *Geflüchtete*, *Migrant*, *Asylant*, *Asylwerber*, *Asylbewerber*}. We then removed articles that were: 1) duplicated, 2) from non-political sections such as *Sport*, and 3) with a ratio of the 'refugee'-synonyms lower than 0.01. Criterion 3) was experimentally defined: it allowed us to remove most articles that mention the European Refugee Crisis only as a side-topic. Table 1 summarizes the final dataset.

Source	Type	#Articles	#Tokens
BILD	C, T	12,107	3,188,561
FAZ	C, Q	6,686	3,432,080
SZ	L, Q	4,536	1,812,835

Table 1: Dataset overview. (C = conservative; L = liberal; T = tabloid; Q = quality)

4 Operationalizing Framing

As we do not have any annotation of frames available for our dataset - moreover, it is prohibitive to conduct such annotation considering the enormous labor cost, we use a set of theoretically derived topical and rhetorical features to conduct a data-driven exploratory framing analysis on the document level. The proposed rhetorical features (Section 4.2) also aim to fill the research gap in investigating the linguistic properties of framing. The features and their relevance to framing are described below.

4.1 Topical Framing

We apply the *Refugees and Migration Framing Vocabulary* (RMFV) by Yu and Fliethmann (2022) as a proxy to measure the topical frames in different newspapers. RMFV contains vocabularies for the following 9 frame categories specifically designed for the issue of refugees and migration:

- ECONOMY, IDENTITY, LEGAL, MORALITY, POLICY, POLITICS, PUBLIC OPINION, SECURITY, WELFARE

For each article, we compute the ratio of the vocabularies of each frame category F. An article is considered as having a stronger emphasis on the topical frame F if the vocabularies of F show a higher ratio, i.e., occur more often.

4.2 Rhetorical Framing

(I) Arousal Former research in political communication has found that framing an issue with emotionally charged language can make a persuasive impact on the addressee (Gross, 2008; Cheng, 2016; Nabi et al., 2018). Thus, we incorporate the AROUSAL degree of the language as one dimension of rhetorical framing. To this end, we apply the arousal ratings of German lemmas by Köper and Schulte im Walde (2016), which include a large range of 350,000 tokens. For each article, we measure the average arousal rating of all its tokens.

(II) Presupposition In natural language, a speaker often *presuppose* certain information, i.e., assume that the information is already part of the *common ground* (shared belief) between them and the addressee (Stalnaker, 2002). In political discourse, presuppositions can bring up attitudinal messages in a hidden manner. Example (2) shows such a case: the adverb 'even' triggers the presupposition that other measures have already been taken to alleviate the overcrowded infrastructure, and that setting up tents was the most unexpected measure (see the semantics of 'even' in Giannakidou, 2007; Szabolcsi, 2017). The message that the city already needs the most surprising measure renders the consequence of refugee influx as dramatic.

(2) *Die Einrichtung dort* [in Giessen] *ist überfüllt. Nun wurden sogar Zelte aufgestellt.*
'The infrastructure there [in Giessen] is overcrowded. Even tents were set up.'

As presupposition is extremely widespread in natural language (e.g., the usage of person names also presupposes the existence of the referred persons), we cannot include all possible types of presupposition triggers in our study. Here, we specifically focus on two types of presupposition triggers:

- SCALAR PARTICLES: e.g., *sogar* 'even', *nicht einmal* 'not even'
- ADVERBS FOR ITERATION OR CONTINUATION: e.g., *wieder* 'again', *andauernd* 'continuously'. Especially in the discourse of a crisis, adverbs of continuation such as 'continuously' are typical devices used to frame the event as being long-standing, which is often connected to criticism.

We compiled a list for triggers of these two types based on seed items found in König (1981) and Yu (2022), and their synonyms found using GermaNet (Hamp and Feldweg, 1997; Henrich and Hinrichs, 2010). For each article, we calculate the ratio of each trigger type, defined as their count divided by the article's token amount.

(III) Modal Particles German has a rich inventory of *modal particles*: they are words that do not contribute to the propositional content (i.e., descriptive, or truth-conditional content) of an utterance, but indicate how the speaker thinks that the content of an utterance relates to the common ground with the addressee (Thurmair, 1989; Zimmermann, 2011; Bross, 2012). Thus, they subtly manipulate how a proposition should be received by the addressee, constituting framing devices par excellence. We explore the usage of the following types of modal particles:

- MODAL PARTICLES SIGNALING COMMON GROUND: *ja* (literal translation: 'yes'). Expressions in the form of *ja*(φ) (i.e., *ja* modifying a proposition φ) convey that the speaker believes φ to be uncontroversial (Zimmermann, 2011).[3]
- MODAL PARTICLES SIGNALING RESIGNED ACCEPTANCE: *eben* (lit. 'even/flat'), *halt* (lit. 'stop'). *eben/halt*(φ) conveys that the speaker believes φ to be obvious and can not be altered, and therefore has to be accepted (Bross, 2012).
- MODAL PARTICLES SIGNALING WEAKENED COMMITMENT: *wohl* (lit. 'probably'). *wohl*(φ) conveys that speaker considers φ to be highly probable or plausible, but φ could also possibly be falsified (Zimmermann, 2011).

As mentioned in Section 1, there is no real English equivalence for the German modal particles discussed here. Nevertheless, to illustrate their effects clearer, we provide coarse paraphrases of their meaning (adapted from Hautli-Janisz and El-Assady, 2017) in Example (3) below:

(3) *Die Flüchtlinge müssen ja / eben (halt) / wohl zunächst Deutsch lernen.*
'The refugees must learn German first, as we all know/that's how it is/I assume.'

For each article type, we calculate the ratio of each modal particle category. Here we do not count their usage in direct or indirect quotations as marked respectively by quotation marks or the German *subjunctive I*, because the stances conveyed by the modal particles are always attributed to their speakers (see descriptions above), and we are only interested in investigating the stances of the newspaper article authors: for instance, if a newspaper article author writes the sentence *Peter sagt: "Die Flüchtlinge müssen eben Deutsch lernen."* (Peter says: "The refugees must learn German - that's how it is."), the resigned acceptance conveyed by the modal particle *eben* is attributed to Peter, not the author.[4]

(IV) Sentence Type In news articles, while declarative sentences are the most often used, the usage of questions and exclamatory sentences also has its own cognitive and rhetorical effects. Questions can add an interactive style to a text (Scheffler, 2017): especially, we observe that newspaper articles occasionally use questions, typically at the beginning of the article, to bring up a topic and trigger the readers to think along. Exclamatory sentences carry a two-fold function: besides the obvious function of expressing strong emotion, they

[3] Whereas another German modal particle *doch* also signals common ground, we refrain from incorporating it into our analysis, because *doch* is ambiguous between many senses and it is often difficult to disambiguate them without prosodic information.

[4] As the effects of the features in (I), (II) and (V) regarding framing are not affected by such perspective shift when used in quotations, we do not exclude their quotation usage.

also mark the propositional content of the utterance as evident (Faure, 2017). For each article, we calculate the ratio of QUESTION and EXCLAMATORY SENTENCES, defined as their count divided by the article's total sentence amount. We exclude their usage in quotations due to the same reason as described in (III) above.

(V) Information Structure The political information acquisition of individuals concerns not only the *factual knowledge*, i.e., whether one correctly knows certain events or political figures, but also the *structural knowledge*, i.e., how the factual information is interrelated and organized (Tolochko et al., 2019). In natural languages, the usage of DISCOURSE CONNECTIVES, i.e., words or phrases that link together two or more utterances in a discourse and signal the relationship between them, has a crucial function of revealing coherence between events and conveying instructions about how to integrate this information (Gernsbacher, 1997; Graesser et al., 2004). In terms of German, a recent empirical study by Blumenthal-Dramé (2021) shows that the presence of discourse connectives benefits German speakers in recognizing the discourse relation. Therefore, we assume that using discourse connectives in news articles facilitates the reader's acquisition of structural knowledge. For each article, we calculate the cumulative ratio of the following types of DISCOURSE CONNECTIVES: *adversative* (e.g., *jedoch* 'yet'), *causal* (e.g., *da* 'because'), *concessive* (e.g., *obwohl* 'though') and *conditional* (e.g., *wenn* 'if').

5 Experimental Setup

5.1 Automated Feature Annotation

The detection for many features in Section 4 is straightforward, as it can be either based on existing lexical resources or unambiguous cue words. Nonetheless, reliably identifying the German modal particles and discourse connectives is extremely challenging due to their highly ambiguous nature: for instance, the causal connective *da* also has the locative adverb usage 'there'. However, there are very few previous NLP work we can build on. To our best knowledge, by now there is still no labeled dataset that covers a comprehensive enough range of German modal particles or discourse connectives, which could enable us to train machine learning models. The only exception is El-Assady et al. (2017), who integrate a rule-based annotation system of these features into the visual discourse analysis tool *VisArgue*.

The cue list and disambiguation rules of VisArgue are curated by experts of linguistics and thus theoretically valid, but the implementation of the disambiguation rules is rather inaccurate: it is mainly based on the position of a target cue in a sentence and its adjacent words. We inherit the cue list and disambiguation rules from VisArgue, but optimize the disambiguation by incorporating information of part-of-speech, morphological features and dependency relation provided by the neural-network NLP pipeline *Stanza* (Qi et al., 2020).

5.2 Determining Most Predictive Features

To quantify which features discussed in Section 4 are most distinctive in each newspaper source (BILD, FAZ and SZ), for each source we fit a binary logistic regression model using the source as response variable (e.g., `is_BILD` = 0 vs.1) and all features described in Section 4 as predictors. All feature values are standardized by removing the mean and scaling to unit variance. As the topical feature WELFARE shows a relatively strong correlation to ECONOMY (Spearman's $\rho = 0.63$, $p < 0.001$) whereas the vocabulary of ECONOMY has a broader coverage, we discard the feature WELFARE. Among the other feature pairs, no strong correlation was found (Spearman's $\rho < |0.40|$; see Figure 1 for all feature correlations).

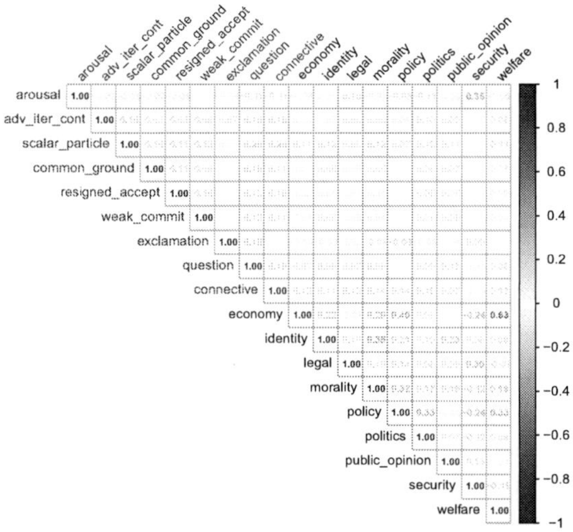

Figure 1: Correlation matrix of all features. The number in each cell shows Spearman's ρ. Blue tick labels mark the rhetorical framing features.

As inspired by Frassinelli et al. (2021), we inspect the z-value of each feature to find the most predictive features for each source. The z-value is defined as the ratio of the coefficient estimate divided by its standard error: a larger absolute value indicates a less uncertain estimate, which in turn implies that the distributional difference of the feature is larger between the articles belonging to the source and those not belonging to the source. Moreover, the sign of the z-value indicates the direction of effect, i.e., a positive sign indicates that the feature is predictive for articles belonging to the source, and a negative sign indicates that the feature is predictive for articles not belonging to the source.

6 Results and Discussion

Figure 2 shows the within-source frequency of each feature, computed as the count of a feature divided by the total token amount of a source. It can be observed that the rhetorical framing features are extremely sparse, especially the modal particles.[5]

Yet, the logistic regression analysis reveals interesting contrast between the usage of the features in each newspaper. Figure 3 shows the z-values of all significant features in predicting each source. The detailed results are provided in Appendix A. In what follows, we summarize the major findings from the logistic regression analysis.

6.1 Topical Framing

Among all topical features, SECURITY and MORALITY show significant effects in predicting all three newspapers, either in a positive direction or a negative direction (see Figure 3): SECURITY shows a positive effect in predicting articles from the tabloid-newspaper BILD, whereas MORALITY shows a positive effect in predicting articles from the two qualities newspapers FAZ and SZ. Considering that different items within the same vocabulary can carry different connotations and thus frame the issue in different directions, we further inspected which items within the vocabularies of these frames are most representative of each newspaper. To this end, we adapted the measure of *PMI-freq* (Jin et al., 2020) to calculate the association strength of an item i in each vocabulary set and a newspaper N. *PMI-freq* is derived from the concept of *pointwise mutual information* (PMI), but it overcomes PMI's shortage of preferring rare words by incorporating the frequency of an item into the calculation. The definition of *PMI-freq* is shown below, where $f(i)$ stands for the overall frequency of i in the whole dataset:

$$\textit{PMI-freq}(i;\, N) = \begin{cases} \log(f(i)) \log \frac{P(i,N)}{P(i)P(N)} & \text{if } f(i) \geq 50 \\ 0, & \text{otherwise} \end{cases}$$

Table 2 shows the top 5 items for SECURITY and MORALITY with the highest *PMI-freq*. The three newspapers show striking differences in the perspectives they emphasize: for SECURITY, all items from BILD are clearly related to criminality or terrorism, rendering the refugees as causing problems for domestic security. Words like 'assault' and 'arson' also suggest that BILD frequently focuses on individual criminal cases. In contrast, all keywords in FAZ are related to the security situation of the refugees on the migration route (e.g., 'human smuggling') or in their countries of origin (e.g., 'war'). This renders the refugees as being threatened instead of as a threat. SZ shows a mixed focus on both security situation on the migration route (e.g., 'coast guard') and illegal issues in the asylum procedure ('abuse of asylum'). Regarding MORALITY, top 3 of the 5 items in BILD are related to xenophobia. The other two items indicate a focus on the acceptance capacity ('upper limit') and the impact of refugees on the welfare system ('Hartz IV'; an unemployment benefit in Germany). This contrasts especially strongly with SZ, where most items are related to humanitarian aid and solidarity. FAZ displays a mixed focus on both humanitarian aspects ('voluntary', 'moral') and broader politico-economic issues ('economic migrant', 'international law').

6.2 Rhetorical Framing

Though the topical framing features already reveal strong differences between the newspapers, the rhetorical framing features allow us to detect more subtle framing strategies on a deeper level. In what follows, we illustrate the results with selected examples for clarity purposes, but most of the described framing effects of the features arise from their intrinsic semantics (described in Section 4.2), and thus generate beyond the selected examples.

Among all three newspapers, BILD shows the most distinctive characteristics regarding the rhetorical framing features. The positive z-values of EXCLAMATORY SENTENCES and QUESTION show an emotional and interactive language usage in BILD.

[5]This is unsurprising given that modal particles in German are more prevalent in spoken texts.

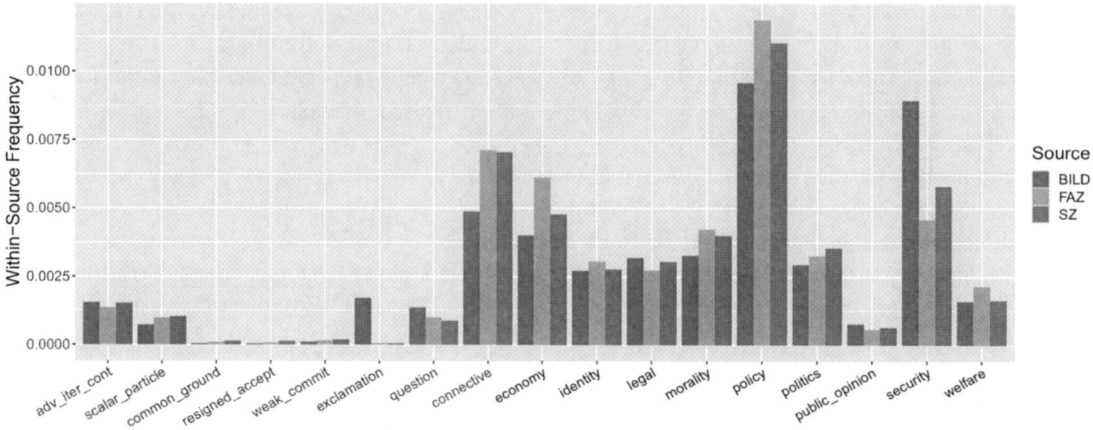

Figure 2: Within-source frequency of each feature. Blue tick labels mark the rhetorical framing features.

Figure 3: Z-values of each feature for BILD-, FAZ-, and SZ-articles. Only significant features are shown.

	Security	**Morality**
BILD	*ISIS*, *U-haft* 'custody', *Körperverletzung* 'assault', *Brandstiftung* 'arson', *Totschlag* 'homicide'	*fremdenfeindlich* 'xenophobic', *Anfeindung* 'hostility', *ausländerfeindlich* 'hostile to foreigners', *Hartz IV*, *Obergrenze* 'upper limit'
FAZ	*Verfolgte* 'persecuted', *Menschenschmuggel* 'human smuggling', *Verfolgung* 'persecution', *unbegleitete Minderjährige* 'unaccompanied juveniles', *Krieg* 'war'	*ehrenamtlich* 'voluntary', *moralisch* 'moral', *Wirtschaftsmigrant* 'economic migrant', *Völkerrecht* 'international law', *Verpflichtung* 'obligation'
SZ	*Schutzstatus* 'protected status', *inhaftieren* 'detain', *Asylmissbrauch* 'abuse of asylum', *Minderjährige* 'juveniles', *Küstenwache* 'coast guard'	*human* 'humane', *Humanität* 'humanity', *Existenzminimum* 'subsistence level', *Konvention* 'convention', *Solidarität* 'solidarity'

Table 2: The top 5 keywords in the vocabulary of security and morality with highest *PMI-freq* to each newspaper. The words are sorted in descending order by *PMI-freq*.

Even though their usage within quotations is not included when fitting the logistic regression model, exclamatory sentences still show a strong predictive power for BILD-articles as reflected by the large z-value. This indicates that exclamatory sentences are systematically employed in BILD. Here it is worth pointing out the powerful effect of exclamatory sentences in framing a message as evident or factive: e.g., Example (4) not only conveys a sensational flavor, but also emphasizes that *it is a fact* that the refugees do not want to be accommodated in the gymnasiums. This covertly prevents the readers from further questioning the plausibility of the information.

(4) *Viele Flüchtlinge wollen gar nicht in den Turnhallen wohnen!* (BILD)
'Many refugees don't want to be accommodated in the gym!'

The positive z-values of AROUSAL and ADVERBS FOR ITERATION OR CONTINUATION also reflect a sensational language style in BILD. Especially, the positive effect of adverbs for iteration or continuation indicates that BILD is more likely to render certain events or aspects as long-lasting or repeating. This has an especially strong framing effect in the context of negative consequences of the refugee influx: e.g., in Example (5), the adverb 'continuous' insinuates that the chaotic situation should have been long since solved but still is not, shedding a negative light on the administrations.

(5) *Das seit Monaten <u>andauernde</u> unwürdige Chaos bei der Aufnahme von Flüchtlingen in Berlin hat zu personellen Konsequenzen geführt.* (BILD)
'The <u>continuous</u> undignified chaos in refugee reception in Berlin has led to personnel consequences.'

Overall, it can be observed that BILD systematically applies emotionally charged language. This is also reinforced by BILD's focus on criminality and xenophobia as mentioned in 6.1, which are both inherently emotional topics.

FAZ and SZ exhibit a more structuralized and sophisticated reporting style. CONNECTIVES, together with most of the presupposition triggers and modal particles, turn out to be predictive features for FAZ- and SZ-articles. Regarding the usage of presupposition triggers, they exhibit an interesting contrasting behavior to BILD: whereas adverbs for iteration or continuation are predictive for BILD-articles, SCALAR PARTICLES are found instead to be predictive for FAZ- and SZ-articles. Scalar particles have an inherent attitudinal characteristic. Consider Example (6): the scalar particle 'not even' presupposes that among all tasks in processing refugee cases, fingerprint collection is the most basic one. This evokes a strongly attitudinal inference that the capacity shortage in the countries under discussion has been extremely acute.

(6) *Die Staaten an der Südgrenze der EU [...] schaffen es noch <u>nicht einmal</u>, von jedem Ankömmling einen Fingerabdruck zu nehmen.* (FAZ)
'The states on the southern border of the EU [...] <u>do not even</u> manage to take a fingerprint of every arrival.'

Last, intriguing characteristics in the usage of modal particles can also be observed from FAZ and SZ. Even though modal particles are rather typical in speech instead of highly-edited written texts, and we did not consider their usage within quotations, most of the modal particle categories still show a significant effect in predicting FAZ- and SZ-articles. This implies that there is indeed an intentional usage of them by journalists of the two newspapers. Modal particles for COMMON GROUND, i.e. *ja*, are predictive for both FAZ- and SZ-articles. As *ja* conveys that the propositional content of the sentence is already in the common ground between the author and the readers, its usage frames a message as uncontroversial and covertly makes the message difficult to refute. For instance, the *ja* in Example (7) renders the author's stance *Merkel is right* as being already accepted by all readers, thereby tricking the readers to agree with him.

(7) *Merkel hat <u>ja</u> recht: Deutschland kann seine Grenzen nicht schließen.* (SZ)
'Merkel is <u>*ja*</u> right: Germany cannot close its borders.'

However, FAZ and SZ differ in their usage of modal particles for RESIGNED ACCEPTANCE and WEAKENED COMMITMENT: modal particles for resigned acceptance, i.e., *eben* and *halt*, have a high positive z-value in predicting SZ-articles but not FAZ articles. As such modal particles modify a proposition as obvious and unchangeable, they have a strong effect in imposing the reader to accept the proposition. This effect is especially typical in argumentative context: e.g., in Example (8), the model particle *eben* conveys that the author's reasoning of the death cases is obvious and thus must be accepted. Rendering the argumentation as uncontroversial subtly closes the possibility of any further challenges or discussions.

(8) *Im Mittelmeer wird derweil weiter gestorben – weil es <u>eben</u> für Flüchtlinge und Migranten keinen legalen Weg nach Europa gibt.* (SZ)
'Meanwhile, there are further death cases

at the mediterranean sea – because there is <u>eben</u> no legal route to Europe for refugees and migrants.'

In contrast, the modal particle for WEAKENED COMMITMENT, i.e., *wohl*, is shown to be predictive for FAZ-articles but not SZ-articles. *Wohl* as a two-faceted function: it renders a proposition as highly probable, but also conveys that the author is not fully committed to its truth. Consider Example (9): *wohl* there conveys that the author has enough plausible evidence to support his assertion that no alternative solution could be found, but also signals that this assertion is not absolutely true and could be defeated. This tactfully relieves the author from being liable for the validity of his claim.

(9) *Es gibt <u>wohl</u> gar keine andere Lösung , als die Flüchtlinge in den jeweiligen Ländern so schnell wie möglich in Arbeitsverhältnisse zu bringen.* (FAZ)
'There is <u>wohl</u> no other solution than to get the refugees into employment in the respective countries as quickly as possible.'

Whereas *eben/halt* has a strengthening effect, *wohl* rather weakens a proposition. Taking together the different properties of these two modal particle types and the high positive z-value of AROUSAL in SZ, it can be observed that SZ tends to use more intensive language than FAZ.

7 Conclusion and Outlook

Previous research in framing detection has focused heavily on topical framing, leaving the effect of individual linguistic devices in framing understudied. Addressing this weakness, we theoretically derived a set of in-depth semantic and pragmatic features relevant to framing, and implemented an automatic annotation pipeline for identifying them. Combining them with shallow topical framing cues enabled us to identify deeper differences in framing strategies employed by different German newspapers in the discourse of the European Refugee Crisis.

The advantage of our approach is its linguistic depth and explainability: to our best knowledge, all the proposed features have still not been studied in respect of framing in a large-scale fashion. Our work contributes to both NLP and social sciences by extending the knowledge of linguistic aspects of framing. For future NLP work on framing detection, this work has two indications: first, framing detection should not be restricted to topical frames. Many linguistic devices also play crucial roles in framing by affecting how a message should be received by individuals. Second, though handcrafted feature sets have multiple restrictions, a more in-depth framing detection can still benefit from consciously incorporating theoretically derived features. As shown by our study, the distribution of many important linguistic devices could be extremely sparse, whose effects might thus be challenging for NN-based algorithms to capture.

This work is not without limitations. First, the various types of modal particles involved in this work do not exist in all languages, and their taxonomy in different languages can vary from the one applied here. Our automated annotation pipeline is also German-specific by now. However, other rhetorical framing devices and their effects discussed in this work are language-independent and can thus be applied to framing analysis for other languages. Second, this work only covers a limited range of linguistic features: due to the lack of existing tools or annotated datasets, we adopt a rule-based approach for the automated feature identification. Some relevant cues for the rhetorical framing features are left out because their disambiguation is highly context-dependent and difficult to realize with rules. Future work will consider using our automated annotation pipeline as a weak-labeling assistance and creating datasets for detecting the linguistic features with supervised methods. Moreover, for modal particles and presupposition triggers, a more fine-grained analysis direction would be to identify the actors involved in sentences containing these devices, and detect frames using discourse network analysis on the actors (following van Atteveldt et al., 2017). Despite these limitations, we hope that our initial work on rhetorical framing strategies will facilitate future work on investigating the deeper linguistic dimensions of framing.

Acknowledgements

This work was funded by the Deutsche Forschungsgemeinschaft (DFG - German Research Foundation) under Germany's Excellence Strategy – EXC-2035/1 – 390681379. The author also thanks the valuable comments and suggestions from the anonymous reviewers of LaTeCH-CLfL 2023.

References

Afra Feyza Akyürek, Lei Guo, Randa Elanwar, Prakash Ishwar, Margrit Betke, and Derry Tanti Wijaya. 2020. Multi-label and multilingual news framing analysis. In *Proceedings of the 58th Annual Meeting of the Association for Computational Linguistics*, pages 8614–8624, Online. Association for Computational Linguistics.

Eric Baumer, Elisha Elovic, Ying Qin, Francesca Polletta, and Geri Gay. 2015. Testing and comparing computational approaches for identifying the language of framing in political news. In *Proceedings of the 2015 Conference of the North American Chapter of the Association for Computational Linguistics: Human Language Technologies*, pages 1472–1482, Denver, Colorado. Association for Computational Linguistics.

Vibhu Bhatia, Vidya Prasad Akavoor, Sejin Paik, Lei Guo, Mona Jalal, Alyssa Smith, David Assefa Tofu, Edward Edberg Halim, Yimeng Sun, Margrit Betke, Prakash Ishwar, and Derry Tanti Wijaya. 2021. OpenFraming: Open-sourced tool for computational framing analysis of multilingual data. In *Proceedings of the 2021 Conference on Empirical Methods in Natural Language Processing: System Demonstrations*, pages 242–250, Online and Punta Cana, Dominican Republic. Association for Computational Linguistics.

Alice Blumenthal-Dramé. 2021. The online processing of causal and concessive relations: Comparing native speakers of English and German. *Discourse Processes*, 58(7):642–661.

Amber E. Boydstun, Dallas Card, Justin H. Gross, Philip Resnik, and Noah A. Smith. 2014. Tracking the development of media frames within and across policy issues. `https://homes.cs.washington.edu/~nasmith/papers/boydstun+card+gross+resnik+smith.apsa14.pdf`, last accessed on February 20, 2023.

Fabian Bross. 2012. German modal particles and the common ground. *Helikon. A Multidisciplinary Online Journal*, 2(1):182–209.

Dallas Card, Amber E. Boydstun, Justin H. Gross, Philip Resnik, and Noah A. Smith. 2015. The media frames corpus: Annotations of frames across issues. In *Proceedings of the 53rd Annual Meeting of the Association for Computational Linguistics and the 7th International Joint Conference on Natural Language Processing (Volume 2: Short Papers)*, pages 438–444, Beijing, China. Association for Computational Linguistics.

Maria Cheng. 2016. The power of persuasion: Modality and issue framing in the 2012 Taiwan presidential debates. *Discourse & society*, 27(2):172–194.

Dennis Chong and James N Druckman. 2007. Framing theory. *Annu. Rev. Polit. Sci.*, 10:103–126.

Dorottya Demszky, Nikhil Garg, Rob Voigt, James Zou, Jesse Shapiro, Matthew Gentzkow, and Dan Jurafsky. 2019. Analyzing polarization in social media: Method and application to tweets on 21 mass shootings. In *Proceedings of the 2019 Conference of the North American Chapter of the Association for Computational Linguistics: Human Language Technologies, Volume 1 (Long and Short Papers)*, pages 2970–3005, Minneapolis, Minnesota. Association for Computational Linguistics.

James N Druckman. 2011. What's it all about? Framing in political science. *Perspectives on framing*, 279:282–296.

Mennatallah El-Assady, Annette Hautli-Janisz, Valentin Gold, Miriam Butt, Katharina Holzinger, and Daniel Keim. 2017. Interactive visual analysis of transcribed multi-party discourse. In *Proceedings of ACL 2017, System Demonstrations*, pages 49–54, Vancouver, Canada. Association for Computational Linguistics.

Robert M. Entman. 1993. Framing: Toward clarification of a fractured paradigm. *Journal of communication*, 43(4):51–58.

Richard Faure. 2017. Exclamations as multi-dimensional intersubjective items. *Revue de Sémantique et Pragmatique*, 40(40):7–15.

Anjalie Field, Doron Kliger, Shuly Wintner, Jennifer Pan, Dan Jurafsky, and Yulia Tsvetkov. 2018. Framing and agenda-setting in Russian news: a computational analysis of intricate political strategies. In *Proceedings of the 2018 Conference on Empirical Methods in Natural Language Processing*, pages 3570–3580, Brussels, Belgium. Association for Computational Linguistics.

Diego Frassinelli, Gabriella Lapesa, Reem Alatrash, Dominik Schlechtweg, and Sabine Schulte im Walde. 2021. Regression analysis of lexical and morpho-syntactic properties of kiezdeutsch. In *Proceedings of the Eighth Workshop on NLP for Similar Languages, Varieties and Dialects*, pages 21–27, Kiyv, Ukraine. Association for Computational Linguistics.

Peter Furko. 2017. Manipulative uses of pragmatic markers in political discourse. *Palgrave Communications*, 3(1):1–8.

William A Gamson. 1985. Goffman's legacy to political sociology. *Theory and society*, 14(5):605–622.

Morton Ann Gernsbacher. 1997. Coherence cues mapping during comprehension. *Processing interclausal relationships. Studies in the production and comprehension of text*, pages 3–22.

Anastasia Giannakidou. 2007. The landscape of even. *Natural Language & Linguistic Theory*, 25(1):39–81.

Arthur C Graesser, Danielle S McNamara, Max M Louwerse, and Zhiqiang Cai. 2004. Coh-metrix: Analysis of text on cohesion and language. *Behavior research methods, instruments, & computers*, 36(2):193–202.

Kimberly Gross. 2008. Framing persuasive appeals: Episodic and thematic framing, emotional response, and policy opinion. *Political Psychology*, 29(2):169–192.

Birgit Hamp and Helmut Feldweg. 1997. GermaNet - a lexical-semantic net for German. In *Automatic information extraction and building of lexical semantic resources for NLP applications*, pages 9–15.

Mareike Hartmann, Tallulah Jansen, Isabelle Augenstein, and Anders Søgaard. 2019. Issue framing in online discussion fora. In *Proceedings of the 2019 Conference of the North American Chapter of the Association for Computational Linguistics: Human Language Technologies, Volume 1 (Long and Short Papers)*, pages 1401–1407, Minneapolis, Minnesota. Association for Computational Linguistics.

Annette Hautli-Janisz and Mennatallah El-Assady. 2017. Rhetorical strategies in German argumentative dialogs. *Argument & Computation*, 8(2):153–174.

Verena Henrich and Erhard W. Hinrichs. 2010. GernEdiT - the GermaNet editing tool. In *Proceedings of the Seventh Conference on International Language Resources and Evaluation (LREC 2010)*, pages 2228–2235.

Valentin Hofmann, Xiaowen Dong, Janet Pierrehumbert, and Hinrich Schuetze. 2022. Modeling ideological salience and framing in polarized online groups with graph neural networks and structured sparsity. In *Findings of the Association for Computational Linguistics: NAACL 2022*, pages 536–550, Seattle, United States. Association for Computational Linguistics.

Pere-Lluís Huguet Cabot, Verna Dankers, David Abadi, Agneta Fischer, and Ekaterina Shutova. 2020. The Pragmatics behind Politics: Modelling Metaphor, Framing and Emotion in Political Discourse. In *Findings of the Association for Computational Linguistics: EMNLP 2020*, pages 4479–4488, Online. Association for Computational Linguistics.

Yangfeng Ji and Noah A. Smith. 2017. Neural discourse structure for text categorization. In *Proceedings of the 55th Annual Meeting of the Association for Computational Linguistics (Volume 1: Long Papers)*, pages 996–1005, Vancouver, Canada. Association for Computational Linguistics.

Yiping Jin, Dittaya Wanvarie, and Phu T.V. Le. 2020. Learning from noisy out-of-domain corpus using dataless classification. *Natural Language Engineering*, pages 1–31.

Shima Khanehzar, Trevor Cohn, Gosia Mikolajczak, Andrew Turpin, and Lea Frermann. 2021. Framing unpacked: A semi-supervised interpretable multi-view model of media frames. In *Proceedings of the 2021 Conference of the North American Chapter of the Association for Computational Linguistics: Human Language Technologies*, pages 2154–2166, Online. Association for Computational Linguistics.

Ekkehard König. 1981. The meaning of scalar particles in German. *Words, worlds, and contexts*, pages 107–132.

Maximilian Köper and Sabine Schulte im Walde. 2016. Automatically generated affective norms of abstractness, arousal, imageability and valence for 350 000 German lemmas. In *Proceedings of the Tenth International Conference on Language Resources and Evaluation (LREC'16)*, pages 2595–2598, Portorož, Slovenia. European Language Resources Association (ELRA).

Siyi Liu, Lei Guo, Kate Mays, Margrit Betke, and Derry Tanti Wijaya. 2019. Detecting frames in news headlines and its application to analyzing news framing trends surrounding U.S. gun violence. In *Proceedings of the 23rd Conference on Computational Natural Language Learning (CoNLL)*, pages 504–514, Hong Kong, China. Association for Computational Linguistics.

Julia Mendelsohn, Ceren Budak, and David Jurgens. 2021. Modeling framing in immigration discourse on social media. In *Proceedings of the 2021 Conference of the North American Chapter of the Association for Computational Linguistics: Human Language Technologies*, pages 2219–2263, Online. Association for Computational Linguistics.

Robin L Nabi, Abel Gustafson, and Risa Jensen. 2018. Framing climate change: Exploring the role of emotion in generating advocacy behavior. *Science Communication*, 40(4):442–468.

Nona Naderi and Graeme Hirst. 2017. Classifying frames at the sentence level in news articles. In *Proceedings of the International Conference Recent Advances in Natural Language Processing, RANLP 2017*, pages 536–542, Varna, Bulgaria. INCOMA Ltd.

Viet-An Nguyen, Jordan Boyd-Graber, Philip Resnik, and Kristina Miler. 2015. Tea party in the house: A hierarchical ideal point topic model and its application to republican legislators in the 112th congress. In *Proceedings of the 53rd Annual Meeting of the Association for Computational Linguistics and the 7th International Joint Conference on Natural Language Processing (Volume 1: Long Papers)*, pages 1438–1448, Beijing, China. Association for Computational Linguistics.

Peng Qi, Yuhao Zhang, Yuhui Zhang, Jason Bolton, and Christopher D. Manning. 2020. Stanza: A Python natural language processing toolkit for many human languages. In *Proceedings of the 58th Annual Meeting of the Association for Computational Linguistics: System Demonstrations*, pages 101–108.

Tatjana Scheffler. 2017. Conversations on Twitter. *Researching computer-mediated communication: Corpus-based approaches to language in the digital world*, pages 124–144.

Robert Stalnaker. 2002. Common ground. *Linguistics and philosophy*, 25(5/6):701–721.

Anna Szabolcsi. 2017. Additive presuppositions are derived through activating focus alternatives. In *Proceedings of the 21st Amsterdam Colloquium*, pages 455–465.

Maria Thurmair. 1989. *Modalpartikeln und ihre Kombinationen*, volume 223. Walter de Gruyter.

Petro Tolochko, Hyunjin Song, and Hajo Boomgaarden. 2019. "That looks hard!": Effects of objective and perceived textual complexity on factual and structural political knowledge. *Political Communication*, 36(4):609–628.

Oren Tsur, Dan Calacci, and David Lazer. 2015. A frame of mind: Using statistical models for detection of framing and agenda setting campaigns. In *Proceedings of the 53rd Annual Meeting of the Association for Computational Linguistics and the 7th International Joint Conference on Natural Language Processing (Volume 1: Long Papers)*, pages 1629–1638, Beijing, China. Association for Computational Linguistics.

Wouter van Atteveldt, Tamir Sheafer, Shaul R Shenhav, and Yair Fogel-Dror. 2017. Clause analysis: Using syntactic information to automatically extract source, subject, and predicate from texts with an application to the 2008–2009 Gaza War. *Political Analysis*, 25(2):207–222.

Qi Yu. 2022. "again, dozens of refugees drowned": A computational study of political framing evoked by presuppositions. In *Proceedings of the 2022 Conference of the North American Chapter of the Association for Computational Linguistics: Human Language Technologies: Student Research Workshop*, pages 31–43, Hybrid: Seattle, Washington + Online. Association for Computational Linguistics.

Qi Yu and Anselm Fliethmann. 2022. Frame detection in german political discourses: How far can we go without large-scale manual corpus annotation? *Journal for Language Technology and Computational Linguistics*, 35(2):15–31.

Caleb Ziems and Diyi Yang. 2021. To protect and to serve? analyzing entity-centric framing of police violence. In *Findings of the Association for Computational Linguistics: EMNLP 2021*, pages 957–976, Punta Cana, Dominican Republic. Association for Computational Linguistics.

Malte Zimmermann. 2011. Discourse particles. In *Volume 2*, pages 2012–2038. De Gruyter Mouton.

A Logistic Regression Results

Table 3-5 shows the logistic regression results of all features for BILD, FAZ and SZ (see Section 5.2). The significant level is set to 0.05 in the experiment. The features in each table are sorted by the estimate in descending order (*: $p \leq 0.05$; **: $p \leq 0.01$; ***: $p \leq 0.001$).

Feature	Estimate	Std. Error	z-Value	p
exclamation	5.145	0.187	27.486	< 2e-16***
security	0.276	0.020	14.041	< 2e-16***
question	0.069	0.018	3.773	0.00016***
public_opinion	0.049	0.015	3.183	0.00146**
arousal	0.048	0.017	2.899	0.00374**
adv_iter_cont	0.043	0.015	2.837	0.00455**
economy	0.004	0.016	0.245	0.80623
legal	-0.014	0.017	-0.831	0.40574
politics	-0.017	0.016	-1.058	0.29013
policy	-0.020	0.018	-1.104	0.26961
identity	-0.026	0.016	-1.677	0.09351
weak_commit	-0.055	0.016	-3.421	0.00062***
morality	-0.102	0.016	-6.382	1.75e-10***
scalar_particle	-0.171	0.017	-10.241	< 2e-16***
common_ground	-0.224	0.028	-8.147	3.74e-16***
resigned_accept	-0.266	0.034	-7.893	2.95e-15***
connective	-0.408	0.017	-24.664	< 2e-16***

Table 3: Logistic regression results of BILD.

Feature	Estimate	Std. Error	z-Value	p
connective	0.262	0.015	17.061	< 2e-16***
economy	0.108	0.016	6.721	1.81e-11***
scalar_particle	0.084	0.015	5.518	3.42e-08***
morality	0.062	0.016	3.874	0.00011***
common_ground	0.049	0.016	3.115	0.00184**
weak_commit	0.033	0.015	2.175	0.02964*
identity	0.029	0.017	1.745	0.08095
policy	0.019	0.019	1.047	0.29529
resigned_accept	0.012	0.019	0.607	0.54414
question	-0.008	0.017	-0.453	0.65051
legal	-0.009	0.019	-0.487	0.62613
politics	-0.034	0.017	-2.053	0.04011*
adv_iter_cont	-0.063	0.017	-3.693	0.00022***
public_opinion	-0.069	0.018	-3.728	0.00019***
arousal	-0.182	0.018	-10.110	< 2e-16***
security	-0.254	0.023	-10.921	< 2e-16***
exclamation	-3.874	0.198	-19.605	< 2e-16***

Table 4: Logistic regression results of FAZ.

Feature	Estimate	Std. Error	z-Value	p
connective	0.185	0.017	11.152	< 2e-16***
resigned_accept	0.151	0.022	6.912	4.76e-12***
arousal	0.136	0.019	7.052	1.76e-12***
scalar_particle	0.103	0.016	6.528	6.66e-11***
common_ground	0.082	0.017	4.813	1.49e-06***
politics	0.062	0.017	3.543	0.000396***
morality	0.053	0.017	3.036	0.0024**
weak_commit	0.030	0.016	1.892	0.05849
legal	0.023	0.019	1.232	0.21792
adv_iter_cont	0.013	0.017	0.774	0.4389
public_opinion	0.007	0.017	0.385	0.70009
identity	0.005	0.018	0.274	0.78409
policy	0.002	0.020	0.108	0.91433
question	-0.089	0.025	-3.587	0.00033***
security	-0.145	0.023	-6.343	2.25e-10***
economy	-0.167	0.020	-8.244	< 2e-16***
exclamation	-4.433	0.302	-14.684	< 2e-16***

Table 5: Logistic regression results of SZ.

Named Entity Annotation Projection Applied to Classical Languages

Tariq Yousef * **Chiara Palladino** † **Gerhard Heyer** * **Stefan Jänicke**‡

*Leipzig University †Furman University ‡University of Southern Denmark

<tariq.yousef@uni-leipzig.de>

Abstract

In this study, we demonstrate how to apply cross-lingual annotation projection to transfer named-entity annotations to classical languages for which limited or no resources and annotated texts are available, aiming to enrich their NER training datasets and train a model to perform NER tagging. Our approach employs sentence-level aligned corpora of ancient texts and the translation in a modern language, for which high-quality off-the-shelf NER systems are available. We automatically annotate the text of the modern language and employ a state-of-the-art neural word alignment system to find translation equivalents. Finally, we transfer the annotations to the corresponding tokens in the ancient texts using a direct projection heuristic. We applied our method to ancient Greek and Latin using the Bible with the English translation as a parallel corpus. We used the resulting annotations to enhance the performance of an existing NER model for ancient Greek.

1 Introduction

Named Entity Recognition (NER), like other NLP tasks, has benefited from the advances in language modeling and the availability of large annotated corpora. Numerous high-quality NER models are available for modern languages. However, classical and ancient languages lack adequate annotated data and language models essential for training NER models. Therefore, annotation projection can be employed over parallel text corpora to overcome this problem and transfer the annotation from modern languages for which accurate off-the-shelf NER systems are available.

The core concept of annotation projection is to perform automatic or manual linguistics annotation on a text and project the annotation to its translation using mapping heuristics that link the entities with their correspondences. Translation alignment has been used for this purpose to transfer various linguistic annotations, such as Semantic Role labels (Padó and Lapata, 2009; Kozhevnikov and Titov, 2013), Part-of-Speech (Huck et al., 2019; Tiedemann, 2014; Wisniewski et al., 2014), Named Entities tags (David et al., 2001; Ni et al., 2017; Jain et al., 2019), Relations and Arguments (Kim et al., 2010, 2014; Faruqui and Kumar, 2015; Lou et al., 2022), Semantic Parsing (Shao et al., 2020; Hinrichs et al., 2022), Syntactic and Dependency parsing (Xiao and Guo, 2015; Guo et al., 2015; Tiedemann, 2015). Recently, neural translation alignment models were able to produce accurate alignments for a variety of modern and classical languages, even with no or a small amount of training data profiting from contextualized multilingual language models.

In this paper, we present a processing pipeline to transfer NE annotations from a text in modern languages to parallel texts in classical or low-resourced languages. We use accurate NER models for modern languages and employ state-of-the-art neural alignment models at the word level to find the translation equivalents. Further, we propose a direct projection heuristic that maps the annotations from source to target tokens considering various alignment types. We used the obtained entities to improve the accuracy of existing NER models for ancient Greek. The proposed approach works for any language pair provided the parallel corpora are available and aligned at the sentence or paragraph level.

2 Related Work

Cross-lingual annotation projection of named entities in a parallel corpus has two main scenarios: The first scenario incorporates machine translation to translate the detected named entities of the source text and tries to look up the translated entities in the corresponding parallel sentence using various matching heuristics based on orthographic and phonetic similarity and edit distance text sim-

Proceedings of the 7th Joint SIGHUM Workshop on Computational Linguistics for Cultural Heritage, Social Sciences, Humanities and Literature (LaTeCH-CLfL2023), pages 175–182

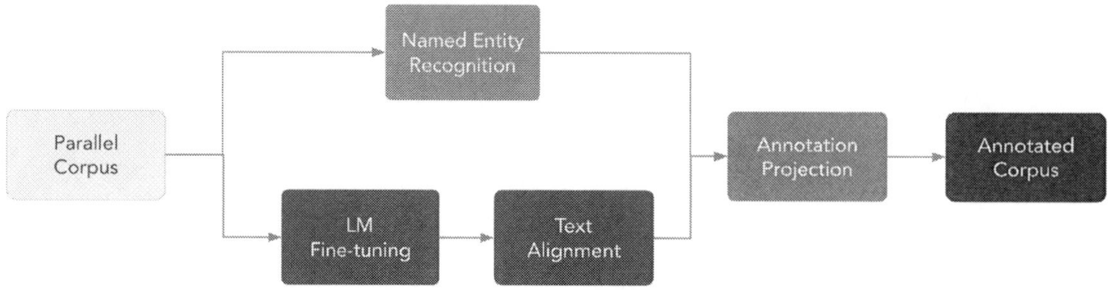

Figure 1: An overview of the proposed pipeline.

ilarity (Ehrmann et al., 2011; Jain et al., 2019). The second scenario employs automatic word alignment to find the translation equivalents of the detected entities in the parallel sentence and project the annotation (Ni et al., 2017; Agerri et al., 2018). On NER in Digital Classics: The Classical Language Toolkit (CLTK) is the largest Python library to perform NLP tasks on ancient languages, including NER (Johnson et al., 2021). However, the lack of adequately annotated datasets for most classical languages is a fundamental hindrance to the high performance of this task. Other efforts have been made, starting from large annotated datasets of specific sources, using semantic annotation platforms and Machine Learning (Berti, 2019). Yousef et al. (2023b) trained a transformer-based NER for ancient Greek; however, the model performed poorly on multi-token entities since the training data used in the training process is composed of single-token entities.

3 Methodology

Figure 1 illustrates the proposed pipeline, it consists of three main components. We start with collecting and preparing a parallel corpus of ancient languages and at least one modern language, such as English, for which a high-quality off-the-shelf NER annotation tool is available. The corpus must be aligned at the sentences or paragraph level. Then we use a NER tool such as *spaCy*[1], *AllenNLP*[2] (Gardner et al., 2017), or *flairNLP*[3] (Akbik et al., 2019) to annotate the text of the modern language. In parallel, we use a state-of-the-art automatic alignment model to align the parallel sentences and extract the translation equivalents. An unsupervised fine-tuning using the parallel corpus can be employed using different training objectives to improve the word alignment accuracy. Subsequently, we find the corresponding translations of the detected named entities and project the annotation using a direct mapping heuristic. In our experiment, we used the Bible in Ancient Greek, Latin, and English.

3.1 Corpus Collection

The Bible is an ideal source of parallel texts and is available in several modern and ancient languages. The corpus includes 31,102 verses (23,145 verses in the Old Testament and 7,957 in the New Testament). Further, the corpus is aligned at the verse level thanks to its hierarchical structure (Book/Chapter/Verse), which allows for producing accurate alignments at the word level. It is also rich in named entities, especially persons and locations. Nevertheless, the Bible corpus has its limitations regarding the language style and text diversity.

We used the *Bible Corpus* repository[4] to build our parallel corpus. The repository includes translations of the Bible in over 100 languages (Christodouloupoulos and Steedman, 2015). For our experiment, we used ancient Greek and Latinwith the English translation. Every verse has a unique ID that encapsulates the information of the book, chapter, and verse; This ID is unified among all translations. The ancient Greek translation was unavailable in the repository; therefore, we collected it from the *Perseus Digital Library*[5]. We followed the same naming convention to assign verse IDs.

[1] https://spacy.io/

[2] https://allenai.org/allennlp

[3] https://github.com/flairNLP/flair

[4] https://github.com/christos-c/bible-corpus

[5] https://scaife.perseus.org/library/urn:cts:greekLit:tlg0031/

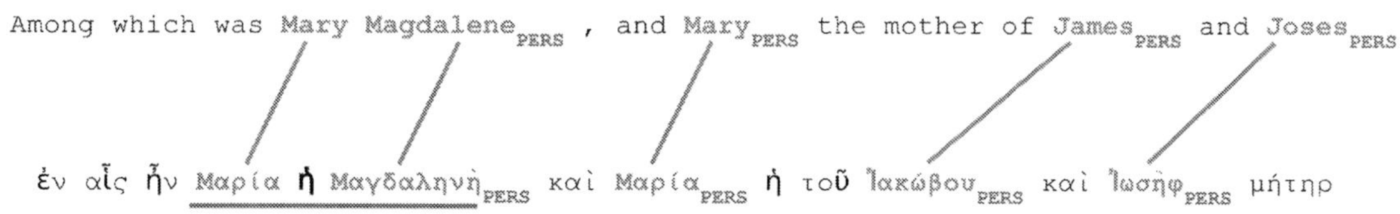

Figure 2: Annotation projection example.

3.2 Automatic NER Tagging

Recently, tremendous progress has been made in the field of NER tagging with the advent of transformer models and the availability of training datasets of adequate size. Several NER Tagging systems were developed for many languages, especially modern European languages, and achieved high accuracy. However, these models are trained on modern texts, and their performance varies when annotating classical texts, such as the Bible.

Therefore, we benchmarked three state-of-the-art NER tagging tools for English, *SpaCy*, *AllenNLP*, and *flairNLP*, to select the best model that delivers the highest accuracy on the biblical text[6]. The comparison revealed that *AllenNLP* and *flairNLP* significantly outperformed *spaCy*, and their performance was so close (Figure 3). In this study, we used *AllenNLP* NER tagger with four entity classes (PERS, LOC, ORG, MISC).

3.3 Automatic Translation Alignment

Translation alignment aims to link words/tokens in the source text with their correspondences in the translation. With the recent advances in multilingual transformer models and neural machine translation, a new era of alignment models has begun. Neural models, which significantly outperformed the statistical models, achieved state-of-the-art performance on a variety of language pairs (Zenkel et al., 2020; Jalili Sabet et al., 2020; Dou and Neubig, 2021; Garg et al., 2019; Chen et al., 2021), including ancient languages (Yousef et al., 2022a,c).

In our experiment, we employed an automatic alignment workflow that utilizes cross-lingual semantic similarity among tokens based on contextualized embeddings derived from multilingual language models such as mBERT (Devlin et al., 2018) or XLM-RoBERTa (Conneau et al., 2019) and derive the word-level alignments from the obtained similarity matrix using various heuristics auch as ARGMAX, ITERMAX (Jalili Sabet et al., 2020), SOFTMAX, ENTMAX (Dou and Neubig, 2021), and OPTIMAL TRANSPORT (OS) (Chi et al., 2021).

Various training objectives can be employed to fine-tune the language model supervised and unsupervised in order to enhance the cross-lingual transfer of the word embeddings and improve the alignment accuracy consequently. For instance, Translation Language Modeling (TLM) (Conneau and Lample, 2019), Self-training (SO) and Parallel Sentence Identification (PSI) objectives (Dou and Neubig, 2021),and Denoising Word Alignment (DWA) (Chi et al., 2021).

We trained a multilingual language model[7] that performed well on ancient Greek, Latin, and English language pairs (Yousef et al., 2022a). We finetuned XLM-RoBERTa unsupervised with a large corpus of parallel sentences in ancient languages and supervised with manually aligned translation pairs extracted from Ugarit database (Yousef et al., 2022b). We employed this language model in our experiment to derive word embeddings, COSINE SIMILARITY as a similarity measure, and ITERMAX as an alignment extraction heuristic since it achieved the best Phrase Alignment Accuracy (PAC) with large margin (Yousef et al., 2023a) and the second lowest Alignment Error Rate (AER) (Yousef et al., 2022a) on the ancient Greek-English dataset.

3.4 Annotation Projection

The basic premise from which we start is that named entities are informative components of any text and contribute to its meaning; therefore, a good translation should preserve the named entities of the original text and their relations. Suppose we have a sentence pair $S = \{s_1, s_2, \cdots, s_n\}$ and its translation $T = \{t_1, t_2, \cdots, t_m\}$. S is already NER annotated and $E = \{(s_k, Loc), (\{s_j, s_{j+1}\}, Pers) \cdots\}$ is the set of detected entities, and S, T are already aligned at word level and $A = \{(s_i, t_j), \cdots, (s_n, t_m)\}$ is the set of translation pairs. In order to project the

[6]More information is available in the appendix

[7]https://huggingface.co/UGARIT/grc-alignment/

annotations from S to T, we followed a simple mapping heuristic that considers the different alignment types:

When the entity $e(s_i, Cat) \in E$, whether a single- or multi-token entity, is aligned to:

- a single token t_j $(s_i, t_j) \in T$ (one-to-one or many-to-one alignments). We assign t_j the same category as the source entity (t_j, Cat). For instance, *Mary*-Μαρία, *James*-Ἰακώβου, and *Joses*-Ἰωσὴφ in Figure 2.

- multiple tokens $\{(s_i, t_j), (s_i, t_k)\} \subset T$ (one-to-many or many-to-many alignments), in this case, if the corresponding tokens are consecutive $|j - k| = 1$, they will be considered as one multi-token entity $(\{t_j, t_k\}, Cat)$. Otherwise, we annotate the range of tokens from j to k as one entity $(\{t_j, \cdots, t_k\}, Cat)$. However, if $|j - k| > 2$, we create two separate entities (t_j, Cat) and (t_k, Cat). For instance, *Mary Magdalene* and Μαρία ἡ Μαγδαληνὴ in Figure 2.

- $NULL$, i.e. the entity has no correspondence in the target language (one-to-null or many-to-null alignments), then no projection is required.

4 Results

We employed the projection approach to the 7950 verses of the new testament and resulted in 6,567 ancient Greek entities (6,104 single-token and 463 multi-token entities) and 6481 Latin entities (5940 single-token an 541 multi-token).

We performed qualitative evaluation to estimate the quality of the produced annotations on two language pairs: English-Ancient Greek and English-Latin. Two domain experts manually assessed 100 random verses, which corresponded to about 550 extracted entities per language, and assigned a score to each detected entities. Table 1 summarizes the evaluation results: The performance on Ancient Greek achieved the highest accuracy (86.63%) followed by Latin (82.34%).

The automatic NER annotation of English text achieved over 94% accuracy and the entities alignment on Ancient Greek-English achieved the highest accuracy (91.9%), since the alignment model is optimized for this language pair. However, the entities classification errors were common for personal names classified as locations and vice versa. In some cases, a Greek or Latin noun would be misclassified as a consequence of the English translation, which adopted a different type of entity: many ethnonyms, which would be classified as MISC in our dataset, were translated in English as location names, and therefore classified as LOC. Additionally, incomplete or partial alignments were frequent in the dataset (9 cases in Ancient Greek, 28 in Latin)especially in multi-token entities such as "Jesus Christ", "Simon Zelotes", or "Pontius Pilate".

Further, we used the resulted annotations to extend the available NER training dataset for ancient Greek[8] and fine-tune the existing ancient Greek NER models proposed by Yousef et al. (2023b)[9]. The obtained model achieved a higher F1, and a better performance on multi-token entities as reported in Table 2.

5 Conclusion

In this experiment, we used translation alignment to project NER annotations from texts in modern languages to texts in ancient languages in order to create NER datasets for such languages, enrich the available datasets, or annotate texts where the existing NER models fail to create accurate annotations. The proposed approach can be employed to any parallel corpus, not only the Bible. However, many factors might affect the annotation performance, such as the translation quality, text genre, and performance of the NER tool of the modern language used in the parallel corpus. Also, the proposed method can be applied to low-resourced modern languages to enrich the annotated NER training dataset. The automatic alignment accuracy varies between language pairs; It is not surprising that the English-Ancient Greek alignments are more accurate than the English-Latin since the language model used in the experiment is mainly fine-tuned on Ancient Greek texts. This experiment is a proof of concept, and due to limited computational resources, we used a subset of the Bible corpus (New Testament only). Using the entire corpus with other parallel corpora will result in more named entities and accurate NER models.

[8] https://scaife.perseus.org/reader/urn:cts:greekLit:tlg0008.tlg001.perseus-grc4

[9] https://huggingface.co/UGARIT/flair_grc_bert_ner

Score	Ancient Greek	Latin
correct alignment / correct NER	86.63%	82.34%
incorrect alignment / correct NER	7.26%	12.87%
correct alignment / incorrect NER	5.28%	3.96%
incorrect alignment / incorrect NER	0.83%	0.83%

Table 1: Manual evaluation of 100 randomly selected verses.

6 Limitations

The proposed approach requires accurate parallel corpora to achieve good results. Further, it employs two automatic components, and getting accurate results is subject to the performance of the two components and their success in annotating and aligning the texts. However, the workflow depends, in the first place, on the accuracy of the automatic NER tagger because if it can not detect the entity, it will not be projected. Replacing one or both automatic components with manual annotation or alignment would significantly enhance performance. Another obstacle is that multilingual language models do not support all languages and alphabets. We tested the projection approach on Coptic and Syriac translations of the Bible, and the results were terrible. The alignment workflow failed to generate accurate alignments since the language model we used to derive the embeddings is fine-tuned XLM-RoBERTa model, whose vocabulary is limited and does not support Coptic and Syriac alphabets.

References

Rodrigo Agerri, Yiling Chung, Itziar Aldabe, Nora Aranberri, Gorka Labaka, and German Rigau. 2018. Building named entity recognition taggers via parallel corpora. In *Proceedings of the Eleventh International Conference on Language Resources and Evaluation (LREC 2018)*, Miyazaki, Japan. European Language Resources Association (ELRA).

Alan Akbik, Tanja Bergmann, Duncan Blythe, Kashif Rasul, Stefan Schweter, and Roland Vollgraf. 2019. FLAIR: An easy-to-use framework for state-of-the-art NLP. In *NAACL 2019, 2019 Annual Conference of the North American Chapter of the Association for Computational Linguistics (Demonstrations)*, pages 54–59.

Monica Berti. 2019. Named entity annotation for ancient greek with inception. In *CLARIN Annual Conference Proceedings*, pages 1–4, Leipzig. CLARIN.

Chi Chen, Maosong Sun, and Yang Liu. 2021. Mask-align: Self-supervised neural word alignment. In *Proceedings of the 59th Annual Meeting of the Association for Computational Linguistics and the 11th International Joint Conference on Natural Language Processing (Volume 1: Long Papers)*, pages 4781–4791, Online. Association for Computational Linguistics.

Zewen Chi, Li Dong, Bo Zheng, Shaohan Huang, Xian-Ling Mao, Heyan Huang, and Furu Wei. 2021. Improving pretrained cross-lingual language models via self-labeled word alignment. In *Proceedings of the 59th Annual Meeting of the Association for Computational Linguistics and the 11th International Joint Conference on Natural Language Processing (Volume 1: Long Papers)*, pages 3418–3430, Online. Association for Computational Linguistics.

Christos Christodouloupoulos and Mark Steedman. 2015. A massively parallel corpus: the bible in 100 languages. *Language resources and evaluation*, 49(2):375–395.

Alexis Conneau, Kartikay Khandelwal, Naman Goyal, Vishrav Chaudhary, Guillaume Wenzek, Francisco Guzmán, Edouard Grave, Myle Ott, Luke Zettlemoyer, and Veselin Stoyanov. 2019. Unsupervised cross-lingual representation learning at scale. *CoRR*, abs/1911.02116.

Alexis Conneau and Guillaume Lample. 2019. Cross-lingual language model pretraining. *Advances in neural information processing systems*, 32.

Yarowsky David, Ngai Grace, Wicentowski Richard, et al. 2001. Inducing multilingual text analysis tools via robust projection across aligned corpora. In *Proceedings of the First International Conference on Human Language Technology Research*, pages 1–8.

Jacob Devlin, Ming-Wei Chang, Kenton Lee, and Kristina Toutanova. 2018. BERT: pre-training of deep bidirectional transformers for language understanding. *CoRR*, abs/1810.04805.

Zi-Yi Dou and Graham Neubig. 2021. Word alignment by fine-tuning embeddings on parallel corpora. In *Proceedings of the 16th Conference of the European Chapter of the Association for Computational Linguistics: Main Volume*, pages 2112–2128, Online. Association for Computational Linguistics.

Maud Ehrmann, Marco Turchi, and Ralf Steinberger. 2011. Building a multilingual named entity-annotated corpus using annotation projection. In *Proceedings of the International Conference Recent Advances in Natural Language Processing 2011*, pages

118–124, Hissar, Bulgaria. Association for Computational Linguistics.

Manaal Faruqui and Shankar Kumar. 2015. Multilingual open relation extraction using cross-lingual projection. In *Proceedings of the 2015 Conference of the North American Chapter of the Association for Computational Linguistics: Human Language Technologies*, pages 1351–1356.

Matt Gardner, Joel Grus, Mark Neumann, Oyvind Tafjord, Pradeep Dasigi, Nelson F. Liu, Matthew Peters, Michael Schmitz, and Luke S. Zettlemoyer. 2017. Allennlp: A deep semantic natural language processing platform.

Sarthak Garg, Stephan Peitz, Udhyakumar Nallasamy, and Matthias Paulik. 2019. Jointly learning to align and translate with transformer models. In *Proceedings of the 2019 Conference on Empirical Methods in Natural Language Processing and the 9th International Joint Conference on Natural Language Processing (EMNLP-IJCNLP)*, pages 4453–4462, Hong Kong, China. Association for Computational Linguistics.

Jiang Guo, Wanxiang Che, David Yarowsky, Haifeng Wang, and Ting Liu. 2015. Cross-lingual dependency parsing based on distributed representations. In *Proceedings of the 53rd Annual Meeting of the Association for Computational Linguistics and the 7th International Joint Conference on Natural Language Processing (Volume 1: Long Papers)*, pages 1234–1244.

Nicolás Hinrichs, Maryam Foradi, Tariq Yousef, Elisa Hartmann, Susanne Triesch, Jan Kaßel, and Johannes Pein. 2022. Embodied metarepresentations. *Frontiers in neurorobotics*, 16:836799.

Matthias Huck, Diana Dutka, and Alexander Fraser. 2019. Cross-lingual annotation projection is effective for neural part-of-speech tagging. In *Proceedings of the Sixth Workshop on NLP for Similar Languages, Varieties and Dialects*, pages 223–233, Ann Arbor, Michigan. Association for Computational Linguistics.

Alankar Jain, Bhargavi Paranjape, and Zachary C Lipton. 2019. Entity projection via machine translation for cross-lingual ner. *arXiv preprint arXiv:1909.05356*.

Masoud Jalili Sabet, Philipp Dufter, François Yvon, and Hinrich Schütze. 2020. SimAlign: High quality word alignments without parallel training data using static and contextualized embeddings. In *Findings of the Association for Computational Linguistics: EMNLP 2020*, pages 1627–1643, Online. Association for Computational Linguistics.

Kyle P. Johnson, Patrick J. Burns, John Stewart, Todd Cook, Clément Besnier, and William J. B. Mattingly. 2021. The Classical Language Toolkit: An NLP framework for pre-modern languages. In *Proceedings of the 59th Annual Meeting of the Association for Computational Linguistics and the 11th International Joint Conference on Natural Language Processing: System Demonstrations*, pages 20–29, Online. Association for Computational Linguistics.

Seokhwan Kim, Minwoo Jeong, Jonghoon Lee, and Gary Geunbae Lee. 2010. A cross-lingual annotation projection approach for relation detection. In *Proceedings of the 23rd International Conference on Computational Linguistics (Coling 2010)*, pages 564–571, Beijing, China. Coling 2010 Organizing Committee.

Seokhwan Kim, Minwoo Jeong, Jonghoon Lee, and Gary Geunbae Lee. 2014. Cross-lingual annotation projection for weakly-supervised relation extraction. *ACM Transactions on Asian Language Information Processing (TALIP)*, 13(1):1–26.

Mikhail Kozhevnikov and Ivan Titov. 2013. Cross-lingual transfer of semantic role labeling models. In *Proceedings of the 51st Annual Meeting of the Association for Computational Linguistics (Volume 1: Long Papers)*, pages 1190–1200.

Chenwei Lou, Jun Gao, Changlong Yu, Wei Wang, Huan Zhao, Weiwei Tu, and Ruifeng Xu. 2022. Translation-based implicit annotation projection for zero-shot cross-lingual event argument extraction. In *Proceedings of the 45th International ACM SIGIR Conference on Research and Development in Information Retrieval*, pages 2076–2081.

Jian Ni, Georgiana Dinu, and Radu Florian. 2017. Weakly supervised cross-lingual named entity recognition via effective annotation and representation projection. In *Proceedings of the 55th Annual Meeting of the Association for Computational Linguistics (Volume 1: Long Papers)*, pages 1470–1480.

Sebastian Padó and Mirella Lapata. 2009. Cross-lingual annotation projection for semantic roles. *Journal of Artificial Intelligence Research*, 36:307–340.

Bo Shao, Yeyun Gong, Weizhen Qi, Nan Duan, and Xiaola Lin. 2020. Multi-level alignment pretraining for multi-lingual semantic parsing. In *Proceedings of the 28th International Conference on Computational Linguistics*, pages 3246–3256.

Jörg Tiedemann. 2014. Rediscovering annotation projection for cross-lingual parser induction. In *Proceedings of COLING 2014, the 25th International Conference on Computational Linguistics: Technical Papers*, pages 1854–1864, Dublin, Ireland. Dublin City University and Association for Computational Linguistics.

Jörg Tiedemann. 2015. Improving the cross-lingual projection of syntactic dependencies. In *Proceedings of the 20th Nordic Conference of Computational Linguistics (NODALIDA 2015)*, pages 191–199, Vilnius, Lithuania. Linköping University Electronic Press, Sweden.

Guillaume Wisniewski, Nicolas Pécheux, Souhir Gahbiche-Braham, and François Yvon. 2014. Cross-lingual part-of-speech tagging through ambiguous learning. In *Proceedings of the 2014 Conference on Empirical Methods in Natural Language Processing (EMNLP)*, pages 1779–1785, Doha, Qatar. Association for Computational Linguistics.

Min Xiao and Yuhong Guo. 2015. Annotation projection-based representation learning for cross-lingual dependency parsing. In *Proceedings of the Nineteenth Conference on Computational Natural Language Learning*, pages 73–82.

Tariq Yousef, Gerhard Heyer, and Stefan Jänicke. 2023a. Evalign: Visual evaluation of translation alignment models. In *Proceedings of the 17th Conference of the European Chapter of the Association for Computational Linguistics: System Demonstrations*.

Tariq Yousef, Chiara Palladino, and Stefan Jänicke. 2023b. Transformer-based named entity recognition for ancient greek. *The Book of Abstracts of DH2023*.

Tariq Yousef, Chiara Palladino, Farnoosh Shamsian, Anise D'Orange Ferreira, and Michel Ferreira dos Reis. 2022a. An automatic model and gold standard for translation alignment of ancient greek. In *Proceedings of the Language Resources and Evaluation Conference*, pages 5894–5905, Marseille, France. European Language Resources Association.

Tariq Yousef, Chiara Palladino, Farnoosh Shamsian, and Maryam Foradi. 2022b. Translation alignment with ugarit. *Information*, 13(2).

Tariq Yousef, Chiara Palladino, David J. Wright, and Monica Berti. 2022c. Automatic translation alignment for ancient greek and latin. In *Proceedings of the Second Workshop on Language Technologies for Historical and Ancient Languages*, pages 101–107, Marseille, France. European Language Resources Association.

Thomas Zenkel, Joern Wuebker, and John DeNero. 2020. End-to-end neural word alignment outperforms GIZA++. In *Proceedings of the 58th Annual Meeting of the Association for Computational Linguistics*, pages 1605–1617, Online. Association for Computational Linguistics.

A Appendix

NER models benchmarking

For benchmarking, we used spaCy with *en_core_web_lg* model, flairNLP[10] with *ner-english-large* model, and AllenNLP with *tagging-elmo-crf-tagger*. We annotated 100 random verses of the Bible and evaluated the results manually. The precision of the three models was close, but regarding the Recall, spaCy underperformed the other models significantly. From 7937 verses of the new testament, spaCy detected 3,788 entities, AllenNLP 6,403 entities, and flairNLP 6,883 entities. This explains why spaCy achieved low Recall.

Automatic Text Alignment

Embeddings: We used *UGARIT/grc-alignment*[11] language model as source of embedddings and Cosine similarity to create the similarity matrix.

Alignment Extraction: We used *Itermax* (Jalili Sabet et al., 2020) to extract the translation pairs from the similarity matrix. We used the code as it is provided by authors[12].

Fine-tuning: To fine-tune the language models we used the training objectives proposed by Dou and Neubig. The code for fine-tuning is available on the authors Github repository[13].

NER model Trainig

To train a NER model for ancient Greek with the results of the annotation projection process, we used Flair framework[14] (Akbik et al., 2019) and $pranaydeeps/Ancient-Greek-BERT$ language model using 75% of the data for training, 12.5% for testing, and 12.5% as development dataset. We trained the models 10 epochs and used Conditional Random Field (CRF) for prediction. The size of the training dataset is (18,276 PERS, 6,655 MISC, 3,415 LOC, and 61 ORG)

[10]https://github.com/flairNLP/flair

[11]https://huggingface.co/UGARIT/grc-alignment/

[12]https://github.com/cisnlp/simalign

[13]https://github.com/neulab/awesome-align

[14]https://github.com/flairNLP/

		Our Model			UGARIT/flair_grc_bert_ner		
		Precision	**Recall**	**F1-score**	**Precision**	**Recall**	**F1-score**
Traing	PER	92.87 %	94.31 %	93.59 %	91.24%	94.45%	92.82%
	MISC	84.49 %	82.32 %	83.39 %	80.92%	83.17%	82.03%
	LOC	82.99 %	82.99 %	82.99 %	86.86%	78.35%	82.38%

Table 2: Training results.

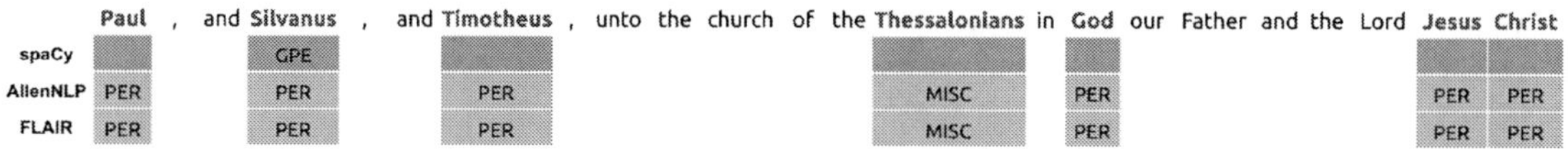

Figure 3: A performance comparison between three STOA NER models on biblical text (1 Thessalonians 1:1).

Author Index

Association for Computational Linguistics
209 N. Eighth Street
Stroudsburg, Pennsylvania 18360

ISBN 978-1-7138-7384-6

9 781713 873846

CURRAN ASSOCIATES INC.
proceedings.com